Democratic Constitutional Design and Public Policy

Democratic Constitutional Design and Public Policy

Analysis and Evidence

edited by Roger D. Congleton
and Birgitta Swedenborg

The MIT Press
Cambridge, Massachusetts
London, England

MIT Press books may be purchased at special quantity discounts for business or sales promotional use. For information, please email special_sales@mitpress.mit.edu or write to Special Sales Department, The MIT Press, 55 Hayward Street, Cambridge, MA 02142.

This book was set in Palatino on 3B2 by Asco Typesetters, Hong Kong.
Printed and bound in the United States of America.

Library of Congress Cataloging-in-Publication Data

Democratic constitutional design and public policy : analysis and evidence / edited by Roger D. Congleton and Birgitta Swedenborg.
p. cm.
Papers originally presented at a conference sponsored by the Center for Business and Policy Studies.
Includes index.
ISBN 0-262-03349-6 (alk. paper) — ISBN 0-262-53280-8 (pbk. : alk. paper)
1. Comparative government—Congresses. 2. Political science—Decision making—Congresses. 3. Rational choice theory—Congresses. 4. Political planning—Congresses. 5. Policy sciences—Congresses. 6. Economic policy—Congresses. 7. Constitutional law. I. Congleton, Roger D. II. Swedenborg, Birgitta, 1941–
JF51.D46 2006
320.6—dc22 2005056241

10 9 8 7 6 5 4 3 2 1

Contents

Contributors

John Charles Bradbury
Assistant Professor of Economics
University of South Sewanee

Roger D. Congleton
Professor of Economics and
Senior Research Associate
Center for Study of Public Choice
George Mason University

W. Mark Crain
Simon Professor of Political Economy
Department of Economics
Lafayette College

Daniel Diermeier
IBM Professor of Regulation
Departments of Managerial Economics and Political Science
Northwestern University

Hülya Eraslan
Assistant Professor of Finance
The Wharton School
University of Pennsylvania

Lars P. Feld
Professor of Economics
University Marburg
Marburg, Germany

Bruno S. Frey
Professor of Economics
Institut für Empirische Wirtschaftsforschung
University of Zurich

Randall G. Holcombe
DeVoe Moore Professor of Economics
Department of Economics
Florida State University

Brian Knight
White Assistant Professor of Economics and Public Policy
Brown University

Antonio Merlo
Klein Professor of Economics and
Director of PIER
University of Pennsylvania

Dennis C. Mueller
Professor of Economics
University of Vienna

Professor Torsten Persson
Professor of Economics and
Director of the Institute for International Economic Studies
Stockholm University

Bjørn Erik Rasch
Professor of Political Science
University of Oslo

Thomas Stratmann
Professor of Economics
Center for Study of Public Choice
George Mason University

Alois Stutzer
Research Fellow
Institut für Empirische
Wirtschaftsforschung
University of Zurich

Birgitta Swedenborg
Research Director
Center for Business and Policy
Studies (SNS)
Stockholm

Guido Tabellini
Professor of Economics
President of IGIER
Universita Bocconi

Stefan Voigt
Professor of Economic Policy
University of Kassel

Barry R. Weingast
Professor of Political Science and
Chair
Department of Political Science
Stanford University

Acknowledgments

The genesis of the present volume was a conference on constitutional design sponsored by the Center for Business and Policy Studies (Studieförbundet Näringsliv och Samhälle, SNS) as part of its constitutional project. The conference was organized jointly by Roger D. Congleton, Center for Study of Public Choice, George Mason University, and Birgitta Swedenborg, Center for Business and Policy Studies (SNS), Stockholm. Its purpose was to take stock of recent empirical research on constitutional political economy and add to our understanding of the effects of constitutions on policy outcomes by promoting discussion among leading researchers from public choice, the new political economy, and political science.

The participants agreed that a volume that surveyed the empirical results of the new rational choice-based constitutional analysis would be very useful, and with that in mind, the papers included in the present volume were solicited, revised, and edited. The Persson and Tabellini paper was subsequently published in the *Journal of Economic Perspectives* (2004) and appears with the permission of the American Economic Association.

The editors wish to acknowledge financial support from the Jan Wallander and Tom Hedelius Foundation. Additional research support was provided to Professor Congleton by the Center for Study of Public Choice at George Mason University, the Faculteit der Sociale Wetenschappen at the Universiteit Leiden, Nuffield College of Oxford University, and the Faculty of Law at the University of Rome.

Roger D. Congleton and Birgitta Swedenborg

1 Introduction: Rational Choice Politics and Political Institutions

Roger D. Congleton and
Birgitta Swedenborg

1.1 Introduction

Democracies are not all created equal. Political institutions differ greatly among countries that can legitimately call themselves democratic. Electoral systems may be based on proportional representation or plurality rule or any combination of the two. The executive may be accountable to the legislature, as in parliamentary systems, or directly elected by the people, as in presidential systems. The legislature may have one or two chambers, the judiciary may be more or less independent of the other branches of government, and local and regional governments may be more or less autonomous. Democratic governance may be subject to more or fewer constitutional and legal constraints. The potential variety is very large, regarding both the broad institutional architecture of governance and institutional details.

Do these differences matter? If "the people" spoke with a single voice, it is possible that the institutional details of democratic governance would matter little. Policy choices might be identical under all democratic systems if a single essentially unanimous voice ultimately determined policy or selected representatives—provided that these representatives were able and willing to carry out faithfully the people's wishes. However, the people do not speak with a single voice and elected representatives do not always faithfully represent the interests of their supporters. Consequently differences in constitutional procedures and constraints are very likely to affect public policy.

Citizens may or may not have preferences about political processes, but they most certainly have preferences regarding policy outcomes. Therefore knowing the policy effects of alternative political institutions is an important prerequisite for informed constitutional choice.

This volume surveys and extends recent empirical evidence on the policy effects of alternative democratic constitutional designs. Its purpose is to take stock of what we know about the political and economic effects of constitutional design with special emphasis on the accumulating empirical evidence. The focus is on the rational choice–based literature, and the papers, for the most part, belong to the field of political economy, although they also include contributions from the rational choice strand of political science. The contributors to the present volume have all made substantial contributions to the new research on constitutional design, and several are among the pioneers in this field of research.

The empirical analysis focuses for the most part on the experience of the OECD countries. These countries have had relatively stable forms of constitutional democracy for half a century or more and also have extensive reliable data sets on which to base empirical analysis. These features make them excellent laboratories in which to assess the impact of small differences in democratic design. In the OECD countries it is likely that the strategies used by politicians, political parties, and politically active interest groups are mature reflections of their political institutions rather than historical accidents or temporary experiments of one kind or another. This allows the equilibrium effects of alternative democratic constitutional designs on public policy and prosperity to be estimated and compared. Evidence from broader international studies is largely consistent with the OECD experience and is also reviewed and extended in several of the chapters.

The book is about constitutional design, but the term *constitution* as used here is not limited to the formal procedures and constraints included in a country's written constitution. A political constitution is defined more broadly as the fundamental and durable procedures and constraints through which laws and public policies are adopted. For representative democracies these include election laws (which are often not part of a nation's written constitution), the general architecture of government, statements of citizen rights and obligations, the legal system, and the formal procedures for reforming those procedures and constraints. Great Britain does not have a written constitution and lacks a formal process of amendment, but clearly has constitutional governance, as the political and historical literatures on *the* English constitution clearly attest.

This introductory chapter is organized as follows: Sections 1.2 through 1.4 provide an overview of the rational choice analysis of democratic constitutional design. The literature review sets the contributions of this volume in perspective and provides the reader with a sense of the origins, breadth, depth, and pace of the new literature. More complete surveys can be found in Mueller (2003) and Persson and Tabellini (2000b), although they do not focus on the constitutional literature as such. Section 1.5 notes how the rational choice research program has divided into at least three clusters of researchers. This volume brings together leading scholars from these more or less independent research groups—specifically the public choice, new institutionalist, and new political economy groups—in order to assess what we have learned from recent empirical research on democratic constitutional design. Section 1.6 contains brief summaries of the individual chapters. Section 1.7 concludes the overview.

Five general areas of empirical research on constitutional design are analyzed in this volume. Part I analyzes the effects of electoral systems on public policy. Part II analyzes the effects of alternative decision-making processes within the legislatures of representative democracies, including the effects of bicameral legislatures. Part III analyzes the effects of decentralization on public policy formation. Part IV examines the economic effects of a nation's legal and regulatory setting, what might be considered a nation's "economic constitution." Part V analyzes dynamic aspects of constitutional design.

Overall, the empirical research surveyed and extended by this volume implies that even relatively small differences in the fundamental procedures and constraints of democratic governance can have relatively large effects on politics, public policies, and prosperity.

1.2 The Rational Choice Approach to Constitutional Analysis

What Is New in the New Literature?

Analysis of the properties and relative merits of alternative political institutions is approximately as old as government itself. Every ruling council and every ruler confronts the problem of organizing governance, and nearly all are interested in effective rules and routines for governmental decision making. Analysis of alternative ways of organizing public policy making is therefore a very ancient field of research.

Scholarly work on constitutional design is a somewhat more recent phenomenon, but has been an important part of social science from its inception. For example, Aristotle's pioneering study of the constitutions of 158 Greek city-states continues to draw attention more than 2,000 years after its completion. Scholarly analysis of the merits and demerits of alternative political institutions continued for the next two thousand years, albeit with interruptions, and played an important role in the democratic constitutional revolutions of the eighteenth, nineteenth, and twentieth centuries.

Given the long history of constitutional research, one might reasonably ask whether modern work can add anything truly new to this enormous body of work. However, there is much that is new in recent research. New methods of analysis have generated new models of political behavior, new empirical evidence, and new research questions—all of which advance our understanding of the relationships among institutions, political processes, and public policies. Analysis of politics and political institutions from the long-standing legal and historical perspectives is limited to the constitutional documents, politically active persons, and circumstances actually observed in history. However detailed the information about a specific event or set of institutions and however carefully an inductive analysis is undertaken, the conclusions cannot easily be generalized beyond the specific events or institutions analyzed. In contrast, the point of departure for much of the new literature is an analytical model rather than a specific case history. The model characterizes the behavior of rational individuals within a particular institutional context, and the effects of institutions on political outcomes are determined by changing institutional assumptions. This deductive approach allows constitutional analysis to take place in an "other things being equal" environment that isolates the effects of decision rules and constraints from the wide variety of personalities, culture, and crises that infuse politics in historical settings.

The "rational choice" approach thus represents a sharp break with the longstanding historical approach to constitutional analysis—indeed a paradigm shift. It allows sharp hypotheses about the *general* effects of institutions on public policy formation to be formulated, tested for logical consistency, and subjected to statistical analysis.

The use of game theory and rational choice models to analyze politics and constitutional design tends to focus attention on many technical issues of narrow interest to model builders. Are there stable electoral equilibria and dominant political strategies within democracies? If equilibria exist, how are equilibrium strategies affected by electoral rules and other constitutional procedures and constraints? What does it mean to be rational within the context of a specific model?

What is the appropriate way to think about equilibria, knowledge limits, and error?

Answers to many of these narrow technical questions have broad implications for real institutions. The effects of constitutional rules on political equilibria imply that constitutions may systematically affect policy choices in a manner that is independent of culture or history. The existence or absence of equilibrium strategies may reveal that some forms of government are fundamentally more stable and more durable than others.

The subsequent use of statistical methods to determine whether the relationships discovered analytically are present in the real world also breaks with historical analysis of constitutional design in several ways. Most statistical methods require both models and *quantitative* data, whereas traditional historical techniques do not. Contemporary statistical techniques consequently encourage the development of new models of institutions and the collection of new historical facts about those institutions. In the long run the research cycle of model, test, and revision yields conclusions that are increasingly robust to modeling assumptions, data sets, and statistical techniques. The ultimate aim of the new approach is a science of constitutional design.

The Rational Choice Approach to Political Analysis

The rational choice–based approach to constitutional analysis has its roots in the economic analysis of politics that emerged shortly after World War II. The first rational choice models of democratic decision making implied that when two parties compete for elective office, their proposed platforms tend to converge to that preferred by the median voter (Black 1948; Downs 1957). Duverger (1954) suggests that two-party systems tend to emerge in "first-past-the-post" electoral systems and also suggests that coalition governments are more likely under proportional representation (PR) than under first-past-the-post systems. Majority coalitions must also please the median voter, but they generally adopt policies that reflect the bargaining power and positions of the parties included in those coalitions (Riker 1962). Unfortunately, pluralistic collective decision rules may lack a definite equilibrium (Black 1948a, b; Arrow 1954; Plott 1967). In the absence of ideological and constitutional restrictions, rational choice models suggest that majoritarian decision making tends to be unstable and unsystematic.[1]

During the same early postwar period the public economics literature (Samuelson 1954; Riker and Tiebout 1956) demonstrated that public policies can improve on the results of private markets in cases where private transactions fail to obtain Pareto-efficient results. These results provided analytical foundations for the theory of the productive state, where the state could intervene to correct market failures and thus increase efficiency. These same results, however, also made it clear that actual governmental policies did not always resemble those of the productive state. Tax and transfer systems had clear excess burdens, many externality problems were ignored, and many others were misregulated.

During the 1960s and 1970s, rational choice–based political research attempted to explain why existing public policies were less effective than public economics implied they could and should be. Two types of explanations were developed. Voters may fail to understand fully the consequences of public policies and institutions or fail to monitor and sanction their elected representatives completely (Downs 1957). As a consequence electoral mistakes are made and political agency problems go unpunished.

Alternatively, politically active interest groups (Olson 1965) and the bureaucracy (Downs 1965; Niskanan 1971; Breton and Wintrobe 1975) may cause governments to adopt policies that advance narrow interests, rather than those of the median voter. Cases exist where governmental regulators are "captured" by the industries they are charged to regulate (Stigler 1971; Peltzman 1976). Interest group efforts to influence government tax and regulatory policies not only reduce economic efficiency and redistribute income in undesirable ways but can also consume considerable resources (Tullock 1967; Krueger 1974; Posner 1975).[2]

The electoral and interest group analyses of democratic politics remained largely independent literatures during the 1970s and early 1980s, although significant extensions of the electoral and interest group models took place. For example, Breton (1974) explicitly considered polycentric policy making within democracies and argued that bargaining among centers of authority and within coalitions determines public policies. Browning (1975) pioneered intergenerational analysis of elections and demonstrated that long-term public policies such as social security are affected by the timing of program benefits and similarities in the interests of successive generations of voters as they approach retirement. Meltzer and Richards (1981) demonstrated that an integrated economic and electoral analysis can explain the magnitude of redistributive programs within democracies. Becker (1983) developed a more comprehensive model of interest group politics, whereas Denzau and Munger (1986) showed how unorganized interest "groups" might also influence democratic politics.

In the late 1980s and early 1990s several more complete models of democratic politics were developed that incorporated interest groups and informational problems into electoral models (Austin-Smith 1987; Congleton 1989; Coughlin, Mueller, and Murrell 1990; Grossman and Helpman 1996). These more complete models also generally implied that elected officials in open democracies are not always completely faithful agents of their electorates.

Statistical tests of the hypothesized relationships between economic and political variables and policy outcomes were undertaken using a variety of national data. For example, the median voter, spatial voting, and complete models received considerable empirical support (Holcombe 1977; Denzau and Grier 1980; Congleton and Shughart 1990; Poole and Rosenthal 1991). For the most part, however, the theoretical literature outpaced its empirical counterpart.

The extent of political agency problems, however, continued to be controversial. On the one hand, research such as Weingast and Moran (1983) and Wittman (1995) suggests that political agency problems are not as bad as some of the early theoretical work implied or at least no worse than in the private sector. On the other hand, a substantial literature suggests governmental bureaucracies are generally less productive than their private counterparts (Davies 1971; Crain and Zardkoohi 1978; Boardman and Vining 1989; Laffont and Tirole 1991). Research on government corruption also suggested that political agency problems can be severe (Rose-Ackerman 1978, 1999).

Regardless of whether agency problems are worse in the public sector than in the private sector, however, an important institutional design question is whether political agency problems can be reduced by an appropriate choice of political institutions. That important question was also addressed by the rational choice literature and is addressed at several places in the present volume.

1.3 Rational Choice, Constitutional Design, and Public Policy

From a game theoretic perspective, it is natural to think of constitutions as the "rules of the political game" and public policy as a consequence of the equilibrium strategies adopted by politicians, voters, and the bureaucracy under those rules. This allows the relative merits of alternative constitutional designs to be analyzed using tools developed from game theory and public economics. Insofar as the rules of a game partly determine the outcome of a game, different constitutions may lead to different public policies. If constitutions affect public policies and some policies are better than others, then some constitutions are better than others. In particular, constitutional designs can potentially improve democratic governance by better aligning the equilibrium strategies of elected officials with the shared long-term policy interests of the electorate.

Game theoretic representations of policy formation require that a government's basic procedures and constraints be sufficiently stable that they can be taken "as given" during the course of ordinary day-to-day politics, but they do not require the "rules of the political game" to be above politics per se. Political institutions are not exogenous in the sense that the rules of an established parlor game tend to be. Ultimately they are also chosen by the players or a subset of the players themselves.

The stability of a particular constitution is partly determined by its ability to advance the interests of those who play under its rules and partly by the procedures for changing those rules. The latter are partly determined by the constitution itself through its amendment procedures, which provide rules that govern the political contest over political procedures and constraints. The consequences of alternative rules together with the available methods for changing those rules determine the extent to which particular procedures and constraints are likely to remain in place.

Buchanan and Tullock (1962) use such reasoning to explain the use of a variety of voting rules within modern repesentative democracies. When downside risks associated with new public policies are relatively large, supermajority approval will protect the shared interests of the electorate. When these risks are small or the benefits of immediate action are large, minority or executive decision making may be employed to reduce decision-making costs. Similarly Oates (1972) demonstrates that decentralized forms of government decision making and finance tend to produce public policies that cannot be worse than those associated with centralized control and may well be better, unless there are substantial economies of scale in the production of government services. Tullock (1980) argues that different judicial systems may have systematic effects on crime and the extent of litigation. Shepsle and Weingast (1981) and Hammond and Miller (1987) demonstrate that institutions can reduce uncertainty about policy outcomes by increasing the policy domain in which democratic politics have stable equilibria. The internal organization of the legislature—committees and memberships of those committees—were also shown to have significant effects on the formation of public policies (Ferejohn 1974; Strom 1975; Holcombe and Zardkoohi 1981).

Empirical work on the policy effects of political institutions during this period was for the most part focused on Switzerland and the United States, because their federal systems and histories have generated significant institutional variation among their regional governments. For example, the variation among Swiss cantons with respect to their use of the institutions of direct democracy allows an analysis of the effects of town meetings, popular initiatives, and referenda. Within the United States, variation in the details of state budgetary processes, fiscal constraints, and use of referenda allow the effects of these institutions to be assessed. These intranational variations allow the effects of referenda, balanced budget rules, and gubernatorial veto power to be assessed statistically (Abrams and Burton 1986; Holtz-Eakin 1988; Crain and Miller 1990; Carter and Schap 1990). In general, the findings suggest that referenda reduce political agency problems, but the effects of other fiscal institutions were empirically less robust. The political and policy effects of those institutions, if any, were evidently more complex than the early analyses assumed.

A parallel literature in macroeconomics investigated the relationship between institutional structures and a nation's macroeconomic policies. Even well-behaved democratic governments are evidently inclined to misuse macroeconomic policy tools in the short run and to expand the public debt and monetary base more rapidly than in the long-term national interest (Nordhaus 1975; Hibbs 1977; Toma and Toma 1986; Grier 1989; Alesina and Tabellini 1990). There is often a tension between democratic politics and effective stabilization policies (Nordhaus 1975; Buchanan and Wagner 1977). Deficits may be controlled to some extent by constitutional structures such as direct democracy (Pommerehne 1978), balanced budget rules (Brennan and Buchanan 1980), and the line item veto (Carter and Schap 1990) within limited circumstances. Tendencies toward inflationary monetary policies may also be resolved institutionally with rule-based policies (Kydland and Prescott 1977; Cukierman and Meltzer 1986) or an independent central bank (Banaian, Laney, and Willett 1983; Rogoff 1985), although the institutions that ensure independence are not immediately obvious. The latter led to a good deal of innovative theoretical and empirical research on credible commitment to rules and on institutional designs that can assure central bank independence (Waller 1989; Cukierman 1992).

Prior to 1990, however, it is fair to say that the effects of constitutional architecture on political agency problems and public policy were largely neglected by theoretical and empirical work in the rational politics tradition, although a very large literature used rational choice models, game theory, and sophisticated statistical techniques to understand politics and policy formation within democracies.

1.4 Acceleration of Constitutional Research after 1990

Several factors contributed to a heightened interest in the role of political institutions in the 1990s. The end of the cold war and the dissolution of the old Soviet empire led to a great wave of constitutional reform in eastern Europe, Asia, Africa, and South America in the 1990s. These along with the gradual political centralization of the European Union brought constitutional issues to the fore. The pressing need for new constitutions revealed the limits of existing rational choice–based constitutional theories, which were unable to provide more than general structural advice that was perhaps more based on historical studies and intuition than a substantial body of careful empirical research. Moreover a growing realization among economists that public policies failed to produce what they should led increasing numbers of economists to examine the effects of political institutions. Public deficits, inflation, unemployment, and inefficient transfer programs were increasingly seen as policy failures caused by the incentives faced by politicians and public servants rather than a lack of information regarding the appropriate policies to pursue. These incentives, in turn, were seen to depend on "the rules of the political game."

The 1990s consequently witnessed a great new wave of innovative constitutional research. For example, many books were written that deepened the rational choice analyses of political institutions. Barnett, Hinich, and Schofield (1993) survey and extend the principal rational choice–based analyses of democratic political institutions. Alesina and Rosenthal (1995) analyze how staggered election cycles affect macroeconomic policies and the political composition of the legislature.

Laffont and Tirole (1993) and Dixit (1996) explore possible contractual and institutional solutions to agency costs within the unelected portion of modern governments. Laver and Shepsle (1996) summarize and extend the literature on government formation within multiparty parliamentary systems. Mueller (1996) provides a careful normative analysis of the relative merits of alternative features of modern democratic constitutional design. Tsebelis and Money (1997) explore the effects of bicameral legislatures on public policies. Cox (1997) analyzes the coordination of voters and parties necessary to make policy decisions within a variety of constitutional settings. Buchanan and Congleton (1998) demonstrate that a constitutional requirement of uniform taxation and public service can make democratic political outcomes more efficient. Wintrobe (1998) examines the political and informational constraints that authoritarian regimes confront. Gordon (1999) establishes historical links between the division of power and the extent of civil liberties in republican government. Przeworski et al. (2000) develop an extensive international study of the effects of constitutional designs on political stability and a nation's economic growth. Persson and Tabellini (2000b) provide an extensive overview and synthesis of the politics of government policy formation with special attention to institutions governing macroeconomics and public finance. Brennan and Hamlin (2000) suggest that democratic constitutional designs should account for ethical behavior as well as self-interest. Tsebelis (2003) examines how the number of veto players incorporated into a nation's political institutions affects political outcomes. Congleton (2003) analyzes the political and policy effects of four Swedish constitutional regimes over the course of nearly two centuries. Mesquita et al. (2003) develop and test a model of policy choice that takes account of a continuum of constitutional designs in each of which the risk of internal and external overthrows are significant concerns.

The production of shorter pieces continued apace as several journals opened their pages up to the new constitutional research and several new journals were founded that focus on rational choice politics, including one, *Constitutional Political Economy*, devoted to constitutional analysis.

The rational choice research program continued to be driven in large part by its own methodology and results as models were extended to address new choice settings and as richer models of human behavior and political institutions were explored. Many of the new models used extensive rather than normal form games so that interdependencies between series of decisions within a given institutional setting could be better represented and understood. And, perhaps paradoxically, some strands of the new research became increasingly narrow and specialized, while other strands became increasingly broad and interdisciplinary. Overall, however, the new theoretical research on constitutions remained conceptual and deductive and addressed both analytical and normative propositions concerning constitutional design.

Of particular interest for the purposes of this book is the large volume of empirical work that tested the new theories using new international and historical data sets and new statistical techniques. For example, Grier and Tullock (1989) provide evidence that relatively more democratic countries tend to grow faster than relatively more authoritarian ones, other things being equal. Knack and Keefer's very influential work (1995, 1997) suggests that culture—social capital—as well as institutional factors affect economic growth. This led to an extensive empirical literature that attempted to evaluate the relative importance of political institutions, culture, and economic variables in determining economic growth rates.

Unfortunately, as is often the case with empirical work in the social sciences, the results were not always as clear-cut as one might have hoped. Przeworski and Limongi (1993) and Temple (1999) suggest that the link between growth and indexes of political liberties is less than completely robust, although economic freedom and political stability appear to encourage economic growth. The ambiguity of the effects of institutions are consistent with economic theory, which implies that political institutions will have systematic economic effects only if they systematically affect political equilibria and the subsequent policy choices of governments. Gwartney, Lawson, and Holcombe (1999) provide evidence that economic policies rather than political institutions or culture are the decisive variables.

The first efforts to assess the effects of institutions had neglected to determine which policies were affected by which institutional differences. Subsequent theoretical and empirical research attempted to isolate the effects of particular political institutions on particular public policies. For example, insofar as voters disagree about public policy, many public policies are determined partly by election law, because variation in election law will induce changes in the identity of the pivotal voter. The latter systematically affects public policy insofar as candidates and parties propose public policies in order to attract the pivotal voter's vote. Lott and Kenny (1999) find the expansion of women's suffrage increased the effective demand for social insurance programs. Mueller and Stratmann (2003) find similar effects for rules that increase electoral turnout, which also change the identity of the pivotal voter, who generally becomes younger and poorer as turnout increases.

Unfortunately, the policy effects of political institutions are often difficult to untangle, and progress required the development of more sophisticated models, data sets, and empirical techniques. This research program rapidly became one of the most ambitious and innovative of the new lines of constitutional research. For example, the two most widely used rules for determining representation, plurality votes in single-member districts and proportional representation in multimember districts, have a variety of significant, but subtle, effects on electoral politics, government formation, and the public policies that emerge. Persson and Tabellini (1999) demonstrate that the relatively smaller size of districts within plurality systems increases the electoral advantages of targeted expenditures within plurality-based systems relative to proportional representation (PR) systems. The larger number of parties supported by PR systems also implies that coalition government is the rule rather than the exception. Lupia and Strom (1995) and Diermeier, Eraslan, and Merlo (2002) demonstrate that the stability of ruling coalitions within PR systems is affected by the rules under which governments are formed and dissolved. Coalition governments may choose to be larger than the minimal majority coalitions implied by Riker's analysis (1962), because larger coalitions are more resistant to destabilizing external shocks. Persson and Tabellini (1999) note that the larger number of parties in government in PR systems tends to reduce incentives to attend to the overall program results, which encourages the expansion of government expenditures and deficits. Moreover the fiscal commons problem also tends to increase with the size of a nation's legislature (Gilligan and Matsusaka 1995, 2001).

The general architecture of governance and the division of power within a system of representative democracy also have a variety of subtle effects on politics and the selection of public policies. For example, the division of policy-making authority affects the flow of information available to voters. Federalism allows individuals to observe the fiscal package available in neighboring communities and punish officials at the ballot box for providing services less efficiently than their neighbors or providing less attractive fiscal packages (Shleifer 1985; Salmon 1987; Besley and Case 1995). Similarly a divided government can produce useful information about public policy, which potentially reduces the magnitude of political agency problems (Persson and Tabellini 1997).

Of course, not all of the new constitutional research during recent decades was undertaken by scholars using the rational choice approach. The effects of major and minor differences in political institutions have attracted increased attention from scholars working in a wide range of methodologies. Notable among the many other contributions are multiple-volume historical studies of government by Finer (1997) and of the law by Berman (2003). Moreover the borders among the historical, legal, and rational choice traditions are not sharp, and complementary contributions to the new constitutional research program have been made by, for example, Ostrom (1990), Shughart (1992), Lijphart (1994), Cooter (2000), and Powell (2000).

Again, the aim of the present overview is not to provide an exhaustive survey of the field but to provide the reader with a sense of the breadth and accelerated pace of constitutional research undertaken in the recent decades. More extensive reviews are undertaken in the individual chapters below.

1.5 Independence of the New Research Programs

Overall, the past two decades of rational choice analysis have produced a bountiful harvest of constitutional research. However, much of that work was independently conceived and undertaken.

During the 1970s the rational choice approach to politics and its associated literature came to be known as "public choice," and ties among researchers were strengthened as public choice societies were founded in the United States, Europe, and Japan. As the rational choice research program on politics and political institutions became more widely accepted, increasing numbers of economists and political scientists employed game theoretic models of political competition and interest group behavior to analyze problems central to their research. Such models were applied in subfields of economic policy analysis, including taxation, regulation, international trade, economic history, economic development, and macroeconomics. The originality and importance of this new research program has been widely recognized. For example, several researchers have received the Nobel Prize, in part, because of their contributions to the economic analysis of politics. Among those may be counted Arrow, Becker, Buchanan, Sen, and

Stigler. To these may be added Coase, Hayek, and North whose research also included rational choice analyses of political and legal institutions.

As the breadth of research expanded and the number of researchers increased, however, more specialized models and applications were developed and connections among scholars dwindled. Although most contemporary models and empirical work continue to reflect the insights of the pioneers, the same roots support many branches of research. Consequently there is a broad overlap in the methodology and conclusions of recent work on constitutional design, but there is not yet a unified field of constitutional political economy.

At least three clusters of constitutional researchers within the rational choice tradition can be identified. In general, the three major research clusters use somewhat different models, data sets, and empirical techniques; refer to different scholarly traditions of research; and address somewhat different historical and technical questions concerning constitutional design. They publish in different journals and participate in different conferences. They are members of different academic associations and are often from different parts of the world. All three groups nonetheless use rational choice models and sophisticated statistical techniques, and all are interested in political decision making, institutions, and the interaction of political and economic variables. The research of these three groups tends to be known as "public choice," "the new institutionalism," and "the new political economy," although many other labels would work as well.[3]

The independence of these research programs has several advantages for advancing our knowledge of constitutions. The existence of several independent research programs allows researchers to pursue particular lines of research more aggressively than would be possible in a unified framework or within a single circle of researchers. Smaller, more homogeneous research circles allow new work to be encouraged by fellow travelers rather than impeded by the various conceptual, methodological, ideological, and personal conflicts that often exist among fellow researchers in larger groups. Beyond ease of research, independence also implies that any similarities in conclusions and results are also independent and thus more likely to reflect underlying features of the phenomena under study, rather than blinders imposed or necessitated by particular research programs or groups. In areas where a broad convergence exists among models and results, convergence implies that some methods of thinking about constitutional design are more fruitful than others and that truly general results are possible.

Independent research programs, however, also have disadvantages. When research groups are too independent, they may not be aware of parallel developments in other groups and so fail to recognize the generality or limits of their results. New ideas and methods are less widely discussed and disseminated, and research questions at the margins of the individual groups may be neglected. This volume seeks to encourage a broader synthesis and dissemination of the new constitutional research by including researchers from the three major research circles.

1.6 An Overview of the Book: The New Constitutional Research

It is clear that more rigorous models, new data sets, and more powerful statistical tools can potentially extend and deepen our understanding of the political and economic effects of political institutions. However, whether increased rigor actually adds anything substantive to our accumulated stock of constitutional knowledge is itself an empirical question. This volume addresses that empirical question by providing an overview of the new empirical research.

Our aim in assembling the present volume is to take stock of what recent research teaches us about the political and economic effects of alternative democratic constitutional designs. As previously noted, the term "political constitution" is broadly construed as a country's fundamental and durable political procedures and constraints, rather than that subset of its core procedures and constraints that are included within a country's formal constitutional documents. Five major areas of constitutional design are analyzed: electoral systems, legislative structure, federalism, the legal system, and the amendment process. Each chapter is written by a different researcher or team of researchers, and each summarizes existing theoretical and empirical research, although the emphasis is often on the research undertaken by their particular group. The contributors to the present volume are prominent researchers in the areas analyzed and leading representatives of the three main rational choice–based research programs. The careful reader will note that many of the chapter reference lists overlap only slightly, although broad areas of agreement exist in tone and substance. In most cases the chapters also extend the areas of research surveyed.

Except for the last two chapters the analyses assume that the constitutional settings are exogenously determined in order to focus on the properties of particular institutions. The present volume thus neglects radical changes in government, partly because its aim is to explore a single form of governance, namely constitutional democracy, and partly because relatively little empirical work on processes of major constitutional reform has been undertaken by rational choice–based research.[4]

Electoral Systems: Direct and Indirect Democracy

The voting system is the most fundamental political institution in a democracy. Voting rules determine who can vote, how votes are counted, what matters are voted on, and thereby, which citizen interests are actually represented in elected assemblies and advanced through public policies. Eligibility rules and electoral cycles also affect the degree of political competition that takes place, and thereby largely determine the extent to which voters are able to hold representatives accountable. Indeed the term democracy is often defined in terms of voting rules. If democracy matters, then a polity's election system will have systematic effects on public policy. There is considerable evidence of such effects, as noted above and further developed in chapters 2 through 4.

In chapter 2, Bruno Frey and Alois Stutzer provide an overview of empirical studies of direct democracy and discuss their relevance for constitutional design, especially for current constitution making within the European Union. A central question in research on elections is the extent to which voting over representatives differs from voting directly over policies. If elected representatives perfectly represent their constituencies, voters can safely delegate policy making to elected representatives. The Swiss research on direct democracy provided the first clear demonstration of the effects of different electoral feedback systems on public policies and continues to provide convincing evidence that substantial political agency problems exist within representative democratic systems.

In general, the results indicate that public services are provided more efficiently and in a manner more pleasing to voters by canton governments that make the greatest use of the institutions of direct democracy, rather than those that rely more on conventional representative institutions. Similar results have been found at the state level in the United States, where popular initiatives and referenda are also used, albeit less extensively than in Switzerland. The results of this extensive literature as well as recent contributions by the authors themselves clearly indicate that elected representatives often advance interests that differ significantly from those of their electorate. The authors conclude that the institutions of direct democracy are an important corrective for such agency problems, and, therefore, greater use of direct democracy would improve government performance.

In chapter 3, Torsten Persson and Guido Tabellini provide an overview of research on the effects of constitutional architecture on political equilibria and public policy, emphasizing the contributions made by the new political economy school. This literature, to which the authors themselves have made many significant contributions, demonstrates that agency problems vary with electoral systems (proportional representation or plurality) and the forms of government (presidential or parliamentary). Theory suggests that the effects of electoral systems can be both direct and indirect. Direct effects arise from the different incentives provided representatives in different systems. Voters vote for national parties in PR systems and for individual regional candidates in single member–district plurality systems. Indirect effects arise from changes in party structure and government formation (single-party or coalition government). The authors hypothesize that the extent of agency problems will be evident in, for example, the degree of corruption and fiscal policies. Empirical tests of these hypotheses use large international data sets (50–60 countries during 30–40 years covering about 500 elections) and a variety of statistical methods. The findings are consistent with political agency models. For example, plurality voting is associated with more accountability (less corruption), and PR systems tend to have somewhat broader programs of expenditures than plurality systems, in which representatives tend to target their own electoral districts. Coalition governments, a result of PR systems, tend to have larger aggregate government expenditures as well as deficits than single-party governments. Parliamentary governments tend to spend more than presidential governments.

Whether electoral systems directly affect the behavior of representatives elected under them, however, is only indirectly indicated by these broad aggregate measures. In chapter 4, Thomas Stratmann investigates whether the manner in which representatives are elected has significant effects on their behavior in office. Within mixed-member systems, some representatives are elected from single-member districts and others are elected from party lists, as within ordinary PR systems. Using data from the German mixed-member system, Stratmann's estimates suggest that electoral systems have observable effects on member behavior. Members elected from single districts are less inclined to vote along party lines and more inclined to serve on committees making targeted grants to local governments than are members elected under PR rules.

Government Formation and the Structure of the Legislature

Public policy is only partly determined by the identity and interests of those elected to office. The formal and informal process of intragovernmental decision-making matters as well, because those procedures largely determine the relative influence of office holders as in the case of presidential compared with parliamentary systems. Part II of the book explores the effects of legislative rules and architecture on political equilibrium and policy choices. Does it matter whether a parliamentary government requires majority support to form and whether it is subject to votes of confidence once formed? Does it matter whether the legislature is composed of one chamber or two, and, if so, why?

In chapter 5, Daniel Diermeier, Hülya Eraslan, and Antonio Merlo survey recent work on the effects of constitutional "micro" rules on coalition governments in parliamentary democracies. Specifically, they analyze how the rules for forming and dissolving governments within parliamentary systems affect the composition and durability of government. Using a game theoretic model of a "formateur" interacting with coalition members, they demonstrate that coalition governments are not necessarily less stable than those formed by single parties, because stability can be achieved by creating larger majorities. A trade-off consequently exists among the size of the majority, the stability of the government, and the control exercised by dominant parties. These trade-offs are affected by a number of features of the process by which governments are formed and dissolved: the electoral cycle, bicameralism, and the stochastic political environment in which governments operate. Tests of these theoretical relationships, unfortunately, cannot be conducted using "off-the-shelf" statistical methods. Using estimators developed directly from their stochastic political models on cross-sectional data (9 European countries during 42 years), the authors find that the most stable parliamentary systems have constitutionally fixed electoral cycles and require the ongoing support of a majority of the legislature and new governments to be formed immediately after a vote of no confidence.

The stability and composition of public policies are also affected by the structure of legislatures. In chapter 6, Roger Congleton surveys the small literature on bicameralism and uses simulated elections to explore how election cycles affect policy choices in bicameral and unicameral systems. Bicameralism is often predicted to lead to more stable policies, reflecting broader interests and more carefully considered proposals. These predictions are normally based on the assumption that the chambers represent somewhat different interests. However, Congleton's simulations demonstrate that bicameralism can reduce political agency problems and increase stability, even if the chambers are elected in the same way. Policies adopted by bicameral systems are less affected by electoral cycles and partisan politics than are unicameral systems, insofar as bargaining between the chambers reduces policy variation induced by external random factors. This effect is evident in the experiences of Denmark and Sweden, both of which switched from bicameral to unicameral parliaments in 1953 and 1970 respectively. Using postwar time series data from Denmark (1930–1976) and Sweden (1960–1997), Congleton finds that their respective time series of government expenditures are significantly less volatile in the period of bicameralism than in their periods of unicameralism.

In chapter 7, Mark Crain and Charles Bradbury provide additional evidence that bicameral legislatures affect public policies. Drawing on the work of Money and Tsebelius (1997), they argue that the effects of bicameralism tend to be largest in cases in which the interests represented in the two chambers are substantially different. Using both international and US pooled cross-sectional data sets, they find that bicameralism has a larger effect on public policies when the groups represented in the two chambers differ. They also find that bicameralism reduces the "fiscal commons problem," that is, the fact that governmental expenditures tend to rise with size of its legislature.

Federalism and Decentralization

Another significant structural variation among democracies is the extent to which policy-making power is centralized within a unified national government or is distributed among the central, regional, and local governments. Part III explores the effects of decentralization on government policy making. The literature on fiscal federalism is the largest and one of the oldest of the rational choice literatures on constitutional design. An extensive theoretical and empirical literature has analyzed the extent to which competition among local governments encourages the efficient provision of government services or discourages it.

In chapter 8, Dennis Mueller summarizes the normative case for federalism and reviews empirical studies of the effects of decentralization within federal systems. Mueller notes that both decentralized and centralized forms of federalism may potentially have advantages. The normative case for decentralization is that competition among local governments efficiently elicits information about voter preferences and reduces political agency problems. The normative case for centralization is that local determinations of public services ignore effects on individuals living outside the local jurisdiction, which may generate externality problems that are difficult to correct within decentralized systems. Whether decentralized or centralized federal systems, on balance, more effectively promote citizen interests is consequently an empirical question.

The empirical literature on fiscal federalism generally finds that relatively decentralized governments are more effective at meeting citizen demands than are more centralized governments. The evidence on intergovernmental grants (the "flypaper effect" literature) suggests that central grants do "stick" to the targeted areas of local expenditures, which allows a central government to address fiscal equity concerns and encourage local governments to solve externality problems that might otherwise be neglected. However, central grants may also encourage excessive spending at the local level by creating "common pool problems." In general, efficiency requires that spending and financing decisions be made at the same level. Mueller also reviews evidence that the efficiency-increasing effect of federalism is larger in systems in which local governments are more responsive to local demands, as in jurisdictions where referenda are used for key policy decisions.

Of course, not only local governments are affected by decentralization. In chapter 9, Brian Knight analyzes how central government policies may be influenced by local government interests in cases in which representatives are elected from regional or local districts. Common pool problems exist when local governments (and local voters) do not pay the full price for centrally provided local services. In such cases locally elected representatives tend to take account of their constituent's local tax prices and local service levels and evaluate national policies on the basis of local rather than global considerations. Moreover, if representatives elected to the central government actually represent local rather than national interests, they will favor local over national programs at the margin and overrepresented seats will obtain relatively greater resources from the central government. Knight provides evidence that this is the case within the United States, and furthermore that disproportionality in the seats in the American legislature favors small states over larger states.

Judicial Independence, Civil Law, and the Rule of Law

Besides political decision-making procedures a variety of other institutions and political constraints of a more or less constitutional nature affect the range of public policies that can be adopted. For examples, most modern democracies include a bill of rights that rules out various kinds of policies (arbitrary arrest, discrimination, censorship, etc.), while mandating others (national defense, education, and social insurance). Other durable constraints are implicit in a nation's civil law and judicial system and in the long-term nature of the policies themselves. Insofar as a polity's constitution may be thought of as its collection of durable decision-making procedures and constraints, such laws may be regarded as constitutional in nature whether formally codified in a nation's constitutional documents or not. Constitutional constraints, however adopted, may not bind a government unless some form of electoral or judicial feedback assures compliance with those constraints.

Part IV of the book explores the effects of judicial independence and other long-term constraints on a nation's public policies and prosperity. Does judicial independence within a democracy affect public policy? Can depoliticizing some areas of law encourage prosperity in well-functioning democracies?

In chapter 10, Stefan Voigt and Lars Feld survey the literature on judicial independence, which suggests that judicial independence can have positive effects on economic development by depoliticizing the implementation of public policy and law enforcement. Uniform enforcement of civil, criminal, and regulatory law tends to reduce economic and political risks as well as private transaction costs, which tends to increase investment rates and specialization. Judicial independence, however, cannot be readily deduced from a nation's formal constitutional documents, because the formal relationships between the government and court system allow a variety of fiscal and political pressures to be placed on the judiciary and because not all governments follow the rules of their constitutional documents. Voigt and Feld create indexes of de jure and de facto judicial independence for the highest courts of appeal in 80 countries and assemble other economic, political, and cultural data for those countries for 1980 to 1998. Adjusting for country differences, their estimates indicate that de facto, rather than de jure, judicial independence increases economic growth rates.

Overall, the effects of a nation's system of public and private law define a nation's economic constitution—the rules under which private economic decisions are made. In chapter 11, Randall Holcombe, Robert Lawson, and James Gwartney survey empirical work on the effects of durable features of a nation's civil and regulatory legal system on national growth rates, giving particular attention to studies that include indexes of economic freedom. The results of that research program suggest that the worldwide variation in economic prosperity is substantially explained by institutions and laws that reduce uncertainty and transaction costs. Previous index-based research has examined the effects of economic policy and institutions on economic performance for more than a hundred countries. Their new research determines whether those results hold for the subset of developed countries when focused more narrowly on public policies with a quasi-constitutional status. Based on data from 18 OECD countries, their new results indicate that economic growth rates are higher in countries with constitutional provisions and durable public policies that support market transactions (or at least do not discourage them). Holcombe, Lawson, and Gwartney conclude that even generally well-performing economic systems can benefit from reform of their economic constitutions.

Constitutional Dynamics and Stability

Constitutions are not chiseled in stone but are amended from time to time. Constitutions may be revised using formal amendment procedures specified in constitutional documents, or they may be implicitly revised through judicial interpretation and reinterpretation and as informal norms, rules, and ordinary legislation change through time. If a polity's fundamental political procedures and constraints can affect public policies, as indicated above, and if public policies affect individual wealth and well-being, it is clear that individuals and groups will have an interest in modifying their existing constitutions to advance both narrow and general interests. In the long run the constitutional rules governing day-to-day politics in a particular nation are also political decisions. Nonetheless, this level of politics is also constitutionally constrained, insofar as formal amendment procedures are applied.

Part V explores some dynamic issues in constitutional design that have not received much attention in the rational choice literature. How important are formal amendment processes? What characteristics do stable constitutions have? Is constitutional durability and stability a consequence of a well-designed amendment process or of other constraints that limit the domain of public policy?

In chapter 12, Bjørn Rasch and Roger Congleton survey the relatively small literature on constitutional amendment procedures. A wide variety of formal amendment procedures are used by democratic countries. These vary from relatively easy majoritarian procedures, as in Sweden and the United Kingdom, to relatively more demanding and inclusive procedures, as in Denmark and the United States. Evidence from the OECD countries suggests that the stability of a nation's formal constitution increases as the number of veto points in the amendment process increases.

The link between the stringency of amendment procedures and overall constitutional stability, however, is not clear. This is, in part, because not all constitutional reforms are equally important, and consequently simply counting the number of reforms provides only a rough measure of the extent to which fundamental political procedures and constraints change through time. It is also because constitutions can be reformed informally as well as formally, and informal changes are difficult to discern and quantify. For example, the hard-to-amend US Constitution has changed considerably through time as the result of judicial interpretation rather than formal amendments.

Moreover informal agreements can be very important determinants of a nation's constitutional stability although they are often unappreciated in constitutional research. In chapter 13, Barry Weingast analyzes how a self-enforcing constitution can fail when the "stakes" of public policy suddenly increase. Using examples from American and Spanish constitutional history, he argues that constitutional stability depends partly on informal pacts among political elites. Both formal and informal pacts among elites are more likely to stand the test of time when they remove particularly threatening policies from the domain of constitutionally permitted legislation. Such informal rules as well as the formal "takings" clauses of modern constitutions increase political stability by keeping the political stakes relatively low, which tends to reduce the extent and intensity of distributive conflicts.

1.7 Conclusion: Democratic Constitutional Design Affects Public Policy

The rational choice literature on constitutional design is very much a work in progress, and recent publication rates suggest that much remains to be analyzed and tested. The rapidly accumulating research, however, has already made substantial additions to its rational choice precursors and to longstanding historical and legal research on democratic constitutional design. Overall, the results suggest that subtle variations in democratic constitutional design can have systematic and quantifiable effects on national politics, public policies, and long-term national prosperity. For example:

- Electoral systems affect public policy both directly and indirectly. Political representatives tend to be more accountable to the electorate under plurality voting than under proportional representation.
- Direct democracy reduces political agency problems even further, affecting both spending patterns and budget deficits.
- Popular initiatives and referenda stimulate policy debate and citizen involvement, making citizens better informed about policy issues, more satisfied with policy outcomes and less distrustful of politicians.
- Government spending patterns differ under PR and plurality systems.
- Polities with proportional representation tend to have larger government sectors and larger budget deficits than those with first-past-the-post systems. This is evidently caused, at least in part, by the prevalence of coalition governments under proportional representation.
- The size and stability of a coalition government is affected by a number of "micro" rules determining government formation.
- Bicameral systems tend have more predictable public policies, and are somewhat less susceptible to the fiscal commons problem.
- Federal systems tend to be more responsive to variations in local demands. They can also enhance efficiency through institutional com-

petition among local governments. On the other hand, they may contribute to fiscal commons problems at the national level.

• Polities tend to be more prosperous if civil law is depoliticized and protected via an independent judiciary.

An important finding, which runs through many of the contributions in this volume, is that representative systems of governance are subject to a variety of political agency problems. Elected representatives do not always represent the shared interests of their electorate. Agency problems can be reduced through several institutional features, although a trade-off often exists between benefits and drawbacks of particular institutions. Institutions that can reduce political agency problems tend to be those that ensure some kind of division of power, and include:

• Direct democracy
• Divided government (bicameralism or presidentialism)
• Decentralization (fiscal federalism)
• An independent judiciary.

It is not the division of power itself that reduces agency problems, of course, but rather the additional information generated and the productive forms of competition engendered by that division.

The stability of a particular government depends, as noted, on a number of micro rules determining government formation and dissolution. Constitutional stability similarly depends on both formal and informal procedures of amendment. Democratic constitutions tend to be more stable if unproductive conflicts about political decisions are avoided by depoliticizing some potential areas of policy, whether formally in constitutional documents or with informal agreements among political elites.

Of course, the conclusion that "political institutions matter" has long been present in comparative political research, and it has also long been implied by the rational choice analyses of constitutional design. In this respect the new empirical research provides additional support for those strands of research that accord significance to a nation's institutions. Agreement, of course, is not the same as redundancy. That scholars from different academic backgrounds independently reach largely similar conclusions suggests that the effects of constitutions are real rather than imagined.

The new work differs from the old, moreover, in its attempt to understand the effects of political institutions as products of self-interested behavior by rational individuals rather than as consequences of broad historical and cultural trends or of the personalities of the particular persons who rise to positions of power. It attempts to model political relationships analytically and quantify the effects of those relationships using new and increasingly powerful statistical tools and extensive data sets. The new research consequently provides increasingly rigorous models of the processes by which institutions affect political outcomes and stronger quantitative evidence of the magnitude of those effects, and thus sheds new light on the trade-offs involved in constitutional design.

The research surveyed in this volume is also of interest because not all modern work in the economic, legal, and historical traditions attributes much importance to political institutions or constitutional documents. A good deal of economic analysis continues to ignore the effects of political institutions on public policies and thereby on prosperity. And many histories have been written that devote very few pages to constitutional and institutional developments. The research surveyed in the present volume implies that such economic and historical accounts underestimate the importance of durable political institutions and changes to them.

Democratic constitutions often change through time, although they may remain democratic, as has been evident throughout Europe, eastern Asia, and North America in the twentieth century. It is evident from the work presented in this book that not all such reforms are improvements or mere symbols of their times. Neither constitutional history nor political economy stops when a nation becomes "democratic," because the details of democratic constitutional design matter.

Notes

1. It is sometimes said that the new rational choice models were borrowed from economics. It would be more accurate to say that such models have emerged more or less simultaneously in all the social sciences as tools from applied mathematics became available. Here one may note that Condorcet (1785) and Borda (1781) were developing rigorous models of political decision making at about the same time that Adam Smith (1776) was developing his well-reasoned, but intuitive theory of the wealth of nations (Mclean 1995). The postwar literature rediscovered and reenergized the rational choice approach to political analysis.

Note also that the application of mathematical models and game theory to politics is approximately as old as rational choice politics. The game theoretic models of Black

(1948), Arrow (1954), and Duverger (1954) emerged at about the same time that game theory (Luce and Riaffa 1957) and general equilibrium theory (Debreu 1957) gained wide currency among economists and other social scientists.

2. It may be surprising to some readers that the work of economists accounts for so much of the rational choice–based political research of the postwar years. However, relatively few political scientists or constitutional scholars were trained to use rational choice models and statistical analysis. Economists, by contrast, not only share an analytical approach based on rational choice but also have a shared interest in the economic effects of public policy and have become increasingly interested in the effects of political institutions on those policies.

Although the contributors to the rational choice research program have this in common, there are also significant methodological differences, as is evident in the individual contributions to the literature and to this volume. Overall, however, there is broad agreement that the details of constitutional design have quantifiable effects on a nation's ongoing politics and public policies.

3. The term "new political economy" was evidently first used by Inman and Fitts (1990, p. 81) to describe the entire rational choice politics research program in terms with which economists would be more comfortable. Moreover each research cluster could be further subdivided. For example, the public choice group could be divided into European and American communities, or into Virginia and Rochester schools, whose members also tend to publish in different journals and tend to work more or less independently of one another. The new institutionalism can be divided into rational choice, historical, and sociological perspectives (Hall and Taylor 1996). The new political economy might usefully be subdivided into microeconomic and macroeconomic research programs. Moreover it bears noting that the groups overlap somewhat; thus, as with colors, it is sometimes difficult to determine to which group particular scholars or pieces of research at the margins should be assigned.

4. Theoretical work on transitions from one form of government to another has begun. See, for example, Voigt (1999), Acemoglu and Robinson (2001), and Congleton (2001).

References

Abrams, B., and W. Dougan. 1986. The effects of constitutional restrains on government spending. *Public Choice* 49: 101–16.

Acemoglu, D., and J. A. Robinson. 2001. A theory of political transitions. *American Economic Review* 91: 938–63.

Alesina, A., and G. Tabellini. 1987. Rules and discretion with noncoordinated monetary and fiscal policy. *Economic Inquiry* 25: 619–30.

Alesina, A., and G. Tabellini. 1990. A positive theory of fiscal deficits and government debt. *Review of Economic Studies* 57: 403–14.

Alesina, A., and H. Rosenthal. 1995. *Partisan Politics, Divided Government, and the Economy*. Cambridge: Cambridge University Press.

Anderson, G., D. T. Martin, W. F. Shughart, and R. D. Tollison. 1990. Behind the veil: The political economy of constitutional change. In W. M. Crain and R. D. Tollison, eds., *Predicting Politics: Essays in Empirical Public Choice*. Ann Arbor: University of Michigan Press.

Aristotle. [150 BC] 1962. *The Politics*, tr. T. A. Sinclair. New York: Penguin.

Arrow, K. 1951. *Social Choice and Individual Values*. New York: Wiley.

Austen-Smith, D. 1987. Interest groups, campaign contributions, and probabilistic voting. *Public Choice* 54: 296–321.

Baldwin, R. 1982. The political economy of protectionism. In J. N. Bhagwati, ed., *Import Competition and Response*. Chicago: University of Chicago Press.

Banaian, K., L. O. Laney, and T. D. Willett. 1983. Central bank independence: An international comparison. *Economic Review*, Federal Reserve Bank of Dallas (March): 1–13.

Barnett, W. A., M. J. Hinich, and N. J. Schofield, eds. 1993. *Political Economy: Institutions, Competition, and Representation. Proceedings of the Seventh International Symposium in Economic Theory and Econometrics*. New York: Cambridge University Press.

Becker, G. S. 1983. A theory of competition among pressure groups for political influence. *Quarterly Journal of Economics* 98: 371–400.

Beghin, J. C., and M. Kherallah. 1994. Political institutions and international patterns of agricultural protection. *Review of Economics and Statistics* 76: 482–89.

Berman, H. J. 2003. *Law and Revolution II*. Cambridge: Harvard University Press.

Besley, T., and A. Case. 2003. Political institutions and policy choices: Evidence from the United States. *Journal of Economic Literature* 61: 7–73.

Besley, T., and S. Coate. 1995. Incumbent behavior: Vote-seeking, tax-setting, and yardstick competition. *American Economic Review* 85: 25–45.

Besley, T., and S. Coate. 1997. An economic model of representative democracy. *Quarterly Journal of Economics* 88: 139–56.

Black, D. 1948a. On the rationale of group decision-making. *Journal of Political Economy* 56: 23–34.

Black, D. 1948b. The decisions of a committee using a special majority. *Econometrica* 16: 245–61.

Boardman, A., and A. R. Vining. 1989. Ownership and perfomance in competitive environments: A comparison of the performance of private, mixed, and state-owned enterprises. *Journal of Law and Economics* 32: 1–33.

Borda, J. C. 1781. Mémoire sur les elections au scrutin. *Histoire de l'Academie Royale des Sciences*. Paris.

Brennan, G., and J. M. Buchanan. 1980. *The Power to Tax*. Cambridge: Cambridge University Press.

Brennan, G., and A. Hamlin. 2000. *Democratic Devices and Desires*. Cambridge: Cambridge University Press.

Breton, A. 1974. *The Economic Theory of Representative Government*. Chicago: Aldine.

Breton, A., and R. Wintrobe. 1975. The equilibrium size of a budget-maximizing bureau. *Journal of Political Economy* 83: 195–207.

Browning, E. 1975. Why the social insurance budget is too large in a democracy. *Economic Inquiry* 22: 373–88.

Buchanan, J. M., and R. D. Congleton. 1998. *Politics by Principle Not Interest: Toward Nondiscriminatory Democracy*. Cambridge: Cambridge University Press.

Buchanan, J. M., and G. Tullock. 1962. *The Calculus of Consent*. Ann Arbor: University of Michigan Press.

Buchanan, J. M., and R. Wagner. 1977. *Democracy in Deficit*. New York: Academic Press.

Carter, J. R., and D. Schap. 1990. Line-item veto: Where is thy sting? *Journal of Economic Perspectives* 4: 103–18.

Condorcet, Marquis de. 1785. *Essai sur l'application de l'analyse à la probabilité des décisions redues a la plu alite des voix*. Paris: L'Imprimerie Royale.

Congleton, R. D. 1989. Campaign finances and political platforms: The economics of political controversy. *Public Choice* 62: 101–18.

Congleton, R. D. 2001. On the durability of king and council: The continuum between dictatorship and democracy. *Constitutional Political Economy* 12: 193–215.

Congleton, R. D. 2003. *Improving Democracy through Constitutional Reform*. Dordrecht: Kluwer Academic.

Congleton, R. D., and W. F. Shughart. 1990. The growth of social security: Electoral demand or political pull? *Economic Inquiry* 28: 109–32.

Cooter, R. 2000. *The Strategic Constitution*. Princeton: Princeton University Press.

Coughlin, P., D. C. Mueller, and P. Murrell. 1990. Electoral politics, interest groups and the size of government. *Economic Inquiry* 28: 682–705.

Cox, G. 1987. Electoral equilibria under alternative voting institutions. *American Journal of Political Science* 31: 82–108.

Cox, G. 1997. *Making Votes Count*. Cambridge: Cambridge University Press.

Crain, W. M., and J. C. Miller. 1990. Budget process and spending growth. *William and Mary Law Review* 31: 1021–46.

Crain, W. M., and R. D. Tollison. 1979. Constitutional change in an interest group perspective. *Journal of Legal Studies* 8: 165–75.

Crain, W. M., and A. Zardkoohi. 1978. A test of the property-rights theory of the firm: Water utility companies in the United States. *Journal of Law and Economics* 21: 395–408.

Cukierman, A. 1992. *Central Bank Strategy, Credibility and Independence: Theory and Evidence*. Cambridge: MIT Press.

Cukierman, A., and A. H. Meltzer. 1986. A positive theory of discretionary polity, the cost of a democratic government, and the benefit of a constitution. *Economic Inquiry* 24: 367–88.

Davies, D. G. 1971. The efficiency of public versus private firms: The case of Australia's two airlines. *Journal of Law and Economics* 14: 149–65.

Debreu, G. 1957. Theory of value: An axiomatic analysis of economic equilibrium. New Haven: Yale University Press.

Diermeier, D., H. Eraslan, and A. Merlo. 2002. Coalition governments and comparative constitutional design. *European Economic Review* 46: 893–907.

Denzau, A., and K. Grier. 1980. Determinants of local school spending: Some consistent estimates. *Public Choice* 44: 385–83.

Denzau, A., and M. Munger. 1986. Legislators and interest groups: How unorganized interests get represented. *American Political Science Review* 80: 89–106.

Dixit, A. 1996. *The Making of Economic Policy: A Transactions Cost Politics Perspective*. Cambridge: Cambridge University Press.

Dixit, A., G. Grossman, and E. Helpman. 1997. Common agency and coordination, general theory and application to government policy making. *Journal of Political Economy* 105: 752–69.

Downs, A. 1957. An economic theory of political action in a democracy. *Journal of Political Economy* 65: 135–50.

Downs, A. 1965. A theory of bureaucracy. *American Economic Review* 55: 439–46.

Duverger, M. 1954. *Political Parties, Their Organization, and Activity in the Modern State*. New York: Wiley.

Finer, S. 1997. *The History of Government from the Earliest Times*, vol. 3. Oxford: Oxford University Press.

Ferejohn, J. 1974. *Pork Barrel Politics: Rivers and Harbors Legislation, 1947–68*. Stanford: Stanford University Press.

Frey, B. S. 1994. The role of democracy in securing just and prosperous societies. *American Economic Review* 84: 338–42.

Frey, B. S., and A. Stutzer. 2000. Happiness, economy, and institutions. *Economic Journal* 110: 918–38.

Frey, B. S., and A. Stutzer. 2002. *Happiness and Economics: How the Economy and Institutions Affect Well-being*. Princeton: Princeton University Press.

Gilligan, T. W., and J. G. Matsusaka. 1995. Deviations from constituent interests: The role of legislative structure and political parties in the states. *Economic Inquiry* 33: 383–401.

Gilligan, T. W., and J. G. Matsusaka. 2001. Fiscal policy, legislature size, and political parties: Evidence from state and local governments in the first half of the 20th century. *National Tax Journal* 54: 57–82.

Glazier, A. 1989. Politics and the choice of durability. *American Economic Review* 79: 1207–14.

Gordon, S. 1999. Controlling the state: Constitutionalism from ancient Athens to today. Cambridge: Harvard University Press.

Grier, K. 1989. On the existence of a political monetary cycle. *American Journal of Political Science* 33: 379–89.

Grier, K. B., and G. Tullock. 1989. An empirical analysis of cross-national economic growth, 1951–80. *Journal of Monetary Economics* 24: 259–76.

Grossman, G. M., and E. Helpman. 1996. Electoral competition and special interest politics. *Review of Economic Studies* 63: 265–86.

Gwartney, J. D., R. A. Lawson, and R. G. Holcombe. 1999. Economic freedom and the environment for economic growth. *Journal of Institutional and Theoretical Economics* 155: 643–63.

Hall, P. A., and R. C. R. Taylor. 1996. Political science and the three new institutionalisms. *Political Studies* 46: 936–57.

Hammond, T. H., and G. J. Miller. 1987. The core of the constitution. *APSR* 81: 1155–74.

Hibbs, D. 1977. Political parties and macroeconomic policy. *American Political Science Review* 71: 1467–87.

Hillman, A. L., and H. W. Ursprung. 1988. Domestic politics, foreign interests, and international trade policy. *American Economic Review* 78: 719–45.

Holcombe, R. G. 1977. The Florida system: A Bowen equilibrium referendum process. *National Tax Journal* 30: 77–84.

Holcombe, R. G., and A. Zardkoohi. 1981. The determinants of federal grants. *Southern Economic Journal* 48: 393–99.

Holtz-Eakin, D. 1988. The line item veto and public sector budgets: Evidence from the states. *Journal of Public Economics* 36: 269–92.

Inman, R. P., and M. A. Fitts. 1990. Political institutions and fiscal policy: Evidence from the U.S. historical record. *Journal of Law, Economics, and Organization* 6: 79–132.

Knack, S., and P. Keefer. 1995. Institutions and economic performance: Cross-country tests using alternative institutional measures. *Economic and Politics* 7: 207–27.

Knack, S., and P. Keefer. 1997. Does social capital have an economic payoff? A cross-country investigation. *Quarterly Journal of Economics* 112: 1251–88.

Kramer, G. H. 1971. Short-term fluctuations in U.S. voting behavior, 1896–1964. *American Political Science Review* 65: 133–43.

Kruger, A. O. 1974. The political economy of the rent-seeking society. *American Economic Review* 54: 291–303.

Kydland, F., and E. Prescott. 1977. Rules rather than discretion: The inconsistency of optimal plans. *Journal of Political Economy* 85: 473–90.

Laffont, J. J., and J. S. Tirole. 1993. *A Theory of Incentives in Procurement and Regulatios.* Cambridge: MIT Press.

Landes, M., and R. A. Posner. 1975. The independent judiciary in an interest group perspective. *Journal of Law and Economics* 18: 875–901.

Laver, M., and K. A. Shepsle. 1996. *Making and Breaking Governments: Cabinets and Legislatures in Parliamentary Democracies.* Cambridge: Cambridge University Press.

Lijphart, A. 1990. The political consequences of electoral laws 1945–85. *American Political Science Review* 84: 481–96.

Lijphart, A. 1994. *Electoral Systems and Party Systems: A Study of Twenty-Seven Democracies, 1945–1990.* New York: Oxford University Press.

Lipset, S. M. 1959. Some social requisites of democracy: Economic development and political legitimacy. *American Political Science Review* 53: 69–105.

Lott, J. R., and L. W. Kenny. 1999. Did women's suffrage change the size and scope of government? *Journal of Political Economy* 107: 1163–98.

Luce, R. D., and H. Raiffa. 1957. *Games and Decisions: Introduction and Critical Survey*. New York: Wiley.

Lupia, A., and K. Strom. 1995. Coalition termination and the strategic timing of parliamentary elections. *American Political Science Review* 89 (3): 648–69.

Matsusaka, J. G. 1995. Fiscal effects of the voter initiative: Evidence from the last 30 years. *Journal of Political Economy* 103: 587–623.

Matsusaka, J. G. 2000. Fiscal effects of the voter initiative in the first half of the twentieth century. *Journal of Law and Economics* 43: 619–50.

Mclean, I. 1995. *Classics of Social Choice*. Ann Arbor: University of Michigan Press.

McCubbins, M. D., R. G. Noll, and B. R. Weingast. 1989. Administrative procedures as instruments of political control. *Journal of Law Economics and Organization* 3: 243–77.

Meltzer, A. H., and S. F. Richard. 1981. A rational theory of the size of government. *Journal of Political Economy* 89: 914–27.

Mesquita, B. B., A. Smith, R. M. Siverson, and R. D. Morrow. 2003. *The Logic of Political Survival*. Cambridge: MIT Press.

Mueller, D. C. 1996. *Constitutional Democracy*. New York: Oxford University Press.

Mueller, D. C. 2003. *Public Choice III*. New York: Cambridge University Press.

Mueller, D. C., and T. Stratmann. 2003. The economic effects of democratic participation. *Journal of Public Economics* 87: 2129–55.

Niskanen, W. A. 1971. *Bureaucracy and Representative Government*. Chicago: Aldine Press.

Nordhaus, W. D. 1972. The political business cycle. Discussion Paper 333. Cowles Foundation.

North, D. C. 1985. The growth of government in the United States: An economic historian's perspective. *Journal of Public Economics* 28: 383–99.

North, D. C., and B. Weingast. 1989. Constitutions and commitment: The evolution of institutions governing public choice in seventeenth-century England. *Journal of Econmic History* 69: 803–32.

Oates, W. 1972. *Fiscal Federalism*. New York: Harcourt Brace Jovanovich.

Olson, M. 1965. *The Logic of Collective Action: Public Goods, and the Theory of Groups*. Cambridge: Harvard University Press.

Olson, M. 1993. Dictatorship, democracy, and development. *American Political Science Review* 87: 567–76.

Ostrom, E. 1990. *Governing the Commons: The Evolution of Institutions for Collective Action*. Cambridge: Cambridge University Press.

Peltzman, S. 1976. Toward a more general theory of regulation. *Journal of Law and Economics* 19: 211–40.

Peltzman, S. 1993. George Stigler's contribution to the economic analysis of regulation. *Journal of Political Economy* 101: 818–32.

Persson, T., and G. E. Tabellini. 1999. The size and scope of government: Comparative politics with national politicians. *European Economic Review* 43: 699–735.

Persson, T., and G. E. Tabellini. 2000a. Comparative politics and public finance. *Journal of Political Economy* 108: 1121–61.

Persson, T., and G. E. Tabellini. 2000b. *Political Economics: Explaining Economic Policy.* Cambridge: MIT Press.

Persson, T., G. Roland, and G. E. Tabellini. 1997. Separation of powers and political accountability. *Quarterly Journal of Economics* 112: 1163–1202.

Piketty, T. 1999. The information aggregation approach to political institutions. *European Economic Review* 43: 791–800.

Plott, C. R. 1967. A notion of equilibrium and its possibility under majority rule. *American Economic Review* 57: 787–806.

Pommerehne, W. W. 1978. Institutional approaches to public expenditure: Empirical evidence from Swiss municipalities. *Journal of Public Economics* 9: 225–80.

Pommerehne, W. W. 1990. The empirical relevance of comparative institutional analysis. *European Economic Review* 34: 458–69.

Poole, K. T., and H. Rosenthal. 1991. Patterns of congressional voting. *American Journal of Political Science* 35: 228–78.

Posner, R. A. 1975. The social cost of monopoly and regulation. *Journal of Political Economy* 83: 807–27.

Poterba, J. M. 1996. Budget institutions and fiscal policy in the U.S. states. *American Economic Review* 86: 395–400.

Powell, G. B. 2000. *Elections as Instruments of Democracy: Majoritarian and Proportional Visions.* New Haven: Yale University Press.

Przeworski, A. 2000. *Democracy and Development: Political Institutions and Well-being in the World, 1950–1990.* Cambridge: Cambridge University Press.

Przeworski, A., and F. Limongi. 1993. Political regimes and economic growth. *Journal of Economic Perspectives* 7: 51–69.

Rees, A. H., S. Kaufman, J. Eldersveld, and F. Friedel. 1962. The effect of economic conditions on congressional elections 1946–58. *Review of Economics and Statistics* 44: 458–65.

Riker, W. H. 1955. The senate and American federalism. *American Political Science Review* 49: 452–69.

Riker, W. H. 1962. *The Theory of Political Coalitions.* New Haven: Yale University Press.

Riker, W. H. 1982. The two-party system and Duverger's law. *American Political Science Review* 76: 753–66.

Rogoff, K. 1985. The optimal degree of commitment to an intermediate monetary target. *Quarterly Journal of Economics* 100: 1169–90.

Rose-Ackerman, S. 1978. *Corruption.* New York: Academic Press.

Rose-Ackerman, S. 1999. *Corruption and Government.* Cambridge: Cambridge University Press.

Salmon, P. 1987. Decentralisation as an incentive scheme. *Oxford Review of Economic Policy* 3: 24–43.

Samuelson, P. A. 1954. The pure theory of public expenditures. *Review of Economics and Statistics* 36: 387–89.

Shepsle, K. A., and B. R. Weingast. 1981. Structure-induced equilibrium and legislative choice. *Public Choice* 37: 503–19.

Schumpeter, J. 1947. *Capitalism, Socialism, and Democracy*. New York: Harper and Bros.

Schap, D. 1986. Executive veto and informational strategy: A structure-induced equilibrium analysis. *American Journal of Political Science* 30.

Shleifer, A. 1985. A theory of yardstick competition. *Rand Journal of Economics* 16: 319–27.

Shugart, M., and J. Carey. 1992. *Presidents and Assemblies: Constitutional Design and Electoral Dynamics*. Cambridge: Cambridge University Press.

Stigler, G. 1971. The theory of economic regulation. *Bell Journal of Economics and Management Science* 2: 3–21.

Stratmann, T. 1992. The effects of logrolling on congressional voting. *American Economic Review* 82: 1162–76.

Stratmann, T. 1996. Instability of collective decisions? Testing for cyclic majorities. *Public Choice* 88: 15–28.

Strom, G. 1975. Congressional policy making: A test of a theory. *Journal of Politics* 37: 711–35.

Tiebout, C. M. 1956. A pure theory of local expenditures. *Journal of Political Economy* 64: 416–24.

Temple, J. 1999. The new growth evidence. *Journal of Economic Literature* 37: 112–56.

Toma, E., and M. Toma. 1986. *Central Bankers, Bureaucratic Incentives, and Monetary Policy*. Dordrecht: Martinus Nijhoff.

Toma, M. 1982. Inflationary bias of the Federal Reserve System: A bureaucratic perspective. *Journal of Monetary Economics* 10.

Tocqueville, A. [1835] 1972. *Democracy in America*. New York: Knopf.

Tsebelis, G. 2002. *Veto Players: How Political Institutions Work*. Princeton, NJ: Princeton University Press.

Tsebelis, G., and J. Money. 1997. *Bicameralism*. Cambridge: Cambridge University Press.

Tullock, G. 1965. *The Politics of Bureaucracy*. Washington, DC: Public Affairs Press.

Tullock, G. 1967. The welfare costs of tariffs, monopolies, and theft. *Western Economic Journal* 5: 224–32.

Tullock, G. 1980. *Trials on Trial*. New York: Columbia University Press.

Voigt, S. 1999. *Explaining Constitutional Change: A Positive Economics Approach*. Cheltenham: Edward Elgar.

Waller, C. J. 1989. Monetary policy games and central bank politics. *Journal of Money, Credit, and Banking* 21: 422–31.

Weingast, B. R., and M. J. Moran. 1983. Bureaucratic discretion of congressional control? Regulatory policy making in the FTC. *Journal of Political Economy* 91: 765–800.

Weingast, B. R., and W. Marshall. 1988. The industrial organization of congress, or why legislatures, like firms, are not organized as markets. *Journal of Political Economy* 89: 642–64.

Wintrobe, R. 1998. *The Political Economy of Dictatorship*. Cambridge: Cambridge University Press.

Wittman, D. 1995. *The Myth of Democratic Failure: Why Political Institutions are Efficient*. Chicago: University of Chicago Press.

I

Voting Systems, Agency, and Public Policy

2 Direct Democracy: Designing a Living Constitution

Bruno S. Frey and Alois Stutzer

2.1 Introduction

In this chapter we analyze the competition between various interests to control the state, including the power to change its basic laws. We apply a comparative view to evaluate initiatives and referendums as mechanisms for institutional change. The reference standard is a purely representative democratic system (as is still dominant in most countries) in which members of parliament decide on constitutional issues such as basic rights, the scope of democratic decision-making and of market exchange, and the organization of the judiciary and federal structure of the country. Section 2.2 briefly describes direct democratic decision making in general, and lists where it has been applied. Section 2.3 analyzes the effects of providing for direct citizen involvement through initiatives and referenda. We focus on three aspects: (1) the difference induced in the principal–agent relationship between citizens and politicians, when citizens have agenda control via initiatives and can ask for a referendum on new legislation; (2) the process of direct democratic decision making; and (3) the protecting influence of referenda against the risk of overcentralization. Empirical evidence for all three aspects is provided in section 2.4. Section 2.5 discusses arguments for and counterarguments against direct democracy. Issues for designing a constitution that includes direct participation rights for the citizens, especially in the context of the European Union, are taken up in section 2.6. Last section 2.7 offers some concluding remarks.

Direct democracy fundamentally changes the *process* of political decision making. It is not only that politicians are more restricted to follow citizens' preferences, but the direct involvement of the people changes their motivation when they act as voters, taxpayers or fellow citizens (Frey 1997). This can explain systematic differences as to how well aware of political issues people are, whether they can build up a relationship based on trust to public authorities, and whether they have a preference for, and gain procedural utility from, direct democratic participation rights as such.

The Proposal by the Convention of the European Union delivered in June 2003 presents a *unique chance to write a constitution for this century*, and for those to come.[1] It represents a rare window of opportunity for designing a constitution for one of the major political units of the world. It is very likely that few, if any, ground rules of such relevance can be written in the near future. The Convention could not start from scratch—no designers of any constitution ever can. In the case of the European Union there are various previous treaties, such as those of Maastricht, Nice, and Amsterdam, as well, of course, as the founding Treaty of Rome in 1956, that have to be taken into account. Nevertheless, the entry of ten new member states in 2004, as well as the likely future entry of five or so additional countries, should have allowed the Convention to draft pathbreaking new rules for the future European Union.

This opportunity was missed. The Convention understood its task quite differently, namely as an *exercise in compromise*. Granted, the Convention had a difficult task to fulfill. The new EU constitution has to meet with the agreement of all the member countries. So the support of the existing 25 members must be sought. This is no small task, considering that the interests of the nations can differ in a great many respects. Most important, two fundamentally different interpretations of the European unification clash with each other. The *first* interpretation sees the European enterprise as essentially an *economic* one. The Union is to guarantee *free trade* in terms of the movement of goods, services, labor, and capital. Political interventions should only serve to keep the borders open, to prevent trade distortions by subsidization, and other interferences distorting relative prices. The *second* interpretation sees the goal of the European enterprise as a *political* one. Europe is to move to "an ever closer union" (in the words of the former president of the Commission, Jacques Delors) and end up as a "United States of Europe."

Accepting the "necessity" of a compromise, the focus should already today lie on the development of the European constitution in the future, namely on the question of *amending constitutions*. This chapter suggests that direct democracy should play a central role in every constitution's amendment process.

2.2 Direct Democratic Decision Making and Its Diffusion

There are many different meanings, conceptions, and also misunderstandings about what "direct democracy" is. The two crucial features of the term "direct democracy" are discussed here.[2]

Referenda and Initiatives as Additional Rights

Direct democracy (or, more precisely, semi-direct democracy) does not substitute for parliament, government, courts, and all the other features known in representative democracies. Instead, it shifts the final rights in determining issues to the citizens. The extent of direct participation rights may vary, but they always include constitutional changes, normally by an obligatory referendum. Optional referenda and initiatives (allowing citizens to put issues on the political agenda) require a predetermined number of signatures by the citizens before they can take place.

From a historical perspective, three main stages of democracy may be distinguished:

• Classical democracy, first developed in Athens and other Greek city-states. Participation rights were restricted to male citizens, thereby excluding a large number of the population, and extended only over a small area of a town. Yet the principles of democracy still revered and used today were developed there.

• The French Revolution extended democracy over a large area. The principle of representation made it possible to introduce indirect political participation to the nation state.

• Direct democracy combines these two earlier types of democracy by giving every citizen the right to decide on certain issues. The extreme (classical) form of having citizens decide on each and every issue is practiced nowhere today, but the number of issues on which citizens may vote varies widely between countries.

Over the period 1990 to 2000, no less than 405 popular referendums on the *national level* were recorded (see Gross and Kaufmann 2002; Butler and Ranney 1994). More than half took place in Europe, namely 248 (and again half of them in Switzerland); 78 in America, 37 in Africa, 26 in Asia, and 16 in Oceania.[3] In the decade before (1980 to 1990), there were only 129 national referenda. Up until August 2002 issues of European integration led to no less than 30 national referenda.[4] There are a very large number of popular referenda at lower levels of government. In the German state of Bavaria, there were as many as 500 since its adoption. In Switzerland, there are thousands of referenda at all three levels of government: local, cantonal, and federal. In the United States, the initiative and referendum process is available to citizens in 24 states. Since 1904 when the first statewide initiative appeared on Oregon's ballot, approximately 2,021 measures have been placed on the voting agenda and many more referenda (Waters 2003).

Most democracies do not allow the general electorate to participate in taking important decisions. Nowhere (except in Switzerland and Liechtenstein) are popular referenda used in a regular and systematic way at the national level. In the United States, despite its many local popular decisions, and its frequent use in some states, such as California and Oregon, there is no referendum at the national level. Many important decisions shaping a country's fate for decades to come are not subject to a popular referendum. A telling example is Germany. The citizens had no say either with respect to the conditions for the integration of the former GDR or the dumping of the deutsche mark and introducing the euro. Directly democratic decisions are in many cases not taken seriously by the politicians in power. A revealing example is the Irish vote on the Nice Treaty of the European Union. The citizens rejected it in June 2001. Before the second vote on the issue, due to take place in August 2002, EU politicians made it clear that they would go ahead with the Treaty's program, regardless of whether the Irish vote be positive or negative (though unanimity within the European Union is required).

Referenda and Other Forms of Consultation of Citizens

Referenda are a right given to the citizens by the constitution. Government and parliament are bound by these rights: they are not free to ask the opinion of the citizens only when it suits them. This distinguishes referenda from plebiscites undertaken by governments to ex post sanction a decision already taken by them. With plebiscites, the citizens are not asked to decide on an issue, but only to express their support of the government. Referenda also fundamentally differ from opinion surveys, which are on the spot views of people, without any consequences for the government: they can choose to act in accordance with the results or disregard them. In contrast, when citizens have taken a decision in a referendum, the constitution obliges the government to put the corresponding policy into practice.

2.3 Working of the Direct Democratic Process

Direct Democracy against the Politicians' Cartel

Politicians against the Voters
Persons acting within the confines of the political system have incentives to exploit it to their advantage. Politicians are not "bad," or any worse than other persons, but they tend to be—as everyone else—self-regarding. They endeavor to further their own interests, which consist not only of material wealth but also of recognition and prestige.

In a democracy, politicians can use three main ways of gaining benefits at the citizens' expense, or "exploiting" the general population:

• Politicians may take decisions that they know to *deviate from the voters' preferences*. Political actors may do so because they have an ideology of their own, because they reap material and nonmaterial advantages by so doing, or because they have insufficient information. For instance, politicians systematically prefer direct interventions in the economy to employing the price system because regulations generally allow them to derive larger rents.

• Politicians secure themselves *excessive privileges* in the form of direct income for themselves or their parties, pensions, and fringe benefits such as cars and houses.

• Citizens' exploitation may take the form of *corruption*, namely of direct payments for special services provided to payers but not to others.

Politicians have a common interest to protect and extend these rents where possible. That means they have an incentive to form a *cartel* against the ordinary citizens. There is, however, a public good problem involved: an individual politician has an incentive to break out, if such action is positively sanctioned by the electorate. Such action can regularly be observed in democracies, but it is rarely of much consequence for the cartel. The politicians in many countries form a close-knit group of people clearly differentiated from the rest of the population. Their main contacts are within the group, so that the social disapproval of the few who dare to break out of the cartel is acutely felt and carries a high cost. Moreover the cartel is administered by the leaders of the parties so that in most countries and time periods, only a small number are involved, and the breakout of a politician is quickly and effectively sanctioned by the other members of the cartel, for instance, by restricting access to parliamentary positions (in particular membership of powerful commissions) or by reducing the monetary support provided by the state to the parties. Individual politicians find it equally hard not to be a part of the cartel because the leaders of their parties have many means at their disposal to control their politicians, including enforced resignation.

Constitutional Provisions against the Politicians' Cartel All the actors involved, in particular the voters, are well aware that there are strong and ubiquitous incentives for the politicians to form a cartel and to exploit the voters. In response, one finds three quite different forms of institutions in democratic constitutions designed to check such action:

1. *Rules* prohibiting the (excessive) appropriation of rents by the politicians, the most stringent ones being to prevent corruption. Obviously such rules are only effective if they cannot easily be circumvented and if they are well enforced. Such provisions are completely useless against the first type of exploitation mentioned, namely the systematic deviation from citizens' preferences. As the privileges accorded by the politicians to themselves are of an extremely varied kind and are difficult to detect (especially with respect to pensions), experience shows that politicians' rent seeking can thereby scarcely be prevented. With respect to corruption, only the most blatant cases are found out. It must be concluded that while such rules are of some use, they certainly are not able to prevent the exploitation of citizens to any significant extent.

2. The establishment of special *courts*, with the task of preventing citizens' exploitation. All democratic countries know some institution of courts of accounts, but it may well be shown that they fulfill their role only to a limited extent. They are obviously the less effective, the more directly they depend on the politicians they are supposed to control. In this respect it does not help much if the members of the court of accounts are elected and must answer to the parliament (instead of to the government) because the cartel includes politicians inside and outside the government. Even courts of accounts, formally independent of

government and parliament, have little incentive and possibility of checking the exploitation of the citizens by the politicians. This applies particularly to the deviation from citizens' preferences; it may indeed be shown that courts of accounts, which necessarily have to focus on the formal correctness of politicians' and administrators' behavior, in some respects tend to widen the gap between what politicians provide and what the people want.

3. *Competition between parties* is the classical institution in representative democracies to prevent politicians from pursuing their own goals at the population's expense. Constitutions include various devices to further competition and make a coalition between the politicians more difficult. One is the division of power among the executive, legislative, and jurisdictional branches. Another is the establishment of two houses of parliament. Because of the many types of interactions existing, and the well-defined gains to be expected, these devices are rather ineffective in checking the interests of the *classe politique.*

An important constitutional device for stimulating the competition among parties is to guarantee, and to facilitate, the entry of new politicians and parties into the political system. While this certainly forces the established parties in a democracy to take better care of the people's wishes and to be more careful with regard to privileges and corruption, the effects tend to be short-lived. The previous outsiders quickly realize that many advantages are to be gained by tolerating the politicians' cartel, and even more by participating in it. The experience of many countries supports this theoretical proposition. An example are the "Green" parties, who at first fought against the political establishment, but within a surprisingly short time learned to take advantage of the taxpayers' money for their own purposes.

On the basis of these arguments, it is concluded that neither party competition, nor constitutional rules, nor courts, are particularly successful in reducing the possible exploitation of the general population by the politicians. It is not argued, of course, that the constitutional features elaborated are useless, but that they do not provide a sufficient safeguard against politicians' rent seeking. It is therefore desirable to search for, and to seriously consider, other constitutional means of fighting the politicians' cartel.

Referenda as a Constitutional Provision against the Politicians' Cartel A referendum, which allows all citizens the possibility of participating, meets the crucial requirement that it gives decision-making power to people *outside* the politicians' cartel. The individuals making the decision are not integrated into the *classe politique*, and they avoid the control of politicians. In an *initiative* the demands are explicitly directed against the political establishment represented in parliament and government. Initiatives allow putting issues on the political agenda that members of parliament prefer not to discuss. *Optional* and *obligatory* referenda serve more of a controlling function because, if successful, they overrule the decisions taken by the executive and the legislative bodies.

A popular referendum (in the widest sense of the word) can only serve its purpose if the *classe politique* cannot block it. In many countries the Supreme Court or, even worse, the parliament, has the power to decide whether a referendum is admissible. The criteria appear to be purely formal, but in fact the members of the *classe politique* have a considerable number of possibilities and incentives to forbid referenda threatening the position of the politicians' cartel. Often vague concepts, based on what *they* consider to be the "raison d'état," are employed. In other countries, such as Switzerland, almost no such possibility exists, and therefore issues may be brought to the vote that are not desired, and are sometimes even strongly disliked, by the politicians.

Empirical evidence shows that referenda can break the cartel among the politicians by getting through constitutional provisions and laws totally against the interests of the *classe politique*. The following cases refer to Switzerland, the referenda nation par excellence. The first two cases concern important historical episodes (Blankart 1992).

CASE 1 During the nineteenth century the house of representatives (*Nationalrat*) was elected according to the majority rule. The largest party greatly benefited from that throughout seven decades, the Radical-Democratic Party secured a majority of the seats. When the idea was raised that the elections should follow proportional representation in order to allow small parties to enter parliament, the then *classe politique* among the executives and jurisdiction strongly rejected this proposal for obvious reasons of self-interest. Nevertheless, in 1918, the corresponding referendum was accepted by the majority of the population and the cantons. In the subsequent elections the Radical-Democratic Party lost no less than 40 percent of their seats.

CASE 2 Until the Second World War, Urgent federal laws (*dringliche Bundesbeschluesse*) were not subject to (optional) referenda. In order not to have to seek the people's approval, and in order to pursue policies in their own interests, the *classe politique* in the government and parliament often declared federal laws to be "urgent," even if that was not in fact the case. In 1946 an initiative was started with the objective of preventing this disregard for the interests of the population. Again, the executive and legislative bodies urged the voters to reject the initiative, which was clearly one of self-interest. However, the initiative was accepted by the voters, and the politicians are now forced to take the citizens' interests into account when they decide on federal laws.

The history of Swiss voting provides many more examples of such clashes between the opinions of the leaders and the citizens. The politicians have to make great efforts to endorse as quickly as possible any movements originating from outside the cartel. Sometimes it is established parties (but usually at the fringes of the cartel), or associated interest groups, that initiate referenda. If this strategy is to be successful, the politicians have to at least partially take into account the population's preferences, and have to reduce the extent of their rent seeking. The *institution* of referendum in this case leads indirectly to the desired outcome that the cartel of politicians has less leeway.[5]

Politicians are well aware that the institution of popular referendum severely restricts their possibility of "exploiting" the citizens/taxpayers, and they therefore oppose introducing elements of direct democracy.

Referenda as a Process

It would be mistaken to consider a referendum just to be a vote. Indeed two important stages before and after the vote need to be considered.

The Pre-referendum Process

The constitutional setting determines to a large extent which issues are put on the political *agenda* and which are prevented from appearing. In representative democracies, politicians are often skilled at not letting problems, which are to their disadvantage, be discussed in the democratically legitimized institutions. As has been shown, both theoretically and empirically, agenda setting power has a significant effect on voting outcomes.[6]

An important feature of referenda is the *discussion process* stimulated among the citizens, and between politicians and citizens.[7]

Pre-referendum discussions may be interpreted as an exchange of arguments among equal persons taking place under well-defined rules. This institutionalized discussion meets various conditions of the "ideal discourse process," as envisaged by Habermas (1983). The relevance of discussion for politics induces citizens to participate, depending on how important the issue in question is considered to be. The experience of Switzerland shows indeed that some referenda motivate intense and far-reaching discussions (e.g., referenda on whether to join the European Economic Space with a participation rate of almost 80 percent, compared to an average of roughly 40 percent). Other referenda considered to be of little importance by the voters engender little discussion and low participation rates (as low as 25 percent). This variability in the intensity of discussion and participation overrides the much studied "paradox of voting" (Tullock 1967; Riker and Ordeshook 1973).

The main function of the pre-referendum process is certainly to raise the level of information of the participants (for empirical evidence, see the next section). It may moreover be hypothesized that the exchange of arguments also forms the participants' preferences. What matters most is that this preference formation can be influenced by, but not controlled by, the *classe politique*.[8]

A further important aspect of the referendum process is going beyond outcome considerations. Citizens may benefit from the process as such, as it is well established that people have a preference for participation in decision making because it enhances individuals' perception of self-determination (e.g., Pateman 1970; for an extensive survey, see Lane 2000, ch. 13). With regard to direct democracy, Cronin (1989, p. 11), for example, notes, that "giving the citizen more of a role in governmental processes might lessen alienation and apathy." Moreover the political discussion induced by initiatives and referendums generates a common understanding for different political opinions and positions. This strengthens the social contract based on consensus and motivates people to go beyond acting out of narrow self-interest. Participation possibilities are thus considered an important source of perceived procedural fairness, shaping individual behavior.

Post-referendum Adjustments

In a referendum a political decision is formally made, but this does not necessarily mean that the politicians and the public administration take the appropriate action to implement it. In fact there is substantial variation on how they react to winning referendums and in particular to initiatives (Gerber et al. 2001, 2004; Bali 2003). Initiatives that are drafted in order to overcome inaction of the government or the parliament often face opposition from the latter actors in the post-referendum process. The groups who launch and support winning initiatives are not authorized to implement and enforce them. They must rather delegate these tasks to the members of parliament or the administration. The position of the initiators is relatively stronger if they are linked to a political party represented in the legislature or if they can rely on an existing and permanent infrastructure. It is most difficult (or impossible) to oversee the implementation and enforcement of initiatives for ad hoc groups and committees that disband after the ballot. The costs for the legislatures and the bureaucrats to oppose winning initiatives in the post-referendum process thereby are the higher, the more legitimate the constitution is taken to be in a political system. The politicians may in particular fear of not being reelected by the voters if they undermine citizens' democratic rights. However, ultimately the extent of implementation depends on whether the constitutional rules are voluntarily obeyed by the persons in power.

The question of which side gets a majority in a referendum is not the only thing that matters. A referendum also clearly reveals how the population feels about the matter, and where and how large the minorities are. Groups dissenting from the majority are identified; their preferences become visible and become part of the political process (see Gerber 1997). This makes it more likely that particular parties start to champion their cause in order to win additional support, and for referenda to take place in particular regions.

Switzerland again provides a suitable example. In 1989 a popular initiative demanded that the Swiss Army be completely disbanded. Many Swiss considered this to be an attack on one of the almost "sacred" institutions of the country. The *classe politique* was totally against the initiative, and the generals threatened that they would retire if the initiative was not overwhelmingly rejected (they spoke of a percentage of no-votes between 80 and 90 percent). The referendum outcome was a surprise to everybody, because one third of the voters (and a majority among the young voters eligible for military service) voted for the dissolution of the army. After a short period of shock, several parties suggested changes in the army which were implemented within a short time—changes which, before the referendum, were considered by everyone to be impossible to achieve.

Referenda and the Protection of Federalism

The institution of citizens directly deciding on an issue and the decentralization of decision making are closely connected. On the one hand, federalism is an *alternative* means for better fulfillment of the voters' preferences: individuals tend to turn away from unsatisfactory jurisdictions, while they are attracted to those caring for the people's preferences at low cost. The possibility to vote with one's feet (Tiebout 1956; see also Buchanan 1965; Hirschman 1970) tends to undermine regional cartels by politicians.

Federalism is, at the same time, *facilitating* effective referenda rather than substituting them. In small communities much of the knowledge needed for informed political decision making is acquired in everyday life. The citizens are well aware of the benefits and costs of particular public programs (see also Mueller, chapter 8 in this volume). As taxpayers they have to carry the burden, provided that there is a sufficient amount of fiscal equivalence (Olson 1969, 1986).

It is crucial for the beneficial functioning of federalism that the constitution explicitly assigns competence to spend money, *as well as* to levy taxes, to all the different levels of the state. However, this is not enough, because politicians oppose federal competition as it restricts them in following their own interests. Therefore subcentral governments try to form tax and expenditure cartels that are protected by the central government. As a result there is a tendency toward government centralization beyond the point where citizens benefit the most (e.g., Blankart 2000). The problem of overcentralization also exists for other reasons (see Eichenberger 1994; Vaubel 1994) and is difficult to control. Rather than protect the federal system in the United States, the Supreme Court allowed a broad interpretation of activities assigned to the federal level that led to substantial centralization (Niskanen 1992). A referendum system, in contrast, is the constitutional provision that is most likely to protect a decentralized government.[9]

2.4 Empirical Evidence on the Consequences of Direct Democracy

Direct democracy changes the political process in three important ways, compared to a purely representative democracy, as was argued in the last section: (1) Due to a restriction of established politicians' power, an *outcome* of the political process can be expected that is closer to the citizens' preferences. (2) The participatory character of direct democratic decision making provides incentives to voters to inform themselves about political issues, and changes their relationship to authorities and fellow citizens. The referendum *process* might thus be a source of procedural utility. (3) Direct democracy affects *institutional* change, and protects rules that favor the citizens; in particular, it is a safeguard against the risks of overcentralization.

In order to substantiate these hypotheses, systematic empirical analyses are necessary. A number of studies exist for both Switzerland and the United States (e.g., for surveys, see Bowler and Donovan 1998; Eichenberger 1999; Kirchgässner, Feld, and Savioz 1999; Gerber and Hug 2001; Matsusaka 2004). The two countries are particularly suited for comparative empirical analyses because direct democratic rights are developed to a very different extent at the level of Swiss cantons and US states respectively. While we briefly mention a wide range of results, some particularly important findings are presented in greater detail.

Effects on Policy Outcomes

In order to study whether direct democracy makes a difference to the outcomes of the political process, a natural starting point is to begin with public expenditures and revenues. Fiscal decisions are the central activities of most governments, and policy priorities are to a large extent formed in the budgeting process.

In a study covering the 26 Swiss cantons and the years between 1986 and 1997, Feld and Kirchgässner (2001) measure the effects of a mandatory fiscal referendum on aggregate expenditure and revenue. In 217 cases of the totally 312 annual observations, cantons adopted a mandatory referendum on new expenditure above a given threshold. It is found that expenditure and revenue in cantons with fiscal referendums are lower by about 7 and 11 percent respectively, compared to cantons that do not have this institutional provision.[10] In a sample of 132 large Swiss towns in 1990, the same authors replicated their test for the mandatory referendum on budget deficits. In cities where a budget deficit has to be approved by the citizenry, expenditure and revenue, on average, are lower by about 20 percent, while public debt is reduced by about 30 percent. With an extended panel data set from 1980 to 1998, the effect of the mandatory expenditure referendum is analyzed, taking the spending threshold into account (Feld and Matsusaka 2003). At the median threshold of 2.5 million Swiss francs (SFR), spending per capita is reduced by 1,314 SFR, namely by 18 percent for an average expenditure level of 7,232 SFR (compared to cantons that either have an optional financial referendum or no referendum on new public expenditure).[11] The difference in overall spending significantly varies between cantons, applying a low threshold of 0.5 million SFR (25th percentile) and a high threshold of 15 million SFR (75th percentile). For the former, expenditure is estimated to be lower by 1,389 SFR, while for the latter the reduction is 845 SFR. Moreover it is found that the mandatory financial referendum has less effect when it is easier for citizens to launch an initiative for a new law or to change an existing law (measured by the signature requirement). Thus there is a substitutive relationship between the two institutions with regard to their consequences on cantonal fiscal outcomes.

Very similar results are found for analyses across US states (Matsusaka 1995, 2004). In a panel from 1970 to 1999, including all states except Alaska, the effect of the initiative right is estimated on public expenditure, as well as on revenue. The institutional variable (a dummy variable) captures any type of initiative, whether it is statutory or for a constitutional amendment. After controlling for the average income in the state, federal aid, population size and growth, the percentage of metropolitan population, and whether it is a southern or western state, initiative states, on average, have lower expenditure, as well as lower revenue, than non-initiative states. States with the initiative spend $137 less per capita than states that do not provide the initiative, ceteris paribus. They also raise less revenue, $117 per capita compared to non-initiative states. Both effects are about 4 percent, compared to average expenditure and revenue respectively. The effects are, however, significantly different when the signature requirements to launch an initiative are taken into consideration. States with a 2 percent requirement are estimated to levy $342 less taxes and fees per capita than non-initiative states (for the modal signature requirement of 5 percent, revenue is 6 percent lower and expenditure is 5 percent lower; Matsusaka 2004, ch. 3). These effects reflect robust results that can be assigned to the referendum process and not, for example, to the ideology of a state's electorate. Controlling for roll call voting of state senators, as a proxy for voters' conservatism, does not change the results in a substantive manner; if anything, the effects for the institutional variable increase (Matsusaka 2004, ch. 3).

Often these kinds of results are interpreted as clear evidence that direct democracy produces favorable outcomes for the citizens. However, they mainly provide clear evidence against a simple median voter world, in which representatives implement the preferred expenditure and revenue levels of the median voter, and referendums and initiatives would have no effect.[12] It could well be that low expenditure and revenue levels mainly serve some well-organized interests (e.g., rich people) that rely less on public services. Therefore the efficiency in the provision of public goods has to be analyzed.

The cost efficient use of public money under different institutional settings can be directly studied for single publicly provided goods. In a careful study on waste collection, Pommerehne (1983, 1990) finds that this service is provided at the lowest cost in Swiss towns that have extended direct democratic participation rights and choose a private contractor. If the services are provided by the town instead of a private company, costs are about 10 percent higher. Efficiency losses are about 20 percent in purely representative democratic towns (compared to direct democratic ones). The average cost of waste collection is the highest in towns that rely on representative democratic decision making only, as well as on publicly organized collection (about 30 percent higher than in the most efficient case).

A hint on the efficiency of public services comes from a study that relates fiscal referendums to economic performance in Swiss cantons (Feld and Savioz 1997). For the years 1984 until 1993 a neoclassical production function is estimated that includes the number of employees in all sectors, cantonal government expenditure for education including grants, as well as a proxy for capital based on investments for building and construction. The production function is then extended by a dummy variable that identifies cantons with extended direct democratic participation rights in financial issues at the local level. Total productivity—as measured by the cantonal GDP per capita—is estimated to be 5 percent higher in cantons with extended direct democracy, compared to cantons where these instruments are not available.

Based on an aggregate growth equation, Blomberg et al. (2004) analyze to what extent public capital (utilities, roads, education, etc.) is productively provided and whether there is a difference between initiative and non-initiative states in the United States. Data on gross state product, private and public capital, employment and population, are for 48 US states between 1969 and 1986. They find that non-initiative states are only about 82 percent as effective as states with the initiative right in providing productive capital services, meaning approximately

20 percent more government expenditure is wasted where citizens have no possibility to launch initiatives, compared to states where this institution is installed.

Interesting indirect evidence for the efficiency of referendums and initiatives offers a comparative study of land prices in 91 municipalities in Connecticut (Santerre 1986). Property prices are significantly higher in municipalities that provide direct democratic rights, compared to municipalities that do not.

In section 2.3 we outlined a politicoeconomic process in which politicians form a cartel against citizens. Previous results could, however, also be explained by imperfect information that leads benign representatives to implementing inferior policies, which happens less frequently in cantons, municipalities, and states with direct democratic rights. While we do not reject the notion of well-intentioned representatives, differences in the level of efficiency are hypothesized to be due to differences in legislative shirking. Corresponding evidence is provided by a study on corruption in US states in 1998 (Alt and Lassen 2003). The misuse of public office for private gains is measured based on a survey of state house reporters' perception of public corruption. It is found that in addition to a number of control variables, there is a statistically significant effect of voter initiatives on perceived corruption. In initiative states, corruption is lower than in non-initiative states, and this effect is the larger, the lower the signature requirement to launch an initiative. The result is further qualified, as there is only a negative effect on corruption for direct initiatives (but not for indirect initiatives, that have to be approved by the legislator).

Beyond the efficient provision of public goods and services, the consequences of direct political participation rights can be studied for citizens' happiness. Individuals not only have preferences for material affluence but also with regard to freedom, equal opportunities, social justice, and solidarity. Whether, overall, individuals' preferences are better served in direct democracies than in representative democracies can be conjectured, but not deduced, based on the extensive previous evidence. In contrast, the analysis of people's reported subjective well-being (for an introductory survey, see Frey and Stutzer 2002b) can offer important evidence on whether people in direct democracies are happier.

In a study for Switzerland in the early 1990s, the effect of direct democratic participation rights on people's reported satisfaction with life is empirically analyzed (Frey and Stutzer 2000, 2002a). Survey answers are from more than 6,000 interviews. The proxy measure for individual utility is based on the following question: "How satisfied are you with your life as a whole these days?" People answered on a scale from one (completely dissatisfied) to ten (completely satisfied). The institutionalized rights of individual political participation are measured at the cantonal level, where there is considerable variation. A broad index is used that measures the different barriers preventing citizens from entering the political process via initiatives and referenda across cantons.[13] The main result is a sizable positive correlation between the extent of direct democratic rights and people's reported subjective well-being (after taking important sociodemographic and socioeconomic variables into account). An increase in the index of direct democracy by one standard deviation raises the proportion of people indicating very high satisfaction with life by approximately 3.4 percentage points (or about 0.14 unit on the 10-point scale). This effect is more than a third as large as the difference in life satisfaction between the lowest income category and the one reporting the highest life satisfaction. As the improvement affects everybody, the institutional factor capturing direct democracy is important in an aggregate sense.

Effects on the Process of Political Decision Making

It is widely believed that well-informed citizens are an essential prerequisite for a well-functioning and stable democracy. If citizens do not have sufficient information about the policies or candidates they vote for, they may be disappointed by the actual consequences of their decisions, which in turn can undermine the acceptance and legitimacy of democracy as a political system. However, collecting information in order to make an informed decision at the poll is a public good that citizens are only willing to make to a limited extent. On the one hand, it can be debated whether a direct democratic decision on a particular issue demands more or less information than the choice of a candidate, given the institutions that lower citizens' information costs.[14] On the other hand, it can be asked whether the level of voter information itself is dependent on the political system in which citizens live. We have theoretically argued in the last section that a political system that gives citizens more political participation possibilities will change the demand for political information, as well as the supply of it. An illustrative example is the introduction of the Maastricht Treaty in various European countries. In the countries where citizens had the right to vote on it (e.g., Denmark), politicians had to engage much more in explaining the Treaty to the citizens than in countries where no referendum took place (e.g., Germany). For the citizens the incentives to be informed were greater, as the intense discussions before the referendum partly transformed 'having a reasoned opinion' into a private good. Casual observation suggests that as a consequence information levels on the content of the Treaty were high among Danish citizens. While this example offers suggestive evidence that voters are better informed when they have a larger say in the political process, Benz and Stutzer (2004) provide more systematic evidence.

They study voter information in two different contexts. First, survey data from the Eurobarometer series is used to systematically investigate how referenda in several European countries affected citizens' information on the European Union. The results indicate that people in countries with a referendum are in fact "objectively" better informed (according to ten questions about the European Union in the 1996 Eurobarometer), as well as feeling "subjectively" better informed about the European Union after a referendum (Eurobarometer 1992–1997).

Second, they look at voter information in Switzerland. As a proxy measure for citizens' awareness of political issues, the number of correct answers to the following three questions is used: (1) "How many parties are in the Federal Council?" (2) "Who was the president of the Federal Council in 1995?" And (3) "How many signatures are required for an initiative?" Data are obtained from a large survey conducted among the Swiss electorate in 1996. Differences across cantons are explained by a measure for the extent of citizens' participation rights, as well as a number of sociodemographic control variables. In this study the same broad index is used as in the work on direct democracy and life satisfaction in Switzerland (described in the last subsection). A raw correlation is presented in figure 2.1.

As the figure shows, on average, citizens living in more direct democratic jurisdictions are objectively better informed about politics. The result holds in a multiple regression framework and indicates that the effect is sizable. For the full range of the institutional variable, an effect is estimated that is comparable to an increase in education from mere compulsory education to having attended a college providing a diploma at the end.

The study by Benz and Stutzer (2004) also indicates that political participation possibilities raise discussion intensity which, in the literature, is seen as an important transmission channel that leads to higher voter information.

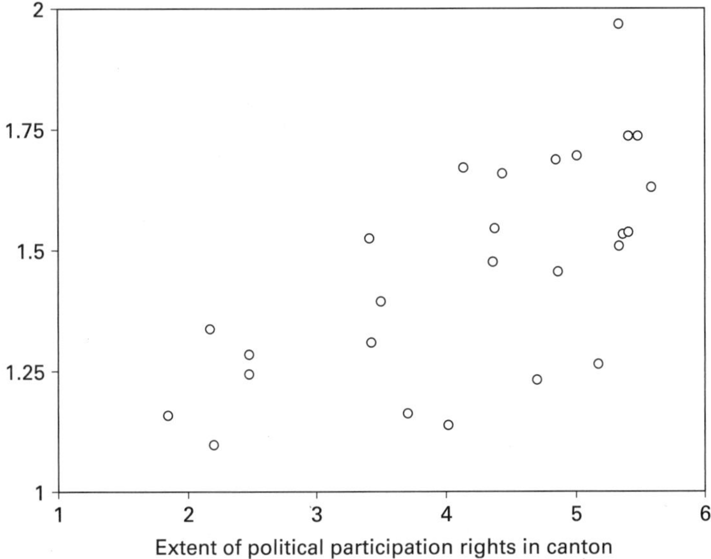

Figure 2.1
Correlation between voter information and political participation rights in Swiss cantons, 1995. Source: Benz and Stutzer (2004), based on Selects 1996.

People's satisfaction with the provision of public services in direct democracies is likely to influence their behavior as voters collecting information or as taxpayers. However, the process of decision making may also change people's trust in authorities (this can be seen as a psychological contract; see Feld and Frey 2002) and their motivation to obey the law. It has, for example, been shown that with more extensive democratic participation rights, people have higher tax morale and evade taxes less. Based on survey data from the World Values Study, Torgler (2003) finds that, in more direct democratic Swiss cantons, citizens are more likely to agree with the statement that "cheating on taxes if you have a chance" is never justifiable. Pommerehne and Weck-Hannemann (1996) directly study tax evasion in Swiss cantons and find that it is substantially lower where citizens have a direct impact on budgetary policy.

Citizens' experience with direct democracy has further been found to form positive attitudes about their abilities to influence what government does (Bowler and Donovan 2002). Thus direct democracy strengthens citizens' feelings of political efficacy.

The evidence mentioned in this subsection leads to the hypothesis that citizens might benefit from the process of direct democracy, beyond its political outcomes.[15] Frey and Stutzer (2005) extend the study mentioned above on direct democracy and life satisfaction to address this hypothesis. In order to disentangle outcome effects and procedural effects that make for the positive correlation between participation rights and reported subjective well-being, foreigners are used as a control group. Foreigners benefit from favorable outcomes but are excluded from procedural benefits. In fact it is found that the positive effect of direct democratic participation rights is about three times as large for citizens as it is for foreigners.

Effects on Government Centralization

The relation between direct democracy and federalism is not restricted to the common goal of a better fulfillment of citizens' preferences. Rather, the two institutions are mutually dependent. In particular, the citizens are interested in a working federal competition between jurisdictions. In order for the citizens to defend themselves against politicians' interests in the case of centralization, they need strong political rights. Blankart (2000) explains the stronger centralization in Germany, compared to Switzerland, after World War II by the missing direct democratic instruments at the federal level in Germany. He documents the centralization process by comparing Germany's Basic Law in 1949 with the one in 1999. With regard to taxation, for example, tax bases in 1949 were allocated exclusively to each of the three levels of government. In 1999, almost all the relevant taxes are under federal legislation, and separation of taxes is replaced by revenue sharing. This is reflected in a percentage of centralized taxes of 93.0 percent in 1995 compared to 61.2 percent in 1950. While, in Switzerland, a parliamentary system with two chambers exists that is similar to the one in Germany, there is a significant difference in the process of constitutional change. In the case of tax issues, for example, "since 1917, the citizens have been called no less than 23 times to vote on federal income and turnover taxes. Forty percent of the proposals have been declined in the first round" (Blankart 2000, p. 32). Accordingly, centralized taxes account for 47.4 percent in Switzerland in 1995, which is a much smaller proportion than in Germany (although both countries had similar levels in 1950: 60.1 percent in Switzerland and 61.2 percent in Germany).

The effect of direct democracy on government decentralization is also empirically documented for the lower levels of government. In an extension of the work on spending across US states from 1970 to 1999, Matsusaka (2004, ch. 4) studies how the initiative changes the division between state and local expenditure. While initiative states, on average, spend 13 percent less per capita at the state level than non-initiative states, they spend 4 percent more at the local level. The result is more decentralized spending patterns in states that adopt the initiative. Similar results are obtained for Swiss cantons in a panel over the period 1980 to 1998 (Schaltegger and Feld 2001). Rather than expenditure per capita, the proportion of cantonal expenditure in percent of total state and local spending is related to the development of the financial referendum. It is found that cantons with fewer obstacles to launching a budget referendum are less centralized with regard to expenditure, as well as revenue. The effect on expenditure is to a large extent due to more decentralized spending on education in more direct democratic cantons.

Direct democracy is not only affecting the process of fiscal centralization, but also spatial centralization. Martin and Wagner (1978) find that there are fewer municipal incorporations in US states, where direct democratic processes involve residents in incorporation decisions.

2.5 Arguments against and Counterarguments for Referenda

Systematic evidence has been accumulated that direct democracy is a process and provides outcomes that are more in line with citizens' preferences than are a purely representative democratic process and its outcomes. Nevertheless, referenda can hardly be considered a popular institution in democracies, not to speak of authoritarian systems. Not surprisingly, the members of the *classe politique* are quick to raise many objections because they realize that referenda constitute a threat to their position, by limiting their rent-seeking potential. Many intellectuals—even those who do not share in the spoils of the politicians' cartel, and those opposing the political establishment—also reject referenda, with a variety of arguments. The basic reason is that they consider themselves to be better judges of what is good for the people than the citizens themselves. They tend to see themselves in the role of "philosopher-king," determining what "social welfare" is. Consequently they prefer decision-making systems where they have a larger say. Thus they oppose referenda for the same reasons as they oppose the market.

The following ten arguments are often raised against the institution of the referendum. In addition to the empirical evidence in the last section, we respond to these claims with additional arguments.

Citizens Fail to Understand the Complex Issues

It is argued that the average voter is not well informed nor well educated, so he or she cannot reasonably be allowed to determine political issues. Therefore policy making is the task of a specialized group, the politicians, who represent the voters.

This view can be refuted for various reasons: First of all, it is inconsistent to trust citizens to be able to choose between parties and politicians in elections but not between issues in referenda. If anything, the former choice is more difficult, as one must form expectations on how politicians will decide on future issues. Second, the voters need not have any detailed knowledge about the issues at stake. Rather, they only need to grasp the main questions involved. These main questions are not of a technical nature but involve decisions of principle, which a voter is as qualified to make as a politician. Third, the general intelligence and qualifications of politicians should not be overrated. They can hardly be considered to be consistently superior to other people. Moreover the average member of parliament has little choice; he or she is normally forced to vote according to what the party superiors and a few specialists have decided in advance. Fourth, a number of institutions have emerged in direct democracies, helping citizens to reach reasoned decisions. The parties and interest groups give their recommendations concerning decision making, which the citizens may take into consideration. Even more important, the discourse in the prereferendum stage brings out the main aspects and puts them in perspective. Finally, as shown in the last section, citizens' information on political issues has to be taken endogenously. Direct democracy provides incentives for the citizens to privately collect information, and for the political actors and the media to provide it.

Citizens Have Little Interest in Participating

Participation in initiatives and referenda is often low and varies with the size of jurisdictions (e.g., see Hansen et al. 1987). Sometimes only a few eligible voters go to the polls. It can be concluded from that that citizens are not interested in the issues to be decided on.

This is, however, a wrong conclusion for three reasons: First, the voting participation is not always so low. When the citizens feel that the issue is important, the voting participation rises considerably. This holds also in large jurisdictions where political mobilization is at a disadvantage. Switzerland provides a good example of this variability: while average participation for all issues at the federal level is around 45 percent, it can be as low as 25 percent. But sometimes it goes up to 80 percent and more, as was the case in 1992, when the Swiss citizens had to decide whether or not they want to join the European economic area.

Second, high voting participation is not necessarily a good thing. Citizens are perfectly rational not to participate when they find the issues unimportant or when they are undecided. It can even be argued that it is socially beneficial that citizens do not participate under these conditions but rather leave the decision to those for whom the issue really matters. Voting participation then reflects citizens' preference intensities, which makes the vote socially more valuable. Third, it is naive to think that *freely chosen* voting participation in parliaments is very different from how citizens behave with respect to popular referenda. Today's members of parliament are highly specialized and seriously consider the pros and cons of only a few issues. In the case of all other issues, they (have to) follow the dictate of the party leadership, so they do not cast a voluntary vote. This is reflected in the often extremely low participation in a parliamentary session. The members of parliament have to be herded together from the lobby or their offices to cast the dictated vote.

Citizens Are Easy to Manipulate

Financially strong parties and pressure groups are better able to start initiatives and to engage in referendum propaganda than are financially poor and nonorganized interests. This cannot be denied. However, the perspective is wrong because it takes an absolute stance: it is *always* true that the rich and well-organized groups wield more power. The crucial question is whether they have *more* or *less* power in a direct than in a representative democracy. It is well known that well-organized and financed pressure groups exert considerable power over the politicians sitting in parliament and in government. It may even be argued that it is cheaper to influence the small number of legislators and government politicians than the total electorate.

Citizens Are Prone to Decide Emotionally

Voters are often supposed to be unduly influenced by emotional considerations. Again, this charge must be considered in a comparative perspective. There is little reason to believe that politicians are less subject to emotions. After all, parliaments are known to have highly emotional debates, sometimes even erupting into fist fighting. For that reason many parliaments have formal procedures to debate a proposal two or even three times, with considerable time elapsing in between. The same holds for popular referenda. Before taking the vote, there must be time for intensive discussion, which allows the various sides of a question to be brought up. This strongly increases the chances of a decision dominated by rational aspects.[16]

There Are Too Many Referenda Confusing the Voters

When the citizens have to simultaneously decide on a great many issues (e.g., in California the voters often have to deal with 20 or even more propositions), they focus on a few clear issues. The decisions on all other issues are then haphazard and lack rationality.

This is indeed a situation to be avoided. However, the number of referenda put to the vote can be steered by the number of weekends with ballots over the year and by the number of signatures required for an initiative or optional referendum. If the number of issues to be decided on gets too large, the number of signatures required can be raised. Such a decision should be taken by a constitutional referendum to prevent the *classe politique* from fixing such a high number of signatures that referenda become improbable.

Political Leadership Is Impossible

Politicians are sometimes supposed to make unpopular decisions. An example would be a restrictive fiscal policy, when the budget deficit is getting too high or when inflation soars. Such policy pays off only over the medium or even long term. It is argued that such unpopular policies would be impossible in a direct democracy.

This conclusion, however, does not necessarily hold. In a direct democracy the politicians are forced to explain their policies to the citizens. If they can give good reasons why they propose to undertake such a seemingly unpopular policy, the citizens will not oppose it.

There are many examples in Switzerland where the citizens are prepared to support policies burdening them, provided that the politicians make an effort to explain why the sacrifice is necessary to improve the situation over the long term. Empirical evidence presented in the last section, for example, shows that fiscal stability is higher in Swiss cantons and US states with more extensive direct democratic participation rights.

Referenda Are Inadequate for Major Issues

As the voters are taken to be poorly educated and ill informed, subject to manipulation and to emotional decisions, it is often argued that referenda should only be used for small and unimportant issues. In contrast, issues of great consequence—such as changes in the constitution—should be left to the professional politicians.

The opposite makes more sense. Major issues can be reduced to the essential content. Evaluation is then not a matter of (scientific) expertise but of value judgments. Following methodological individualism, only the citizens may be the final judges when it comes to preferences, and a substitution by representatives is, at most, a second-best solution. As the politicians have a systematic incentive to deviate from the voters' preferences, a substitution leads to biased outcomes.

Referenda Hinder Progress

Asking the population to make a decision is often rejected because it is argued that the "ordinary citizens" do not like changes, and that they prevent the adoption of "bold, new ideas."

It may well be true that many new propositions are rejected in referenda, but this does not mean that this constitutes a disadvantage. The fact that proposals contain new ideas is no proof of their quality. Indeed the citizens are right in rejecting them when they are in favor of the *classe politique.* The concept of "bold, new" solutions is not rarely the result of technocratic thinking and of a planning mentality. They strengthen the politicians' and bureaucrats' position but need not necessarily be in the voters' interests.

Referenda are well proved to break deadlocks in societal decision making and, in this sense, are progressive. There are cases where a referendum helped clear an issue that was difficult to resolve in parliament and government. The prime example is the demands by regions for more independence. These demands are often accompanied by considerable violence and bloodshed. The Basque country is just one of many cases. In a direct democracy such heated issues may be brought to a resolution acceptable to a large majority. In Switzerland, for instance, the secession of the Jury from the canton Bern was achieved by undertaking a number of referenda. While some minor violence took place, the issue was settled with much less strife and bloodshed than normally occurs in representative democracies, let alone autocratic systems.

Referenda Destroy Civil Rights

One of the fundamental problems of democracy is the "tyranny of the majority." This danger is seen to be particularly acute in the case of referenda where the will of the majority is unrestricted. As a result civil rights may be thwarted. But this is not necessarily the case. Most important, if there are economic, social, and political cross cleavages, no group of citizens is *always* in the majority, and therefore will be careful not to antagonize other social groups. Empirically some evidence for the suppression of civil rights has been found in local and state ballots in the United States (Gamble 1997), but there is also contrary evidence for the United States and Switzerland (Cronin 1989; Frey and Goette 1998). In a study on 51 California ballot propositions, the notion of cross cleavages is supported. Hajnal et al. (2002) find that black, Latino, and Asian American voters are only about 1 percent less likely than white voters to be in the winning majority of the vote.

Referenda Are Expensive

The last argument against referenda is the alleged high cost of undertaking them from an administrative point of view. It is argued that parliamentary decisions are much less expensive and should therefore be favored.

There are two reasons why this reasoning is fallacious: First, referenda are not expensive compared to the large cost of running a professional parliament with its accompanying party system (e.g., see von Arnim 1988 for Germany). As in a direct democracy the final say is with the citizens, and less money needs to be spent on parliament and the parties. Moreover the administrative costs of referenda are not high because several propositions can be dealt with in one weekend, and citizens can be asked to actively participate in organizing the vote and counting the votes. While the citizens drafted suffer some opportunity cost, such a participation has the advantage of getting them more directly involved in governing their state, which tends to raise their sense for citizens' duties. Second, the administrative cost of running referenda is immaterial compared to their major advantage, namely to significantly reduce the deviation of political decisions from individual preferences.

2.6 Issues for Constitutional Design

The Case of the European Constitution

While the designers of the European constitution are well advised when they are inspired by the US constitution, in particular its revolutionary vision, they should not repeat the mistakes of the founders of the American Republic when dealing with constitutional amendments. The constitutional history of the United States shows that in the case of three major transformations, each has broken the rules for constitutional amendment (Ackerman 1998): (1) The convention that wrote the US constitution ignored the rules that allowed for the amendment of the Articles of the Confederation. (2) The amendments, which freed the slaves and provided them with citizenship, did not result from a procedure designed for amending the constitution. (3) The great extension of the competence of central government vis-à-vis the states in the 1930s was backed by Supreme Court judgments rather than a formal amendment. Article V of the US constitution thus does not seem appropriate to handling constitutional change under the rule of law. The first option, to call a convention in order to amend or replace the constitution, was never chosen. The second option, a two-thirds support for an amendment in both Houses of the Congress, and ratification by three-quarters of the states, was sometimes applied but was disregarded for major changes.[17]

The proposal for the new European constitution in Article IV-7 defines the "Procedure for revising the Treaty establishing the constitution." The process is designed as follows:

1. The government of any Member State, the European Parliament or the Commission may submit proposals to the Council of Ministers for the amendment of the Treaty establishing the Constitution.

2. If the European Council, after consulting the European Parliament and the Commission, adopts by a simple majority a decision in favor of examining the proposed amendments, the President of the European Council shall convene a Convention.... The European Council may decide by a simple majority, after obtaining the consent of the European Parliament, not to convene the Convention, should this not be justified by the extent of the proposed amendments.

3. The Convention shall examine the proposal for amendments and shall adopt by consensus a recommendation to the conference of representatives of the governments of the Member States....

4. The conference of representatives of the government of the Member States shall be convened by the President of the Council of Ministers for the purpose of determining by common accord the amendments to be made to the Treaty establishing the Constitution.

5. The amendments shall enter into force after being ratified by all the Member States in accordance with their respective constitutional requirements.

These citations capture the most relevant aspects of article IV-7. Two characteristics are essential. There is *no direct role for citizens* in deciding on the basic law to which they are supposed to adhere. *Unanimous consent* (in the Convention and in the conference of representatives of the governments of the member states) is the only principle for a formal constitutional amendment.

The fact that the European constitution has to meet the *unanimous consent* of all member states means that it can practically *not be changed.* Such unanimity is correct behind the veil of ignorance. But most member countries are far from ignorant about what their interests will be in the future. The requirement of unanimous consent means that formal adjustments and amendments to the constitution will not occur.[18] But such changes are crucial in order to prevent the ossification of the fundamental rules guiding the Union.

Citizens' preferences and the economic and social conditions of the European Union will certainly evolve in the future. If the EU constitution is immutable, due to the exclusion of citizens' direct involvement and unanimity requirements, the necessary changes will take place *outside* the constitution, as has been observed in the United States. Three decision-making bodies will gradually adjust the rules actually followed in the political process. Contrary to a constitutional process geared to fulfill citizens' preferences, these three groups of actors will change institutions and laws more in the direction of their own ideologies and interests. Common tendencies will be the exclusion of "disturbing" influences on the par of the citizenry and the restriction of competition between regions and nations within the Union, resulting in centralization.

The *European Constitutional Court* will form the ground rules by interpreting the existing constitution in a particular way. The respective constitutional developments may well be superior to an immutable set of rules. But the decisions taken will have special features. The members of the Constitutional Court being elected by representative bodies are far from being responsive to citizens' preferences. Even if the members are elected for long terms, or for life, their incentives are unlikely to be directed to meeting citizens' desires. Experience with the US Supreme Court supports this conclusion. Judges do not effectively protect citizens from government intervention. In contrast, the Court tends to support centralization and governmental action against citizens' rights.

The members of the *European Parliament* (MEPs) are elected directly, but the corresponding elections are generally considered to be unimportant. The MEPs do not really have to convince the citizens about their position, but they are elected on the basis of their belonging to a particular party. Nevertheless, MEPs see themselves as the "true" representatives of "Europe." They tend to identify with the European bodies and support the European centralization process, even if it is inconsistent with the voters' wishes. They fight hard to prevent their legislative powers being eroded, in particular, if they are intended to be curbed by the direct participation rights of the citizens.

The *European Commission* and the *European public service* have a direct and strong interest in interpreting and adjusting the constitution in a way that provides more competence for them. Increased centralization of decision making raises their importance and power. For the same reason, both bodies resist direct interventions in decision making by the citizens.

The development of the rules outside the written European constitution thus disregards the interests of the citizens. Binding rules favor the interests of the particular bodies able to informally establish these rules.

While a living constitution is important, its development must be based on the *rule of law*. This means that a crucial part of a constitution is making provision for how to change it. The procedures must not be left to whatever body is trying to capture them. Rather, the procedures for changing the constitution must give the *citizens well-defined rights to participate in that process*. A straightforward way would be to require a double simple majority, both among all the voters in the European Union *and* among the member states.[19] It is, of course, also possible to require qualified majorities, either among the voters or member states, or both. According to our point of view, the essential requirement is that the citizens' participation is fully guaranteed and, in particular, that they (and not the federal government) have the power to assign legislative competence to bodies and state levels, the so-called competence competence. This includes the right to start constitutional changes via popular initiatives, with the courts and parliament having only minor, and clearly delineated, possibilities of intervention with respect to the issues proposed. The right must also extend to accepting or rejecting constitutional changes suggested by the parliament.[20]

Precondition in Society

There are many politicoeconomic obstacles to introducing political institutions that restrict the competence and influence of established interests. However, in societal crisis, or after a revolution (like in the former communist countries in Europe), there is a window of opportunity for institutional change and new basic rules for society. In order to successfully introduce direct democracy during these periods of time, a civic culture is necessary that facilitates the use of referenda and initiatives. It is impossible to successfully run directly democratic institutions where there is no adequate basis in society. One condition under which direct democracy[21] works well is when there are strong crosscutting cleavages (e.g., with respect to per capita income, religion, and culture or language). This guarantees that it is not always the same group of persons that finds itself in the minority and therefore feels exploited. As has also been emphasized, the citizens must have sufficient trust in the politicians that they actualize the referendum decision, and the politicians must trust that the citizens take reasonable decisions when voting on issues. This trust must develop over time and cannot simply be instilled from outside. Therefore the "grand" solution of jumping from a representative democracy straight into a fully developed direct democracy is both unrealistic and undesirable. Rather, direct participation rights for the citizens should be gradually introduced[22] so that a *learning process* can take place between the citizens, parliament and government. The use of initiatives and referenda by the citizens is, however, also a major factor in raising civic culture, especially in the form of the trust citizens have in their government. Direct democracy thus helps to create the necessary conditions for its own smooth functioning, provided that the learning effect does take place.

Gradual Introduction

There are several ways in which directly democratic rights can be gradually introduced. Most of them restrict the application of direct democratic decision making and constitute a considerable danger for direct democracy. Most important, the restrictions introduced may stay for good. In the case of several of the restrictions this would amount to destroying the whole idea of citizens' participation in political decision making. The institutions of direct democracy cannot develop their strengths. The outcome of politics would not correspond more closely to citizens' preferences than under a traditional representative system. Moreover the citizens are unable to learn the special features of direct democracy properly. Five approaches for a gradual introduction are briefly discussed.

Size of Majority

Passing a proposal in a popular vote may require a *super majority*, for instance, two-thirds of the participants. Alternatively, one may require a simple majority of the *whole* electorate, including those abstaining. Such quorums exist in Italy and many transition economies. In several of these countries referenda received a majority of the votes cast but not of the electorate. In Italy these quorums led to the perverse situation that opponents of a referendum called people to abstain from voting and were thus undermining the institution of direct democracy as such.

A strong restriction on popular initiatives and optional referenda is the number of signatures required. A balance between requiring a low number (and therefore having many referenda) and a high number (and therewith excluding citizens) is needed.

Issue Domain

Some questions can be excluded from direct voting or can be protected with the use of qualified majorities, for fear of "irresponsible" or "uncontrollable" outcomes. One could restrict the domain in the following way:

• Basic parts of the *constitution,* such as those referring to human, political, and civil rights, could be excluded.[23]

• Supposedly *sensitive* issues could be removed from citizens' voting. This may refer to problems relating to particular minorities, ethnic, or religious groups but also, for example, to the death penalty (as in Germany).

• Issues that are thought to be beyond the *competence* of the citizens. This could, for instance, be assumed to hold for economic problems, such as taxation. (In Germany the recent proposal to introduce national referenda excluded tax issues from the very beginning).

These restrictions are probably most dangerous for a successful application of direct democratic decision making, since they undermine the institution from the beginning. If only very unimportant issues are put to the vote, or if the number of signatures required for an initiative or optional referendum is far too high, the citizens cannot experience the advantages of direct democracy. On the other hand, the politicians can always claim that they gave direct democracy a chance but that it did not work. In the case of tight restrictions a vicious circle may develop. The way popular participation is introduced leads to unsatisfactory results and experiences, providing the opponents of direct democracy (in particular, the politicians in power) with a good reason to introduce even more severe restrictions. Of course, under these circumstances direct democracy cannot work.

Decision Level

Direct democratic elements can be restricted by initially granting them only on a particular level of the state.

One possibility is to start at the *local level,* giving citizens the right to launch initiatives and vote in referendums in political communes. This allows the citizens to benefit from everyday or impacted information in order to form a reasoned opinion. Moreover the issues are often of immediate relevance to the population. But this procedure only makes sense if the political communes have a sufficient amount of autonomy. Preferably they should be able to decide both on taxes and public expenditures. Recently, in the case of EU member states, there have been introduced quite extensive referendum rights in some of the German Länder (in particular, in Bavaria and the new Länder; e.g., see Luthardt und Waschkuhn 1997).[24]

Another possibility is to start at the *national level* when major issues are at stake. This has indeed happened in several European countries, where the decisions of whether to join the European Union or to join one of the several treaties have been relegated to the citizens as a whole. As these decisions are of crucial importance, the citizens are well aware of their relevance and will certainly be inclined to participate in the vote.

The limitations on the levels at which elements of direct democracy are to be introduced make most sense. The rights for initiatives and referenda should first be introduced at the local level, and at the same time at the national level, and perhaps only later at the regional level. At the local level the citizens tend to be well informed about the issues in question, while at the national level the decisions to be taken are of obvious importance. These are indeed the levels where direct democratic elements have been introduced in several transition economies, though only to a limited extent (Gross and Kaufmann 2002).

Time

The referendum process may be shaped by requiring a sufficient amount of time to pass between the start of an initiative or referendum process, the actual vote and the resulting decision becoming effective. This is a move toward the constitutional idea (e.g., Mueller 1996) of putting people behind the veil of uncertainty, and therefore inducing them to take a more "objective" position.

A more innovative idea is to proceed, as (many) parliaments do, namely to have a first, second, and sometimes even a third reading of a law. In a direct democracy one could first have an *informative* vote, and after sufficient time has elapsed to allow for a discussion of the outcome, a *decisive* vote could be cast.

Co-determination

The citizens' decision may only become effective if it is supported by a corresponding vote in the parliament (and perhaps even in the two houses). This would, however, reduce referenda to a plebiscite. Another possibility would be to accord a veto right either to the citizens or to the parliament. One could also consider a double majority in the form of the popular vote and votes in the regions (cantons or states). This latter requirement applies, for instance, in Switzerland, where both the majority of all the Swiss voters and the majority of the cantons must approve a constitutional referendum.

2.7 Concluding Remarks

The crucial question is *who governs* the step by step introduction of directly democratic instruments. Ideally it would be a constitutional assembly. Its members are not directly involved in current politics, so they take a more objective stance. They do not have to fear a reduction in their own power if direct democracy is introduced in the future. In reality, however, a considerable number of the members are likely to belong to the *classe politique*. They either served in political decision making in the past, currently do so, or hope to do so in the future. In all cases they tend to oppose popular participation in political decision making.

For these reasons the active involvement of the citizens in amending the constitution, as well as in more general political decision making, cannot be substituted by resorting to representation. Giving citizens rights to directly participate in political decision making can be based on two different types of reasoning. The first takes such political rights as a *value as such*, which must not be legitimized any further. Direct democracy is then taken as the next logical major step from the introduction of democracy in the classical Athenian city-state and its broadening over whole nations in the wake of the French Revolution. The second type of reasoning considers the favorable consequences of giving the citizens the right to directly participate in political decision making. This chapter identifies two sources of benefits:

1. *Procedural utility.* Direct participation rights raises citizens' utility, quite independent of the outcomes reached. Empirical evidence suggests that citizens' subjective reported well-being (ceteris paribus) is the higher, the more extensive their participation rights are.
2. *Outcome utility.* When the citizens are allowed to directly participate in political decisions, the policies undertaken yield more favorable results for them.

Extensive empirical evidence for Switzerland and the United States (the leaders in direct democracy) suggests that more extensive participation rights via popular initiatives and referenda lead to a lower tax burden and lower public expenditures, to higher efficiency and productivity in the provision of public goods and services, and to higher overall satisfaction (happiness) of the population.

The following arguments are often raised against direct democratic institutions: the citizens fail to understand the complex issues, they have little interest in participating, they are easy to manipulate, they tend to decide emotionally, the large number of referenda lead to confusion, leadership is made impossible, and direct democracy is inadequate for major issues, hinders progress, destroys civil rights, and is very expensive. This chapter shows that these arguments should be rejected, in particular, if a comparative stance is taken, that is, if decision making in direct democracy is contrasted with that in representative democracy.

Elements of direct democracy can be introduced gradually, and there are many possibilities for varying the required majority, the issue domain, the time, and the extent of codetermination of citizens and parliament, as well as whether to start at the local, national or supranational level.

The chapter concludes that increasing the direct democratic political participation rights of the citizens is an important step for a future democracy. It is, in particular, a crucial requirement for a future European constitution committed to democracy.

Notes

1. The draft of the European Constitution is electronically available at http://european-convention.eu.int/, July 31, 2003.

2. See, for example, Magleby (1984), Cronin (1989), Butler and Ranney (1994), Frey (1994), Dubois and Floyd (1998), Kirchgaessner, Feld, and Savioz (1999), and Frey, Kucher, and Stutzer (2001).

3. Some of these referenda certainly do not meet the requirement of leaving the (final) decision on an issue to the general electorate, but are rather plebiscites, meaning votes where the government wants the support of the population for a decision already taken.

4. An up-to-date account of the referendum experience around the world is provided by C2D—Research and Documentation Centre on Direct Democracy at the University of Geneva (http://c2d.unige.ch/, August 6, 2003). Additional information about direct legislation in the United States is collected by the Initiative and Referendum Institute in Washington (http://www.iandrinstitute.org/, August 6, 2003). Its partner organization in Europe (http://www.iri-europe.org/, August 6, 2003) provides information on the state of direct democracy in European countries (with a special focus on transition economies).

5. Citizens' initiatives also allow an "unbundling" of issues, compared to the bundled issues typical for representative democracies. This induces policy outcomes that have a closer relationship with popular preferences (see Besley and Coate 2000).

6. See Romer and Rosenthal (1978, 1982) for Oregon school budget referendums, and Weingast and Moran (1983) for congressional committees. The two groups of researchers do not consider the general role of referenda in agenda setting, but concentrate on its

effect on bureaucratic decisions. Our emphasis is on its role as a means to break the politicians' cartel.

7. The essential role of discussion in direct democracy is more fully discussed in Frey and Kirchgaessner (1993) and Bohnet and Frey (1994). For democracy in general, see Dryzek (1990).

8. The quality of the discourse process is, however, periled if multiple initiatives on the same issue are drafted and put on the ballot simultaneously. The strategic drafting of initiatives, for example, as observed in California, makes it difficult for voters (1) to catch on the meaning of the proposals from the title or wording of the initiatives and (2) to anticipate the actual policy change if more than one measure on the same topic passes (Silva 2000).

9. In their proposal for a "New Democratic Federalism for Europe," Frey and Eichenberger (1999) develop a model of federalism that is based on functional overlapping competing jurisdictions (FOCJ) that rely to a large extent on direct democracy.

10. While these findings imply larger deficits and higher public debt in cantons with a fiscal referendum, ceteris paribus, the respective empirical results neither show statistically significant effects on the former measure nor on the latter one (Feld and Kirchgässner 2001, p. 354).

11. In the regression equation the following are controlled for: income level in the canton, federal aid, age structure of the population, population size, population density, unemployment rate, as well as whether people are German-speaking or not.

12. In contrast, Pommerehne (1978) provides strong evidence that the median voter model performs better in Swiss towns with extended direct democratic rights than in representative democratic cities. While, for the former category containing 48 of the 110 towns in the data set, a statistically significant demand elasticity for aggregate public expenditure with respect to income is estimated in 1970, this is not the case for representative democracies. Thus public expenditure seems to match median voter's preferences better in direct democratic jurisdictions.

13. The index is based on the four main legal instruments for directly influencing the political process in Swiss cantons: (1) the initiative to change a canton's constitution, (2) the initiative to change a canton's laws, (3) the compulsory or optional referendum to prevent new law or the changing of law, and (4) the compulsory or optional referendum to prevent new state expenditure. Obstacles are measured in terms of (1) the number of signatures necessary to launch an instrument (absolute and relative to the number of citizens with the right to vote), (2) the legally allowed time span in which to collect the signatures, and (3) the level of new expenditure per head allowing a financial referendum. Each of these restrictions is evaluated on a six-point scale: "one" indicates a high obstacle, "six" a low one (compulsory referenda are treated like referenda with the lowest possible obstacle). Average nonweighted ratings represent the measure used for direct democratic rights in Swiss cantons.

14. Voters can use party ideologies to proxy for the consequences of their vote. They also pay attention to the previous performance of a government, they judge the reputation of candidates (Lupia and McCubbins 1998), they evaluate voting recommendations by interest groups (Schneider 1985; Lupia 1994), or they collect political information as a byproduct of mass media consumption.

15. For a general account on procedural utility, see Frey, Benz, and Stutzer (2004).

16. In July 2002 the German Bundestag debated (and rejected) a proposal to introduce elements of direct democracy at the federal level. For fear of emotional decisions, the introduction of the death penalty was excluded right from the very beginning as a subject for a referendum. This overlooks that an extensive discussion among the citizens, and with experts and politicians, brings to the fore all sides of the issue. A purely emotional decision is unlikely to occur. Moreover many countries using the death penalty follow the representative principle (e.g., the United States), while the country with most extensive direct democracy (Switzerland) prohibits the death sentence.

17. For a discussion, see Mueller (1999).

18. If the veil of ignorance is lifted and transaction costs are taken into account, unanimity is not an optimal decision rule (Buchanan and Tullock 1962). Instead, an optimal majority has to be found that is minimizing the sum of costs due to externalities composed of minority and transaction costs.

19. This corresponds to the rules in the Swiss constitution requiring that constitutional changes must be approved by the simple majority of the Swiss voters and the Swiss cantons. This has resulted in a great number of constitutional changes over the course of time and has contributed to ground rules adapting to evolving requirements. The many changes are partly due to the fact that at the federal level, popular initiatives are possible only for changes in the constitution but not for changes in laws. Therefore the constitution became overburdened with issues of lesser importance better suited for the level of laws. Recently this provision has been changed, and it is now possible to undertake general popular initiatives that leave the decision to the legislator whether the initiative is formulated as a constitutional amendment or as federal law.

20. We are, of course, not the only ones who are proposing elements of direct democracy for the new European constitution. See more recently, for example, Feld and Kirchgässner (2003), Mueller (2002, 2003), or Hug (2002, ch. 7) for a survey on previous proposals.

21. This condition is not only specific to direct democracies but also holds for all types of democracy.

22. To gradually introduce direct democratic elements in a political system dominated by the government may, however, induce the risk that the government on purpose undermines its functioning in order to "demonstrate" to the citizens that it cannot work.

23. Such restriction may make sense also in fully developed direct democracies, but it should be noted that this is not the case in Switzerland. It should immediately be added that the Swiss voters have had no inclination to cheat where such basic rights are concerned.

24. The referendum experience in other European countries is described in Gallagher and Uleri (1996).

References

Ackerman, B. 1998. *We the People 2: Transformation.* Cambridge, MA: Belknap Press.

Alt, J. E., and D. Dreyer Lassen. 2003. The political economy of institutions and corruption in American states. *Journal of Theoretical Politics* 5 (3): 341–65.

Bali, V. A. 2003. Implementing popular initiatives: What matters for compliance? *Journal of Politics* 65 (4): 1130–46.

Benz, M., and A. Stutzer. 2004. Are voters better informed when they have a larger say in politics? Evidence for the European Union and Switzerland. *Public Choice* 119 (1–2): 31–59.

Besley, T., and S. Coate. 2000. Issue unbundling via citizens' initiatives. Mimeo, Department of Economics, London School of Economics.

Blankart, Ch. B. 1992. Bewirken Referenden und Volksinitiativen einen Unterschied in der Politik? *Staatswissenschaften und Staatspraxis* 3 (4): 509–24.

Blankart, Ch. B. 2000. The process of government centralization: A constitutional view. *Constitutional Political Economy* 11 (1): 27–39.

Blomberg, S. B., G. D. Hess, and A. Weerapana. 2004. The impact of voter initiatives on economic activity. *European Journal of Political Economy*, forthcoming. 20 (1): 207–26.

Bohnet, I., and B. S. Frey. 1994. Direct-democratic rules: The role of discussion. *Kyklos* 47 (3): 341–54.

Bowler, S., and T. Donovan. 1998. *Demanding Choices: Opinion, Voting, and Direct Democracy*. Ann Arbor: University of Michigan Press.

Bowler, S., and T. Donovan. 2002. Democracy, institutions and attitudes about citizen influence on government. *British Journal of Political Science* 32 (2): 371–90.

Buchanan, J. M. 1965. An economic theory of clubs. *Economica* 32 (1): 1–14.

Buchanan, J. M., and G. Tullock. 1962. *The Calculus of Consent. Logical Foundations of Constitutional Democracy*. Ann Arbor: University of Michigan Press.

Butler, D., and A. Ranney, eds. 1994. *Referendums around the World. The Growing Use of Direct Democracy*. Washington, DC: AEI Press.

Cronin, T. E. 1989. *Direct Democracy. The Politics of Initiative, Referendum and Recall*. Cambridge: Harvard University Press.

Dryzek, J. S. 1990. *Discursive Democracy: Politics, Policy and Political Science*. Cambridge: Cambridge University Press.

Dubois, P. L., and F. Feeney. 1998. *Lawmaking by Initiative: Issues, Options and Comparisons*. New York: Agathon Press.

Eichenberger, R. 1994. The Benefits of Federalism and the Risk of Overcentralization. *Kyklos* 47 (3): 403–20.

Eichenberger, R. 1999. Mit direkter Demokratie zu besserer Wirtschafts- und Finanzpolitik: Theorie und Empirie. In Hans Herbert von Arnim, ed., *Adäquate Institutionen: Voraussetzung für "gute" und bürgernahe Politik?* Schriftenreihe der Hochschule Speyer. Berlin: Duncker and Humblot.

Feld, L. P., and B. S. Frey. 2002. Trust breeds trust: How taxpayers are treated. *Economics of Governance* 3 (2): 87–99.

Feld, L. P., and G. Kirchgässner. 2001. The political economy of direct legislation: Direct democracy and local decision-making. *Economic Policy* 16 (33): 329–63.

Feld, L. P., and G. Kirchgässner. 2003. The role of direct democracy in the European Union. Presented at the CESifo Conference on "A Constitution for the European Union," Munich, February 7–8, 2003.

Feld, L. P., and J. G. Matsusaka. 2003. Budget referendums and government spending: Evidence from Swiss cantons. *Journal of Public Economics* 87 (12): 2703–24.

Feld, L. P., and M. R. Savioz. 1997. Direct democracy matters for economic performance: An empirical investigation. *Kyklos* 50 (4): 507–38.

Frey, B. S. 1994. Direct democracy: Politico-economic lessons from Swiss experience. *American Economic Review* 84 (2): 338–48.

Frey, B. S. 1997. A constitution for knaves crowds out civic virtues. *Economic Journal* 107 (443): 1043–53.

Frey, B. S., M. Benz, and A. Stutzer. 2004. Procedural utility: Not only what, but also how matters. *Journal of Institutional and Theoretical Economics* 160 (3): 377–401.

Frey, B. S., and R. Eichenberger. 1999. The new democratic federalism for Europe: Functional overlapping and competing jurisdictions. Cheltenham, UK: Edward Elgar.

Frey, B. S., and L. Goette. 1998. Does the popular vote destroy civil rights? *American Journal of Political Science* 42 (4): 1343–48.

Frey, B. S., and G. Kirchgässner. 1993. Diskursethik, Politische Ökonomie und Volksabstimmungen. *Analyse und Kritik* 15 (2): 129–49.

Frey, B. S., M. Kucher, and A. Stutzer. 2001. Outcome, process and power in direct democracy: New econometric results. *Public Choice* 107 (3–4): 271–93.

Frey, B. S., and A. Stutzer. 2000. Happiness, economy and institutions. *Economic Journal* 110 (446): 918–38.

Frey, B. S., and A. Stutzer. 2005. Beyond outcomes: Measuring procedural utility. *Oxford Economic Papers* 57 (1): 90–111.

Frey, B. S., and A. Stutzer. 2002a. *Happiness and Economics. How the Economy and Institutions Affect Human Well-Being*. Princeton: Princeton University Press.

Frey, B. S., and A. Stutzer. 2002b. What can economists learn from happiness research? *Journal of Economic Literature* 40 (2): 402–35.

Gallagher, M., and P. V. Uleri, eds. 1996. *The Referendum Experience in Europe*. London: Macmillan.

Gamble, B. S. 1997. Putting civil rights to a popular vote. *American Journal of Political Science* 41 (1): 245–69.

Gerber, E. R. 1997. *The Populist Paradox: Interest Groups and the Promise of Direct Legislation.* Princeton: Princeton University Press.

Gerber, E. R., and S. Hug. 2001. Legislative Response to Direct Legislation. In M. Mendelsohn and A. Parkin, eds., *Referendum Democracy: Citizens, Elites and Deliberation in Referendum Campaigns.* New York: Palgrave, pp. 88–108.

Gerber, E. R., A. Lupia, and M. D. McCubbins. 2004. When does government limit the impact of voter initiatives? The politics of implementation and enforcement. *Journal of Politics* 66 (1): 43–68.

Gerber, E. R., A. Lupia, M. D. McCubbins, and D. R. Kiewiet. 2004. *Stealing the Initiative: How State Government Responds to Direct Democracy.* Upper Saddle River, NJ: Prentice Hall.

Gross, A., and B. Kaufmann. 2002. *IRI Europe Country Index on Citizen Lawmaking 2002.* Amsterdam: IRI (Initiative and Referendum Institute Europe).

Habermas, J. 1983. Diskursethik—Notizen zu einem Begründungsprozess. In J. Habermas, ed., *Moralbewusstsein und kommunikatives Handeln.* Frankfurt: Suhrkamp, pp. 53–125.

Hajnal, Z. L., E. R. Gerber, and H. Louch. 2002. Minorities and direct legislation: Evidence from California ballot proposition elections. *Journal of Politics* 64 (1): 154–77.

Hansen, S., T. R. Palfrey, and H. Rosenthal. 1987. The Downsian model of electoral participation: Formal theory and empirical analysis of the constituency size effect. *Public Choice* 52 (1): 15–33.

Hirschman, A. O. 1970. *Exit, Voice and Loyalty*. Cambridge: Harvard University Press.

Hug, S. 2002. *Voices of Europe: Citizens, Referendums and European Integration.* Lanham: Rowman and Littlefield.

Kirchgaessner, G., L. Feld, and M. R. Savioz. 1999. *Die direkte Demokratie: Modern, erfolgreich, entwicklungs- und exportfähig*. Basel: Helbing and Lichtenhahn/Vahlen/Beck.

Lane, R. E. 2000. *The Loss of Happiness in Market Economies*. New Haven: Yale University Press.

Lupia, A. 1994. Shortcuts versus encyclopedias: Information and voting behavior in California insurance reform elections. *American Political Science Review* 88 (1): 63–76.

Lupia, A., and M. McCubbins. 1998. *The Democratic Dilemma: Can Citizens Learn What They Need to Know*? New York: Cambridge University Press.

Luthardt, W., and A. Waschkuhn. 1997. Plebiszitäre Komponenten in der repräsentativen Demokratie: Entwicklungsstand und Perspektiven. In: Ansgar Klein und Rainer Schmalz-Bruns (Hrsg.). *Politische Beteiligung und Bürgerengagement in Deutschland: Möglichkeiten und Grenzen*. Baden-Baden: Nomos, pp. 59–87.

Magleby, D. B. 1984. *Direct Legislation. Voting on Ballot Propositions in the United States.* Baltimore: Johns Hopkins University Press.

Martin, D., and R. Wagner. 1978. The institutional framework for municipal incorporation: An economic analysis of local agency formation commissions in California. *Journal of Law and Economics* 21 (2): 409–25.

Matsusaka, J. G. 1995. Fiscal effects of the voter initiative: Evidence from the last 30 years. *Journal of Political Economy* 103 (2): 587–623.

Matsusaka, J. G. 2004. *For the Many or the Few: The Initiative, Public Policy, and American Democracy*. Chicago: University of Chicago Press.

Mueller, D. C. 1996. *Constitutional Democracy*. New York: Oxford University Press.

Mueller, D. C. 1999. On amending constitutions. *Constitutional Political Economy* 10 (4): 385–96.

Mueller, D. C. 2002. Constitutional issues regarding European Union expansion. In B. Steunenberg, ed., *Widening the European Union*. London: Routledge, pp. 41–57.

Mueller, D. C. 2003. Rights and citizenship in the European Union. Presented at the CESifo Conference on "A Constitution for the European Union," Munich, February 7–8, 2003.

Niskanen, W. A. 1992. The case for a new fiscal constitution. *Journal of Economic Perspectives* 6 (2): 13–24.

Olson, M. 1969. The principle of "fiscal equivalence": The division of responsibilities among different levels of government. *American Economic Review* 59 (2): 479–87.

Olson, M. 1986. Toward a more general theory of governmental structure. *American Economic Review* 76 (2): 120–25.

Pateman, C. 1970. *Participation and Democratic Theory*. Cambridge: Cambridge University Press.

Pommerehne, W. W. 1978. Institutional approaches to public expenditure: Empirical evidence from Swiss municipalities. *Journal of Public Economics* 9 (2): 225–80.

Pommerehne, W. W. 1983. Private versus öffentliche Müllabfuhr: Nochmals betrachtet. *Finanzarchiv* 41: 466–75.

Pommerehne, W. W. 1990. The empirical relevance of comparative institutional analysis. *European Economic Review* 34 (2–3): 458–69.

Pommerehne, W. W., and H. Weck-Hannemann. 1996. Tax rates, tax administration and income tax evasion. *Public Choice* 88 (1–2): 161–70.

Riker, W. H., and P. C. Ordeshook. 1973. *An Introduction to Positive Political Theory*. Englewood Cliffs, NJ: Prentice Hall.

Romer, T., and H. Rosenthal. 1978. Political resource allocation, controlled agendas, and the status quo. *Public Choice* 33 (4): 27–43.

Romer, T., and H. Rosenthal. 1982. Median voters or budget maximizers: Evidence from school expenditure referenda. *Economic Inquiry* 20 (4): 556–78.

Santerre, R. E. 1986. Representative versus direct democracy: A Tiebout test of relative performance. *Public Choice* 48 (1): 55–63.

Schaltegger, C. A., and L. P. Feld. 2001. On government centralization and budget referendums: Evidence from Switzerland. CESifo Working Paper 615, Munich.

Schneider, F. 1985. *Der Einfluss der Interessengruppen auf die Wirtschaftspolitik: Eine empirische Untersuchung für die Schweiz*. Bern: Haupt.

Silva, J. F. 2000. The California initiative process: Background and perspective. Occasional paper, Public Policy Institute of California.

Tiebout, Ch. M. 1956. A pure theory of local expenditure. *Journal of Political Economy* 64 (5): 416–24.

Torgler, B. 2003. Direct democracy matters: Tax morale and political participation. In *National Tax Association Papers and Proceedings*, Orlando, 2002. Washington, DC: National Tax Association.

Tullock, G. 1967. *Toward a Mathematics of Politics*. Ann Arbor: University of Michigan Press.

Vaubel, R. 1994. The political economy of centralization and the European community. *Public Choice* 81 (1–2): 151–90.

von Arnim, H. H. 1988. *Macht macht erfinderisch*. Zürich: Fromm.

Waters, M. D. 2003. *The Initiative and Referendum Almanac.* Durham: Carolina Academic Press.

Weingast, B. R., and M. J. Moran. 1983. Bureaucratic discretion or congressional control? Regulatory policymaking by the Federal Trade Commission. *Journal of Political Economy* 91 (5): 765–800.

3 Constitutions and Economic Policy[1]

Torsten Persson and
Guido Tabellini

3.1 Introduction

At the rare moments in history when a nation debates constitutional reform, the key issues often concern how the reforms might affect economic policy and economic performance. For example, Italy abandoned a system of pure proportional representation, where legislators were elected according to the proportions of the popular national vote received by their parties, and moved toward including ingredients of plurality rule, where legislators are elected in each district according to who receives the highest number of votes. Key Italian political leaders are now considering proposals to introduce elements of presidentialism, where the head of government is elected by direct popular vote, rather than the current parliamentary regime. A common argument in Italy was that the electoral reform would help stifle political corruption and reduce the propensity of Italian governments to run budget deficits.

In the 1990s constitutional reforms have been debated and implemented in a number of other countries too. For instance, New Zealand moved away from a pure system of plurality rule in single-member districts to a system mixing elements of proportional representation. Japan also renounced its special form of plurality rule (the so-called single nontransferable vote) in favor of a system that mixes elements of proportional and plurality representation. Similar proposals have been debated in the United Kingdom. In Latin America questions have been raised as to whether the poor and volatile economic performance of many countries can be traced to their presidential form of government.

Until very recently social scientists have not directly addressed the question of how the constitution affects economic performance and other economic policy outcomes. Political scientists in the field of comparative politics have spent decades working on the fundamental features of constitutions and their political effects, of course. But they have mainly focused on political phenomena and not systematically asked how constitutional rules shape economic policies. Economists in the field of political economics have studied the determinants of policy choices, but they have not paid much attention to institutional detail.

This chapter discusses theoretical and empirical research on how two constitutional features, electoral rules and forms of government, affect economic policy making. We begin by outlining some key objectives of democratic political constitutions, and by pointing out the inertia and systematic selection that characterize real world constitutions. We then introduce the main concepts used to categorize work on constitutions: different kinds of electoral rules and forms of government. We discuss how these elements of constitutions affect the accountability of government and the size of political rents and corruption, as well as the representativeness of government and a variety of fiscal policy choices.

Our main message is that constitutional rules systematically shape economic policy. When it comes to the extent of political corruption, the devil is in the details, especially the details of electoral systems. When it comes to fiscal policy, in particular the size of government, the effects are associated with broad constitutional categories. The constitutional effects are often large enough to be of genuine economic interest.

3.2 Constitutional Objectives

Democratic constitutions have many objectives, including the desire to formulate and protect some fundamental rights of citizens. Here we focus on the rules that are directly relevant for policy formation. In a representative democracy elected officials determine policy. The constitution spells out which offices have decision-making rights over policies, how access is gained to those offices through elections or political appointments, and what are the procedures for setting policies. In turn these rules determine how well voters can hold politicians accountable, and which groups in society are more likely to see their interests adequately represented.

A common theme in this chapter and in the related literature is that constitution design entails a trade-off between accountability and representation (e.g., see Bingham Powell 2000; Prezworski et al. 1999). Constitutional features that clarify policy responsibilities and make it easy to replace an incumbent government strengthen accountability, but at the same time increase the political influence of the groups to whom policy makers are accountable. Electoral rules demonstrate this tendency. Elections by plurality rule, whereby legislators are elected in many small districts by majority rule, translate swings in voter sentiment into larger changes in legislative majorities than elections using proportional representation, where legislators are often elected by the share of a national vote received. As a result the politicians are motivated to please the voters, and to seek smaller political rents and avoid corruption. But since the stronger accountability is achieved by making political candidates more responsive to the wishes of pivotal groups of voters, this greater accountability also raises the propensity to target benefits to narrow constituencies, at the expense of broad spending programs. As we will see, a similar trade-off between accountability and representation also arises in the choice between presidential and parliamentary forms of government.

Constitutional Inertia and Systematic Selection

Despite the flurry of actual or debated constitutional reforms in the 1990s, the broad features of constitutions have changed very seldom in the post–World War II period within the group of democracies. In the sample of sixty democracies between 1960 and 1998 considered by Persson and Tabellini (2003), no democratic country changed its form of government, and only two enacted important reforms of their electoral system before 1990 (Cyprus and France)—although more time variation is observed if one considers marginal constitutional reforms and transitions from nondemocratic states to some form of democracy.

The observed cross-country variation in constitutions is strongly correlated with stable country characteristics: for example, presidential regimes are concentrated in Latin America, former British colonies tend to have UK style electoral rules (plurality rule in single-member constituencies), and continental Europe is predominantly ruled by parliamentary systems with proportional representation elections. These constitutional patterns make it difficult to draw causal inferences from the data. Constitutional inertia means that experiments with constitutional reforms are very seldom observed, and cross-country estimates risk confounding constitutional effects with other country characteristics. Self-selection of countries into constitutions is clearly nonrandom, and most likely correlated with other unobserved variables that also influence a country's policy outcomes.

These difficulties are similar to those encountered by labor economists who evaluate the effects of job-training programs. People who enter a job-training programs may have a greater level of motivation and initiative than observationally equivalent people who do not enter such a program, and a careful evaluation of the program must take these unobserved differences into account. Moreover, if the job-training program has heterogeneous effects across individuals, treatment and control groups must be chosen to have similar observable characteristics, so as not to bias the estimated effects.

In our work (e.g., Persson and Tabellini 2003) we have exploited the econometric methodology developed by labor economists, adapting it to our inference problem: namely how to estimate causal effects of the constitution on policy outcomes from cross-country comparisons when countries self-select into constitutions. Thus we rely on instrumental variables to try and isolate exogenous variation in electoral rules and forms of government. If constitutions change very seldom, they are largely determined by historical circumstances. We have used the broad period in which the constitution was adopted as an instrument for the constitutional feature of interest. Since there are "fashions" in constitutional design, the period of birth of the current constitution is related its broad features. Our identifying assumption is that controlling for other determinants of policy (including the age of democracy), the birth period of the constitution is not directly related to current policy outcomes. We also use techniques suggested by Heckman and others to adjust the estimates for possible correlation between the random components of policy outcomes and constitution selection. We also exploit "matching methods," so called in which countries are ranked in terms of their probability of adopting a specific constitutional feature, called a "propensity score." Comparisons of countries with similar propensity scores, but with different constitutions, receive more weight. This method avoids biased estimates due to heterogeneous treatment effects and nonlinearities. In Persson and Tabellini (2003) these estimation methods that adjust for self-selection of countries into constitution or account for nonlinearities are used whenever the constitution is measured by a binary variable, such as presidential compared with parliamentary forms of government, or majoritarian compared with proportional elections. If instead the constitution is measured by a continuous variable, such as the detailed features of electoral rules described below, then our inferences described below are based on ordinary least square estimates.

3.3 Categorizing Political Institutions

Arguably the most fundamental aspects of any modern constitution, and certainly the two aspects most studied in comparative politics, are its electoral rules and its form of government. Our exposition focuses on these two dimensions. We therefore leave out many potentially important constitutional features, including judicial arrangements, subnational institutions, vertical arrangements in federations, budgetary procedures, delegation to independent agencies, and referenda. We refer the reader to Besley and Case (2003), Poterba and Von Hagen (1999), and Djankov et al. (2003) for more references on these issues.

Electoral Rules

The political science literature commonly emphasizes three dimensions in which electoral rules for legislatures differ. *District magnitudes* determine the number of legislators (given the size of the legislature) acquiring a seat in a typical voting district. One polar case is when all legislators are elected in districts with a single seat, like the US House of Representatives, the other when all legislators are all elected in a single, all-encompassing district, like the Israeli Knesset. *Electoral formulas* translate votes into seats. Under plurality rule only the winner(s) of the highest vote share(s) get represented in a given district. In contrast, proportional representation awards seats in relation to votes in each district. To ensure closeness between overall vote shares and seat shares, a district system of plurality rule is often amended by a system of "adjustment seats" at the national level. *Ballot structures*, finally, determine how citizens cast their ballot. One possibility is that they get to choose among individual candidates. Another common possibility is that each voter chooses among lists of candidates drawn up by the parties participating in the election. If an electoral district has ten seats and party A wins, say, four of these seats, the first four candidates on the list of party A get elected.[2]

While these three aspects are theoretically distinct, they are correlated across countries. Anglo-Saxon countries often implement plurality rule with voting for individual candidates in single-member districts. On the other hand, proportional representation is often implemented though a system of party lists in large districts, sometimes a single national district. This pattern has lead many observers to adopt a classification into two archetypical electoral systems, labeled "majoritarian" and "proportional" (or "consensual"). But the correlations are certainly not perfect and a number of "mixed" electoral systems occur. In Germany, for example, voters cast two ballots, electing half the Bundestag by plurality in single-member districts, and the other half by proportional representation at a national level, to achieve proportionality between national vote and seat shares. Furthermore some proportional representation systems, such as the Irish system, do not rely on party lists.[3] Blais and Massicotte (1996) and Cox (1997) give good overviews of world electoral systems.

Forms of Government

Researchers in comparative politics emphasize the distinction between two main forms of government: presidential and parliamentary regimes. In a presidential regime, the citizens directly elect the (top) executive; in a parliamentary regime, an elected parliament appoints the executive—a government.

One distinction between presidential and parliamentary government has to do with the allocation of executive and proposal power to individuals or offices. In a parliamentary democracy, where the legislature appoints the executive, the government has executive powers and acts as the agenda setter, initiating all major legislation and drafting the budget. In a presidential democracy with separation of powers like the United States, the president has full executive powers, but smaller agenda-setting powers. For domestic policy, the president has a veto, but the power to propose and amend typically rests with Congress. A second key distinction has to do with how executive and agenda-setting powers are preserved over time. In parliamentary democracies, the government remains in office only as long as it enjoys the support of a majority in the legislative assembly. In presidential democracies, by contrast, the holders of these powers are separately elected and hold on to them throughout an entire election period.

Many real-world constitutions can easily be classified as presidential or parliamentary based on these two criteria. In most countries with an elected president, the executive can hold onto its powers without the support of a legislative majority. Likewise, in many real-world parliamentary regimes, government formation must be approved by parliament, parliament can dismiss the government by a vote of no-confidence, and legislative proposals by the government get preferential treatment in the legislative agenda. Nevertheless, even more than with electoral rules, several mixed systems are observed, depending on exactly how prerogatives are divided between the executive and the legislature, and on the detailed rules for forming and dissolving governments. Shugart and Carey (1992) and Strom (1990) extensively discuss these other constitutional features. In this chapter we consider the simple distinction based on two factors: (1) whether the powers to propose and veto legislative proposals are dispersed among various political offices (like congressional committees), as in most presidential systems, or whether the government proposes legislation, as in most parliamentary systems, and (2) whether the executive can be dismissed by the legislature through a vote of no-confidence, as in parliamentary systems, or whether the executive serves a fixed term regardless of legislative support, as in presidential systems.

3.4 Political Accountability

How do electoral rules and forms of government affect accountability? In this section we only consider policies evaluated in roughly the same way by all voters, leaving the problem of how elected officials react to disagreement among voters for the next section that focuses on representation. In this context accountability refers to two things. It gives voters some control over politicians who abuse their power: voters can punish or reward politicians through re-election or other career concerns, and this creates incentives for good behavior.[4] Accountability also refers to the ability of voters to select the most "able" candidate, where ability can refer to some mix of integrity, technical expertise, or other intrinsic features valued by voters. In particular, in economic policy making, we need to know how the constitution affects corruption, rent seeking, and electoral budget cycles.

Political Accountability and Electoral Rules

The details of electoral rules have *direct* effects on the incentives of politicians. They also have *indirect* effects through the party structure and, more generally, by determining who holds office. In this section we discuss direct and indirect effects of the three aspects of electoral rules mentioned above: ballot structure, district magnitude, and the electoral formula.

Politicians may have stronger direct incentives to please the voters if they are held accountable individually, rather than collectively. Thus party lists discourage collective effort by officeholders, essentially because they disconnect individual efforts and re-election prospects. Persson and Tabellini (2000) write down a model that formalizes this idea and predict political rents will be higher under electoral systems that rely on list voting, compared to elections where voters directly select individual candidates. The same argument also implies that *open* lists (where voters can modify the order of candidates) should be more conducive to good behavior than *closed* lists (that cannot be amended by voters), as should preferential voting (where voters are asked to rank candidates of the same party).

What does the evidence say? If higher political rents are associated with illegal benefits, then one can ask whether corruption by public officials in different countries is systematically correlated to the electoral rule. Of course, corruption is only an imperfect proxy for political rents. Furthermore corruption is measured with error and is determined by many other country features. Yet the cross-sectional and panel data suggest some connections. Persson and Tabellini (2003) and Persson, Tabellini, and Trebbi (2003) study about 80 democracies in the 1990s, measuring perceived corruption by different surveys of surveys assembled by the World Bank, Transparency International, and private risk services. They control for several country characteristics that earlier studies have found to correlate with corruption, such as per capita income, openness to international trade, the citizens' education and religious beliefs, a country's history as captured by colonial heritage, and geographic location as measured by a set of dummy variables. By their estimates, voting for individuals does indeed correlate with lower corruption: a switch from a system where all legislators are elected on party lists to a system of plurality rule, where all legislators are individually elected can reduce perceptions of corruption by as much as 20 percent—about twice the estimated effect of being a country in Latin America. They also find that the decline in corruption is stronger when individual voting is implemented by plurality rule rather than by preferential voting or open lists in a proportional rule electoral systems. Of course, the result may be due to the effects of the electoral formula (as discussed below) rather than the ballot structure alone. Kunicova and Rose Ackerman (2001) obtain similar empirical results, but they single out closed-list, proportional representation systems as the most conducive to corruption.

Some of these conclusions run counter to those in Carey and Shugart (1995) and Golden and Chang (2001), who instead emphasize the distinction between inter-party and intra-party competition. Competition between parties is desirable, as it leads to legislation that pleases voters at large. Competition within parties is not, as it leads candidates to provide favors to their constituencies, through patronage and other illegal activities—the Italian and Japanese electoral systems before the 1990s reforms exemplify this problem. Measuring corruption by judicial inquiries against Italian members of parliament, Golden and Chang (2001) show that they are more frequent in districts with more intense intra-party competition. Thus they conclude that open-list systems are worse than closed-list systems, and suggest that the empirical results by Kunicova and Rose Ackerman (2001) reflect a misspecified model (see also Golden and Chang 2003, mentioned below).

Summarizing, both theory and evidence suggest that individual accountability under plurality rule strengthens the incentives of politicians to please the voters and is conducive to good behavior. But the effects of individual accountability under proportional representation, implemented with open rather than closed lists, are more controversial.

The electoral formula (and district magnitude) can also create behavioral incentives for politicians along other channels. Under plurality rule, the mapping from votes to seats becomes steep if electoral races are close. This connection ought to produce strong incentives for good behavior: a small improvement in the chance of victory would mean a large return in terms of seats. The incentives under proportional representation are weaker, as additional effort has a lower expected return on seats (or on the probability of winning). If electoral races have likely winners, however, incentives may instead be weaker under plurality than proportional representation; if seats are next to certain, little effort goes into pleasing the voters of those districts.[5] Aggregating over all districts (and thus over races of different closeness), the relative incentives to extract rents under different electoral formulas become an empirical question. Related to these arguments, Strömberg (2003) uses a structural model of the US electoral college to study the effects of a (hypothetical) reform to a national vote for president. Given the empirical distribution of voter preferences, he finds that the incentives for rent extraction are basically unaffected by such reform.

Electoral systems (and in particular district magnitude) can also have indirect effects on accountability, by altering the set of candidates that have a chance to be elected, or more generally by changing the party system. One theoretical model suggests that these indirect effects encourage political rent seeking; another that it may reduce political rent seeking.

Myerson (1993) presents a model in which barriers to entry allow dishonest candidates to survive. He assumes that parties (or equivalently, candidates) differ in two dimensions: honesty and ideology. Voters always prefer honest candidates but disagree on ideology. With proportional representation and multimember districts, an honest candidate is always available for all ideological positions, so dishonest candidates have no chance of being elected. But in single-member districts, only one candidate can win the election. Voters may then cast their ballot, strategically, for dishonest but ideologically preferred candidates, if they expect all other voters with the same ideology to do the same: switching to an honest candidate risks giving the victory to a candidate of the opposite ideology. Thus plurality rule in single-member districts can be associated with dishonest incumbents, who are difficult to oust from office.

But electoral systems that make it easy for political parties to be represented in parliament (e.g., multiple-member districts and proportional representation) may actually encourage rent seeking, rather than reducing it, through another channel. If many factions are represented in parliament, the government is more likely to be supported by a coalition of parties rather than by a single party. Under single-party government voters know precisely whom to blame or reward for observed performance. Under coalition government, voters may not know whom to blame, and the votes lost for bad performance are shared among all coalition partners; this dilutes the incentives of individual parties to please the voters. Persson, Roland, and Tabellini (2003) show that proportional representation and multimember districts lead to a higher incidence of coalition governments and thereby higher political rents, compared to plurality rule and small district magnitude. Bingham Powell (2000) reaches a similar conclusion through informal reasoning.

Do the data shed light on these alternative ideas? The hypothesis that coalition governments are associated with more corruption remains untested, as far as we know, although some of the blatant corruption scandals in Europe—Belgium and Italy—have been intimately associated with such governments. The evidence does support the idea that barriers to entry raise corruption, however. Persson and Tabellini (2003) and Persson, Tabellini, and Trebbi (2003) find corruption to be higher in countries and years with small district magnitude (i.e., few legislators elected in each district), again with large quantitative effects. Alt and Lassen (2002) show that restrictions on primaries in gubernatorial elections, making the barriers to entry for candidates higher, are positively associated with perceptions of corruption in US states.

So far we have emphasized the implications of the electoral rule for political rents and corruption. But a strong incentive of political representatives to please the voters can also show up in other ways, such as electoral cycles in taxation, government spending, or macroeconomic policies stimulating aggregate demand. Persson and Tabellini (2003) consider panel data from 1960 covering about 500 elections in over 50 democracies. They classify countries in two groups according to the electoral formula and estimate the extent of electoral cycles in different specifications, including fixed country and time effects as well as a number of time-varying regressors. Governments in democracies that use plurality rule cut taxes, as well as government spending, during election years—the magnitude of both cuts is on the order of 0.5 percent of GDP. In proportional representation democracies, tax cuts are somewhat less pronounced, and no spending cuts are observed. This finding may be consistent with better accountability allowing voters to punish governments for high taxes and spending either because they are fiscal conservatives (as in Peltzman 1992) or because they are subject to a political agency problem (as in Besley and Case 1995).

Political Accountability and Forms of Government

The accountability effects of alternative forms of government have been studied in less detail than have the effects of electoral rules. Here we summarize the main ideas relating to the crude comparison between presidential and parliamentary regimes, neglecting the finer constitutional aspects.

From a theoretical perspective, accountability is likely to be stronger in presidential than parliamentary democracies, for two related reasons (Persson, Roland, and Tabellini 1997, 2000). First, the chain of delegation is simpler and more direct under presidential government, since the executive is directly accountable to the voters. The scope for collusion among political representatives at the voters' expense is accordingly greater under parliamentary government, where the executive is not directly accountable to the voters. Second, many presidential regimes have a strong separation of powers—between the president and Congress but also between congressional committees holding important proposal powers in different spheres of policy. In parliamentary regimes, instead, the government concentrates all the executive prerogatives as well as important powers of initiating legislation. Checks and balances are thus stronger under presidential government. These checks and balances improve accountability and strengthen the politicians' resolve for good behavior, since voters can exploit conflict between different offices to prevent abuse of power or to reduce information asymmetries between them and the policy makers. These arguments apply only in well-functioning democracies, however.

Are these predictions consistent with the evidence? Only to a degree, and depending on the quality of democracy (which can be measured by constraints on the executive, political participation and other institutional data produced by standard sources such as Freedom House or the Polity IV project). Among good democracies Persson and Tabellini (2003) find that presidential regimes have less widespread corruption than parliamentary regimes, but that the result does not extend to regimes classified as bad democracies.[6] Since many presidential regimes fall in the latter group, the negative correlation between corruption and presidentialism in the sample of good democracies is due to relatively few observations, and hence not very robust. For example, Kunicova and Rose-Ackerman (2001) classify presidential countries in a slightly different way, and obtain more negative empirical results: presidentialism seems to be associated with more widespread corruption, rather than less.

Overall Lessons

What does all this imply about the consequences of constitutional reforms for corruption? When it comes to the form of government, our knowledge is not yet precise enough to give a solid answer. When it comes to electoral rules, the devil is in the details. If we pose the question in terms of a large-scale reform from "proportional" to "majoritarian" elections, the answer is ambiguous, because such a reform would affect several features of the electoral rule. A switch from proportional representation to plurality rule, accompanied by a change in the ballot structure from party lists to voting over individuals, would strengthen political incentives for good behavior, both directly and indirectly through the type of government. But these welfare-improving effects might be offset if the reform diminishes district magnitude, thus erecting barriers to entry to the detriment of honest or talented incumbents. The net effects of electoral reform thus depend on which channel is stronger, and on the precise architecture of reform. This nuanced conclusion is also supported by the empirical evidence in Persson and Tabellini (2003) and Persson, Tabellini, and Trebbi (2003), who find no robust difference in corruption across a broad classification between majoritarian and proportional electoral systems, after controlling for other variables and taking into account the self-selection of countries into constitutions.

3.5 Political Representation

Economic policy generates conflicts of interest. Individuals and groups in society have different levels and sources of income, different sectors and occupations, different geographic homes, and different ideologies. As a result people differ in their views about the appropriate level and structure of taxation, the preferred structure of tariffs, subsidies, and regulations; the support for programs aimed at different regions; and so on. Political institutions aggregate such conflicting interests into public policy decisions, but the weight given to specific groups varies with the constitution. In this section we discuss how this happens with regard to fiscal policy.

Electoral Rules and Incentives for Politicians and Voters

Single-member districts and plurality vote tend to pull in the direction of narrowly targeted programs benefiting small geographic constituencies. Conversely, multimember districts and proportional representation pull in the direction of programs targeting broad groups. Building on this insight, some recent theoretical and empirical papers have studied the influence of district magnitude and the electoral formula on the composition of government spending.

For example, Persson and Tabellini (1999, 2000, ch. 8) study a model with two opportunistic, office-seeking parties (candidates), where policy is determined in electoral platforms before the election. Multimember districts and proportional representation diffuse electoral competition, giving the parties strong incentives to seek electoral support from broad coalitions in the population through general public goods or universalistic redistributive programs such as public pensions or other welfare state programs. In contrast, single-member districts and plurality rule typically make each party a sure winner in some of the districts, concentrating electoral competition in the other pivotal districts; this creates strong incentives to target voters in these swing districts. This effect is reinforced by the winner-takes-all property of plurality rule, which reduces the minimal coalition of voters needed to win the election. Under plurality rule, a party needs only 25 percent of the national vote to win: that is, if it wins 50 percent of the vote in 50 percent of the districts, it can receive zero percent in the other districts and still control a majority of the legislature. Under full proportional representation, a party needs 50 percent of the national vote to control the legislature, meaning that politicians have stronger incentives to internalize the policy benefits for larger segments of the population.

A number of models revolve around this point in differing analytical frameworks. Lizzeri and Persico (2001) provide a model with binding electoral promises, where candidates can use tax revenue to provide either (general) public goods or targeted redistribution. Persson and Tabellini (2000a, ch. 9) consider a broad or narrow policy choice by an incumbent policymaker trying to earn re-election. Strömberg (2003) considers the effect of the electoral college on the allocation of campaign resources or policy benefits in a structural model of the election for US president. He shows empirically that this election method implies a much more lopsided distribution across states, where spending is focused on states where a relatively small number of votes might tip the entire state, rather than a (counterfactual) system of a national vote. Milesi-Ferretti et al. (2002) obtain similar results in a model where policy is set in postelection bargaining among the elected politicians. They also predict that proportional elections lead to a bigger overall size of spending.

Is the evidence consistent with the prediction that proportional electoral systems lead to more spending in broad redistributive programs, such as public pensions and welfare spending? Table 3.1 (upper panel) suggests that it is. Confining attention to parliamentary democracies, and without controlling for other determinants of welfare spending, legislatures elected under proportional electoral systems spend more in social security and welfare by as much as 8 percent of GDP, compared to legislatures elected under majoritarian elections. Milesi-Ferretti et al.

Table 3.1
Political and economic outcomes in parliamentary democracies classified by electoral rules

	Majoritarian	Proportional
Economic policy outcomes		
Government spending	25.94	35.12
	(9.05)	(9.30)
Social security and welfare spending	5.37	13.15
	(4.98)	(5.40)
Budget deficit	2.92	3.86
	(3.81)	(4.17)
Political outcomes		
Party fragmentation	0.54	0.70
	(0.17)	(0.09)
Coalition governments	0.24	0.55
	(0.41)	(0.47)
Single-party governments	0.63	0.17
	(0.47)	(0.37)
Number of observations	138	187

Sources: Persson and Tabellini (2003) and Persson, Roland, and Tabellini (2004).
Notes: Simple averages; standard deviations in parenthesis. Fiscal policy variables refer to central governments and are measured as percentages of GDP. Observations were pooled across countries and legislatures. The number of observations refers to the political outcomes (some observations are missing for the policy outcomes).

(2002) and Persson and Tabellini (2003, 2004) show that a statistically significant (but smaller) effect of the electoral systems remains after controlling for other determinants of social security and welfare spending, such as the percentage of the elderly in the population, per capita income, the age and quality of democracy, and so on. They rely on different data sets—based on postwar OECD and IMF data, respectively—that include presidential democracies. Persson and Tabellini (2003, 2004) use a data set with seventy democracies in the 1990s; they allow for a separate effect of presidentialism on policy outcomes and take into account the self-selection of countries into different electoral systems. According to their findings, a reform from plurality rule to proportional representation would boost welfare spending (in a country drawn at random) by about 2 percent of GDP, an economically and statistically significant effect.

If politicians have stronger incentives to vie for electoral support through broad spending programs under proportional representation than under plurality rule, we might expect to observe systematic differences around election time in the two systems. Persson and Tabellini (2003) indeed find a significant electoral cycle in welfare-state spending—expansions of such budget items in election and postelection years—in proportional representation systems but not in plurality systems.

Electoral Rules, Party Formation, and Types of Government

The papers discussed so far focus on the incentives of individual politicians, but as many studies of comparative politics point out, electoral rules also shape party structure and types of government. Plurality rule and small district magnitude produce fewer parties and a more skewed distribution of seats than proportional representation and large district magnitude (e.g., Duverger 1954; Lijphart 1990). Moreover in parliamentary democracies fewer parties mean more frequent single-party majority governments and less frequent coalition governments, in contrast to many parties (Taagepera and Shugart 1989; Strom 1990). The evidence shown in table 3.1 (lower panel) suggests that these political effects of the electoral rule can be large. In parliamentary democracies proportional electoral rule is associated with a more fragmented party system, more frequent coalition governments, and less frequent governments ruled by a single-party majority.

It would be surprising if such large political effects did not also show up in the economic policies implemented by these different party systems and types of government. Indeed a few recent papers have argued that the more fractionalized party systems induced by proportional elections lead to a greater overall size of government spending. For example, Austen-Smith (2000) studies a model where redistributive tax policy is set in postelection bargaining. He assumes that there are fewer parties under plurality rule (two parties) than under proportional representation (three parties). The coalition of two parties is more likely to have higher taxes and to redistribute than is a single party.

Persson, Roland, and Tabellini (2003) and Bawn and Rosenbluth (2003) obtain a similar prediction that proportional representation leads to more government spending than plurality rule, but they treat the number of parties as endogenous and emphasize how electoral competition differs under different types of government. When the government relies on a single-party majority, the main competition for votes is between the incumbent and the opposition; this dynamic pushes the incumbent toward efficient policies, or at least toward policies that benefit the voters represented in office. If instead the government is supported by a coalition of parties, voters can discriminate between the parties in government and this dynamic creates electoral conflict inside the governing coalition. Under plausible assumptions, inefficiencies in bargaining induce excessive government spending.

As shown in table 3.1 (upper panel) these theoretical predictions are supported by the data: on average, and without conditioning on other determinants of fiscal policy, legislatures elected under proportional representation spend about 10 percent of GDP more than legislatures elected under plurality rule. Careful estimates obtained from cross-country data confirm this result. Persson and Tabellini (2003, 2004) consider a sample of 80 parliamentary and presidential democracies in the 1990s. They control for a variety of other policy determinants (including the distinction between presidential and parliamentary government) and allow for self-selection of countries into electoral systems.[7] Their estimates are very robust, and imply that proportional representation rather than plurality rule raises total expenditures by central government by a whopping 5 percent of GDP.

Persson, Roland, and Tabellini (2003) focus on 50 parliamentary democracies (the same ones used to produce table 3.1 above), identifying the effect of electoral rules on spending either from the cross-sectional variation, or from the time-series variation around electoral reforms. They find spending to be higher under proportional elections, and by an amount similar to that found by Persson and Tabellini (2003, 2004), but they suggest the effect to be entirely due to a higher incidence of coalition governments in proportional electoral systems. This conclusion is reached by testing an overidentifying restriction that follows from the underlying theoretical model. Several features of the electoral rule—such as the electoral formula, district magnitude, and minimum thresholds for being represented in parliament—are jointly used as instruments for the type of government. The data cannot reject the restriction that all these measures of electoral systems are valid instruments for the type of government; that is, the electoral rule only influences government spending through the type of government, with no direct effects of the electoral rule on spending.

This result is a feature of the data illustrated in figure 3.1, where each observation corresponds to a country average in the sample of fifty parliamentary democracies during the 1990s. The horizontal axis

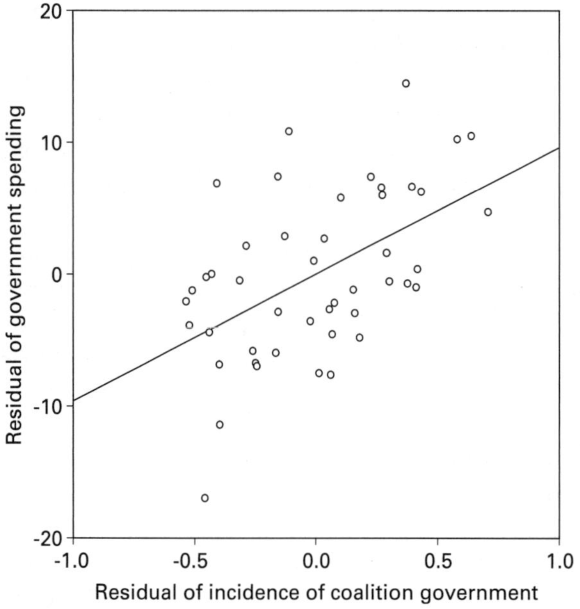

Figure 3.1
Total government spending and incidence of coalition governments. The residuals are obtained by regressing total spending by central government (as percentage of GDP) and the incidence of coalition governments, respectively, on the following variables: per capita income, openness to international trade, the proportion of the elderly in the population, ethnolinguistic fractionalization, UK colonial origin, a dummy variable for federal political structures. The sample refers to 50 parliamentary democracies in the 1990s. Source: Persson, Roland, and Tabellini (2003).

measures the *residuals* of total spending by the central government as percentage of GDP. The vertical axis measures the residuals of the incidence of coalition governments during the 1990s—the incidence varies from 0 (no coalition government) to 1 (coalition governments all the time). By construction, both residual variables have a mean of zero; hence each axis measures the respective variable in deviation from its conditional mean. For instance, a value of −1 on the horizontal axis of figure 3.1, would correspond to a country that was predicted to have coalition governments all the time but instead turns out to be ruled by single-party government throughout the 1990s. The residuals have been obtained by regressing each variable on a set of policy determinants listed in the note to figure 3.1, such as per capita income and demographics. Thus figure 3.1 displays the variation in the size of government spending and incidence of coalition variables uncorrelated with these policy determinants. Clearly, more frequent coalition governments are associated with larger government spending. The slope of the solid line in figure 3.1 corresponds to the estimated coefficient of an OLS regression of total government spending on the incidence of coalition government. It depicts the long run effect of being ruled by a coalition government (as opposed to single-party government) on the size of government spending. Instrumental variable estimation (using measures of electoral rules as instruments for the type of government) further increases the estimated effect of coalition governments on total government spending. Earlier empirical papers treating the type of government as exogenous had also found evidence for higher spending by larger coalitions in other data sets (e.g., Kontopoulos and Perotti 1999; Baqir 2002).

As we noted above, the selection of countries into constitutions is certainly not random, and some of the empirical research takes account of this (e.g., Persson and Tabellini 2003, 2004). But Ticchi and Vindigni (2003) and Iversen and Soskice (2003) note a particularly subtle problem: at least in the OECD countries, proportional electoral rule is frequently associated with center-left governments, while right-wing governments are more frequent under majoritarian elections. This correlation, rather than the prevalence of coalition governments, could explain why proportional representation systems spend more. But why should the electoral rule be correlated with the ideological government type? These papers argue that majoritarian elections concentrate power, which tends to favor the wealthy. In such systems, the argument goes, minorities (groups unlikely to benefit from spending, irrespective of who holds office) would rather see fiscal conservatives than fiscal liberals in office, since this reduces their tax burden. Hence, in winner-takes-all systems, conservative parties have an electoral advantage. If electoral rules are chosen on the basis of the policies they will deliver, this might explain the observed correlation: where the center-left voters dominate proportional systems have been selected, whereas majoritarian systems have been selected where conservatives dominate. The empirical results by Persson, Roland, and Tabellini (2003) cast some doubt on this line of thought, however. If indeed the electoral rule influences policy through the ideology of governments, rather than through the number of parties in government, the electoral rule cannot be a valid instrument for the incidence of coalition governments in a regression on government spending—contrary to the findings discussed above.

Finally, if bargaining inefficiencies inside coalition governments lead to high spending, they may also produce other distortions. Several papers have studied intertemporal fiscal policy, treating the type of government as exogenous, but arguing that coalition governments face more severe "common-pool problems." The latter concept refers to the tendency for overexploitation when multiple users make independent decisions on how much to exploit a common resource such as fish; the analogy to this common resource is current and future tax revenue. In reviewing the extensive work on government budget deficits, Alesina and Perotti (1995) draw on the work by Velasco (1999) to argue that coalition governments are more prone to run deficits. Hallerberg and von Hagen (1998, 1999) explicitly link the severity of the common-pool problem to electoral systems and argue that this has implications for the appropriate form of budgetary process. These arguments find some support in the experiences of European and Latin American countries. As coalition governments have more players who could potentially veto a change, they could be subject to some inability to alter policy in the wake of adverse shocks (Roubini and Sachs 1989; Alesina and Drazen 1991). Moreover, in the developed democracies, changes of government or threatened changes of government are empirically more frequent under proportional elections (due to the greater incidence of minority and coalition governments). When governments must often face a vote on their own survival, it could lead to greater policy myopia and larger budget deficits (Alesina and Tabellini 1990; Grilli, Masciandaro, and Tabellini 1991). These ideas are related to those in Tsebelis (1995, 1999, 2002), where a larger number of veto players tends to "lock in" economic policy and reduce its ability to respond to outside shocks. In Tsebelis's conception, proportional elections often lead to multiple partisan veto players in government and thus to more policy myopia, though the electoral rule is not the primitive in his analysis.

Evidence based on larger data sets partly confirms these results and ideas. As shown in earlier in table 3.1, budget deficits are larger by about 1 percent of GDP in legislatures elected under proportional representation, compared to those elected under plurality rule (although this difference is not statistically significant in table 3.1). Persson and Tabellini (2003) consider larger data sets from the 1990s as well as from the 1960s and show that, when controlling for other determinants of policy, this difference grows to about 2 percent of GDP and becomes statistically significant. There is also some evidence that the electoral rule is correlated with the reaction of government to economic shocks: in proportional democracies, spending as a share of GDP rises in recessions but does not decline in booms, while cyclical fluctuations tend to have symmetric impacts on fiscal policy under other electoral systems.

Forms of Government and Political Representation

The defining feature of parliamentary democracies is that the executive can be removed from office at any time by a nonconfidence vote by the legislature. In a parliamentary democracy the government also has strong powers to initiate legislation and set the agenda. The parties represented in government thus hold valuable bargaining powers that they risk losing if a government crisis takes place. Therefore the confidence requirement, together with the agenda-setting prerogatives of governments, creates strong incentives to maintain discipline inside the governing party or coalition, as noted by Shugart and Carey (1992) and formally modeled by Huber (1996) and Diermeier and Feddersen (1998). To use the jargon of the literature, the confidence requirement creates "legislative cohesion"—a stable majority supporting the cabinet and voting together on policy proposals. When the executive cannot be removed by a nonconfidence vote, as in a presidential system, the result is unstable coalitions and less discipline within the majority.

Building on this idea, Persson, Roland, and Tabellini (2000) contrast alternative arrangements for legislative bargaining. In parliamentary democracies, a stable majority of legislators pursues the joint interest of its voters. Spending thus optimally becomes directed toward a broad majority of voters, as in the case of broad social transfer programs or general public goods. In presidential democracies, the (relative) lack of such a majority instead pits the interests of different minorities against each other for different issues on the legislative agenda. As a result programs with broad benefits suffer, and the allocation of spending favors minorities in the constituencies of powerful officeholders, for example, the heads of congressional committees in the United States.

Moreover, in parliamentary regimes, the stable majority of incumbent legislators, as well as the majority of voters backing them, become "residual claimants" on additional revenue; they can keep the benefits of spending within the majority, putting part of the costs on the excluded minority. Both majorities favor high taxes and high spending. In presidential regimes, on the other hand, no such residual claimants

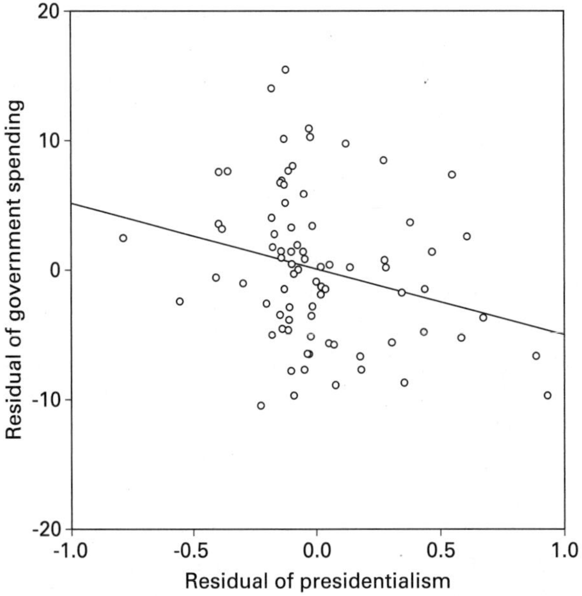

Figure 3.2
Total government spending and the form of government. The residuals are obtained by regressing total spending by central government (as percentage of GDP) and a dummy variable for presidential regimes, respectively, on the following variables: per capita income, openness to international trade, the proportion of the elderly and of the young in the population, ethnolinguistic fractionalization, quality and age of democracy, and dummy variables for plurality-rule elections, federal political structures, OECD countries, continental location and colonial origin. The sample refers to 83 democracies in the 1990s. Source: Persson and Tabellini (2003).

on revenue exist, and the majority of taxpayers and legislators therefore resist high spending, as the benefits would be directed toward different minorities.

Thus presidential regimes are predicted to have lower overall spending and taxation than parliamentary regimes, both because presidential regimes never face the risk of a no-confidence vote and also because of the separation of powers argument in the previous section. Presidential regimes should also be associated with more targeted programs at the expenses of broad spending programs.

The evidence is strongly supportive of some of these predictions. In figure 3.2 we plot total government spending as percentage of GDP against a dummy variable for presidentialism in 83 democracies in the 1990s, after taking into account several other possible determinants of fiscal policy (including the electoral system). As for figure 3.1, the two axes show the residuals of the two variables measured in a regression against the set of policy determinants listed in the note to figure 3.2. By construction, the mean of both variables is zero, and figure 3.2 displays the remaining variation in each variable, uncorrelated with the policy determinants included as regressors. Thus a value of 1 on the horizontal axis corresponds to a country that was predicted to be parliamentary, but turns out to be presidential, and vice versa for the value of −1. Presidential countries are defined as those where the executive is not accountable to the legislature. A strong negative relation is apparent: the slope of the regression line, which corresponds to the OLS coefficient estimate, is about −5. This means that a constitutional reform that switches the form of government from parliamentary to presidential in a country drawn at random from this sample will reduce the total size of government spending by about 5 percent of GDP in the long run—a very large number. Persson and Tabellini (2003, 2004) show that this result is very robust, to the sample of countries, to the specification of the controlling variables, and to the estimation methods (including least squares, instrumental variables, a Heckman-style adjustment, and propensity score matching). As in the case of electoral rules, differences observed today largely result from different rates of growth of government in the last four decades, with spending growing much faster in parliamentary than in presidential democracies.

The containing effect of presidentialism on the size of public spending is also a feature of local governments, and not just of national governments. Baqir (2002) contrasts public spending in US municipalities differing in their form of government. Some are parliamentary in the sense that the chief executive is appointed by the municipal council, and others are presidential, in the sense that the mayor is directly elected. Baqir finds that presidential governments spend less than those where the mayor is accountable to the municipal legislature.

Finally the predicted result that presidential regimes have smaller universalistic welfare programs is found only among the better democracies (see note 6), where presidential democracies indeed spend less, by about 2 percent of GDP.

Types of Government and Political Representation

We are not aware of any formal theoretical analysis that has explicitly tried to contrast the size of the budget deficit or the reaction of policy to economic shocks under presidential, as opposed to parliamentary, form of government. In theory the comparison could go either way. On the one hand, fixed terms of office and greater durability of the executive in presidential regimes could reduce policy myopia, relative to parliamentary regimes, leading to smaller budget deficits and more rapid reactions to adverse events. On the other hand, in a presidential system with divided governments—that is, executives and congressional majorities from different parties—both sides may be gridlocked when responding to adverse shocks to the economy. Some authors such as Alt and Lowry (1994) have even tried to explain the occurrences of budget deficits and the adjustments to shocks in the US states as due to divided government, where governors and majorities in state congresses are controlled by different parties.[8] A common criticism among political scientists of Latin American presidential regimes, namely that they are commonly deadlocked and ineffective, can be read in the same way.

Persson and Tabellini (2003) find no robust evidence for government deficits being systematically influenced by the form of government. But they do uncover systematic differences in the adjustment of fiscal policies to economic and political events. In presidential democracies, spending and deficits are pro-cyclical rather than countercyclical. Moreover a postelection tightening of fiscal policy is observed only in presidential democracies, where spending is cut and deficits improve in the average postelection year by no less than 1 percent of GDP. These results on fiscal policy dynamics are robust to controlling for the overrepresentation of Latin American countries in the set of presidential democracies. How to interpret these institution-dependent patterns in the data is far from clear, however, and probably requires a new round of theoretical work on the dynamics of policy making under different forms of government.

3.6 Concluding Remarks

Constitutional rules appear to shape economic policy. Whether we are economists or political scientists, at the end of the day we are interested not only in government policies per se but also in their overall effect on economic performance. This is a more difficult issue because we know relatively little about the policy determinants of economic performance, and what we know suggests very complex patterns of interaction.

Nevertheless, it is tempting to explore the data to see whether some robust correlations are possible. Persson and Tabellini (2003) uncover some intriguing but preliminary patterns among seventy-five democracies in the 1990s. A broad classification of electoral rules into proportional and majoritarian does not seem to be strongly correlated with economic performance. But a parliamentary form of government is associated with better performance and better growth-promoting policies, measured by indexes for broad protection of property rights and of open borders in trade and finance (the same policies as those considered in a well-known study by Hall and Jones 1999). Growth-promoting policies, in turn, positively affect productivity. It is tempting to interpret these findings as parliamentary democracies generating better provision of public goods, or policies with broadly distributed benefits, because property-rights-protecting regulatory policies and nonprotectionist trade policies can be described in those terms. But the negative effect of presidentialism is only present among the democracies with lowest scores for the quality of democracy; this suggests that it is not presidential government per se that is detrimental to economic performance but rather the combination of a strong and directly elected executive in a weak institutional environment where political abuse of power cannot be easily prevented.

Persson (2003) goes further, extending the sample to panel data and to non-democracies, so as to exploit entry into or exit from different types of democratic constitutions. His preliminary findings are also consistent with a sizable positive effect of parliamentary democracy (relative to presidential democracy as well as non-democracy) on growth-promoting policies and labor productivity. Moreover he shows that an imaginative instrument for growth-promoting policy suggested by Acemoglu, Johnson, and Robinson (2001) induces better expected performance through a higher likelihood of parliamentary democracy (and better growth-promoting policies).[9] The robustness and the precise interpretation of these patterns in the data is an exciting task for future research. A related interesting line of research studies the effects of becoming a democracy on economic performance (e.g., Roll and Talbott 2002; Prezworski and Limongi 1993).

What can be inferred from the literature discussed in this chapter about the overall consequences of constitutional reforms? It suggests that electoral reforms and changes to the form of government often entail a trade-off between accountability and representation, as political scientists have long suggested, and that these trade-offs extend to economic policy outcomes. In particular, plurality rule strengthens accountability by reinforcing the incentives of politicians to please the voters. As a result there are smaller political rents and less corruption.

But plurality rule also makes political candidates more responsive to the wishes of pivotal groups of voters, which increases the propensity to target benefits to narrow constituencies, at the expense of broad and universalistic programs such as welfare-state spending and general public goods. The evidence suggests that both effects are quantitatively important.

In addition small district magnitude combined with plurality rule induces a system with fewer political parties. This too has several implications. On the one hand, it becomes more difficult to oust dishonest or incompetent incumbents because voters will often support such incumbents over honest but ideologically opposed challengers. On the other hand, the incidence of coalition governments is reduced (in parliamentary democracies), and this is likely to lead to more efficient policies. The overall effect on accountability of these changes is ambiguous. But the overall size of government and budget deficits are much larger under coalition governments, and the later are promoted by proportional representation and large district magnitude.

Another important lesson of this line of research, however, is that any real-world electoral reform should pay attention to the finer details of the electoral system and to specific country characteristics. In some cases, it may be possible to combine the broad categories discussed here. For example, in Chile and Mauritius voters cast their ballots for individuals elected by plurality in two- or three-member districts. Such an arrangement might be a way of reaping the benefits both of individual accountability and plurality rule. In other cases, the linkages discussed here may not hold. For example, in some countries like Italy voters may find that single-party legislative districts still end up with a large number of political parties and coalition governments because political preferences reflect geographic location and this allows small parties to be sure winners in some districts. We expect that future research on constitutions and economic policy will show a greater ability to understand and exploit these subtle interactions between the constitution and country-specific characteristics.

Notes

An earlier version of this chapter was published in the *Journal of Economic Perspectives*, American Economic Association, vol. 18(1): 75–98. It is adapted here with permission from the American Economic Assocation.

1. We are grateful to Timothy Taylor, Brad DeLong, Andrei Shleifer, and Michael Waldman for helpful comments on the earlier draft. We also thank the Canadian Institute of Advanced Research for financial support.

2. This description presupposes a system of closed party lists. When lists are open, voters can also express preferences across candidates, which may modify the results. This distinction between open and closed party lists is discussed further below.

3. To achieve proportionality, the Irish "single transferrable vote" system (also used in Malta) relies on votes over individuals in multi-member districts where each voter can only vote for a single candidate, and a complicated procedure where seats are awarded sequentially and votes for losing candidates are transferred from one seat to the next.

4. Besley and Case (1995) provide direct evidence that the desire to be reappointed creates incentives to please the voters. Term limits in gubernatorial elections in US states are associated with higher taxes and higher government spending, compared to states without such limits (or periods in office when the limits are not binding), a finding consistent with the authors' political agency model where unchecked governors tax and spend too much.

5. Of course, districts can be redesigned at will at some intervals, which makes the closeness of elections an endogenous choice. This possibility opens up the door for strategic manipulation, also known as gerrymandering, where protection of incumbents is one of several possible objectives.

6. "Bad" and "good" are defined in terms of democracy scores in the Freedom House and Polity IV data sets, which measure aspects such as consrtraints on the executive's use of powers and freedom of political participation across societies and time.

7. Variables held constant in the underlying regressions include per capita income, the quality and age of democracy, openness of the economy, the size and age composition of the population, plus indicators for federalism, OECD membership, colonial history, and continental location. Estimation is by ordinary least squares, instrumental variables, the Heckit method, or propensity–score matching, with all estimates yielding similar results.

8. A similar idea in the literature on US state fiscal policy is that other legislative institutions—such as a governor's line-item veto—have more bite on taxes, spending and deficits under divided government, an idea that has received some electoral support. Again, we refer the reader to Besley and Case (2003) for an extensive survey of this literature.

9. These authors suggested that (1) the influence on institutions from western European colonization is long lived, (2) whether the colonizers set up productive or extractive institutions depends systematically on living conditions in the colonies, and (3) living conditions in colonized countries are well measured by the (nonmilitary) death rates among the settlers in the early nineteenth century. On these grounds, they suggest that early settler mortality is a good instrument for growth-promoting institutions.

References

Acemoglu, D., S. Johnson, and J. Robinson. 2001. The colonial origins of comparative development: An empirical investigation. *American Economic Review* 91: 1369–1401.

Alesina, A., and A. Drazen. 1991. Why are stabilizations delayed? *American Economic Review* 81: 1170–88.

Alesina, A., and R. Perotti. 1995. The political economy of budget deficits. IMF Staff Papers, March.

Alesina, A., and G. Tabellini. 1990. A positive theory of fiscal deficits and government debt. *Review of Economic Studies*.

Alt, J., and D. Lassen. 2002. The political economy of institutions and corruption in American states. EPRU working paper, University of Copenhagen.

Alt, J., and R. Lowry. 1994. Divided government, fiscal institutions and budget deficits: Evidence from the states. *American Political Science Review* 88: 811–28.

Austen-Smith, D. 2000. Redistributing income under proportional representation. *Journal of Political Economy* 108: 1235–69.

Baqir, R. 2002. Districting and government overspending. *Journal of Political Economy* 110: 1318–54.

Bawn, K., and N. Rosenbluth. 2003. Coalition parties vs. coalition of parties: How electoral agency shapes the political logic of costs and benefits. Mimeo, Yale University.

Besley, T., and A. Case. 1995. Does political accountability affect economic policy choices? Evidence from gubernatorial term limits. *Quarterly Journal of Economics* 110: 769–98.

Besley, T., and A. Case. 2003. Political institutions and policy choices: Evidence from the United States. *Journal of Economic Literature* 42: 7–73.

Bingham Powell, G. 2000. *Elections as Instruments of Democracy: Majoritarian and Proportional Visions*. New Haven: Yale University Press.

Blais, A., and L. Massicotte. 1996. Electoral Systems. In L. LeDuc, R. Niemei, and P. Norris, eds., *Comparing Democracies: Elections and Voting in Global Perspective*. Newbury Park, CA: Sage.

Carey, J., and M. Shugart. 1995. Incentives to cultivate a personal vote: A rank ordering of electoral formulas. *Electoral Studies* 14: 417–39.

Cox, G. 1997. *Making Votes Count*. Cambridge: Cambridge University Press.

Djankov, S., E. Glaeser, R. La Porta, F. Lopez-de-Silanes, and A. Shleifer. 2003. The new comparative economics. *Journal of Comparative Economics* (December).

Diermeier, D., and T. Feddersen. 1998. Cohesion in legislatures and the vote of confidence procedure. *American Political Science Review* 92: 611–21.

Duverger, M. 1954. *Political Parties: Their Organization and Activity in the Modern State*, tr. B. North and R. North. New York: Wiley.

Golden, M., and E. Chang. 2001. Competitive corruption: Factional conflict and political malfeasance in postwar Italian Christian democracy. *World Politics* 53: 558–622.

Golden, M., and E. Chang. 2003. Electoral systems, district magnitude and corruption. Mimeo. UCLA.

Grilli, V., D. Masciandaro, and G. Tabellini. 1991. Political and monetary institutions and public financial policies in the industrialized countries. *Economic Policy* (13).

Hall, R., and C. Jones. 1999. Why do some countries produce so much more output per worker than others? *Quarterly Journal of Economics* 114: 83–116.

Hallerberg, M., and J. Von Hagen. 1998. Electoral institutions and the budget process. In K. Fukasaka and R. Hausmann, eds., *Democracy, Decentralization and Deficits in Latin America*. Paris: OECD.

Hallerberg, M., and J. Von Hagen. 1999. Electoral institutions, cabinet negotiations, and budget deficits in the European Union. In J. Poterba and J. Von Hagen, eds., *Fiscal Institutions and Fiscal Performance*. Chicago: University of Chicago Press.

Holmström, B. 1982. Managerial incentive problems—A dynamic perspective. In *Essays in Economics and Management in Honor of Lars Wahlbeck*. Helsinki: Swedish School of Economics. Reprinted 1999 in *Review of Economic Studies* 66: 169–82.

Huber, J. 1996. The vote of confidence in parliamentary democracies. *American Political Science Review* 90: 269–82.

Iversen, T., and D. Soskice. 2003. Electoral systems and the politics of coalitions: Why some democracies redistribute more than others? Mimeo, Harvard University.

Kontopoulos, Y., and R. Perotti. 1999. Government fragmentation and fiscal policy outcomes: Evidence from the OECD countries. In J. Poterba and J. von Hagen, eds., *Fiscal Institutions and Fiscal Preference*. Chicago: University of Chicago Press.

Kunicova, J., and S. Rose Ackerman. 2001. Electoral rules as constraints on corruption: The risks of closed-list proportional representation. Mimeo, Yale University.

Lijphart, A. 1990. The political consequences of electoral laws 1945–85. *American Political Science Review* 84: 481–96.

Lizzeri, A., and N. Persico. 2001. The provision of public goods under alternative electoral incentives. *American Economic Review* 91: 225–45.

Milesi-Ferretti, G.-M., R. Perotti, and M. Rostagno. 2002. Electoral systems and the composition of public spending. *Quarterly Journal of Economics* 117: 609–57.

Myerson, R. 1993. Effectiveness of electoral systems for reducing government corruption: A game theoretic analysis. *Games and Economic Behavior* 5: 118–32.

Peltzman, S. 1992. Voters as fiscal conservatives. *Quarterly Journal of Economics* 107: 329–61.

Persson, T. 2003. Consequences of constitutions. Presidential address at the 2003 EEA Congress, Stockholm. *Journal of the European Economic Association*, forthcoming.

Persson, T., and G. Tabellini. 1999. The size and scope of government: Comparative politics with rational politicians. 1998 Alfred Marshall Lecture. *European Economic Review* 43: 699–735.

Persson, T., and G. Tabellini. 2000. *Political Economics: Explaining Economic Policy*. Cambridge: MIT Press.

Persson, T., and G. Tabellini. 2003. Economic effects of constitutions. Cambridge: MIT Press.

Persson, T., and G. Tabellini. 2004. Constitutional rules and economic policy outcomes. *American Economic Review*, forthcoming.

Persson, T., G. Roland, and G. Tabellini. 1997. Separation of powers and political accountability. *Quarterly Journal of Economics* 112: 1163–1202.

Persson, T., G. Roland, and G. Tabellini. 2000. Comparative politics and public finance. *Journal of Political Economy* 108: 1121–61.

Persson, T., G. Roland, and G. Tabellini. 2003. How do electoral rules shape party structures, government coalitions and economic policies? Mimeo, Bocconi University.

Persson, T., G. Tabellini, and F. Trebbi. 2003. Electoral rules and corruption. *Journal of the European Economic Association* 1: 958–89.

Prezworski, A., S. Stokes, and B. Manin. 1999. *Democracy, Accountability and Representation*. Cambridge: Cambridge University Press.

Prezworski, A., and F. Limongi. 1993. Political regimes and economic growth. *Journal of Economic Perspectives* (summer).

Poterba, J., and J. von Hagen, eds. 1999. *Fiscal Rules and Fiscal Performance*. Chicago: University of Chicago Press.

Roll, R., and J. Talbott. 2002. Why many developing countries just aren't. Mimeo, Anderson School, UCLA.

Roubini, N., and J. Sachs. 1989. Political and economic determinants of budget deficits in the industrial democracies. *European Economic Review* 33: 903–33.

Shugart, M., and J. Carey. 1992. *Presidents and Assemblies: Constitutional Design and Electoral Dynamics*. Cambridge: Cambridge University Press.

Strom, K. 1990. *Minority Government and Majority Rule*. Cambridge: Cambridge University Press.

Strömberg, D. 2003. Optimal campaigning in presidential elections: The probability of being Florida. Mimeo, IIES.

Taagepera, R., and M. Shugart. 1989. Seats and votes: The effects and determinants of electoral systems. New Haven: Yale University Press.

Ticchi, D., and A. Vindigni. 2003. Endogenous constitutions. Mimeo, IIES, University of Stockholm.

Tsebelis, G. 1995. Decision-making in political systems: Veto players in presidentialism, parliamentarism, multicameralism and multipartyism. *British Journal of Political Science* 25: 289–36.

Tsebelis, G. 1999. Veto players and law production in parliamentary democracies. *American Political Science Review* 93: 591–608.

Tsebelis, G. 2002. *Veto Players: How Political Institutions Work*. Princeton: Princeton University Press.

Velasco, A. 1999. A model of endogenous fiscal deficit and delayed fiscal reforms. In J. Poterba and J. von Hagen, eds., *Fiscal Rules and Fiscal Performance*. Chicago: University of Chicago Press.

4 Party-Line Voting and Committee Assignments in the German Mixed-Member System

Thomas Stratmann

4.1 Introduction

An ideal analysis of electoral rules on legislative behavior would randomly assign candidates to one or another electoral rule under which they would be elected. Such random assignment allows an analysis to determine a causal effect of rules on behavior. Without random assignment, and when estimating the effects of electoral rules across countries, there is the possibility that unobserved country characteristics that are important for legislator behavior are correlated with the electoral rule in the country. If countries use solely a proportional electoral system or solely a majoritarian system, it is impossible to disentangle the effect of country specifics from the effect of the electoral rule on legislative behavior because unobserved country characteristics can be correlated with the electoral rule adopted. Some of these issues can be avoided when one examines countries with mixed-member systems, namely countries in which some legislators are elected through one electoral method and others through a different method.

Only a few countries have a mixed-member system, although there has been a tendency for countries to adopt a mixed system within the last fifteen years. For example Israel, Italy, Japan, New Zealand, and Venezuela have moved from having all of their members elected through solely one electoral system to a mixed-member system (Shugart and Wattenberg 2001). One mixed-member system is in Germany, and this chapter examines the behavior of German legislators in the 1990s.

Most of the literature comparing electoral rules has looked at the macro picture, such as the differences between proportional representation (PR) and a majoritarian system, also known as first pass the post (FPTP), with respect to the number of parties, party strength, the different viabilities of small parties, representation of preferences, and legislative majorities (e.g., see Rae 1971).[1] Few studies, however, have analyzed the micro level, namely the incentives faced by legislators elected under one rule versus another. Examining differences in legislative behavior by electoral rule is of interest because legislative behavior is one of the central inputs into political and economic outcomes.

A key responsibility of legislators is to cast votes on a variety of bills and amendments. Relative to the majoritarian electoral systems where parties are relatively weak, there is a high level of party unity voting in proportional systems. Also in mixed member systems, as in the German system, legislators tend to vote with their parties and most votes are voice votes. However, documented votes that record how each legislator voted exist in the German system. This chapter tests the hypothesis that legislators who are elected through the majoritarian system are more likely to deviate from the party line than legislators elected through a proportional system.

To my knowledge only one previous study has done a quantitative examination of roll call votes in Germany. This study derives a measure of party discipline from roll call votes over the period from 1949 to 1990 and relates this measure to the homogeneity of party members socioeconomic characteristics (Saalfeld 1995). This study did not find systematic patterns in the data, although Saalfeld did not examine voting behavior by the type of electoral rule through which each German legislator became a member of parliament.

Besides voting, legislators craft bills, and this occurs in committees of the German Bundestag. Committees allow legislators to influence language in bills to the benefit of particular groups in society. Legislators have are motivated to support certain groups because of the electoral system through which they are reelected. For example, legislators elected though the FPTP electoral rule are expected to seek benefits for their home constituency, also referred to as pork-barreling (Weingast, Shepsle, and Johnsen 1981). While pork barrel activity has been documented in the United States, it is not clear whether it is primarily attributable to the electoral rule FPTP, used for electing US legislators, or to other characteristics of American politics.[2] This chapter tests whether German FPTP legislators seek committees that put then in an advantageous position to deliver central government funds to their home constituency. This chapter also tests whether PR legislators, whose reelection depends on their ranking in the party and whether they are supported by groups supporting the party, will seek committees that put them in a position to redistribute resources to supporters of their party.

Previous work has found support for the hypothesis that FPTP legislators are members of committees that are particularly suitable to help their home constituencies and that PR legislators are members of committees that help their party consistencies (Stratmann and Baur 2002). This chapter tests this hypothesis for the one electoral period for which I analyze party unity voting.

I find that FPTP legislators are more likely to vote against the party than their PR counterparts. Further FPTP legislators are predominantly on committees where they have influence over the allocation of benefits to their geographic reelection constituency, while PR legislators are members of committees that have control over funds that benefit party reelection constituencies. Thus electoral rules have a significant influence on day-to-day legislative behavior, which in turn affects government policy.

The next section of this chapter discusses the underlying institutions in Germany. Section 4.3 presents hypotheses, and data are described in the section 4.4. Results are presented in section 4.5, and section 4.6 concludes.

4.2 Institutional Background

Electoral System

In Germany's electoral system some representatives are elected through plurality rule from single-member districts and others though proportional representation. Each voter casts a candidate ballot (*Erststimme*) for the district candidate and party list ballot (*Zweitstimme*) for the party.[3] For the party list ballot the voter votes for a party, not a particular member on the party list. The district candidate with the largest number of votes wins and becomes a member of parliament. Thus the German electoral system is party majoritarian due to the fact that the winner of the election in each of the n single-member districts becomes a member of parliament.

Each party receives that fraction of the seats in parliament that is proportional to the percentage of votes that the party receives on the party list ballot. Those seats are allocated first to the winners of district races. If the party receives more seats through the party list ballot than it can fill with winners in district races, party members with the highest rank on the state party list fill those slots. Thus the number of district races won does not influence the overall number of seats obtained by the party except where a party wins more races than the number of seats allocated through the party list ballot. In the latter case the party can keep the extra seats (*Überangsmandate*). District candidates can also appear on the party list ballot. If those candidates win in the district election, they enter the parliament based on winning the district election, not based on having a slot on the party list.

The party ballots are totaled at the state level. For example, suppose that the state of Baden-Württemberg contributes 100 seats to the parliament, which are divided into 50 district seats (implying that this state has 50 district races) and 50 party list seats. Further suppose that the CDU wins 45 percent of the party list ballot votes, the SPD win 42 percent, and the FDP and Greens receive 7 and 6 percent, respectively. Last, assume that the CDU wins in 40 of the 50 district races while the SPD wins in the remaining 10 races. In this case the CDU's district winners fill 40 of the 45 seats and 5 individuals are chosen (those with the highest rank) from the CDU's state party list. Similarly the SPD district winners fill 10 of the 42 seats allocated to the SPD, and the remaining seats are filled from the top spots of the SPD's state party list. Thus the larger the number of FPTP seats won by a party, the fewer the PR seats it receives. The mix of FPTP and PR seats then differs for each party. In this example the FDP and Greens draw their 7 and 6 representatives entirely from their state lists.

If a party has more FPTP seats than it has representatives through the PR system, it can keep these extra seats (*Überhangsmandate*). In the previous example, if the CDU receives 47 seats through the candidate ballot, it can keep the extra two seats and no individuals are chosen from the state party list.[4] For the purpose of the subsequent empirical analysis of committee assignments, this circumstance is of little or no quantitative importance.[5]

In summary, the legislature has $n + m$ seats, where m is the number of legislators chosen from state party lists, and n is the number of plurality rule winners in the district races. Since n is roughly equal to m, approximately half of the legislators are elected by plurality rule (n legislators) and the other half is elected by proportional representation from state (*Länder*) party lists. Germany is divided into 16 states.[6] Each state (s) contributes k_s seats to the legislature, where $\sum k_s = n + m$. The number of seats for each state is determined by the state's population size. The party list ballot determines the final distribution of the $n + m$

seats in the legislature. That is, the mix of FPTP and PR seats differs for each party, depending on the number of district races won, since each party's overall number of seats is determined by the party list ballot. Legislators who are elected through PR or FPTP have identical rights and obligations within the legislature.

Voting

Voting in the German Bundestag can be by either secret ballot or voice vote, where simply the number of yea and nay votes are counted (Geschäftsordnung paragraphs 48 and 51, *einfache Abstimmung, Zählen der Stimmen*) or the recorded roll call vote (Geschäftsordnung paragraph 52—*namendliche Abstimmung*. The recorded roll call vote occurs when one party (*Fraktion*) requests a recorded vote or when 5 percent of the representatives request a recorded vote. Prior to 1980 a different parliamentary rule applied. That rule required a request from a minimum of fifty legislators in order to hold a roll call vote.

The most frequent vote type in the German Bundestag is the voice vote, which does not provide information as to who voted in favor or against the proposition. The literature on recorded votes in the German Bundestag suggests that recorded votes occur when a party expects to achieve political gain from a recorded vote, or when it wants to stake out a clear position, or wants to assure that interest groups and voters know about the party's position (Loewenberg 1971; Borgs-Maiejewski 1986).

Committee System[7]

The German legislature, the Bundestag, has permanent (standing) committees and also special committees and investigatory committees. The issue areas of standing committees mirror, for the most part, the policy issues for which the government ministries are responsible.

Legislation is referred to the committees from these the executive and from the parliamentary parties. Committees are required to make recommendations whether or not a bill should be passed to the entire legislature. The recommendations may include amendments to the legislation. Bills are modified at the committee stage in about 60 percent of all cases. Often bills are in the committee stage for six months (Johnson 1979, p. 124)[8] during which time the committees hold public hearings and take opinions from experts and affected parties. In addition to modifying legislation, committees provide "infrastructure for communications and information between members of parliament, government ministers, bureaucrats, and interest groups" (Saalfeld 1998, p. 58).[9]

"Committees [in the German legislature] play a major part in giving... legislative output its final shape" (Johnson 1979, p. 135). As in the United States, committee members' decisions are typically influenced by party positions. Organized interests attempt to influence legislation by lobbying committee members. Interests also have influence, in part, because committee members are often interest group officials. In fact appointments to committees are often made so as to match legislators who are members of pressure groups with the jurisdiction of committees (Saalfeld 1998, p. 58). For example, the education committee has been dominated by members from the academic community (Johnson 1979).

Committees also work on nonlegislative items such as conducting investigations, holding hearings on particular issues of concern, and prepare reports. They not only work on issues that are referred to them by the Bundestag but also develop their own initiative in holding hearings on matters that they view as important, and they do so as they see fit. During the twelfth Bundestag there have been 3,024 committee meetings (Hübner 1995). German committees also have some oversight functions with respect to the executive. For example, committees investigate government regulations and review activities of the executive branch of government (Johnson 1979).

Committees assignments are made after the general election, at the start of a new legislative session. First legislators indicate their preferences regarding committee assignments, and next the party whips formulate a proposal to the party caucus (*Fraktion*). The party caucus decides on the final committee assignments (Kaack 1990). Parties allocate seats according to personal preferences of legislators, representativeness of various political groups within the party, and representativeness of the various German regions (Johnson 1979; Ismayr 1992, p. 189). If there exists a greater demand for seats on a particular committee than there are slots, intra-party bargaining occurs to achieve an agreement.[10] FPTP members appear to be in a better bargaining position and are more likely to obtain their first choice of committee seat. "Where they [FPTP members] really want to have it their way, mostly in matters of interest to their voting districts, they can... mobilize considerable bargaining power within their parliamentary groups" (Patzelt 2000, p. 38).

Committees are assigned after the election, at the beginning of a new legislative session. Legislators indicate their committee preferences to their party, and the party caucus determines the final committee assignments (Kaack 1990). Legislators can be fairly independent in choosing their committee assignments (Hübner 1995). Parties allocate seats according to personal preferences of legislators, representativeness of various political groups within the party, and representativeness of the various German regions (Johnson 1979, Ismayr 1992: 189). Thus appointments to committees often match legislators who are members of pressure groups with the jurisdiction of committees (Saalfeld 1998, p. 58). For example, the education committee has been dominated by members from the academic community (Johnson 1979).

Once each legislator has voiced his preference, party whips formulate a proposal for committee assignments which requires consent by the party caucus (*Fraktion*). If there exists a greater demand for seats on a particular committee than there are slots, intra-party bargaining occurs to achieve an agreement. FPTP members appear to be in a better bargaining position and are more likely to obtain their first choice of committee seat. "Where they [FPTP members] really want to have it their way, mostly in matters of interest to their voting districts, they can . . . mobilize considerable bargaining power within their parliamentary groups" (Patzelt 2000, p. 38).

As in the United States reelected legislators can retain their seats on the committee on which they previously served. Once a legislator "has secured a committee assignment to his liking, he can usually count on holding on to it" (Johnson 1979, p. 119). Most legislators are members of only one committee. While multiple committee membership is more common among members of smaller parties, a significant fraction of CDU, CSU, and SPD legislators are members of multiple committees. In the 1990s approximately 15 percent of the legislators from major parties were members on multiple committees, while over 15 percent of the legislators from major parties had no committee assignments (as *Ordentliche Mitglieder*).

The seats for each party on each committee are proportional to the number of seats in the Bundestag rather than the share of the popular vote. Each committee has one chairperson who can be from any party. A party's overall number of committee chairs is determined by its share of party list ballot votes. For example, if the Christian Democratic Party receives 40 percent of the popular vote, 40 percent of all committee chairpersons come from that party.

4.3 Hypotheses

Pervious work on mixed member systems has analyzed the determinates as to why countries switch from one type of electoral system to a mixed member system (Shugart and Wattenberg 2001). A few studies have analyzed the consequences of mixed member systems with respect to economic or political outcomes. Two examples of such recent studies are Benoit (2001), who suggests that directly elected candidates in Hungary are more likely to respond to party preferences than to district preferences, and Stratmann (2001), who finds that between 1990 and 2002 German legislators have systematically different committee assignments, depending on whether they were elected from the district or obtained a seat in parliament though the party list. In contrast, Weldon (2001) suggests that in Mexico the possible effects of a mixed system on legislative behavior are overwhelmed by other institutional factors. Other work on mixed member systems has analyzed the effects of split ticket voting (e.g., see Bawn 1999).

Most of the literature on the German parliamentary system has claimed that there are no significant behavioral differences between both legislator types in Germany (see Nohlen 1990; Thaysen 1990; Ismayr 1992). For example, using survey data, Ismayr (1992) finds that PR legislators are approximately as likely to be active in their geographic district as are FPTP legislators, lending support to the hypothesis that there is little behavioral difference between the legislator types and electoral systems. Little emphasis has been placed on the fact that German FPTP and PR legislators face different reelection constraints that may manifest themselves in behavioral differences (Patzelt 2000). One survey study, however, shows that FPTP legislators perceive it as more important to provide projects for reelection purposes than do PR legislators (Lancaster and Patterson 1990).[11]

German PR legislators are chosen from state party lists made up prior to the election. State party congresses determine the ranking of legislators on the lists. The higher a party member's rank on the list, the higher the probability that she or he will become a member of parliament. The ranking on the list is determined, in part, by the party members' prominence, seniority, interest group approval of the nomination, and evidence of longstanding prior party activities (Conradt 1986, p. 124). The top spots on the list are typically reserved for party leadership. Much bargaining occurs to achieve a high rank, and even candidates who run in districts that are considered "safe" seek a high list position, to assure their entry into the legislature in case they are defeated in their district (Conradt 1986).

Voting Behavior

PR legislators' seat in parliament is thus solely due to the fact that they ranked sufficiently high on the party list. If they were not to serve the party and interest groups that support the party, it is likely that they would obtain a lower rank on the party list for the next election. PR legislators are more dependent on having a good standing in the party as opposed to FPTP legislators, whose reelection is a function of whether they provide services to their geographic home constituency. Since PR legislators have a stronger incentive to be loyal to their party and to follow the party line, I predict that PR legislators are more likely to vote with the party than FPTP legislators.

If omitted or unobserved variables cause both voting decision and whether the legislator a PR for FTPT legislator, the point estimate on the legislator type is biased. An omitted variable that could cause such bias is party loyalty. If legislators who are dedicated to serve the party prefer list seats and are also more likely to vote along party lines, an estimate that suggests that list legislators are more likely to vote along party lines has an upward bias. To identify the effect of legislator type on voting behavior, I assume that the type assignment is exogenous with respect to the voting decision. This assumption is most likely to hold for legislators who run both in a district and are also on the party list. This is the sample of legislators that I am studying in the regression analysis.

Committee Assignments

If so-called pork barrel politics are important, then FPTP legislators will seek committees that help them to support specific projects in the interest of their geographic reelection constituencies.[12] Thus committees where FPTP legislators can obtain extra money for the home district are especially attractive to them, and they will avoid committees where they cannot secure specific benefits for their home constituencies. Servicing their constituency does not solely imply having seats on pork barrel committees; it also implies seeking committees where an ombudsman role can be played. These hypotheses imply that the distribution of FPTP and PR legislators on committees differs systematically across committee types.

As noted in my discussion of voting behavior, PR legislators depend on their state party, not on voters, for a seat in the legislature. Therefore PR legislators have incentives to service the constituency supporting their party. This can be done by being a member of specific committees. As noted previously, interest groups have an influence on the ranking of candidates on the party lists. Given their influence, a PR legislator has an incentive to service these groups by sitting on a committee that addresses their interests.

The Construction Committee (Ausschuß für Raumordnung, Bauwesen und Städtebau), Traffic Committee (Ausschuß für Verkehr), and Agriculture Committee (Ausschuß für Ernährung, Landwirtschaft und Forsten) are perhaps the most clear-cut examples of committees where funds can be channeled to the home district and I classify these committees as district committees.[13] Thus we predict that FPTP legislators will seek assignments on these committees. One caveat applies to the Agriculture Committee, since many of the decisions regarding agriculture are not made at the national legislative level but on the European level. I predict that legislators elected through proportional representation will service their constituencies on committees that are designed to help distribute funds to their electoral supporters.

I classify the Women and Youth Committee (Ausschuß für Frauen und Jugend) and the Family and Elderly Committee (Ausschuß für Familie und Senioren) as party committees because they have most clearly group-specific redistributive functions.[14] Legislators elected because they ranked relatively high on the party list have an incentive to work for the party's reelection constituency. Thus I predict that PR legislators will be committee members on the Family Committee and its predecessors.

Further I classify the Health Committee as a party committee. In Germany the Health Committee (Ausschuß für Gesundheit) helps determine national health care prices, serving primarily as an advisory body to the executive government, with respect to national health care laws. This committee provides FPTP legislators with few opportunities to channel geographically concentrated benefits to their districts. Thus we predict that FPTP legislators will avoid this committee. By contrast, since the elderly population comprises a large part of the CDU's reelection constituency, we predict that PR legislators from the CDU will be committee members on the Health Committee.

I classify the remaining committees as neutral because they allow for only limited possibilities in terms of either services in the district or party constituency or because they are low-prestige committees with limited redistributive functions. Those committees comprise the budget, finance, interior, foreign affairs, economics, environment, sports, European Union, election, labor, law, technology, petitions, and education and science.

4.4 Data and Estimation Issues

I study the allocation of seats on committees in the 1990 to 1994 legislative periods. Five parties have were elected to the German parliament in the 1990 to 1994 election cycle: the CDU (Christian Democratic Party outside of Bavaria), the CSU (Christian Democratic Party in Bavaria), the SPD (Social Democratic Party), the Grüne (Green Party), the PDS (Socialist Party), and the FDP (Liberal Party). The Grüne and the FDP legislators have only PR seats. Legislators from the CDU, CSU, SPD, and PDS have obtained their seats either through the FPTP or the PR electoral system. To test for differences in behavior between representatives elected through FPTP and PR, the focus can thus only be on these four parties. Of these parties we will not examine the PDS, because there is little variation with respect to the FPTP and PR distinction. Only 1 of the 20 PDS members in 1990 were elected through FPTP.

In the data examined, 18 percent of the members in the German legislature won the election in their district but were not placed on the party list. Seven percent of the members did not run for election in a district but became a member of parliament because they were ranked above the cutoff number on the state party lists. As explained below, these legislators are not part of the empirical analysis due to data limitations. The remaining members ran in a district for election and had a place on the state party list. Fifty-three percent of those legislators lost the district election and obtained a seat through the PR electoral rule. The fact that losers in district elections often obtain a seat in parliament via the state party list weakens FPTP legislators' incentives to provide direct geographic constituency service because they have a "safety net" in case they lose the election.[15] This circumstance puts the odds against finding a significant difference in the committee seat allocation between both legislator types.

In Germany the government is formed from members of parliament, but these legislators (Minister and Staatssekretäre) are not members of any committees in the legislature. Thus we exclude legislators who are part of the executive branch from the statistical analysis of committee membership.

An analysis of electoral systems on legislators' behavior is subject to at least two endogeneity concerns. First, unobserved country heterogeneity may be a determinant of the electoral system as well as economic outcomes. Second, legislators who, for example, find the proportional representation electoral system particularly suitable to their campaigning style, may decide to run for election on the party list while they would have chosen not to run for election if they would have had to run in a district. This selection effect may lead to biased estimates of electoral rules on outcomes. An analysis of legislator behavior in mixed-member systems avoids the first type of endogeneity. The concern regarding the second type of endogenity is mitigated by just examining those legislators who are both on the party list and at the same time also run in a district. Thus mixed-member systems provide an interesting subject of analysis.

The regression estimated is

$$Y = f(\text{FPTP}, \text{percent in election}, \text{constituency characteristics}, \text{seniority}) + \varepsilon.$$

Here Y is a measure of legislator behavior, namely deviations from the party line or the committee assignment; FPTP is an indicator variable defined to equal one when a legislator won the district election and zero when the legislator entered parliament through the party list. I will also control for the percentage received in the election, as some MPs enter the Bundestag through the party list but also run in the local race. Thus these legislators may also have an incentive to consider their home district in their decisions. I also include seniority of the legislator in the regression equations. Seniority is the number of legislative periods served in the Bundestag. The seniority variable equals zero for newcomers (freshmen), one for legislators who have been a member for two periods, two for legislators who have been a member for three periods, and so forth. Finally I will control for the constituency characteristics, requiring that I drop legislators who are solely elected through the party list from the regression analysis. The constituency data employed are the population employed in industry, the service sector,

Table 4.1
Descriptive statistics means and standard deviations

Number of times a MP voted against his or her party	2.237 (1.792)
District committee	0.094 (0.293)
Party committee	0.109 (0.312)
Percent in general election	43.953 (8.774)
Obtained seat in parliament by winning the district election = 1; 0 otherwise	0.545 (0.499)
Fraction of district working population employed in industry	0.419 (0.859)
Fraction of district working population employed in farming	0.033 (0.027)
Fraction of district working population employed in services	0.371 (0.072)
Seniority	2.205 (2.038)
Number of observations	413

Note: Data are for the 1990–94 German Bundestag.

and farming. Table 4.1 presents descriptive statistics for the variables employed in the regression analysis.

4.5 Results

Table 4.2 presents results where the dependent variable in the Poisson regressions is the number of times a legislator deviated from the party position. A deviation is defined to occur when a legislator votes against the majority of his party. The first column presents results where I include in the regression equation an indicator for whether the legislator was elected through FPTP or PR, the percentage obtained in the district election, seniority, and constituency characteristics. The second column adds party indicators, and the third column adds regional state (*Länder*) indicators.

The results show that the coefficients on the district election indicators are statistically significant at the 6 and 7 percent level in columns 1 and 2 and statistically significant at the 5 percent when regional indicators are included, as in column 3. The coefficient on the indicator variable suggests that legislators who won the district elections, are

Table 4.2
Voting against the party line

	(1)	(2)	(3)
Obtained seat in parliament by winning the district election = 1; 0 otherwise	0.196 (0.106)	0.195 (0.106)	0.220 (0.108)
Percent in general election	−0.019 (0.006)	−0.017 (0.006)	−0.021 (0.006)
Industry employment	0.871 (1.208)	0.930 (1.211)	1.256 (1.507)
Farm employment	0.036 (0.015)	0.038 (0.015)	0.036 (0.018)
Service employment	0.011 (0.015)	0.011 (0.015)	0.013 (0.017)
Seniority	0.021 (0.016)	0.021 (0.016)	0.021 (0.016)
Party indicators	No	Yes	No
State (*Länder*) indicators	No	No	Yes
Number of observations	413	413	413
Log-likelihood	−772.95	−772.11	−762.01

Notes: Asymptotic standard errors are in parentheses. The dependent variable is the number of times the member of parliament did not vote with the party. The estimates are derived from Poisson regressions.

approximately 20 percent more likely to vote against the party line than legislators who do lost the district election.

The coefficients on industry and service employment are statistically insignificant in all specifications and also seniority does not appear to be a determinant of party line voting. Legislators representing farm constituency, however, are more likely to deviate from the party line.

Table 4.3 presents results from the probit regressions that have membership on a district committee as the dependent variable. The point estimates on the FPTP indicator are statistically significant at the 5 percent level, indicating that FPTP legislators are more likely to be members of committees that allow them to direct funds to their home districts than PR legislators. Regardless of the specification the point estimates are similar, suggesting that FPTP legislators have an almost 10 percent higher likelihood to be a member of FPTP committees than their PR counterparts. The results are robust when the percentage of the popular election are excluded from the regressions.[16]

Of the control variables none but seniority is statistically significant. One year of extra seniority reduces the likelihood to belong to a FPTP committee by 1 to 2 percent. When the FPTP indicator is included, the

Table 4.3
Membership on "district committees"

	(1)	(2)	(3)
Obtained seat in parliament by winning the district election = 1; 0 otherwise	0.094	0.097	0.095
	(0.042)	(0.043)	(0.044)
Percent in general election	0.001	0.002	0.001
	(0.003)	(0.003)	(0.003)
Industry employment	0.105	0.178	0.437
	(0.460)	(0.459)	(0.582)
Farm employment	0.250	0.400	0.565
	(0.593)	(0.600)	(0.728)
Service employment	0.092	0.195	0.373
	(0.573)	(0.574)	(0.662)
Seniority	−0.016	−0.016	−0.017
	(0.007)	(0.007)	(0.007)
Party indicators	No	Yes	No
State (Länder) indicators	No	No	Yes
Number of observations	413	413	413
Log-likelihood	−118.99	−118.21	−116.87

Notes: Marginal effects. Asymptotic standard errors are in parentheses. The dependent variable is whether the member of parliament is on a district committee. The estimates are derived from Probit regressions.

coefficient on the percentage of the popular election is positive and statistically significant, indicating that legislators who are elected by large margins are more likely to be a member of FPTP committees. This is perhaps not too surprising, given that the FPTP and the percentage in the election are positively correlated: the reason a legislator is a FPTP legislator is that this legislator won the local election.

Table 4.4 presents the results for determinants of committee membership on the party interest group committees. Here the coefficient on the FPTP indicator is negative, although the point estimates are only statistically significant at the 10 percent level in column 1 and at the 12 percent level in column 2. Given that the percentage in the election and the FPTP indicator are positively correlated, I reestimateed the regression excluding the percentage in the election. Those results (not reported) show that the point estimates on the FPTP dummy are negative and statistically significant at the 5 percent level, in all specification, and that the point estimates are of similar magnitude as reported in table 4.4. Among the control variables and with exception of the point estimates on seniority, the point estimates are statistically insignificant.

Table 4.4
Membership on "party committees"

	(1)	(2)	(3)
Obtained seat in parliament by winning the district election = 1; 0 otherwise	−0.072 (0.046)	−0.068 (0.046)	−0.057 (0.047)
Percent in general election	0.001 (0.003)	0.000 (0.003)	0.000 (0.003)
Industry employment	0.041 (0.482)	0.008 (0.480)	0.219 (0.581)
Farm employment	−0.373 (0.647)	−0.358 (0.645)	−0.603 (0.771)
Service employment	−0.051 (0.600)	−0.107 (0.600)	0.040 (0.668)
Seniority	−0.034 (0.007)	−0.034 (0.007)	−0.035 (0.007)
Party indicators	No	Yes	No
State (Länder) indicators	No	No	Yes
Number of observations	413	413	413
Log-likelihood	−127.50	−126.59	−125.50

Notes: Marginal effects. Asymptotic standard errors are in parentheses. The dependent variable is whether the member of parliament is on a district committee. The estimates are derived from Probit regressions.

The results in table 4.3, and with some caveats the results in table 4.4, are also consistent with the hypothesis that FPTP and PR legislators seek out different committees in their goal to increase their chances of reelection. However, the results are also consistent with the hypothesis that a party assigns committee assignments in a way documented. If parties seek to maximize seats in the electorate, they would want to put FPTP legislators on committees that would help them in their reelection campaigns. The committee data underlying the regressions in tables 4.3 and 4.4 do not serve well in discriminating between the "legislator-choice" model and the "party-choice" model, which arrive at similar predictions regarding committee membership.

4.6 Conclusions

In this chapter, I examined legislator behavior using the variation that is offered by Germany's mixed member system. The fact that approximately half of the German legislators are elected through a majoritarian system and the other half through a proportional system lends itself to testing the hypothesis that electoral rules influence legislator behavior. I analyzed legislative behavior with respect to their voting records and with respect to their committee assignments. With respect to the voting behavior, I examined the number of times legislators vote against their party. With respect to committee assignments, I examined whether committee assignments differ depending on the electoral rule under which a legislator entered the German Bundestag. The estimates show that legislators elected through a majoritarian system (FPTP legislators) are more likely to deviate in their voting behavior from the party line than legislators elected through the proportional system, and thus through their ranking on the party list (PR legislators). Also my findings show that committee membership significantly differs between these two legislator types. While FPTP legislators are members of committees that allow them to direct funds to their home district, PR legislators tend to be members of committees that help them serve their party constituency. Further research could be done on whether the same differences exist in other mixed-member electoral systems.

Notes

1. All these studies are subject to the simultaneous equation bias mentioned earlier.

2. US politicians' incentives to secure federal funds for their home districts have been modeled, for example, by Weingast (1979), Shepsle and Weingast (1981), Weingast, Shepsle, and Johnsen (1981), Ferejohn and Krehbiel (1987), and Inman and Fitts (1990). Evidence on the effectiveness of pork barrel spending for securing reelection has been documented by Levitt and Snyder (1997).

3. For an analysis of voters' responses to this two-vote system, see Bawn (1999).

4. In this case the overall number of seats in the legislature is adjusted.

5. In the 1998, 1994, and 1990 elections the SPD had 13, 4, and 0 extra seats, and the CDU had 0, 12, and 6 extra seats, respectively. Neglecting those extra seats, the German parliament has 656 legislators. Prior to the German unification, the West German parliament had 496 seats.

6. Prior to the unification of East and West Germany, West Germany was divided into 11 states.

7. This section draws on the discussion of German committees in Stratmann and Baur (2002).

8. In contrast to US practice, subcommittees are virtually nonexistent.

9. Compared internationally, German committees are more powerful than the British House of Commons committees but less powerful than American congressional committees.

10. Demand for committee seats cannot exceed the supply of seats. If legislators do not request assignments, they do not get in. Where this is the case the self-selection aspect of choosing committee seats is overstated.

11. FPTP members more frequently claimed success in influencing project allocations than PR legislators (Lancaster and Patterson 1990).

12. In comparing FPTP and PR systems, Rae (1971) hypothesized that "redistributive effects... are usually most intense under first-past-the-post formulae and least intense under P.R. formulae" (Rae 1971, p. 103). A similar hypothesis was developed by Lancaster (1986). Recent work by Persson, Roland, and Tabellini (2000) related electoral systems to government size.

13. Examples of Construction Committee and Traffic Committee work are legislation regarding the building of public housing and streets, and the allocation of subsidies for public transportation. Examples of Agriculture Committee work are legislation on marketing issues in German regions, on implementing European Union regulations within Germany, and on restricting some agricultural imports. Committees that perform such administrative functions are obviously concerned with non–pork barrel activities.

14. These committees work on legislation regarding women's rights in the work place, and gender discrimination issues.

15. Similarly PR legislators who run in districts and lose the election sometimes maintain a district office.

16. A corollary to the hypothesis that PR legislators are more likely to vote along party lines is that state delegations are more unified if they are from small parties than from large, since small parties tend to have most of their elected legislators from the list. However, the data do not lend support to this hypothesis.

References

Bawn, K. 1999. Voter responses to electoral complexity: Ticket splitting, rational voters and representation in the Federal Republic of Germany. *British Journal of Political Science* 29: 487–505.

Benoit, K. 2001. Evaluating Hungary's mixed-member electoral system. In M. S. Shugart and M. P. Wattenberg, eds., *Mixed-Member Electoral Systemts. The Best of Both Worlds?* Oxford: Oxford University Press.

Blais, A., and L. Massicotte. 1996. Electoral systems. In L. LeDuc, R. G. Niemi, and P. Norris, eds., *Comparing Democracies*. Thousand Oaks, CA: Sage.

Borgs-Maiejewski, H. 1986. *Parlamentsorganisation: Institutionen des Bundestages und ihre Aufgaben*. Heidelberg: Decker and Müller.

Conradt, D. P. 1986. *The German Polity*. New York: Longman.

Ferejohn, J., and K. Krehbiel. 1987. The budget process and the size of the budget. *American Journal of Political Science* 28: 297–320.

Grofman, B. 1999. SNTV: An inventory of theoretically derived propositions and a brief review of evidence from Japan, Korea, Taiwan, and Alabama. In B. Grofman, S.-C. Lee, E. A. Winckler, and B. Woodall, eds., *Elections in Japan, Korea, and Taiwan under the Single Non-transferable Vote*. Ann Arbor: University of Michigan Press.

Grofman, B., E. Mikkel, and R. Taagepera. 1999. Electoral systems change in Estonia. *Journal of Baltic Studies* 30 (3): 227–49.

Hübner, E. 1995. Parlamentarische Demokratie II. Heft Nr. 227. Bundeszentrale für politische Bildung.

Inman, R. P., and M. A. Fitts. 1990. Political institutions and fiscal policy: Evidence from the U.S. historical record. *Journal of Law, Economics, and Organization* 6: 70–132.

Ismayr, W. 1992. *Der Deutsche Bundestag: Funktionen Willensbildung, Reformansätze*. Opladen: Leske and Budrich.

Johnson, N. 1979. Committees in the West German Bundestag. In J. A. Lees and M. Show, eds., *Committees in Legislatures: A Comparative Analysis*. Durham, NC: Duke University Press.

Kaack, H. 1990. The social composition of the Bundestag. In U. Thaysen, R. H. Davidson, and R. G. Livingston, eds., *The U.S. Congress and the German Bundestag*. Boulder, CD: Westview Press.

Lancaster, T. D. 1986. Electoral structures and pork barrel politics. *International Political Science Review* (January): 67–81.

Lancaster, T. D. 1998. Candidate characteristics and electoral performance: A long-term analysis of the German Bundestag. In C. J. Anderson and C. Zelle, eds., *Stability and Change in German Elections*. Westport, CT.

Lancaster, T. D., and W. D. Patterson. 1990. Comparative pork barrel politics: Perceptions from the West German Bundestag. *Comparative Political Studies* (January): 458–77.

Loewenberg, G. 1971. *Parlamentarismus im politischen System der Bundesrepublik Deutschland*. Tübingen: Rainer Wunderlich.

Nohlen, D. 1990. *Wahlrecht und Parteiensystem: Über die politischen Auswirkungen von Wahlsystemen*. Opladen: Leske Verlag.

Patzelt, W. J. 2000. What can an Individual MP do in German parliamentary politics. *Journal of Legislative Studies* 5(3). Reprinted in L. D. Longely and R. Y. Hazan, eds., *The Uneasy Relationship between Parliamentary Members and Leaders*. Portand, OR: Cass.

Persson, T., G. Roland, and G. Tabellini. 2000. Comparative politics and public finance. *Journal of Political Economy* 108: 1121–61.

Rae, D. W. 1971. *The political consequences of electoral laws*. New Haven: Yale University Press.

Saalfeld, T. 1995. *Parteisoldaten und Rebellen*. Opladen: Leske and Budrich.

Saalfeld, T. 1998. Germany: Bundestag and interest groups in a "Party Democracy." In P. Norton, ed., *Parliaments and Pressure Groups in Western Europe*. Portland, OR: Cass.

Shugart, M. S., and M. P. Wattenberg. 2001. *Mixed-Member Electoral Systemts: The Best of Both Worlds?* Oxford: Oxford University Press.

Stratmann, T., and M. Baur. 2002. Plurality rule, proportional representation, and the German Bundestag: How incentives to pork-barrel differ across electoral systems. *American Journal of Political Science* (July): 506–14.

Thaysen, U. 1990. Representation in the Federal Republic of Germany. In U. Thaysen, R. H. Davidson, and R. G. Livingston, eds., *The U.S. Congress and the German Bundestag*. Boulder, CO: Westview Press.

Weingast, B. R. 1979. A rational choice perspective on congressional norms. *American Journal of Political Science* 23: 245–62.

Weingast, B. R., K. Shepsle, and C. Johnsen. 1981. The political economy of benefits and costs: A neoclassical approach to distributive politics. *Journal of Political Economy* 79: 642–64.

Weldon, J. A. 2001. The consequences of Mexico's mixed-member electoral system, 1998–1997. In M. S. Shugart and M. P. Wattenberg, eds., *Mixed-Member Electoral Systemts: The Best of Both Worlds?* Oxford: Oxford University Press.

II

Legislative Decisions and Structure and Policy Outcomes

5 The Effects of Constitutions on Coalition Governments in Parliamentary Democracies

Daniel Diermeier, Hülya Eraslan, and Antonio Merlo

5.1 Introduction

In parliamentary democracies the executive receives its mandate from the legislature, which also retains the power to dismiss the executive at any time *via* a vote of no confidence. When more than two parties are represented in parliament, as long as no single party controls an absolute majority of seats, this fundamental feature of parliamentary democracy naturally leads to coalition governments. This is the norm in Western European democracies that elect their parliaments according to proportional representation: for example, Belgium, Denmark, Finland, Germany, Iceland, Italy, the Netherlands, Norway, and Sweden.

Since popular elections underdetermine the selection of the executive in these countries, a detailed understanding of the formation and survival of coalition government is critical to our understanding of parliamentary political systems. The formation and the survival of coalition governments in multiparty parliamentary democracies are the outcomes of a complex bargaining process among the parties represented in parliament. Countries differ, however, with respect to the specific rules in their constitutions that govern this bargaining process (e.g., see Inter-Parliamentary Union 1986; Lijphart 1984; Müller and Strom 2000).

For the nine Western European countries listed above over the postwar period, important constitutional differences that pertain to the way governments form and terminate can be described as follows: A first difference concerns whether the government needs an actual vote by parliament to legally assume office (the *investiture vote*), or whether it can simply assume office after being appointed by the head of state (either a monarch or a president). In Belgium (until 1995) and Italy, after a new government is inaugurated, it has to be approved by a parliamentary majority. The other countries considered here do not have such a requirement.

A second difference concerns whether to remain in power the government needs the continued, explicit support of a parliamentary majority (*positive parliamentarism*), or whether the lack of opposition by a parliamentary majority is sufficient (*negative parliamentarism*). In Denmark, Norway, and Sweden, governments can be sustained as long as there is no explicit majority vote of opposition in parliament. In other words, the government is assumed to have the confidence of the parliament until the opposite has been demonstrated. In the other countries considered here, this is not the case. In particular, to remain in office, the government must maintain the active support of a parliamentary majority (e.g., supporting all major legislative initiatives by the government including the budget) and not just be tolerated by parliament.

A third difference concerns whether the government can simply be voted out of office through a no-confidence vote in parliament, or whether it needs to be immediately replaced by an alternative government (the *constructive vote of no confidence*). In all parliamentary democracies each party represented in parliament can at any time table a vote of no confidence. In all countries except Germany (and, since 1995, Belgium), the government has to resign if defeated by a parliamentary majority leading to a new government formation process. In Germany and more recently in Belgium, on the other hand, a parliamentary majority must not only depose the current government but also simultaneously elect an alternative government which must be specified before the vote takes place.

A fourth difference concerns the time horizon faced by the government. In Norway and Sweden, elections must be held at predetermined intervals (*fixed interelection period*). The constitutions of the other countries considered here, on the other hand, admit the possibility of dissolving parliament before the expiration of the parliamentary term (whose duration varies across countries) and starting a new term by calling early elections.

Finally, if a country has a bicameral legislature (as opposed to a unicameral one), a fifth difference concerns whether the government is responsible to both chambers of parliament (*dual responsibility*) or only to the lower chamber. While Belgium, Germany, Italy, the Netherlands, Norway, and Sweden (until 1970) have bicameral legislatures (Den-

Table 5.1
Constitutional features

	INVEST	NEG	CCONF	FIXEL	DUAL
Belgium[a]	1	0	1	0	1
Denmark	0	1	0	0	0
Finland	0	0	0	0	0
Germany	0	0	1	0	0
Iceland	0	0	0	0	0
Italy	1	0	0	0	1
Netherlands	0	0	0	0	0
Norway	0	1	0	1	0
Sweden[b]	0	1	0	1	1

a. In 1993 Belgium amended its constitution by simultaneously abolishing the investiture vote and dual responsibility and introducing the constructive vote of no-confidence. This constitutional reform went into effect after the 1995 election.
b. Prior to 1970 Sweden was a bicameral parliamentary democracy with dual responsibility. In 1970 Sweden amended its constitution by eliminating its upper chamber and becoming a unicameral parliamentary democracy.

mark, Finland, Iceland, and Sweden after 1970 have unicameral legislatures), only in Belgium (until 1995), Italy, and Sweden (until 1970) the government has to maintain the confidence of both chambers of parliament to stay in power. Table 5.1 summarizes the institutional environment for each of the nine countries we consider, where *INVEST, NEG, CCONF, FIXEL,* and *DUAL* are indicator variables that denote the presence of the investiture vote, negative parliamentarism, the constructive vote of no confidence, a fixed interelection period and dual responsibility, respectively.

Western European parliamentary democracies also differ systematically with respect to the observed duration of their government formation processes, the type (minority, minimum winning, or surplus) and size of the government coalitions that result from these processes, and the relative durability of cabinets. In some countries, like Denmark, minority governments are virtually the norm, whereas, in others, like Germany, they are a rare occurrence. Surplus governments are frequent in Finland, but they never occur in Sweden. Similarly governments in Italy are notoriously unstable, but Dutch governments frequently last the entire legislative period. Tables 5.2 and 5.3 illustrate these differences by reporting the average number of formation attempts, the average government duration, and the average size of the government coalition (table 5.2) and the distribution of minority,

Table 5.2
Government formation and duration

	Average number of attempts	Average government duration (days)	Average government size (%)
Belgium	2.4	495	62
Denmark	1.8	626	41
Finland	1.8	509	55
Germany	1.1	727	57
Iceland	1.6	802	55
Italy	1.8	321	51
Netherlands	2.6	810	62
Norway	1.1	755	47
Sweden	1.2	740	47
Average	1.7	603	53

Table 5.3
Distribution of government types

	% Minority governments	% Minimum winning governments	% Surplus governments
Belgium	12	70	18
Denmark	83	17	0
Finland	31	14	55
Germany	12	71	17
Iceland	19	71	10
Italy	48	2	50
Netherlands	15	40	45
Norway	64	36	0
Sweden	65	35	0
Average	40	36	24

minimum winning, and surplus governments (table 5.3) for each of the nine countries we consider over the period 1947 to 1999.

Several interesting facts emerge from these tables. While minority governments account for 40 percent of all governments, the fraction of minority governments varies from 12 percent in Belgium and Germany to 83 percent in Denmark. A similar variation is observed in the fraction of surplus governments (about one-fourth of all governments), which ranges from 0 percent in Denmark, Norway, and Sweden to 55 percent in Finland. These differences in the distribution of government types across countries help explain the observed variation in the average size of the government coalition, which ranges from 41 percent in Denmark to 62 percent in Belgium and the Netherlands.

Average government duration also varies a great deal across countries and ranges from a little less than a year in Italy to about 2.2 years in the Netherlands. Iceland, Germany, Norway, and Sweden also have average government durations over two years. There is also some variation in the time it takes until a government forms. While almost all negotiations in Germany, Norway, and Sweden succeed during the first attempt, government formations in the Netherlands are on average longer (the average number of attempts is above 2) and may require as many as seven attempts. However, the cross-country variation in the duration of the government formation process is fairly limited.

These observations raise the following important questions: Can constitutional differences account for observed differences in government outcomes? Or, what are the effects of constitutions on the composition and the stability of coalition governments? Providing answers to these questions is very important for the design (or redesign) of constitutions in modern parliamentary democracies. Several "young" democracies, such as the countries that emerged from the collapse of the Eastern European block, are currently facing these issues. Some of the "older" democracies, for example, Belgium and Italy, are also experimenting with changes in their constitution. Moreover the European unification process may lead to the formation of a "European state" whose constitution presumably would draw from the constitutions of the member states. For example, the German constitutional convention created the constructive vote of no confidence with the explicit intent of preventing unstable governments. To achieve the same goal, Belgium in 1995 amended its constitution by simultaneously eliminating the investiture vote and dual responsibility and adopting the constructive vote of no confidence.

Answering these questions has also important economic implications. For example, empirical studies have demonstrated that political instability has a detrimental effect on economic performance and growth (e.g., see Alesina et al. 1996; Barro 1991). For a parliamentary democracy, political instability means short-lived governments and long-lasting negotiations. Moreover recent empirical studies have pointed out that the size and composition of government coalitions have systematic effects on fiscal policies (e.g., see Persson, Roland, and Tabellini (2003)).

In this chapter we present an overview of our recent research where we address the questions we posed above and investigate the effects of constitutions on coalition governments in parliamentary democracies (Diermeier, Eraslan, and Merlo 2002, 2003a, b; henceforth DEM).[1] We begin our survey by describing our approach, which is based on the specification and estimation of a bargaining model of government formation, and placing it in the context of the literature. We then present a general version of our theoretical framework, followed by an example where we focus on the potential implications of dual responsibility for coalition governments in a bicameral parliamentary system. We conclude with a description of our empirical analysis and a summary of our main findings.

5.2 A Structural Approach to the Study of Coalition Governments

The formation and termination of coalition governments are two of the most widely studied phenomena in comparative politics.[2] A distinctive feature of these literatures is a tight connection between theoretical and empirical analyses. Until recently most theoretical studies used some version of cooperative game theory as their formal methodology, relying, for example, on variants of the core as their solution concept (e.g., see Austen-Smith and Banks 1990; Laver and Shepsle 1990). However, over the last decade models of coalition governments have been predominantly using noncooperative game theory (e.g., see Baron 1991, 1993, 1998; Diermeier and Merlo 2000; Diermeier and Stevenson 2000; Lupia and Strom 1995; Merlo 1997).

Most of the early theoretical work on coalition governments has focused on government formation, interpreting coalition governments as the outcome of an elaborate bargaining process between office- or policy-motivated parties and their leaders. In a recent paper Lupia and Strom (1995) argue that a similar approach can be used to study the duration of coalition governments. That is, coalition governments need to be sustained as equilibrium outcomes over time in the presence of potentially destabilizing changes to the political and economic environment, so-called critical events (e.g., see Browne et al. 1984, 1986; King et al. 1990; Merlo 1998; Warwick 1994).

On the one hand, this approach marks a promising shift in the study of cabinet duration. In particular, the specification of explicit models of inter-party bargaining is likely to focus attention on the role of institutional features of the bargaining environment in determining cabinet failure rather than on a list of cabinet attributes (e.g., the number of formation attempts) or general measures of the political environment (e.g., the number of parties represented in parliament) that have been emphasized in the empirical literature on cabinet duration (e.g., see King et al. 1990; Strom 1990; Warwick 1994). This may open the door to a formal study of parliamentary constitutions and their consequences for the quality of governance.

On the other hand, the bargaining approach raises a number of challenging methodological issues. First, Diermeier and Stevenson (2000) show that testing the Lupia-Strom model requires careful specifications of the stochastic model that preclude the usage of "off-the-shelf" event study methods. Second, Merlo (1997) points out that changing expectations about government duration (due to external events such as the release of macroeconomic data) may lead party leaders to delay the formation of a government. Hence governments that actually form should be viewed as the result of strategic selection by the members of the government coalition. Third, as Diermeier and Merlo (2000) show in a game-theoretic model, expectations about government duration may also influence which government is chosen in the first place. Consider the example of a formateur who has to decide whether to form a single-party minority government or to invite another party to form a minimum winning coalition. In this case the formateur needs to identify the optimal trade-off between the degree of control over ministries (which is higher in the case of a single-party government) and the government's expected longevity (which is smaller for minority governments).

Together these results suggest that government type, formation time, and government duration are *all simultaneously determined in equilibrium* subject to institutional constraints. That is, taking the concept of governments as equilibria seriously requires a radical departure from existing empirical approaches that typically rely on reduced-form specifications.

In DEM we propose an alternative, structural approach and develop a theoretical and empirical framework to assess quantitatively the consequences of constitutional features of parliamentary democracy for the formation and dissolution of coalition governments. Our approach relies on the structural estimation of a game-theoretic model. The methodology we use consists of specifying a bargaining model of government formation, estimating the model's parameters, assessing the ability of the model to account for key features of the data, and then using the estimated structural model to conduct (counterfactual) experiments of comparative constitutional design. This approach allows us to interpret important features of the data as equilibrium phenomena and to assess the equilibrium responses of the outcomes of the government formation process to changes in the institutional environment.

5.3 The Theoretical Framework

We model government formation as a multiple-stage stochastic bargaining game. Let $N = \{1, \ldots, n\}$ denote the set of parties represented in the parliament, and let $\pi^C \in \Pi^C = \{(\pi_1^C, \ldots, \pi_n^C) : \pi_i^C \in [0,1], \sum_{i \in N} \pi_i^C = 1\}$ denote the vector of the parties' relative shares in parliamentary chamber $C \in \{H, S\}$, where H denotes the House (lower chamber) and S denotes the Senate (upper chamber).[3] If the parliament has only one chamber (the House), or if the constitution prescribes that the government is only responsible to the House (even when the parliament is bicameral), then we set $\pi^S = (0, \ldots, 0)$.[4]

Each party $i \in N$ has linear von Neumann-Morgenstern preferences over the benefits from holding office $x_j \in R_+$ and the composition of the government coalition $G \subseteq N$,

$$U_i(x_i, G) = x_i + u_i^G, \tag{1}$$

where

$$u_i^G = \begin{cases} \varepsilon_i^G & \text{if } i \in G \\ \eta_i^G & \text{if } i \notin G, \end{cases} \tag{2}$$

$\varepsilon_i^G > \eta_i^G$, $\varepsilon_i^G, \eta_i^G \in R_+$. This specification captures the intuition that parties care both about the benefits from being in the government coalition (e.g., controlling government portfolios) and the identity of their coalition partners. In particular, ε_i^G can be thought of as the utility that a party in the government coalition obtains from implementing government policies. The policies implemented by a government depend on the coalition partners' relative preferences over policy outcomes and on the institutional mechanisms through which policies are determined. In our analysis, we abstract from these aspects and summarize all policy related considerations in equation (2).[5] The assumption that $\varepsilon_i^G > \eta_i^G$ for all $i \in N$ and for all $G \subseteq N$ implies that, ceteris paribus, parties always prefer to be included in the government coalition rather than being excluded. We let $\beta \in (0,1)$ denote the common discount factor reflecting the parties' degree of impatience.

Our analysis begins after an election or the resignation of an incumbent government (possibly because of a general election or because of a no-confidence vote in the parliament). We let $\overline{T}$ denote the *time horizon* to the next scheduled election (which represents the maximum amount of time a new government could remain in office) and $s \in \Sigma$ denote the current *state of the world* (which summarizes the current political and economic situation). While $\overline{T}$ is constant, we assume that the state of the world evolves over time according to an independently and identically distributed (iid) stochastic process σ with state space Σ and probability distribution function $F_\sigma(\cdot)$.

After the resignation of an incumbent government, the head of state chooses one of the parties represented in the parliament to try to form a new government. We refer to the selected party $k \in N$ as the formateur. Following Laver and Shepsle (1996) and Baron (1991, 1993), we assume that the choice of a formateur is nonpartisan and the head of state is nonstrategic.[6] In particular, we assume that each party $i \in N$ is selected to be a formateur with probability

$$p_i(\pi^H, \pi^S, k_{-1}) = \begin{cases} 1 & \text{if } \pi_i^H > 0.5 \text{ or } \pi_i^S > 0.5, \\ & \text{and } \pi_j^H \leq 0.5, \ \forall j \in N \\ \dfrac{\exp(\alpha_0 \pi_i^H + \alpha_1 I_i)}{\sum_{j \in N} \exp(\alpha_0 \pi_j^H + \alpha_1 I_j)} & \text{if } \pi_j^C \leq 0.5, \ \forall j \in N, \\ & \text{for } C = H, S \\ 0 & \text{if } \exists j \neq i \text{: } \pi_j^C > 0.5, \\ & \text{for } C = H \text{ or } C = S, \end{cases} \tag{3}$$

where $k_{-1} \in N$ denotes the party of the former prime minister, and I_i is a dummy variable that takes the value 1 if $k_{-1} = i$ and zero otherwise. This specification captures the intuition that although relatively larger parties may be more likely to be selected as a formateur than relatively smaller parties, there may be an incumbency bias. It also reflects the fact that if a party has an absolute majority in either chamber of the parliament (where an absolute majority in the Senate is relevant only if the constitution specifies dual responsibility), then it has to be selected as the formateur.[7]

The formateur then chooses a proto-coalition $D \in \Delta_k$, where Δ_k denotes the set of subsets of N which contain k.[8] Intuitively a proto-coalition is a set of parties that agree to talk to each other about forming a government together. Let $\pi^D \equiv (\sum_{i \in D} \pi_i^H, \sum_{i \in D} \pi_i^S)$ denote the *size* of proto-coalition D. The proto-coalition bargains over the formation of a new government, which determines the allocation of government portfolios among the coalition members, $x^D = (x_i^D)_{i \in D} \in R_+^{|D|}$. Following Merlo (1997), we assume that cabinet portfolios generate a (perfectly divisible) unit level of surplus in every period a government is in power, and we let $T^D \in [0, \bar{T}]$ denote the duration of a government formed by proto-coalition D.

Government duration in parliamentary democracies is not fixed. Rather, it depends on institutional factors, the relative size of the government coalition, the time horizon to the next election, the state of the political and economic system at the time a government forms, and political and economic events occurring while a government is in power (e.g., see King et al. 1989; Merlo 1998; Warwick 1994). Let Q denote the vector of institutional characteristics (possibly) affecting government duration (i.e., the investiture vote, positive parliamentarism, the constructive vote of no confidence, a fixed interelection period, and dual responsibility). Hence T^D can be represented as a random variable with density function $f(t^D|s, \bar{T}, Q, \pi^D)$ over the support $[0, \bar{T}]$.[9]

Given the current state s and the vector of (time-invariant) characteristics $(\bar{T}, Q, \pi^D)$, let

$$y^D(s, \bar{T}, Q, \pi^D) \equiv E[T^D|s, \bar{T}, Q, \pi^D] \tag{4}$$

denote the *cake* to be divided among the members of the proto-coalition D if they agree to form a government in that state. That is, $y^D(\cdot) \in (0, \bar{T})$ represents the total expected office-related benefits from forming a government in state s. Given proto-coalition D, for any state s let

$$X^D(s, \bar{T}, Q, \pi^D) \equiv \left\{ x^D \in R_+^{|D|} : \sum_{i \in D} x_i^D \leq y^D(s, \bar{T}, Q, \pi^D) \right\} \tag{5}$$

denote the set of feasible payoff vectors to be allocated in that state, where x_i^D is the amount of cake awarded by coalition D to party $i \in D$.

The proto-coalition bargaining game proceeds as follows. Given state s, the formateur chooses either to pass or to propose an allocation $x^D \in X^D(s, \bar{T}, Q, \pi^D)$. If k proposes an allocation, all the other parties in the proto-coalition sequentially respond by either accepting or rejecting the proposal until either some party has rejected the offer or all parties in D have accepted it. If the proposal is unanimously accepted by the parties in the proto-coalition, a government is inaugurated and the game ends. If no proposal is offered and accepted by all parties in the proto-coalition, state s' is realized according to the stochastic process σ and party $i \in D$ is selected to make a government proposal with probability

$$\widehat{p}_i(\pi^H, \pi^S, D) = \begin{cases} 1 & \text{if } \pi_i^H > 0.5 \text{ or } \pi_i^S > 0.5 \\ & \text{and } \pi_j^H \leq 0.5,\ \forall j \in D \\ \dfrac{\exp(\alpha_2 \pi_i^H)}{\sum_{j \in D} \exp(\alpha_2 \pi_j^H)} & \text{if } \pi_j^C \leq 0.5,\ \forall j \in N, \text{ for } C = H, S \\ 0 & \text{if } \exists j \neq i\text{: } \pi_j^C > 0.5, \text{ for } C = H \\ & \text{or } C = S. \end{cases} \tag{6}$$

Let $\ell \in D$ denote the identity of the proposer. The bargaining process continues until some proposed allocation is unanimously accepted by the parties in the proto-coalition.

An outcome of this bargaining game (τ^D, χ^D) may be defined as a stopping time $\tau^D = 0, 1, \ldots$ and a $|D|$-dimensional random vector χ^D that satisfies $\chi^D \in X^D(\sigma_{\tau^D}, \overline{T}, Q, \pi^D)$ if $\tau^D < +\infty$ and $\chi^D = 0$ otherwise. Given a realization of σ, τ^D denotes the period in which a proposal is accepted by proto-coalition D, and χ^D denotes the proposed allocation that is accepted in state σ_{τ^D}. Define $\beta^\infty = 0$. Then an outcome (τ^D, χ^D) implies a von Neumann-Morgenstern payoff to each party $i \in D$ equal to $E[\beta^{\tau^D} \chi_i^D] + \varepsilon_i^D$, and a payoff to each party $j \in N \backslash D$ equal to η_j^D. Let

$$V_k(D, \overline{T}, Q, \pi^D) \equiv E[\beta^{\tau^D} \chi_k^D]. \tag{7}$$

For any formateur $k \in N$, each potential proto-coalition $D \in \Delta_k$ is associated with an expected payoff for party k,

$$W_k(D, \overline{T}, Q, \pi^D) = V_k(D, \overline{T}, Q, \pi^D) + \varepsilon_k^D. \tag{8}$$

Hence party k chooses the proto-coalition to solve

$$\max_{D \in \Delta_k} W_k(D, \overline{T}, Q, \pi^D). \tag{9}$$

Let $D_k \in \Delta_k$ denote the solution to this maximization problem.

The characterization of the equilibrium of this model relies on the general results for stochastic bargaining games contained in Merlo and Wilson (1995, 1998). In particular, the unique stationary subgame perfect equilibrium of this game has the following features. First, the equilibrium agreement rule possesses a *reservation property*: In any state s, coalition D agrees in that state if and only if $y^D(s, \overline{T}, Q, \pi^D) \geq y^*(D, \overline{T}, Q, \pi^D)$, where $y^*(\cdot)$ solves

$$y^*(D, \overline{T}, Q, \pi^D) = \beta \int \max\{y^D(s', \overline{T}, Q, \pi^D), y^*(D, \overline{T}, Q, \pi^D)\}\, dF_\sigma(s'). \tag{10}$$

Hence delays can occur in equilibrium. During proto-coalition bargaining the reservation property implies a trade-off between delay in the formation process and expected duration. Intuitively coalitions may want to wait for a favorable state of the world that is associated with a longer expected government duration and hence a larger cake. On the other hand, the presence of discounting makes delay costly. In equilibrium agreement is reached when these opposite incentives are balanced. Notice that the role of delays is to "screen out" relatively unstable governments. How much screening occurs in equilibrium depends on how impatient parties are (measured by β), their institutional environment (summarized by Q), the length of the time horizon to the next scheduled election (given by $\overline{T}$), the size and composition of the proto-coalition (equal to π^D and D, respectively), and the uncertainty about the future (summarized by the stochastic process σ).

Second, the equilibrium of the bargaining game satisfies the *separation principle* (Merlo and Wilson 1998): any equilibrium payoff vector must be Pareto efficient, and the set of states where parties agree must be independent of the proposer's identity. This implies that in the proto-coalition bargaining stage, distribution and efficiency considerations are independent and delays are optimal from the point of view of the parties in the proto-coalition. In particular, perpetual disagreement is never an equilibrium, and for any possible proto-coalition, agreement is reached within a finite amount of time. Hence, for any $D \in \Delta_k$, if D is chosen as the proto-coalition, then D forms the government.

Third, for any formateur $k \in N$ and for any potential proto-coalition $D \in \Delta_k$, the ex ante expected equilibrium payoff to party k is given by

$$W_k(D, \overline{T}, Q, \pi^D) = \left(\frac{1 - \beta(1 - \hat{p}_k(\pi^H, \pi^S, D))}{\beta}\right) y^*(D, \overline{T}, Q, \pi^D) + \varepsilon_k^D. \tag{11}$$

Hence we obtain that for any formateur $k \in N$, the equilibrium proto-coalition choice $D_k \in \Delta_k$ is given by

$$D_k = \arg\max_{D \in \Delta_k} \left(\frac{1 - \beta(1 - \widehat{p}_k(\pi^H, \pi^S, D))}{\beta} \right) y^*(D, \overline{T}, Q, \pi^D) + \varepsilon_k^D, \tag{12}$$

and D_k forms the government (i.e., $G = D_k$).

When choosing a government coalition, a formateur faces a trade-off between "control" (i.e., its own share of the cake) and "durability" (i.e., the overall size of the cake). That is, on the one hand, relatively larger coalitions may be associated with longer expected durations and hence relatively larger cakes. On the other hand, because of proto-coalition bargaining, by including additional parties in its coalition the formateur party would receive a smaller share of the cake. The equilibrium coalition choice then depends on the terms of this trade-off, which in turn, given the institutional environment Q, depend on the relative desirability of the different options $y^*(\cdot)$, the degree of impatience of the formateur β, its relative "bargaining power" $\widehat{p}_k(\cdot)$, and the formateur's tastes for its coalition partners ε_k^D.

5.4 An Example: Bicameralism and Coalition Governments

To explore the intuition of the equilibrium and some of its properties, we present a simple example. Consider a parliamentary democracy with a bicameral legislature where there are three parties, $N = \{1, 2, 3\}$ with $\pi^H = \left(\frac{1}{5}, \frac{1}{5}, \frac{3}{5}\right)$ and $\pi^S = \left(\frac{1}{5}, \frac{3}{5}, \frac{1}{5}\right)$, and party 1 is the formateur. If agreement is not reached on the formateur's proposal, then for each possible proto-coalition $D \in \Delta_1 = \{\{1\}, \{1, 2\}, \{1, 3\}, \{1, 2, 3\}\}$ the probability that party 1 is selected to make the next proposal is given by $\widehat{p}_1 = 1/|D|$. Further let $\varepsilon_1^{\{1\}} = \varepsilon_1^{\{1,2\}} = \frac{1}{2}$ and $\varepsilon_1^{\{1,3\}} = \varepsilon_1^{\{1,2,3\}} = 0$. Note that coalition $\{1\}$ has minority status in both chambers, coalitions $\{1, 2\}$ and $\{1, 3\}$ have minority status in one chamber but are minimum winning majority coalitions in the other chamber, and coalition $\{1, 2, 3\}$ is a surplus majority coalition in both chambers.

The time horizon to the next election is five periods, $\overline{T} = 5$. There are two possible states of the world, $\Sigma = \{b, g\}$. Each state is realized with equal probability, $\Pr(\sigma = b) = \Pr(\sigma = g) = \frac{1}{2}$. Consider an institutional environment with dual responsibility and suppose that if $s = b$, then governments that have minority status in both chambers are expected to last one period, governments that have minority status in one chamber but majority status in the other chamber are expected to last two periods, and governments that have majority status in both chambers are expected to last three periods: that is, $y^{\{1\}}(b) = 1$ and $y^{\{1,2\}}(b) =$

$y^{\{1,3\}}(b) = 2$ and $y^{\{1,2,3\}}(b) = 3$. If, on the other hand, $s = g$, then each government's expected duration is increased by one period: that is, $y^{\{1\}}(g) = 2$, $y^{\{1,2\}}(g) = y^{\{1,3\}}(g) = 3$, and $y^{\{1,2,3\}}(g) = 4$. This specification is intended to capture an environment where both a government's majority status and the state of the world affect the expected stability of coalition governments.[10]

We begin by analyzing the outcome of proto-coalition bargaining for every possible proto-coalition $D \in \Delta_1$. Consider first the case where $D = \{1\}$. Using equation (10) above, it is easy to verify that if $\beta \leq 2/3$, then $y^*(\{1\}) = 3\beta/2 \leq y^{\{1\}}(b)$, which implies that delays never occur. If, on the other hand, $\beta > 2/3$, then $y^*(\{1\}) = 2\beta/(2-\beta) > y^{\{1\}}(b)$, which implies that delays occur when $s = b$. Hence, using equation (11) above, the equilibrium payoff to party 1 from choosing proto-coalition $\{1\}$ is equal to

$$W_1(\{1\}) = \begin{cases} 2 & \text{if } \beta \leq \frac{2}{3} \\ \frac{2}{2-\beta} + \frac{1}{2} & \text{if } \beta > \frac{2}{3}. \end{cases}$$

Next, consider the cases where $D = \{1,2\}$ or $D = \{1,3\}$. It is easy to verify that if $\beta \leq 4/5$, then $y^*(\{1,2\}) = y^*(\{1,3\}) = 5\beta/2 \leq y^{\{1,2\}}(b) = y^{\{1,3\}}(b)$, which implies that agreement occurs in both states of the world. If, on the other hand, $\beta > 4/5$, then $y^*(\{1,2\}) = y^*(\{1,3\}) = 3\beta/(2-\beta) > y^{\{1,2\}}(b) = y^{\{1,3\}}(b)$, which implies that agreement only occurs when $s = g$. Hence the equilibrium payoff to party 1 from choosing proto-coalition $\{1,2\}$ is equal to

$$W_1(\{1,2\}) = \begin{cases} \frac{5(2-\beta)}{4} + \frac{1}{2} & \text{if } \beta \leq \frac{4}{5} \\ 2 & \text{if } \beta > \frac{4}{5}, \end{cases}$$

and its equilibrium payoff from choosing proto-coalition $\{1,3\}$ is equal to

$$W_1(\{1,3\}) = \begin{cases} \frac{5(2-\beta)}{4} & \text{if } \beta \leq \frac{4}{5}, \\ \frac{3}{2} & \text{if } \beta > \frac{4}{5}. \end{cases}$$

Finally, consider the case where $D = \{1,2,3\}$. It is easy to verify that if $\beta \leq 6/7$, then $y^*(\{1,2,3\}) = 7\beta/2 \leq y^{\{1,2,3\}}(b)$, which implies that agreement occurs in both states of the world. If, on the other hand, $\beta > 6/7$, then $y^*(\{1,2,3\}) = 4\beta/(2-\beta) > y^{\{1,2,3\}}(b)$, which means that agreement only occurs when $s = g$. Hence, the equilibrium payoff to party 1 from choosing proto-coalition $\{1,2,3\}$ is equal to

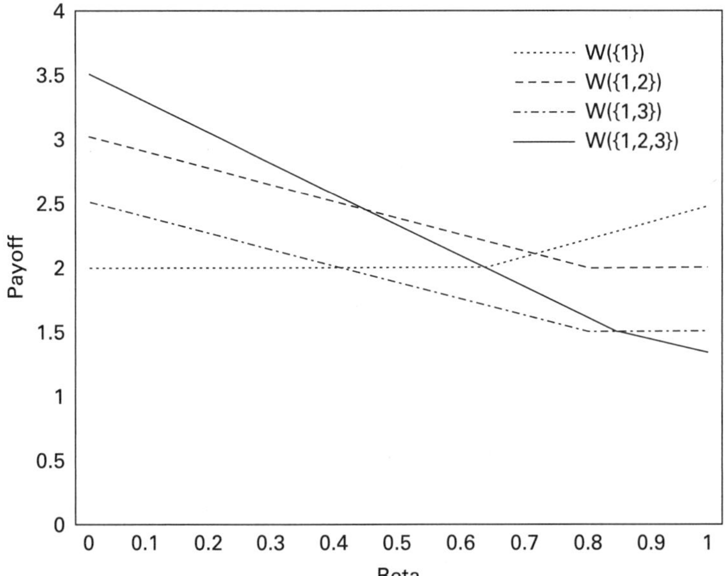

Figure 5.1
Formateur's payoffs with dual responsibility

$$W_1(\{1,2,3\}) = \begin{cases} \frac{7(3-2\beta)}{6} & \text{if } \beta \leq \frac{6}{7}, \\ \frac{4(3-2\beta)}{6-3\beta} & \text{if } \beta > \frac{6}{7}. \end{cases}$$

The equilibrium payoffs to the formateur party 1 associated with all possible proto-coalitions are depicted in figure 5.1 as functions of the parameter β.

Hence the equilibrium proto-coalition choice of the formateur party 1 is given by[11]

$$D_1 = \begin{cases} \{1,2,3\} & \text{if } \beta \in (0, 0.46), \\ \{1,2\} & \text{if } \beta \in (0.46, 0.74), \\ \{1\} & \text{if } \beta \in (0.74, 1). \end{cases}$$

A relatively high degree of impatience would induce the formateur to choose a surplus coalition that would immediately agree to form the government.[12] On average, surplus governments would therefore be observed to last 3.5 periods. For intermediate levels of impatience the formateur would choose a coalition that has minority status in one chamber but is a minimum winning majority coalition in the other chamber. Even in this case the process of government formation would involve no delay and would produce governments that would last, on average, 2.5 periods.[13] Finally, for sufficiently low degrees of impatience, the formateur would choose a coalition that has minority status in both chambers. This government would continue negotiating until the "good" state of the world is realized. Thus the coalition would last, on average, 2 periods.

The example illustrates the two equilibrium selection effects captured by our model. First, when $\beta > 2/3$, the least durable minority governments (i.e., minority governments that come to power in a "bad" state of the world) are "screened out" in equilibrium and never form. This is a consequence of efficient proto-coalition bargaining. Second, when $\beta \in (0.46, 0.74)$, although a more durable option is always available (i.e., a coalition with majority status in both chambers), the formateur chooses a proto-coalition with a smaller expected duration (and no majority status in either of the two chambers) because that maximizes its share of office-related benefits. This is an example of the fundamental trade-off described above between durability (i.e., larger coalitions are typically more durable and hence are associated with larger cakes) and control (i.e., larger coalitions imply smaller shares of the cake for each coalition member) that drives the equilibrium selection of government coalitions subject to institutional constraints. Of course, both effects may work in consort. When β is relatively high (i.e., $\beta \in (0.74, 1)$), because short-lived minority governments are screened out in equilibrium, a minority proto-coalition becomes relatively more attractive compared to proto-coalitions with (at least partial) majority status.

To understand the role played by dual responsibility on the equilibrium selection of government coalitions, consider now a different institutional environment without dual responsibility such that $y^{\{1\}}(b) = y^{\{1,2\}}(b) = 2$, $y^{\{1,3\}}(b) = y^{\{1,2,3\}}(b) = 3$, $y^{\{1\}}(g) = y^{\{1,2\}}(g) = 3$, and $y^{\{1,3\}}(g) = y^{\{1,2,3\}}(g) = 4$, while holding everything else constant. Since the seat shares in the Senate are no longer relevant to determine the majority status of government coalitions, coalitions $\{1\}$ and $\{1,2\}$ are now both minority coalitions, while coalitions $\{1,3\}$ and $\{1,2,3\}$ are both majority coalitions. Relative to the previous case, it is then "as if" all coalitions have majority status in the Senate. Hence, for example, $\{1,2,3\}$ simply corresponds to a surplus majority coalition. As in the case of dual responsibility, this specification is intended to capture an environment that is consistent with some basic empirical regularities about coalition duration. For example, surplus majority coalitions do not necessarily last longer than minimum winning coalitions.[14] Also without dual responsibility the expected duration of each possible coalition is likely to be longer.[15]

As above, we begin by analyzing the outcome of proto-coalition bargaining for every possible proto-coalition $D \in \Delta_1$. Consider first the case where $D = \{1\}$ or $D = \{1,2\}$. It is easy to verify that if $\beta \leq 4/5$, then $y^*(\{1\}) = y^*(\{1,2\}) = 5\beta/2 \leq y^{\{1\}}(b) = y^{\{1,2\}}(b)$, which implies that delays never occur. If, on the other hand, $\beta > 4/5$, then $y^*(\{1\}) = y^*(\{1,2\}) = 3\beta/(2-\beta) > y^{\{1\}}(b) = y^{\{1,2\}}(b)$, which implies that delays occur when $s = b$. Hence the equilibrium payoff to party 1 from choosing proto-coalition $\{1\}$ is equal to

$$W_1(\{1\}) = \begin{cases} 3 & \text{if } \beta \leq \frac{4}{5}, \\ \frac{3}{2-\beta} + \frac{1}{2} & \text{if } \beta > \frac{4}{5}. \end{cases}$$

and its payoff from choosing proto-coalition $\{1,2\}$ is equal to

$$W_1(\{1,2\}) = \begin{cases} \frac{5(2-\beta)}{4} + \frac{1}{2} & \text{if } \beta \leq \frac{4}{5}, \\ 2 & \text{if } \beta > \frac{4}{5}. \end{cases}$$

Next, consider the cases where $D = \{1,3\}$ or $D = \{1,2,3\}$. It is easy to verify that if $\beta \leq 6/7$, then $y^*(\{1,3\}) = y^*(\{1,2,3\}) = 7\beta/2 \leq y^{\{1,3\}}(b) = y^{\{1,2,3\}}(b)$, which implies that agreement occurs in both states of the world. If, on the other hand, $\beta > 6/7$, then $y^*(\{1,3\}) = y^*(\{1,2,3\}) = 4\beta/(2-\beta) > y^{\{1,3\}}(b) = y^{\{1,2,3\}}(b)$, which implies that agreement only occurs when $s = g$. Hence the equilibrium payoff to party 1 from choosing proto-coalition $\{1,3\}$ is equal to

$$W_1(\{1,3\}) = \begin{cases} \frac{7(2-\beta)}{4} & \text{if } \beta \leq \frac{6}{7}, \\ 2 & \text{if } \beta > \frac{6}{7}, \end{cases}$$

and its equilibrium payoff from choosing proto-coalition $\{1,2,3\}$ is equal to

$$W_1(\{1,2,3\}) = \begin{cases} \frac{7(3-2\beta)}{6} & \text{if } \beta \leq \frac{6}{7}, \\ \frac{4(3-2\beta)}{6-3\beta} & \text{if } \beta > \frac{6}{7}. \end{cases}$$

The equilibrium payoffs to the formateur party 1 associated with all possible proto-coalitions are depicted in figure 5.2 as functions of the parameter β.

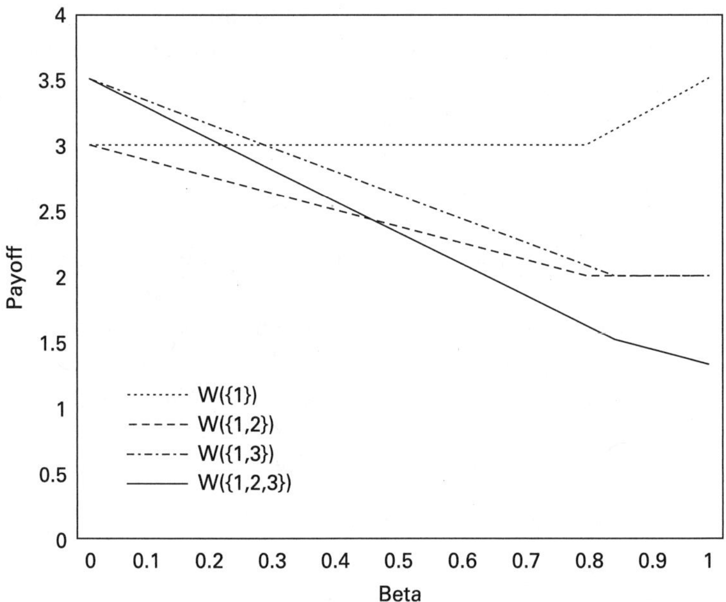

Figure 5.2
Formateur's payoffs with single responsibility

Thus, in this case, the equilibrium proto-coalition choice of the formateur party 1 is given by

$$D_1 = \begin{cases} \{1,3\} & \text{if } \beta \in (0, 0.29), \\ \{1\} & \text{if } \beta \in (0.29, 1). \end{cases}$$

Notice that in this case the formateur will never choose the surplus coalition $\{1,2,3\}$ in equilibrium for any value of β. This follows from the fact that without dual responsibility, adding party 2 to the coalition does not increase expected duration, but (because of proto-coalition bargaining) it decreases the formateur's share of office-related benefits. Hence $\{1,2,3\}$ is dominated by $\{1,3\}$. For a similar reason $\{1,2\}$ is never selected, since in the absence of dual responsibility both $\{1,2\}$ and $\{1\}$ are minority coalitions. Note also that the range of values of β where the minority option $\{1\}$ is chosen in equilibrium is larger. Hence, in this example, removing dual responsibility significantly reduces the occurrence of surplus governments and increases the occurrence of minority governments.

Turning our attention to government duration, note that in the case of $\beta < 0.29$, where a majority government is optimal, there is no

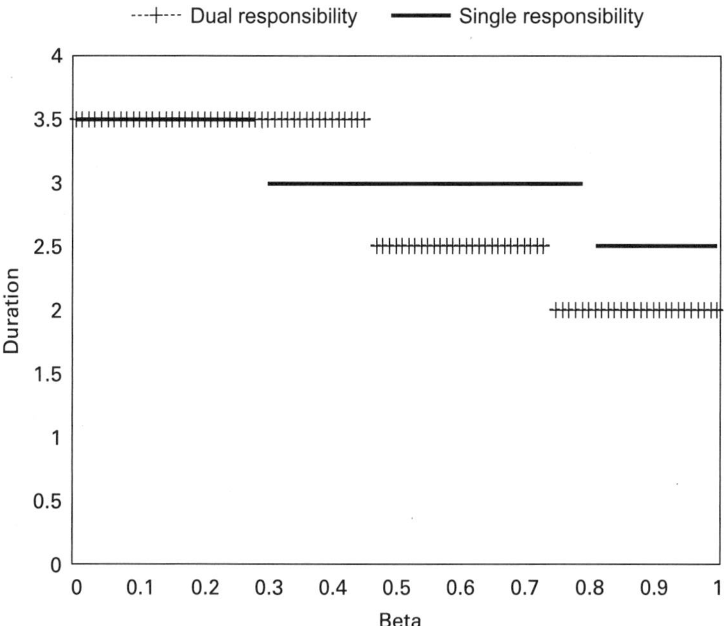

Figure 5.3
Average government duration

proto-coalition "screening." That is, $\{1,3\}$ would be observed to last 3.5 periods on average. For $\beta > 0.8$, minority governments are optimal with proto-coalition screening, resulting in an average duration of 3 periods. For $\beta \in (0.29, 0.8)$, minority governments are also optimal, but it is not worthwhile for the formateur to delay government formation, thus resulting in an average duration of 2.5 periods.

The effect of dual responsibility on government duration is illustrated in figure 5.3. Depending on the parameters of the model, eliminating dual responsibility can either have no effect on government duration (e.g., for $\beta < 0.29$), it can increase government duration (e.g., for $\beta > 0.46$), and it can even *decrease* government duration (e.g., for $\beta \in (0.29, 0.46)$). The last possibility illustrates the potentially powerful consequences of accounting for equilibrium responses by strategic parties. If $\beta \in (0.29, 0.46)$, the formateur party 1 would choose to be in a minority government rather than in the surplus coalition $\{1,2,3\}$ if dual responsibility was abandoned.

The example illustrates an additional equilibrium effect captured by our model. We described above the model's fundamental trade-off between durability (i.e., larger coalitions are typically more durable and hence are associated with larger cakes) and control (i.e., larger coalitions imply smaller shares of the cake for each coalition member) that drives the equilibrium selection of government coalitions subject to the institutional constraints. The terms of this trade-off depend crucially on the relative durability of the different options, which in turn depends on the institutional environment where government formation takes place. Changes in the institutional environment induce changes in the terms of the trade-off that trigger an equilibrium response in the selection of the type of government coalitions that form and their relative stability. When the government is responsible both to the House and the Senate, a vote of no-confidence in either chamber of parliament is sufficient to terminate the government. The equilibrium response to this institutional constraint is to from larger (surplus) coalitions (possibly constituting a majority in both chambers), to achieve the desired level of durability at the cost of a loss of control on the part of the formateur. Removing dual responsibility, while holding everything else the same, removes one source of instability and makes it possible to achieve similar levels of durability by "replacing" larger coalitions with smaller coalitions (*equilibrium replacement effect*).

As evidenced in this example, our model is capable of addressing the issues we discussed in the introduction. However, it should also be clear from the example that the predictions of the model critically depend on the values of the model's parameters. In order to assess quantitatively the effects of dual responsibility (or any other constitutional feature) on the formation and dissolution of coalition governments, we need to estimate the structural model.

5.5 The Empirical Framework

Our sample of observations consists of 255 governments in 9 western European countries over the period 1947 to 1999: Belgium (34 governments), Denmark (30 governments), Finland (29 governments), Germany (24 governments), Iceland (21 governments), Italy (46 governments), the Netherlands (20 governments), Norway (25 governments), and Sweden (26 governments). An observation in the sample is defined by the identity of the formateur party, k, the composition of the proto-coalition, D_k, the duration of the negotiation over the formation of a new government (i.e., the number of attempts), τ^{D_k}, the sequence of proposers (one for each attempt) if the formateur does not succeed to form the government at the first attempt, $\ell_2, \ldots, \ell_{\tau^{D_k}}$, and the duration of the government following that negotiation (i.e., the number of days the government remains in power), t^{D_k}. For each element in the sample we also observe the vector of constitutional characteristics, $Q = (INVEST, NEG, CCONF, FIXEL, DUAL)$, the time horizon to the next scheduled election, $\bar{T}$, the set of parties represented in the parliament, N, the vector of their relative seat shares, π^H and π^S, and the party of the former prime minister, k_{-1}.

Keesings Record of World Events (1944–1999) was used to collect information on the number of attempts for each government formation, the identity of the proposer on each attempt, the time horizon to the next election, and the duration of the government following each negotiation. The list of parties represented in the parliament for each country and their shares of parliamentary seats at the time of each negotiation over the formation of a new government was taken from Mackie and Rose (1990), and for later years in the sample, from Keesings, the *European Journal of Political Research*, and the *Lijphart Elections Archives*.[16] Constitutional characteristics were obtained from Lijphart (1984), Müller and Strom (2000), and from the constitution of each country.[17]

The theoretical model described in section 5.3 implies a probability distribution over endogenous variables conditional on exogenous variables given the model's parameters (i.e., a likelihood function). The model can therefore be estimated by maximum likelihood using the data available. The relationship between the theoretical and the empirical model can be explained as follows: In the bargaining model described in section 5.3, we specified the cake that a generic protocoalition D bargains over in any given period, y^D, to be equal to the expected government duration conditional on the state of the world in that period, s, given the vector of (time-invariant) characteristics, $(\bar{T}, Q, \pi^D)$. Also we characterized the conditions under which agreement occurs in terms of a reservation rule on the size of the current cake. Hence, from the perspective of the political parties that observe the cakes, the sequence of events in a negotiation is deterministic, since they agree to form a government as soon as the current cake is above a threshold that depends only on their expectation about future states of the world and hence future cakes. The only uncertainty concerns the actual duration of the government after it is formed, T^D. The source for this uncertainty are political events (e.g., a scandal or other critical events) occurring while the government is in power. Thus T^D is a random variable with conditional distribution function $F_T(t^D|y^D; \bar{T}, Q, \pi^D)$.

We (the econometricians), however, do not observe the state of the world s.[18] Hence, from the perspective of the econometrician, the cake $y^D(s, \bar{T}, Q, \pi^D) \equiv E[T^D | s, \bar{T}, Q, \pi^D]$ is also a random variable with conditional distribution function $F_y(y^D | \bar{T}, Q, \pi^D)$, which implies that the sequence of events in a negotiation is probabilistic.

Let us now consider the decision problem faced by the formateur party k. For each possible coalition $D \in \Delta_k$, party k can compute its expected equilibrium payoff if D is chosen as the proto-coalition and bargains over the formation of a new government. The formateur's expected payoff depends on the expected outcome of the bargaining process as well as the formateur's tastes for its coalition partners, ε_k^D. Hence, from the perspective of the formateur party that knows its tastes, the optimal coalition choice is deterministic. We (the econometricians), however, again do not observe the formateur's tastes for its coalition partners, ε_k^D. Hence, as before, from the perspective of the econometrician, ε_k^D is a random variable with distribution function $F_\varepsilon(\varepsilon_k^D)$, which implies that the formateur's decision problem is probabilistic.

The likelihood function is then obtained by specifying parametric functional forms for the functions $F_T(t^D | y^D; \bar{T}, Q, \pi^D)$, $F_y(y^D | \bar{T}, Q, \pi^D)$ and $F_\varepsilon(\varepsilon_k^D)$. The contribution to the likelihood function of each observation in the sample is equal to the probability of observing the vector of (endogenous) events $(k, D_k, \tau^{D_k}, \ell_2, \ldots, \ell_{\tau^{D_k}}, t^{D_k})$ conditional on the vector of (exogenous) characteristics $(\bar{T}, Q, N, \pi, k_{-1})$, given the vector of the model's parameters $\theta = (\alpha_0, \alpha_1, \alpha_2, \beta, F_T, F_y, F_\varepsilon)$. From the structure of our model and our equilibrium characterization, this probability can be computed and the parameter vector θ can be estimated by maximum likelihood using the data described above.[19]

5.6 Empirical Results

As we discussed in section 5.2, the estimated structural model can be used to conduct (counterfactual) experiments of comparative constitutional design and assess the effects of specific institutional features of parliamentary democracies (i.e., the investiture vote, positive parliamentarism, the constructive vote of no-confidence, a fixed interelection period, and dual responsibility), on the formation and dissolution of coalition governments.[20]

Our main findings can be summarized as follows: The first set of findings concerns the effects of constitutions on coalition governments in parliamentary democracies with unicameral legislatures. We find that the most stable political system (i.e., the political system with the shortest government formation duration and the longest government duration) has a positive form of parliamentarism with the constructive vote of no-confidence, no investiture vote, and a fixed interelection period. At the opposite end of the spectrum, the least stable political system (i.e., the political system with the longest government formation duration and the shortest government duration) has a positive form of parliamentarism with the investiture vote, no constructive vote of no-confidence, and no fixed interelection period.

The mean government duration in the most stable political system is 1.6 times the mean government duration in the least stable political system. The mean number of attempts in the most stable political system is almost half of the mean number of attempts in the least stable political system. For example, adding the investiture vote to the most stable political system results in an 8 percent increase in the mean number of attempts and a 4 percent decrease in the mean government duration. On the other hand, a removal of both the constructive vote of no-confidence and the fixed interelection period results in a 42 percent increase in the mean number of attempts and a 30 percent decrease in the mean government duration. Eliminating the investiture vote from the least stable political system results in a 19 percent decrease in the mean number of attempts and a 25 percent increase in the mean government duration, while adding the constructive vote of no-confidence results in a 38 percent decrease in the mean number of attempts and a 16 percent increase in the mean government duration. Simultaneously implementing both changes results in a 43 percent decrease in the mean number of attempts and a 43 percent increase in the mean government duration.[21]

With respect to the propensity of different political systems to generate government coalitions of different types, we find that the presence of the constructive vote of no-confidence discourages minority governments from forming, while a negative form of parliamentarism facilitates their formation. Furthermore, a political system with both the investiture vote and the constructive vote of no-confidence is the most conducive to the formation of surplus governments. In general, we find that the constructive vote of no-confidence increases the average size of coalition governments, while a negative form of parliamentarism decreases it. The effects of the investiture vote and a fixed interelection period on the average size of coalition governments are instead negligible.

The second set of findings concerns the effects of dual responsibility on coalition governments in parliamentary democracies with bicameral legislatures. We find that dual responsibility has a negligible effect on government stability, while at the same time producing a sizable impact on the composition of coalition governments. Removing dual responsibility leaves the mean government duration and the mean number of attempts virtually unchanged, but significantly reduces the occurrence of surplus governments and increases the occurrence of minority governments.[22]

5.7 Conclusions

We conclude this survey of our recent work on the effects of constitutions on coalition governments in parliamentary democracies by highlighting the importance of using an equilibrium framework for assessing empirically the consequences of constitutions. To do this, we focus on a prominent constitutional feature that has long played a central role in debates on constitutional reforms: bicameralism.

Previous work on the effects of bicameralism on coalition governments concluded that bicameralism decreases government duration (Tsebelis 2000) and increases the size of government coalitions (Lijphart 1984; Sjölin 1993).[23] The first conclusion follows from the argument that when the agreement of two chambers is required to change the status quo (i.e., there are two "veto players"), the government is relatively more unstable.[24] The second conclusion follows from the argument that in order to pass legislation and hence implement policies, government coalitions need the support of a majority in both chambers of parliament.[25]

Our analysis shows that the prima facie plausible belief that a bicameral system with dual responsibility leads to less stable governments may be misleading. The key oversight is that *both* the type (i.e., minority, minimum winning, or surplus) of the government coalition as well as government duration are equilibrium outcomes. At the heart of our bargaining model there is a fundamental trade-off between durability (i.e., larger coalitions are typically more durable and hence are associated with larger cakes) and control (i.e., larger coalitions imply smaller shares of the cake for each coalition member) which drives the equilibrium selection of government coalitions subject to the constitutional constraints. The terms of this trade-off depend crucially on the relative durability of the different options, which in turn depends on the institutional environment where government formation takes place. Changes in the institutional environment induce changes in the terms of the trade-off that trigger an equilibrium response in the selection of the type of government coalitions that form and their relative stability.

When the government is responsible both to the House and the Senate, a vote of no-confidence in either chamber of parliament is sufficient to terminate the government. The equilibrium response to this institutional constraint is to form larger (surplus) coalitions (possibly constituting a majority in both chambers) to achieve the desired level of durability at the cost of a loss of control. Removing dual responsibility, while holding everything else the same, removes one source of instability, and by making each coalition more durable, it allows the formateur to achieve higher payoffs by forming smaller coalitions (equilibrium replacement effect). Since smaller coalitions are relatively less durable than larger coalitions, the replacement effect compensates the duration-enhancing effect of removing dual responsibility, leading to a negligible change in average government duration. The magnitude of these effects, of course, depends on the estimates of the model's parameters.

Notes

We thank the participants of the SNS Constitutional Design Conference held in Stockholm, Sweden, on August 25–27, 2003, for their helpful comments and suggestions. Financial support from the National Science Foundation is gratefully acknowledged.

1. Our work contributes to a growing area of research in political economy whose aim is to assess the political and economic consequences of political institutions (e.g., see Besley and Coate 2003; Myerson 1993; Persson, Roland, and Tabellini 1997, 2000). For extensive surveys of the literature, see Persson and Tabellini (2000, 2003).

2. For overviews see, for example, Laver and Schofield (1990), Laver and Shepsle (1996), Strom (1990), and Warwick (1994).

3. The shares are determined by the outcome of a general election, which is not modeled here.

4. In the case of bicameral parliaments without dual responsibility (e.g., as in Germany or the Netherlands), the upper chamber only plays a legislative role; it does not participate either in the appointment or the dismissal of the executive.

5. For a richer, spatial model of government formation where government policies are endogenously determined, see Diermeier and Merlo (2000).

6. Note that most constitutions are silent with respect to the rules for selecting a formateur, since they are generally reflected in unwritten conventions and norms. For an empirical analysis of the selection of formateurs, see Diermeier and Merlo (2004).

7. If one party has an absolute majority in the House and another party has an absolute majority in the Senate, we assume that the party that controls the House is selected as the formateur, since the government formation process always initiates in the lower chamber. Note, however, that there are no cases in the data where different parties have absolute majorities in different chambers.

8. Our assumption that parties always prefer to be included in the government coalition implies that the formateur party will never propose a proto-coalition that does not include itself.

9. Here we treat government dissolution as exogenous. For a theoretical model where the decision of dissolving a government is endogenous, see Diermeier and Merlo (2000).

10. See King et al. (1990), Merlo (1997), and Warwick (1994) for empirical evidence.

11. Since ties are zero probability events, we are ignoring here the event of a tie between two alternatives.

12. Notice that when $D = \{1,2,3\}$ and $\beta \in (0, 0.46)$ agreement occurs in both states of the world.

13. Notice that $\{1,3\}$ is never chosen in equilibrium because its expected duration conditional on the state of the world is identical to the one of $\{1,2\}$, but party 1's preferences induce it to prefer $\{1,2\}$.

14. See, for example, Merlo (1997).

15. See, for example, Tsebelis (2000).

16. The archive is available online at http://dodgson.ucsd.edu/lij.

17. For details on the data see DEM.

18. In particular, we do not observe all the relevant elements in the parties' information set when they form their expectations about government durations. Thus we do not observe the cake.

19. For details on the parameterization, derivation, and estimation of the likelihood function, see DEM.

20. For details on the design and execution of constitutional experiments, see DEM.

21. This experiment mimics the constitutional reform implemented in Belgium in 1995, whose explicit intent was to increase the stability of Belgian governments.

22. In 1970 Sweden went from a bicameral system with dual responsibility to a unicameral system. After this constitutional reform, while average government duration changed very little (from 764 to 719 days), the fraction of minority governments more than doubled (from 42 to 86 percent). These observations are consistent with the predictions of our analysis.

23. In a recent empirical study of government formation and duration in western European bicameral parliamentary democracies, Druckman and Thies (2002) find that governments that control a majority of seats in both chambers last substantially longer than those that lack majority status in one of the chambers, but they find little evidence that governments add parties that generate "oversized" coalitions in the lower chamber in order to ensure a majority in the upper chamber. Note, however, that Druckman and Thies do not estimate the effect of bicameralism on government formation and duration.

Rather, they assess how majority status in the upper chamber of a bicameral parliament affects government duration.

24. Tsebelis's (2000) argument is based on empirical evidence that second chambers can make a difference in legislative outcomes even if the party composition of the two chambers is identical (Tsebelis and Money 1997). He argues that governments in bicameral systems are less likely to adapt quickly to exogenous shocks and are thus more likely to fall.

25. Lijphart's (1984) argument, however, only applies to cases where the two chambers are elected by different constituencies. Italy, for example, would be excluded because, even though both Italian chambers share all legislative and electoral powers, the representatives are elected from the same constituencies and thus, according to Lijphart, are expected to represent the same interests. Germany, on the other hand, would qualify because, even though the veto-powers of Germany's upper house are limited, it represents state rather than federal or district-specific constituencies.

References

Alesina, A., S. Ozler, N. Roubini, and P. Swagel. 1996. Political instability and economic growth. *Journal of Economic Growth* 2: 189–213.

Austen-Smith, D., and J. S. Banks. 1990. Stable governments and the allocation of policy portfolios. *American Political Science Review* 84: 891–906.

Baron, D. P. 1991. A spatial bargaining theory of government formation in a parliamentary system. *American Political Science Review* 85: 137–64.

Baron, D. P. 1993. Government formation and endogenous parties. *American Political Science Review* 87: 34–47.

Baron, D. P. 1998. Comparative dynamics of parliamentary governments. *American Political Science Review* 92: 593–609.

Barro, R. J. 1991. Economic growth in a cross section of countries. *Quarterly Journal of Economics* 106: 407–43.

Besley, T., and S. Coate. 2003. Centralized versus decentralized provision of local public goods: A political economy approach. *Journal of Public Economics* 87: 2611–37.

Browne, E. C., J. P. Frendreis, and D. W. Gleiber. 1984. An "events" approach to the problem of cabinet stability. *Comparative Political Studies* 17: 167–97.

Browne, E. C., J. P. Frendreis, and D. W. Gleiber. 1986. The process of cabinet dissolution: An exponential model of duration and stability in western democracies. *American Journal of Political Science* 30: 628–50.

Diermeier, D., H. Eraslan, and A. Merlo. 2002. Coalition governments and comparative constitutional design. *European Economic Review* 46: 893–907.

Diermeier, D., H. Eraslan, and A. Merlo. 2003a. A structural model of government formation. *Econometrica* 71: 27–70.

Diermeier, D., H. Eraslan, and A. Merlo. 2003b. Bicameralism and government formation. Mimeo. University of Pennsylvania.

Diermeier, D., and A. Merlo. 2000. Government turnover in parliamentary democracies. *Journal of Economic Theory* 94: 46–79.

Diermeier, D., and A. Merlo. 2004. An empirical investigation of coalitional bargaining procedures. *Journal of Public Economics* 88: 783–97.

Diermeier, D., and R. T. Stevenson. 2000. Cabinet terminations and critical events. *American Political Science Review* 94: 627–40.

Druckman, J. N., and M. F. Thies. 2002. The importance of concurrence: The impact of bicameralism on government formation and duration. *American Journal of Political Science* 46: 760–72.

Inter-Parliamentary Union. 1986. *Parliaments of the World: A Comparative Reference Compendium*. New York: Facts on File.

King, G., J. Alt, N. Burns, and M. Laver. 1990. A unified model of cabinet dissolution in parliamentary democracies. *American Journal of Political Science* 34: 846–71.

Laver, M., and N. Schofield. 1990. *Multiparty Government: The Politics of Coalition in Europe*. Oxford: Oxford University Press.

Laver, M., and K. A. Shepsle. 1990. Coalitions and cabinet government. *American Political Science Review* 84: 873–90.

Laver, M., and K. A. Shepsle. 1996. *Making and Breaking Governments: Cabinets and Legislatures in Parliamentary Democracies*. Cambridge: Cambridge University Press.

Lijphart, A. 1984. *Democracies: Patterns of Majoritarian and Consensus Government in Twenty-one Countries*. New Haven: Yale University Press.

Lupia, A., and K. Strom. 1995. Coalition termination and the strategic timing of parliamentary elections. *American Political Science Review* 89: 648–69.

Mackie, T., and R. Rose. 1990. *The International Almanac of Electoral History*, 3rd ed. New York: Facts on File.

Merlo, A. 1997. Bargaining over governments in a stochastic environment. *Journal of Political Economy* 105: 101–31.

Merlo, A. 1998. Economic dynamics and government stability in postwar Italy. *Review of Economics and Statistics* 80: 629–37.

Merlo, A., and C. Wilson. 1995. A stochastic model of sequential bargaining with complete information. *Econometrica* 63: 371–99.

Merlo, A., and C. Wilson. 1998. Efficient delays in a stochastic model of bargaining. *Economic Theory* 11: 39–55.

Müller, W. C., and K. Strom, eds. 2000. *Coalition Governments in Western Europe*. Oxford: Oxford University Press.

Myerson, R. 1993. Effectiveness of electoral systems for reducing government corruption: A game-theoretic analysis. *Games and Economic Behavior* 5: 118–32.

Persson, T., G. Roland, and G. Tabellini. 1997. Separation of powers and political accountability. *Quarterly Journal of Economics* 112: 1163–1202.

Persson, T., G. Roland, and G. Tabellini. 2000. Comparative politics and public finance. *Journal of Political Economy* 108: 1121–61.

Persson, T., G. Roland, and G. Tabellini. 2003. How do electoral rules shape party structures, government coalitions, and economic policies? Mimeo. Stockholm University.

Persson, T., and G. Tabellini. 2000. *Political Economics: Explaining Economic Policy*. Cambridge: MIT Press.

Persson, T., and G. Tabellini. 2003. *The Economic Effects of Constitutions*. Cambridge: MIT Press.

Sjölin, M. 1993. *Coalition Politics and Parliamentary Power*. Lund: Lund University Press.

Strom, K. 1990. *Minority Government and Majority Rule*. Cambridge: Cambridge University Press.

Tsebelis, G. 2000. Veto players and institutional analysis. *Governance* 13: 441–74.

Tsebelis, G., and J. Money. 1997. *Bicameralism*. New York: Cambridge University Press.

Warwick, P. 1994. *Government Survival in Parliamentary Democracies*. Cambridge: Cambridge University Press.

6 On the Merits of Bicameral Legislatures: Intragovernmental Bargaining and Policy Stability

Roger D. Congleton

6.1 Contemporary Rational Choice Research on Bicameralism

Bicameral legislatures are characterized by two independently selected chambers, each with some authority over new legislation. Many bicameral systems are symmetric in the sense that the two chambers have essentially equal power to originate and veto legislative proposals, as in the United States and Belgium. Others are asymmetric with one chamber having far less control over legislation than the other, as in Canada, the Netherlands, and France. Moreover the balance of power between the chambers may be constitutionally adjusted through time. The House of Lords was the dominant chamber of the British Parliament for most of the period prior to 1700, a more or less equal partner in legislation during the eighteenth and early nineteenth centuries, and is presently by far the lesser of the two chambers with neither veto power nor authority to originate legislation. Approximately 180 contemporary national governments have a legislature or parliament. About a third of those governments, 61 countries, have legislatures that are bicameral (Patterson and Mughan 1999).

Historical Background

The practice of dividing the authority to create new laws and regulation among two or more legislative chambers is an ancient one. For example, political power in Athens was divided between its assembly (an open town meeting) and its council (staffed by members of the ten tribes of Athens). The Roman Republic divided authority between its Senate and several assemblies. Venice had its Great Council and Senate (Gordon 1999). Multicameralism in modern Europe is nearly as old as parliamentary governance. Parliaments emerged throughout Europe in the thirteenth century. These new assemblies were called *cortes* in Spain, *diets* in Germany, *tings* in Scandanavia, *estates general* in France, and parliaments in the British Isles (Palmer and Coulter 1950). Many of these assemblies were multicameral, as the term "estates" implies, with particular interests (church, town, rural, and noble) represented by separate chambers of the parliament.

Multicameralism remained commonplace within Europe until approximately 1800, after which most European governments gradually became bicameral, partly as a consequence of reforms associated with the French Revolution, but also as a consequence of new constitutional theories and subsequent pressures for constitutional reform. For example, Sweden shifted from an unelected four-chamber parliament to an elected two-chamber parliament in 1866. The British parliament was an exception to this rule. It has been bicameral since early in the fourteenth century, with its upper chamber representing the nobility and clergy (the Lords temporal and spiritual) and its lower chamber representing what might be called federal (town and county) interests during most of its history (Field 2002, ch. 2).

These early parliaments, although representative, were not democratic in the modern sense, because their members were not elected to office by a broad electorate. Rather, their membership was often explicitly or implicitly reserved for members of elite families, and in those cases in which elections were held to select members, the right to vote for representatives was generally reserved for the wealthiest 5 or 10 percent of the population. Nonetheless, membership in these multicameral assemblies was widely dispersed throughout the territitory ruled, which allowed a variety of regional and economic interests to be represented at court.

Because of this history, it not surprising that analysis of the effects of divided government is an ancient field of research, as is evident in Aristotle's 330 BC empirically based argument in favor of divided government. The analysis and arguments of Montesquieu (1748) clearly influenced the constitutional designers of the eighteenth and nineteenth centuries. Such work continues within political science and law, because any effort to improve governance must evaluate the relative merits of alternative forms of political architecture, and multicameralism is one of several methods for representing a broad cross section of national interests.

As national governance came to be increasingly grounded in theories of popular sovereignty in the nineteenth century, however, intellectual and political support for the old multicameral and bicameral systems tended to decline. The old ideas of represented interests gave way to contemporary notions of elected representation. Clearly, granting special powers to a particular class, economic interest group, or to local governments conflicts with the democratic principle of "one man, one vote." Indeed, bicamerals systems are widely regarded to be undemocratic if different interests are represented in legislative chambers, and unnecessarily redundant if they are not.

Contemporary rational choice-based research, however, suggests that bicameral government can advance broad citizen interests in either case. For example, as developed below, "unbiased" bicameral systems can produce public policies that are more faithful to the interests of the electorate, better informed, and more predictable.

Rational Choice Accounts of Bargaining within Bicameral Legislatures

The modern rational choice literature on constitutional design analyzes the bargaining that takes place within and between the chambers of bicameral legislatures. For the most part it analyzes the effects of the formal procedures of interchamber bargaining on both the bargains reached and the policies that emerge from the legislature. A smaller strand of empirical literature attempts to determine which, if any, of the various implications of these bargaining theories are present in real bicameral systems. The analytical literature on bicameralism begins with Tullock (1959) and with Buchanan and Tullock (1962, ch. 16) and continues to the present day, with a substantial increase in the flow of analytical research in the 1990s. Empirical work did not begin in earnest until the 1990s.

Buchanan and Tullock demonstrate that bicameralism indirectly tends to increase the size of the majority required to adopt new legislation. This is clearly true when the chambers are designed to represent different interests, as they typically are. However, they point out that an implicit requirement for supermajorities may arise even in cases where the chambers are not designed to represent different interests, because differences in the two chambers can arise as a consequence of chance events. For example, if some interests are spatially concentrated for whatever reason, those interests will tend to secure greater representation in the "lower" chamber elected from smaller districts than in an "upper" chamber elected from relatively larger districts. If both upper and lower chambers must agree for legislative proposals to become law, legislation will have to advance a broader cross section of interests than that required in a unicameral legislature because two somewhat different majorities have to be assembled. Indeed, bicameralism can be defended as a method for identifying policies with supermajority support.

In a few cases bicameral bargaining can also increase the stability of majoritarian decision making. It has been well known since Duncan Black's work (1948a, b) that majority rule is cycle prone and thus tends to be indecisive. If policy A secures majority support over policy B, in most cases there exists a policy C that can secure policy support over policy A. The possibility of majoritarian indecisiveness has attracted a lot of attention in the academic literature since Black's rediscovery of Condorcet's paradox. As Arrow (1963) points out, indeterminacy—or intransitivity—is not simply a problem with majority rule but with collective choice in general. Several authors have shown that in some circumstances bicameralism can eliminate majoritarian cycles. For example, Hammond and Miller (1987), Brennan and Hamlin (1992), and Riker (1992) demonstrate that if the interests represented within the two chambers are more homogeneous than interests within the legislature as a whole, bicameralism can avoid some problems with democratic cycles.

These papers demonstrate there are circumstances in which a "median" or "pivotal" voter exists for each of the chambers of a bicameral legislature, but no median or pivotal voter exists for the combined legislature. In such cases the pivotal voters of each chamber determine their chamber's policy and negotiation between the medians yields an agreement that lies between the two medians. Bicameralism increases stability insofar as it is generally easier to find Condorcet winners in two homogeneous chambers than in a heterogeneous single chamber. (Political parties and stable coalitions may serve similar purposes.)

More recent work has focused attention on the institutions of interchamber bargaining. It is clear that if each chamber has veto power over new legislation, some form of interchamber negotiation and compromise will be necessary. Tsebelis and Money (1997) demonstrate that the distribution of bargaining power need not be symmetric to affect legislative outcomes. The power to delay implementation of a policy is sufficient to affect legislation within bicameral systems. For example, in cases where the weaker chamber can delay but not veto a proposal, the more "patient" chamber tends to be decisive. The opportunity cost of negotiation might differ because election cycles differ in the two chambers, or because some issues are more pressing for one chamber's voters than the others. In such cases the decisive voter of the chamber prepared to wait the longest for a relatively beneficial outcome can secure a legislative outcome that is relatively closer to his or her ideal point than that of his or her more impatient counterpart.

The distribution of agenda control and veto power clearly affects the bargaining power of the chambers of governance. For example, Steunenberg, Schmidtchen, and Kolboldt (1999) and Steunenberg (2001) demonstrate that the elaborate policy-making procedures of the present European Union (EU) determine the relative power of the Commission, Council, and European Parliament and indirectly the relative power of member states within the EU.

Bicameralism may also affect the internal organization of the legislature. Shepsle and Weingast (1987) demonstrate that intercameral conference committees within the United States (where compromises are worked out) tend to empower legislative committees in both chambers. Diermeier and Myerson (1999) suggest that bicameral systems tend to encourage the development of intracameral veto players insofar as lobbying costs are increased by bicameralism.

Rogers (1998) explores how the power to propose new legislation, a type of agenda control, may affect the course of legislation within bicameral legislatures. He argues that bicameral systems can economize on information costs by allowing the more informed chamber to originate the legislation. He demonstrates that the latter is an equilibrium in the sequential proposal game when information is asymmetric. To the extent that the more informed chamber originates the legislative proposals, bicameral legislatures will tend to make more informed decisions than unicameral ones. His empirical results, based on US state data, are consistent with the theoretical analysis, in that the larger (and he suggests more informed) chamber most often originates legislation. This form of specialization is more evident when a single party controls both chambers of the legislature, as implied by his theoretical analysis.

Persson, Roland, and Tabellini (1997) analyze bargains that might be struck between chambers of a divided government in a setting in which voters can replace incumbents for malfeasance or incompetence. Their analysis takes place in the context of a bipolar government with an independently elected executive and legislature, but their analysis also applies to bargaining between pivotal members of a bicameral legislature subject to reelection pressures. They demonstrate that circumstances exist in which electoral pressures and specific divisions of policy-making responsibilities (agenda control and veto power) can generate improvements in the performance of government relative to a single chamber (player) with complete control over policy making. They also note that different assignments of policy-making power affect the relative bargaining power of the two chambers.

Overall, the rational choice literature on bicameralism predicts that (1) bicameral systems are somewhat more stable than unicameral systems insofar as majority cycles are fewer, (2) levels of consensus required for legislation to be adopted tend to be somewhat higher than under unicameral systems insofar as the interests represented in the two chambers differ, (3) in cases where the chambers each have substantial influence, policy decisions tend to be more informed and faithful to the desires of the electorate, and (4) the effect of bicameralism depends in part on the relative power of the two chambers, which is determined by the formal and informal procedures of negotiation between the chambers and the interests of the pivotal members of the two chambers.

The New Empirical Literature on Bicameralism

The first tests of the theoretical models of bicameralism were often conducted by the theorists themselves, as Tsebelis and Money (1997) and Rogers (1998) attempted to determine whether their theories of the effects of delay and information affected the pattern of intercameral bargaining. Recent empirical studies have focused attention on the policy consequences of bicameralism. Do bicameral bargains yield policies that, on average, differ systematically from unicameral legislatures, and do those policy differences have systematic effects on community welfare?

For example, empirical work by Bradbury and Crain (2002) suggests that the greater the difference in the interests represented by the chambers of a bicameral legislature, the smaller per capita state expenditures tend to be. They argue that when the two chambers represent different interests, legislation requires a broader consensus to pass, which limits opportunities for redistributive politics. Other estimates also imply that modern bicameral systems tend to accord relatively larger bargaining power to the lower (more numerous) chamber. Their estimates imply that the typical lower chamber has about 3.5 times as much bargaining power as the upper chamber. Bradbury and Crain (2001) also find evidence that a small chamber reduces the effect of the "fiscal commons problem" in the larger chamber, although it does not eliminate it. Their estimates suggest that expenditures as a fraction of GDP and in real per capita levels tend to increase as the number of seats in the lower chamber increases, but do so less rapidly in bicameral systems than in unicameral systems. For additional discussion of the fiscal commons problem, see Knight's discussion in chapter 9. The Bradbury and Crain results are discussed at length in chapter 7.

Most empirical work on constitutions and bicameralism is cross-sectional. To isolate the effects of institutions from other differences in circumstances, such studies have to account for a broad array of other differences among countries and states. This problem is reduced in cases where a single country moves from one set of institutions to another, in that cultural and economic conditions are more homogeneous within a single country through time than across countries.

Congleton (2003a, ch. 12) explores the effects of Sweden's switch from bicameral to unicameral institutions in the early 1970s. Those estimates suggest that representative bicameral legislatures tend to have policies that are more stable through time and more broadly supported than those adopted by otherwise similar unicameral legislatures, especially in settings where political parties are important.

Some political theorists suggest that unicameral institutions are more responsive to short-term political demands, which might increase policy uncertainty insofar as voter preferences or turnout varies from year to year. Such an effect might partly explain the very rapid expansion of the social welfare state in Sweden from 1970 to 1985, as a leftward tide of ideology swept through the West. However, estimates of the Swedish demand for public services suggest that the Swedish government became less, rather than more, responsive to electoral demands under unicameralism. Within a proportional representation system, unicameralism tends to concentrates policy-making power in the hands of party leaders within a single chamber, who may implement policies that are somewhat at odds with majoritarian interests. Survey evidence suggests that members of the Riksdag majority often have policy interests that are systematically different from those of their supporters (Esaiasson and Holmberg 1996).

Overall the rational choice literature on bicameralism takes issue with the claim that bicameralism can serve no purpose unless it is an antidemocratic one. Theoretical work suggests that bicameralism can improve public policy by making policy more predictable, more informed, and more responsive to voter interests—especially in settings in which policy deliberations are very partisan. Statistical evidence from Sweden and Denmark, both of which replaced bicameral with unicameral legislatures, are consistent with simulation models of legislation developed below. These results are reviewed at length in sections 6.2 and 6.3 of this chapter.

6.2 Simulated Bicameral Bargains and Public Policy

A bicameral system is unbiased as long as the expected median of the two chambers is the same, as may be true of chambers with differently sized election districts or terms of office, as long as voter preferences are more or less similar among districts and through time. If bicameral effects are present in unbiased systems, they are also likely to be found in biased forms of bicameralism in which interests are given different weights in the two chambers. To explore whether bicameralism, itself, has consequences for policy in the long run, simulation models are developed below.

Simulations allow a variety of constitutional architectures to be analyzed in an artificial environment in which all elements of constitutional design can be controlled. This allows one to determine how policy outcomes are affected by political institutions "on average" as institutions and electoral outcomes vary through time. In addition to the ease with which institutions can be varied and polity outcomes can be modeled, simulations allow the small sample properties of electorates and legislatures to be analyzed. Similar work, of course, can be undertaken using formal mathematical models, although mathematical results are, for the most part, limited to expected values and other "asymptotic cases" in which the number of elections and/or chamber members approach infinity. This limitation suggests that simulation results may be more relevant for constitutional analysis than mathematical analysis, because existing legislature have finite memberships and most democracies have had fewer than 40 national elections. Simulations, however, often require a less general model structure than possible in mathematical analyses, although it bears noting that most dynamic mathematical analyses also tend to rely on fairly narrow concrete models.

A Simulation Model of Bicameral Legislation

The simulations developed below are similar to those developed in Congleton (2003b) but assume different legislature sizes and focus exclusively on the effects that political parties have on policy choices through time. The simulation of policy choices within democractically elected legislatures requires models of voters, parties, elections, and legislative outcomes.

Voters

Voters are assumed to be rational "spatial" voters. Each voter determines his or her ideal government service level within an existing fiscal system, and then votes for the candidate or party whose stated policies are closest to their preferred vector of service levels. For the purposes of the simulations, voter preferences over public services are mapped into a single-dimensioned issue space, interpreted as the voter's preferred growth rate for government services.[1] Voter ideal points within this issue space are assumed to be uniformly distributed between −10 percent a year and +10 percent a year. This distributional assumption implies that the median voter favors the status quo, since the median of the distribution of preferred growth rates for public services is 0. Other voters prefer smaller or larger fiscal packages according to their tastes and circumstances; so they cast their votes for candidates favoring growth rates below or above zero.

Parties

All candidates are assumed to belong to political parties because of electoral advantages associated with party membership. Two-partisan environments are simulated. In the first series of simulations, political parties select "undisciplined" slates of candidates who can vote as they wish without fear of being banished from the party after being elected to office. (This might be regarded as an extreme representation of the US system.) In the second series of simulations, the parties "force" their elected representatives to support their party's platform. (This might be regarded as an extreme representation of list voting in proportional representation systems.)

In both cases it is assumed that only two parties or two viable coalitions exist and that these parties or coalitions have adopted platforms at the Duverger (1954) blocking points. The Duverger blocking positions for the left of center (LoC) and right of center (RoC) coalitions

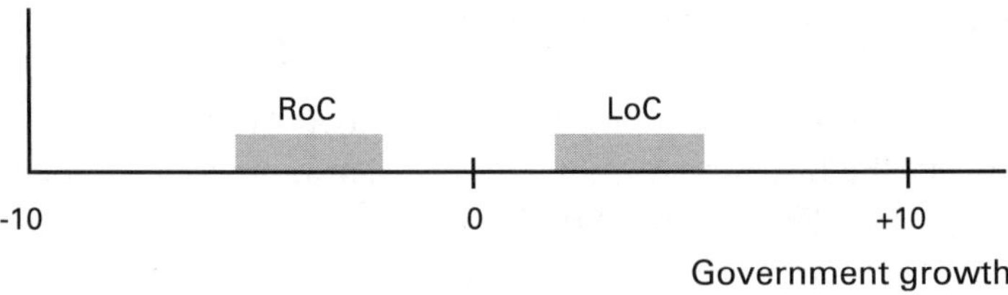

Figure 6.1
Party slates

will be governmental growth rates of 3.33 percent and −3.33 percent respectively given the assumed distribution of voter ideal points.

Political parties are assumed to support candidate with relatively similar policy positions. There are several reasons for doing so. For example, candidates with similar policy preferences will be able to work together more effectively after the election because they have shared interests. It also allows voters to use party labels as information about the policy positions of candidates, which allows voters to economize on information, and also increases candidate incentives to join political parties.

Figure 6.1 characterizes a possible distribution of mainstream candidates from the LoC and RoC parties. In the illustration, party screening and candidate sorting have narrowed the range of viable candidates from the [−10, 10] interval that covers the entire political spectrum to the more moderate [−5.8, 5.8] interval. It seems natural to assume that the RoC candidates all take positions to the right of those of the LoC association of candidates, and that the RoC and LoC parties do not field candidates of the far right or left.[2]

Elections

The election of representatives for the two chambers is simulated as follows. Two candidates are drawn from the distributions of party candidates, and an electoral contest is held. The RoC candidate is selected if the median of the electorate is less then 0; otherwise, the candidate of the LoC party is chosen. This process is repeated for successive pairs of candidates until all the positions in the two chambers are filled. The resulting composition of the legislative bodies is proportional to votes received by the party, as under proportional representation. Similar electoral results would occur under "first past the post" systems if voters are uniformly distributed among electoral districts and screening of candidates is undertaken by national political parties.

Because both parties have adopted Duverger platforms, the two parties (coalitions) receive very similar electoral support, although the positions of the party members who take places in the legislature may differ substantially.

Legislation

Legislative outcomes are determined by the composition of the two chambers, party discipline, and the bargaining process assumed. The median legislator in each chamber determines his or her own chamber's proposed legislation (growth rate). In undisciplined parliaments, the members are free to vote for their own preferred growth rate; in disciplined parties, the median member abides by his or her party's platform. The legislation adopted by a unicameral parliament is that proposed by its median member. Bicameral outcomes are assumed to "split the difference" between the median members of the two chambers; that is to say, an unweighted average of the two chamber medians is adopted.

Simulations of Legislation with Undisciplined Parties

Table 6.1 summarizes the legislative results from a series of 40 electoral cycles for two simulated legislatures with undisciplined political parties. The first legislature has chambers with the number of members for the US Senate and House and the second has those of the old Swedish bicameral legislature. The results allow four unicameral chambers to be compared with two bicameral legislatures, insofar as the median preference in each of the chambers can be interpreted as unicameral outcomes.

Note that the probabilistic pattern of voter turnout and party slates generates policy choices that deviate from the median voter's preferred policy (no change) in particular elections and over the course of the 40 electoral cycles. If we focus on the pseudo–US legislature, the growth rates preferred by the median Senate member range from −1.611 to 2.002 percent a year, whereas the growth rates preferred by the median member of the House varied from −1.343 to 1.371 percent a year. If we focus on the pseudo–Swedish legislature, the growth rates preferred by the median legislature varied from −1.843 to 1.55 percent a year in the first chamber and from −1.15 to 1.41 percent a year in the larger second chamber.

These fluctuations occur even though median voter preferences are completely stable and favor the status quo in each electoral cycle. The

Table 6.1
Bicameral and unicameral outcomes with undisciplined parties: Simulated legislative policy outcome with party slates

	Chamber 1 mean	Chamber 2 mean	Bicameral mean	Chamber 1 median	Chamber 2 median	Bicameral compromise
Statistics for 100-member Senate, 435-member House, 40 elections						
Sample average	0.117	0	0.057	0.49	−0.136	0.177
Standard deviation	0.322	0.203	0.218	1.116	1.054	0.758
Max	1.131	0.424	0.729	2.002	1.372	1.565
Min	−0.52	−0.34	−0.336	−1.612	−1.343	−1.209
Statistics for 151-member First Chamber, 233-member Second Chamber, 40 elections						
Sample average	−0.103	0.044	−0.03	−0.345	0.409	−0.006
Standard deviation	0.322	0.198	0.207	1.137	0.983	0.823
Max	0.484	0.418	0.291	1.546	1.413	1.234
Min	−0.883	−0.396	−0.49	−1.843	−1.152	−1.429

average policy chosen over the course of the 40 elections, however, is approximately that preferred by the median voter. This is true for each chamber and for the bicameral compromise.

The numbers of greatest interest for the purposes of this chapter are the standard deviations of the median member of the various legislative chambers and that of the bicameral compromise. Note that the standard deviation of the median members of the individual chambers tends to fall as the number of members in a chamber increases. This is simply the usual relationship between estimated medians and sample size. As sample size increases, here chamber membership, the median estimate becomes more precise. For similar reasons the standard deviation of the bicameral compromise is always smaller than that of either single chamber.

Insofar as the single chambers can be regarded as unicameral legislatures, the results suggest that *unbiased forms of bicameralism produce public policies that are more faithful to the median preferences of the electorate and more predictable for the electorate as a whole, within a weak party system of governance*. However, in the present case, with undisciplined parties, a similar increase in performance can also be generated by increasing the size of a single chamber, although it bears noting that the use of a single large chamber may induce other problems. For example, it may increase fiscal commons problems.[3]

Simulation of Legislation with Disciplined Parties

Political parties often do more than provide useful information about slates of candidates. The same platform that can be used to provide information about party members during an election can also be used as a legislative agenda after the election. In disciplined parties, party leaders can "force" elected representatives to support the party's announced legislative agenda by conditioning future campaign support (or positions on party lists) in the next election on voting behavior in the current session of parliament. For example, it is clear that party discipline contributed to the similar (although not identical) patterns of voting in the Swedish bicameral parliament (Tsebelis and Money 1997, p. 43).

Any effort by party leaders to coordinate voting within and across chambers reduces the independence of the policies preferred by the two chambers, and might be expected to weaken the statistical case for unbiased bicameralism by increasing chamber congruence.

To explore the effects of partisanship, an extreme form of party discipline is simulated below. In these simulations, each member of each party is assumed to propose its own party's announced platform, represented by its Duverger position. Because the party platforms at Duverger positions are significantly different, this implies that policies will now change significantly whenever the majority party changes. This contrasts with the previous simulations in which the ebb and tide of elections would not generally imply radically different median legislators or policies.[4] In the previous case, the median member of a chamber was always one of the most moderate members of the majority party. In this present case, the party platforms determine the policies proposed and legislated.

Table 6.2 summarizes legislative membership and policy outcomes from a series of 40 pairs of simulated US and Swedish legislatures, selected as in the previous case. Party discipline within the legislature has several striking effects on the simulation results.

The range of policy outcomes is now completely determined by the party platforms and the compromise between them. Consequently only three policy outcomes are observed, rather than a continuum among moderates, the result with undisciplined parties. The average policy observed in the entire series of elections is not significantly affected. On average, the median voter still gets approximately what he or she wants, although *he or she is never directly represented in the Parliament*.

Table 6.2
Disciplined parties: Simulated legislative policy outcomes with party slates and party discipline

	Chamber 1 mean	Chamber 2 mean	Bicameral mean	Chamber 1 outcome	Chamber 2 outcome	Bicameral compromise
Statistics for 100-member Senate, 435-member House, 40 elections						
Sample average	0.054	0.014	0.034	0.322	0.161	0.241
Standard deviation	0.434	0.189	0.222	3.284	3.296	2.137
Max	0.811	0.544	0.418	3.3	3.3	3.3
Min	−0.886	−0.397	−0.641	−3.3	−3.3	−3.3
Statistics for 151-member First Chamber, 233-member Second Chamber, 40 elections						
Sample average	−0.021	−0.011	−0.016	−0.161	0.644	0.241
Standard deviation	0.278	0.212	0.179	3.296	3.235	2.378
Max	0.781	0.446	0.365	3.3	3.3	3.3
Min	−0.621	−0.418	−0.516	−3.3	−3.3	−3.3

However, *the volatility of policy outcomes, measured by the standard deviation of policy outcomes is substantially higher within disciplined partisan legislatures than in undisciplined legislatures.* The standard deviation of the growth rates adopted is approximately three times as large as in the previous simulations. The standard error of the median legislator's policy now exceeds 3.0 in both chambers in both parliamentary systems, whereas previous sample variances had been approximately 1.0.

Bicameralism continues to reduce policy volatility for statistical reasons, but it now has an effect on the *volatility* of policies, as measured by sample variance, that is distinct from the sample size effect present in the first simulations. Note that the standard deviations of decisions by each of the four chambers are all greater than three in this case and *do not diminish with membership.* The sample size effect is not present in this round of simulations because asymptotic limits are evidently more rapidly approached in the binomial case. However, the standard deviations of the bicameral compromise is approximately a third lower than any of the individual chambers in both series of the simulations.

This reduction in volatility occurs because of the occasional necessity of compromise in the bicameral systems. In about half the cases different parties will control the chambers of a bicameral legislature, and compromise is necessary in those cases. These compromises are sufficient to reduce the variation in policy outcomes in the simulations by about a third over that found in the corresponding unicameral system.[5] This *stabilizing effect of bicameralism is not a result of sampling theory, but rather of the necessity of interchamber compromise in bicameral legislatures whenever the interests of the two chambers differ.*

Interparty compromise is unnecessary in unicameral legislatures regardless of chamber size, as long as majority parties or stable majority coalitions exist in the chamber of interest. No matter how large a single legislative chamber is, under the assumed Duverger platforms, the policies adopted by a unicameral legislature with a disciplined and partisan majority tend to oscillate back and forth between dominant party platforms. In partisan environments bicameralism necessarily stabilizes political outcomes relative to unicameralism as long as compromises are worked out. Bicameralism allows intermediate policies to be reached whenever power is divided within the legislature, and consequently yields a more stable time series of policies than the unicameral parliament.[6]

6.3 Statistical Support: Bicameralism and the Median Vote

Within the real world, the median voter does not always favor continuation of the status quo, because her economic and personal circumstances may change through time. If democratic political institutions are "unbiased," however, it remains the case that the pivotal voters get what they want—at least on average. In such cases the volatility of government policy will be jointly determined by the stability of the median voter's demand for government services and the response of government policy makers to variations in that demand.

In the usual rational choice models, voter preferences are not affected by constitutional arrangements. Given this assumption, the demand for government services can be approximated as

$$G_t^d = v(Y_t, I_t),$$

where Y_t is the pivotal voter's income in period t and I_t is an index of the median or average voter's ideology or desire for government services.[7] Within democracies, supply will approximately equal the average voter's electoral demand,

$$G_t^d \approx G_t^s = v(Y_t, I_t) + e_t.$$

The effects of institutions and turnout are reflected in the error term e_t. If institutions are unbiased, the mean of e_t will be zero. If institutions affect the volatility of public policies, the variance of error term e_t will be conditioned on the types of political institutions that are in place.

Several of the theories reviewed above and the simulation results suggest that the variance of e_t will be increased by a shift from bicameralism to unicameralism, although the basis of those predictions differs somewhat. The next two subsections attempt to determine whether this prediction is evident in two European countries that have recently changed from bicameral to unicameral systems.

Effect of the Shift from Bicameralism to Unicameralism in Sweden

Several countries have replaced bicameral institutions with unicameral ones during the past half century: Denmark (1953), Sweden (1970), New Zealand (1951), and Peru (1993) all switched from bicameral to unicameral legislatures. Temporary switches also occurred in Turkey (1982–89), Sri Lanka (1971–72), and Panama (1979–89). Unfortunately, most of these changes in legislative structure took place during politically "extraordinary" times. All but Sweden appear to have adopted or left bicameralism during or immediately following periods of domestic or international crisis. Consequently Sweden's recent constitutional history is likely to provide the best available evidence.

In 1970 the Swedish Constitution (Riksdag Act) was modified after approximately 20 years of peaceful deliberations with very high levels of agreement within the parliament. The revised Riksdag Act effectively merged the two chambers of the 100-year-old Swedish bicameral legislature into a single large chamber.

To determine whether Swedish policies became less predictable after the change from bicameral to unicameral governance, an electoral demand equation is estimated in linear and log linear forms. Increased policy volatility will be evident as an increase in the variance of the residuals of the estimated demand equation.

Government service levels are measured in two ways: as real per capita government consumption and as government consumption as a fraction of Swedish gross domestic product.[8] The median voter's income is approximated by real per capita private consumption. The median voter's preference for government services is represented by average voter ideology, as calculated for Swedish voters by Kim and Fording (1998). Economic data from the World Bank is used for real per capita government consumption levels and for average voter income (after-tax), which is proxied by per capita private consumption.

There is considerable evidence that Sweden's switch from bicameralism to unicameralism in 1970 had significant effects on Swedish politics and thus on Swedish policies. Congleton (2003a) analyzes several effects that Sweden's 1970 constitutional reforms have had on Swedish public policy and welfare. Political leaders became relatively more powerful, the time horizon of policy formation and feedback was reduced (by eliminating the longer terms of the first chamber and adoption of a shorter legislative cycle), and government became less stable. Immergut (2002) reconstructed the majority coalitions that would have emerged had bicameralism been left in place and found that the Social Democrats and their allies on the left would have had a solid majority in the eliminated chamber that would have prevented the center-right coalition from coming to power.

Four estimated supply equations for government services are reported in table 6.3, adjusted for institutional effects. Two of the estimates assume that institution of bicameralism has no systematic effect on the supply of services. The two others allow bicameralism (and the other institutional reforms) to affect service levels directly. The coefficients all have the anticipated signs. Both an increase in after-tax income and an ideological shift to the left increase the demand for and therefore the supply of government services. The negative sign of the interaction term (voter ideology and unicameralism) suggests that the Swedish government became less responsive to short-term changes in voter demand for government services after elimination of the first chamber, possibly by making party leaders and their platforms relatively more important.[9]

Of particular interest for the purposes of this chapter are the residuals of the estimates. The simulations imply that systematic differences will exist in the residual variance of the bicameral and unicameral periods. In each case the White's tests are consistent with this hypothesis. All tests reject the hypothesis that the error term is homoscedastic during the bicameral and unicameral subperiods of the estimates.

The bottom of table 6.3 lists the sample standard deviations of the residuals for the 1960 to 1970 bicameral period and for the 1971 to 1997 unicameral period. In each case the standard error of the unicameral period is greater than that of the bicameral period. Moreover *F*-tests for the hypothesis that the residual variance is not higher in the unicameral period than in the bicameral period can be rejected at the

Table 6.3
Estimated electoral demand for Swedish government services

	Real Swedish government consumption (per capita)	Real Swedish government consumption (per capita)	Real Swedish government consumption (% of GDP)	Real Swedish government consumption (% of GDP)
Constant	−3,586.526	−7,207.25	0.125	−0.090
	(2.60)**	(−26.44)***	(4.05)***	(−4.80)***
Unicameral		7,033.106		0.350
		(4.95)***		(7.46)***
Swedish voter ideology	33.820	67.898	0.0014	0.0027
	(3.36)***	(9.36)***	(6.06)***	(5.65)***
Unicameral* voter ideology		−63.794		−0.0024
		(−4.09)***		(−3.82)***
Real per capita private consumption	0.633	0.8327	4.79e-6	1.90E-5
	(7.04)***	(49.33)***	(2.41)**	(20.10)**
Unicameral* real per capita private consumption		−0.328		−1.94E-5
		(−4.25)***		(−8.30)***
R-squared	0.860	0.93	0.49	0.81
F-statistic	105.56***	85.04***	16.82***	27.42***
Tests for changes in variance of error term				
Whites heteroscadasticity test	8.05***	2.70**	10.80***	3.11**
Bicameral residual standard deviation 1960–70	185.51	67.8	0.01	0
Unicameral residual standard deviation 1970–97	855.91	681.43	0.03	0.02
F-test for equivalence of residual variance	21.29***	101.03***	4.55***	42.50***

Notes: *** Denotes significance at the 0.01 level, ** denotes significance at the 0.05 level, and * denotes significance at the 0.1 level. Newey West standard errors used to calculate *t*-statistics.

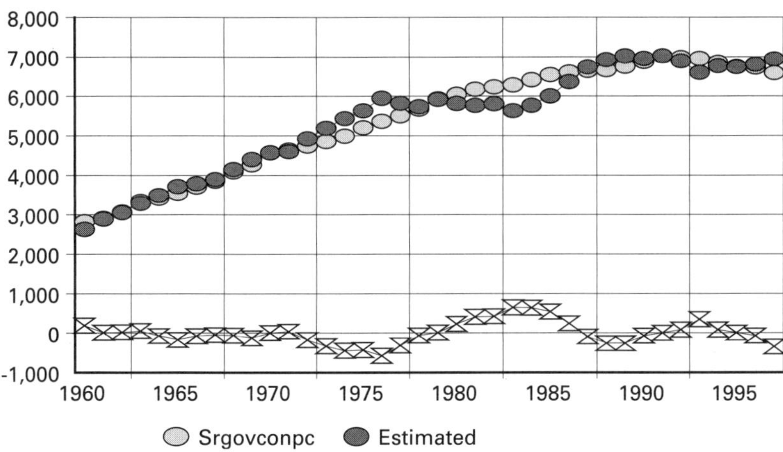

Figure 6.2
Swedish government consumption, real per capita

0.001 level of significance in every case. Overall, the results support the hypothesis that government policy during the unicameral period is less predictable and more highly variable than in the bicameral period.[10]

Indeed, the difference in the policy volatility after the adoption of unicameralism is sufficiently large that it can be directly observed in the data. Figure 6.2 plots the observed and estimated real Swedish per capita government consumption and the residuals. Note that the residuals in the unicameral period after 1970 are noticeably larger than in the bicameral period before 1970. Note also that the increase in the residuals associated with the shift to unicameralism is clearly not the result of a spurious upward trend in residual variance but rather a change in regime.

Further Evidence of Unicameral Policy Volatility from Denmark

Shortly after World War II, Denmark eliminated its long-standing upper chamber, the Landsting, by constitutional amendment, transforming its bicameral Rigsdag to a unicameral system on June 5, 1953. Unfortunately, because the Danish shift occurred relatively shortly after World War II, isolating the effects of the shift to unicameralism is not as straightforward as in the Swedish case. The war might affect both the data collected in the period before the unicameral Riksdag was adopted and the government policies adopted prior to the 1953 constitutional reform.

However, although World War II clearly disrupted ordinary political life, the effects of the German occupation (1941–45) were not as disruptive as in many other countries in Europe. Elections continued to be held, and most national policies were made by the governments elected—except toward the end of the occupation when the government resigned in block, leaving governance for a year or so in the hands of unelected officials. The effects of the war on demands for government services are doubtless present, but the estimates developed below find little that is systematic. (Estimated coefficients for dummy variables for the period of occupation were not statistically different from zero and are not included in the model estimates reported below.) In any case the effect of the turbulent period prior to the 1953 constitutional reform tends to *bias the results away* from finding a significant increase in policy volatility from the subsequent shift to unicameralism.

Another data problem that needs to be confronted in the Danish case is the lack of ideological data for the period of interest. Data on voter preferences for government services are proxied by voter support for the Social Democrats. Voter support for the Social Democrats should be highly correlated with the pivotal voter's increase in expanding government services because Social Democrats routinely support expansion of government services. Increases in their vote share imply that more voters share that view. Increased support suggests that the distribution of voter opinion shifts to the left. Support for the Social Democrats is instumented by regressing vote shares in national elections as a linear function of the previous years' per capita income, a time trend, and unicameralism. The estimated support—the systematic part of voter demands for services—is used as a measure of voter ideology. During the period examined, the Social Democrats were the largest party in the Folkesting.

Economic data were assembled from Mitchell (1992) and political data from Cook and Paxton (1986) for the period 1930 to 1976. The supply of Danish government services is represented by real per capita government consumption. Estimates for linear and (log linear) exponential demand equations are reported. Voter income is represented as real per capita gross domestic product, and voter preferences or ideology is represented as estimated support for the Social Democrats. Several alternative measures and functional forms are reported below in table 6.4.[11] The results are similar to those developed for the Swedish case despite the historical and data problems. Government services

Table 6.4
Estimated voter demand for Danish government services, 1930 to 1976

	Real Danish government consumption (per capita)	Real Danish government consumption (per capita)	Danish government consumption (log per capita)	Danish government consumption (% of GDP)
C	−644.822	−2,015.02	1.088	−232.398
	(−5.31)***	(−2.87)***	(0.81)	(−2.29)**
Real Danish GDP (per capita)	380.624	423.573		63.54
	(7.76)***	(2.02)**		(7.47)***
Estimated Danish voter ideology		30.619		4.307
		(7.40)***		(2.04)**
Log real Danish GDP (per capita)			2.284	
			(19.81)***	
Log estimated Danish voter ideology			0.638	
			(1.85)*	
R-squared	0.88	0.892	0.98	0.88
F-statistic	320.903	169.563	865.315	149.878
Tests for the Effect of Unicameralism on the Predictability of Danish Governance				
Whites heteroscadasticity test	30.354***	15.78***	3.34**	9.312***
Bicameral residual standard deviation 1930–53	85.589	45.76	0.125	11.26
Unicameral residual standard deviation 1954–76	262.902	248.75	0.17	40.378
F-test for equivalence of variance	9.44***	29.55***	1.84*	12.86***

Notes: *** Denotes significance at the 0.01 level, ** denotes significance at the 0.05 level, and * denotes significance at the 0.1 level. Newey-West standard errors used to compute *t*-statistics.

tend to rise as support for the Social Democrats increases and the average voter's income increases.

The variance of the residuals in the bicameral and unicameral periods are analyzed at the bottom of the table. In each case the Whites heterogeneity test statistic again rejects the hypothesis that the residuals are from an error distribution with a constant variance. Inspection affirmed by *F*-tests indicates that the residual variance of the bicameral period is systematically smaller than in the unicameral period. As in the Swedish case, Danish government policy became less predictable after the adoption of its unicameral parliament.

6.4 Conclusion

This chapter has summarized the rational choice literature on bicameralism and recent empirical work on the effects that bicameralism tend to have on public policy. Previous theoretical literature has demonstrated that bicameral legislatures avoid some majority cycling problems, tend to discover policies with supermajority support, and may be more informed and faithful to the policy aims of the electorate.

The chapter also presented in condensed form some results from my own research on bicameralism. That work implies that bicameralism can systematically affect the course of public policy without giving particular interests special consideration. In the circumstances examined, bicameral legislatures adopted policies that were more faithful to the long-run interests of the median voter and more predictable than those adopted by unicameral legislatures. Statistical evidence from Sweden and Denmark is consistent with the simulation analysis. Both nations had somewhat less predictable public policy in the years following their shift to unicameralism. Bicameralism need not overweight some interests nor act as a counter to majoritarian pressures to achieve systematically better performance in terms of advancing median voter's interests.

Nonetheless, the fact that bicameralism makes it possible to design legislatures that address other concerns can be an important consideration. For example, the possibility of overweighting regional interests may be an added advantage when designing new federal states and treaty organizations. Similarly, specifying different electoral periods for the two chambers can ensure a longer term perspective in policy making. Such additional institutional flexibility clearly accounts for recent historical development of bicameral legislatures in a number of countries and, as argued in chapter 7 by Bradbury and Crain, is another reason why bicameralism is widely used in democratic constitutional designs. As this chapter suggests, the process of compromise within bicameral institutions has desirable effects on the course of public policy even in cases in which the two chambers represent similar interests.

Notes

1. The utility-maximizing choice of a typical voter can be represented as follows: Suppose that voters have preferences over government service G and private consumption C. Suppose further that voters are characterized by their income levels Y_i and ideology I_i and that the public service is financed by an income tax $T_i = t(Y_i, G)$. In this case voter i will prefer the service level that maximizes $U_i = u(G, Y_i - t(Y_i, G), I_i)$, which requires G^* to be such that $U_C T_G = U_G$. For the purposes of the simulations, it is assumed that the status quo level of service, G_0, is that preferred by the median voter, as would be the case in a pure median voter model. A voter's demand for government services is $G_i^* = g_i(Y_i, I_i)$, and the preferred change in service level is $(G_i^*/G_0) - 1$.

Voting in this dimension by utilility-maximizing voters is approximately spatial, in the sense that the closer of two candidates is usually preferred to the other. (The distribution of voter ideal growth rates has, in effect, been normalized in the simulations by subtracting the median voter's preferred growth rate from the unnormalized distribution.)

2. There is considerable evidence that policy positions of representatives in the House and Senate of the United States do not converge to identical positions but remain clustered a bit to the right and left of center. See, for example, Poole and Rosenthal (1991) and Francis et al. (1994).

3. These simulations do not attempt to account for the effect that legislative size has on the fiscal commons problem. See the Bradbury and Crain discussion of this in chapter 7. To the extent that an increase in chamber size produces an upward bias in the government spending, dividing a single large chamber into two smaller chambers will produce a smaller bias. In that case bicameralism allows the sampling or representative advantage of increased overall chamber size to realized with a smaller upward bias, than would be associate with a single large chamber.

4. In this setting the random electoral outcomes should be regarded as a consequence of indifference by voters in the middle of the distribution rather than confusion about which party is which. Independence also has a somewhat different interpretation in this setting. Here centrist voters, in effect, toss a coin before casting votes for the upper chamber and then toss the coin again before voting for the second chamber.

5. The theoretical result is exactly half. Under unicameralism, the policy chosen is either -3.3 or $+3.3$ with probability 0.5, which implies a variance of 10.89. Under bicameralism the implied policy is -3.3 or 3.3 with probability 0.25, and 0 with probability 0.5, so the policy variance is exactly half that of unicameralism, 5.45.

6. Note that for this alignment of parties and institutions, the same result would hold if neither party compromised. A compromise generates the status quo, which is the same result that occurs if each chamber simply vetoes every proposal backed by a majority in the other chamber.

7. Recall, as noted above, that a voter's demand for government services can be modeled as follows: Voters are assumed to have preferences over government service G and private consumption C. Voters are characterized by their income levels Y_i and ideology I_i. Public service G is financed by an income tax or other tax that varies with income such as a VAT, $T_i = t(Y_i, G)$. In this case voter i will prefer the service level that maximizes $U_i = u(G, Y_i - t(Y_i, G), I_i)$, which requires G_i^* to be such that $U_C T_G = U_G$. A voter's demand for government services is $G_i^* = g_i(Y_i, I_i)$.

8. In the usual model of consumer choice, consumers are self-interested, and unconcerned with the consumption levels of other individuals. In this case government consumption is what is demanded by the typical voter citizen, and transfers are of interest only insofar as they affect an individual's before tax income. However, if voters are modeled as altruistic, government expenditures, including transfers, would be a better measure of G. For the present analysis, the usual economic assumption is adopted.

9. These statistical results are from Congleton (2003a, ch. 12).

10. Of course, the 1970s are well known for other important international economic events. The Bretton Woods System ended, energy prices increased, and inflation became more problematic. However, similar results are obtained if the performance of Sweden and other small European countries are compared. Moreover, as developed later in this chapter, the increase in variance associated with leaving bicameralism was also present in the Danish experience during the relatively more stable 1950s.

11. These statistical results are from Congleton (2003b).

References

Alesina, A., and H. Rosenthal. 1996. A theory of divided government. *Econometrica* 64: 1311–41.

Aristotle. [330 BC] 1969. *The Politics*. Baltimore, MD: Penguin.

Arrow, K. J. 1963. *Social Choice and Individual Values*, 2nd ed. New Haven: Yale University Press.

Black, D. 1948a. On the rationale of group decision-making. *Journal of Political Economy* 56: 23–34.

Black, D. 1948b. The decisions of a committee using a special majority. *Econometrica* 16: 245–61.

Bradbury, J. C., and W. M. Crain. 2001. Legislative organization and government spending: Cross country evidence. *Journal of Public Economics* 82: 309–25.

Bradbury, J. C., and W. M. Crain. 2002. Bicameralism legislatures and fiscal policy. *Southern Economic Journal* 68: 646–59.

Brennan, G., and A. Hamlin. 1992. Bicameralism and majority equilibrium. *Public Choice* 74: 169–79.

Buchanan, J. M., and G. Tullock. 1962. *The Calculus of Consent.* Ann Arbor: University of Michigan Press.

Cook, C., and J. Paxton. 1986. *European Political Facts 1918–84*. New York: Facts on File.

Congleton, R. D. 2003a. *Improving Democracy through Constitutional Reform: Some Swedish Lessons*. Dordrecth: Kluwer Academic. Also available in Swedish (2002) as *Att Förbätta Demokratin*. Stockholm: SNS Förlag (2002).

Congleton, R. D. 2003b. On the merits of bicameral legislatures: Policy predictability within partisan polities. *Year Book of New Political Economy* 22: 29–49.

De Vanssay, X., and Z. A. Spindler. 1994. Freedom and growth: Do constitutions matter? *Public Choice* 78: 359–72.

Diermeier, D., and R. B. Myerson. 1999. Bicameralism and its consequences for the internal organization of legislatures. *American Economic Review* 89: 1182–96.

Dixit, A., G. Grossman, and F. Gul. 2000. The dynamics of political compromise. *Journal Political Economy* 108: 531–68.

Duverger, M. 1954. *Political Parties, Their Organization and Activity in the Modern State*. London: Wiley.

Esaiasson, P., and S. Holmberg. 1996. *Representation from Above: Members of Parliament and Representative Democracy in Sweden*. Aldershot, England: Dartmouth Publishing.

Ferejohn, J. A., and B. Weingast. 1997. *The New Federalism: Can the States Be Trusted?* Stanford: Hoover Institution Press.

Field, J. 2002. *The Story of Parliament*. London: James and James.

Fording, R., and H. M. Kim. 1998. Voter ideology in western democracies, 1946–1989. *European Journal of Political Research* 33: 73–97.

Gordon, S. 1999. *Controling the State*. Cambridge: Harvard University Press.

Hammon, T., and G. J. Miller. 1987. The core and the constitution. *American Political Science Review* 81: 1155–74.

Immergut, E. M. 2002. The Swedish constitution and social democratic power: Measuring the mechanical effect of a political institution. *Scandinavian Political Studies* 25: 231–57.

Lijphart, A. 1994. *Electoral Systems and Party Systems: A Study of Twenty-seven Democracies, 1945–1990*. New York: Oxford University Press.

Mitchell, B. R. 1992. *International Historical Statistics, Europe 1750–1988*. New York: Stockton Press.

Montesquieu, C. S. [1748] 1966. *The Spirit of the Laws*. New York: Hafner.

Mueller, D. C. 2000. *Constitutional Democracy*. New York: Oxford University Press.

Patterson, S. C., and A. Mughan, eds. 1999. *Senates: Bicameralism in the Contemporary World*. Columbus: Ohio State University Press.

Persson, T., G. Roland, and G. Tabellini. 1997. Separation of powers and political accountability. *Quarterly Journal of Economics* 112: 1163–1202.

Riker, W. H. 1992. The justification of bicameralism. *International Political Science Review* 13: 101–16.

Roger, J. R. 1998. Bicameral sequence: Theory and state legislature evidence. *American Journal of Political Science* 42: 1025–60.

Shepsle, K., and B. Weingast. 1981. Structure-induced equilibrium and legislative choice. *Public Choice* 37: 503–19.

Shepsle, K., and B. Weingast. 1987. The institutional foundations of committee power. *American Political Science Review* 81: 85–104.

Steunenberg, B., D. Schmidtchen, and C. Kolboldt. 1999. Strategic power in the European Union: Evaluating the distribution of power in policy games. *Journal of Theoretical Politics* 11: 339–66.

Tsebelis, G., and J. Money. 1997. *Bicameralism.* Cambridge: Cambridge University Press.

Verney, D. V. 1957. *Parliamentary Reform in Sweden 1866–1921.* Oxford: Oxford University Press.

7 Bicameralism and Political Compromise in Representative Democracy

John Charles Bradbury and W. Mark Crain

7.1 Introduction

The bicameral legislature is a common democratic institution. About one-third of representative democracies in the world employ a bicameral legislative system; however, among developed democracies bicameralism is the dominant institutional form. In the United States, only one state (Nebraska) does not use a bicameral system. The institution of bicameralism is commonplace for several reasons. First, establishing a bicameral legislature with chambers of differing constituents has the effect of constraining transfers in fiscal policy, and may increase spending on public goods. When two chambers must agree on fiscal choices, the policies adopted will be beneficial to majorities in each chamber, which reduces the number of policies likely to survive the legislative process. In essence, adding a second legislative chamber has an impact similar to a supermajority voting rule in a unicameral legislature. Second, bicameral legislatures may increase policy stability and avoid excessive spending that may result from cycling.

In this chapter we discuss the history and origins of bicameralism as well as the theoretical reasons for its success as an institution. Recent empirical and theoretical insights regarding bicameralism tend to support the predictions made about the institution by early political economists. Section 7.2 reviews the theoretical literature on bicameralism, from the classical political economists to modern public choice. Section 7.3 examines the empirical evidence on the impact of bicameralism on fiscal policy. Section 7.4 summarizes the results and offers some concluding comments.

7.2 The History of Bicameral Theory

Classical Political Economy

Political economists in the early twenty-first century tend to favor bicameralism as a desirable legislative structure, although its roots as a virtuous institution are quite old. Many classical economists understood how unanimous agreement between differently composed protects minority interests. Montesquieu, in 1748, was the first individual to note how two chambers of conflicting interests could limit majority exploitation of minorities.

> In a state there are always some people who are distinguished by birth, wealth, or honors; but if they were mixed among the people and if they only had one voice like the others, the common liberty would be their enslavement and they would have no interest in defending it, because most of the representations would be against them. Therefore, the advantages they have in the state, which will happen if they form a body that has the right to check the enterprise of the people, as the people have the right to check theirs.
>
> Thus, legislative power will be entrusted both to the body of the nobles and to the body that will be chosen to represent the people, each of which will have assemblies and deliberations apart and have separate views and interests.

Separating the governing authority into two distinct electoral bodies gives minorities the ability and incentive to check majority tyranny, especially when interests have suspicions of each other. The architects of the US constitution were quite familiar with the work of Montesquieu and undoubtedly proposed a bicameral legislature as a solution to anticipated majority tyranny problems. Indeed, much debate over the US constitution focused on the composition of the Senate and the House of Representatives. Drawing on their past experience with a unicameral legislature under the Articles of the Confederation, the American framers feared assigning legislative power only to states or to the population as a whole would result in the tyranny of majority by small population states or large population states. The eventual compromise over constituent representation was deemed so important to the constitutional convention that it was dubbed the "Great Compromise."

Madison addressed the issue in the Federalist Papers. In Number 62 Madison states, "the improbability of sinister combinations will be in proportion to the dissimilarity of two bodies; it must be politic to distinguish them from each other by every circumstance which will consist with a due harmony in all proper measures." Again in Number 63 Madison states, "the danger [that representatives will betray the interests of the people] will be evidently greater where the whole legislative trust is lodged in the hands of one body of men, than where the concurrence of separate and dissimilar bodies is required in every public act." It is interesting to note the founders also had the results of a natural experiment among colonial legislatures. Although most colonies began operating with unicameral legislatures, all but two states (Pennsylvania and Georgia) had bicameral legislatures at time the US constitution was up for ratification.[1] John Stuart Mill also noted the importance of constituent composition of bicameral outcomes. In *On Representative Government* he comments, "If there are two Chambers, they may be of similar, or dissimilar composition. If of similar, both will obey the same influences, and whatever has a majority in one of the Houses will be likely to have it in the other."

Early Public Choice

Following the lead of classical political economists, modern public choice scholars have found bicameral chambers to be an important democratic institution for familiar and new reasons. Tullock (1959) first noted that a second legislative chamber could dampen the inherent problem of tyranny of majority in democracy in a manner similar to increasing the voting rule toward unanimity, thereby approaching a Pareto optimum. Having to satisfy the legislative preferences of two differently composed chambers raises the decision-making costs of legislatures, thereby reducing majority exploitation of the minority. Continuing this analysis, Buchanan and Tullock (1962) devote an entire chapter of *Calculus of Consent* to separating the legislative branch into two chambers. They find the most important feature of a bicameral structure is the potential to vary constituent preferences between the chambers. The effects of bicameralism are continuous and range from fiscal policy decisions identical to unicameral chambers to chambers with no overlap in legislative preferences. They explain:

> [U]nless the bases for representation are significantly different in the two houses, there would seem to be little excuse for the two house system.... [I]f the basis (sic) of representation can be made significantly different in two houses, the institution of the bicameral legislature may prove to be an effective means of securing a substantial reduction in the expected external costs of collective action without incurring as much added decision-making costs as a more inclusive [supermajority] rule would involve in a single house.

In most cases the true outcome lies between the extremes, meaning that intermediate outcomes result from "the overlapping of the interest-group coalitions in each house." Buchanan and Tullock continue, "If the members of each house were elected from the same constituencies . . . , then the two houses would be identically constituted, and the situation, from our present standpoint, would not differ from a one house legislature." Curiously, contemporaries of Buchanan and Tullock largely ignored or accepted this analysis of bicameralism, since bicameralism received little scrutiny compared to other issues discussed in *Calculus of Consent*. In an early examination of legislatures Stigler (1976) also references the idea that constituent differences between chambers affects policy outcomes. He states "if upper houses were constituted on exactly the same basis of representation as lower houses, the former would provide only the checks on lower houses that come from sampling variability—which should be extremely small in such large samples." In *The Constitution of Liberty*, Hayek devotes a chapter to a discussion of the US constitution and the debate among the founders over its content. Specifically, he praises the use of bicameral chambers by the founders, citing Lord Acton's assertion that a second legislative chamber in the United States "has been found essential for security for freedom in every genuine democracy." In turn, Hayek seizes this idea for his own constitution.

Modern Public Choice

In their important book on bicameralism, Tsebelis and Money (1997) reiterate the argument that agreement between chambers will be less in chambers with differing preferences. "[T]he *political* dimension of bicameralism recognizes that different interests or preferences may be expressed in the two legislative bodies. Where preferences differ, conflict between the two houses arises over the legislative outcome." In sum, the general presumption echoed in all of these statements is that bicameralism serves a purposeful function in democracy only if the chambers are composed of constituent bases of support that differ from one another.

Though diverse interests can be represented in the same unicameral body, it does not have the same limiting effect on policy outcomes as separating interests into separate veto players. More formally, Persson, Roland, and Tabellini (1997) theoretically demonstrate that agreement between chambers is more difficult than agreement within a single chamber because the separate chambers constitute a bilateral monopoly over legislative production. Trades among members of different chambers can occur only at the logrolling equilibriums of both chambers, and the bargaining problems inherent to bilateral monopoly hold. Because either chamber can veto the other, constituent homogeneity affects the extent of the bargaining difficulties. Inter-house trades are subject to intra-house preferences and chamber-specific institutions, making logrolling across chambers difficult. A legislator seeking support from fellow members within his or her own chamber can make trades to achieve the desired outcome. The equilibrium outcome in each house will result where the gains from logrolling are exhausted. However, the interaction between the chambers to reach an agreement alters this analysis. Any attempt by individual representatives to make deals across chambers would be unsuccessful because it disrupts their own chamber's logrolling equilibrium. Such deviations from own-chamber equilibria would be vetoed by intra-house preferences, a result derived in several papers.[2] For example, Diermeier and Myerson (1999) note "legislative chambers in a serial bicameral legislature are more like monopolistic producers of complementary goods than like duopolistic producers of a common good." Though each chamber has its own preferences for policy, political returns are subject to the preferences of the other.[3]

If the composition of chambers leads to differing equilibrium policy preferences, these differences can affect legislative outcomes. For example, similarity in the median legislators implies that the chambers will be more likely to agree on the level and composition of spending drawn from the common pool of government funds. Both chambers must agree on fiscal outcomes; thus bicameral chambers will be more likely to agree on which constituents to tax or subsidize as the constituencies across chambers become more similar. In other words, similarity between the two chambers facilitates inter-cameral agreements (Crain 1979).

As an extreme illustration, suppose the two chambers in a legislature consist of identical constituencies. In this case the policy preferences of the median legislator in each chamber will be identical; thus a 51 percent majority could tax the remaining 49 percent of the population to satisfy majority preferences. When the chambers' constituencies are not identical, the preferences of the majorities in the two chambers diverge. Figure 7.1 shows the difference in constituency homogeneity in two bicameral legislatures using Venn diagrams. In both diagrams

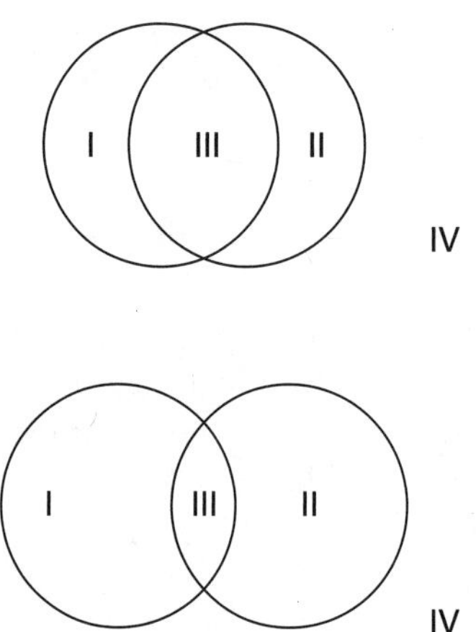

Figure 7.1
(*Top*) constituent homogeneity; (*bottom*) more constituent homogeneity

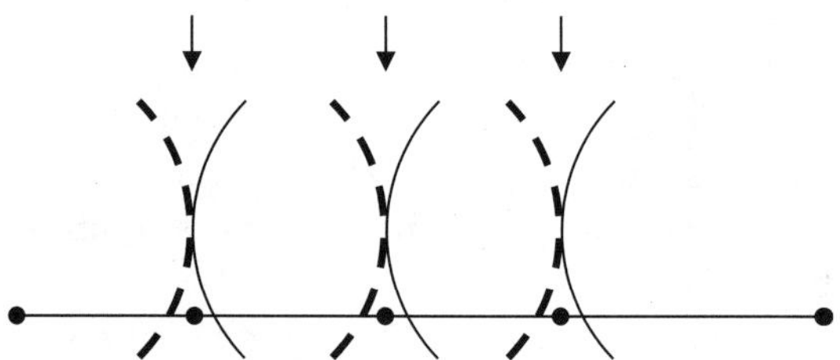

Figure 7.2
Asymmetric power

areas I and II represent the nonoverlapping constituencies of the majority coalitions in the separate chambers. Area III represents the overlap of majority coalitions in the chambers, and area IV represents the rest of the polity that is not represented in the majority coalitions of either chamber. In figure 7.2b the policy preference overlap of constituencies (III) is small compared to the overlap in figure 7.2a; that is, the constituent homogeneity across chambers in the former legislature is less than that in the latter. Additionally the greater the overlap, the larger is the nonrepresented tax base (IV), from which representatives can extract funds. For example, a 41 percent overlap in constituents means that the 10 percent of constituents needed to obtain intra-chamber majorities in the separate bodies will differ; therefore the maximum amount of wealth the bicameral legislature can transfer will be 20 percent less than the amount extracted by a unicameral chamber or identical chambers. To obtain a 51 percent majority in either chamber, each overlapping constituency of 41 percent must attract another 10 percent of constituents to form a majority coalition. Because agreement must be reached for any legislation to pass the legislature, neither chamber can tax the full 49 percent of the minority. Otherwise, one chamber would veto the other. This reduces the total amount of redistributional resources in IV from 49 percent (if either chamber were the unicameral authority) to 29 percent of the polity.

Polities typically design bicameral chambers to represent different constituencies, and this creates differences in policy preferences between the chambers. Different geographic or demographic districts often compose the chambers. In many cases chambers employ differing electoral or appointment procedures to fill the seats.[4] Different constituent preferences means that chambers will be less likely to agree on which groups to tax and subsidize in the legislative process, and power asymmetries affect the ability of each chamber to institute its own legislative preference. This constrains the level of constituent-specific spending below the amount each chamber would prefer individually.

A second reason bicameralism may improve legislative outcomes is stability. Riker (1992) argues the instability of democracy may induce current majorities to exploit their present position. As a result of rotating majorities, current majorities seek to offset predicted future transfer losses by passing inefficiently high levels of spending.[5] A unicameral chamber with a supermajority rule offers a similar protection, except on single-dimensional issues that would always pass under a simple majority rule. Bicameral legislatures have the unique ability to narrow the choice set on multidimensional issues that will cycle to Condorcet winners, while not preventing stable single-dimensional policies from passing. Empirically, legislative stability ought to limit spending on redistributive issues without limiting spending on public goods.

7.3 Empirical Findings

Two empirical predictions arise from the analysis above. First, bicameral legislative chambers will engage in less "unproductive" transfer spending than unicameral chambers. The requirement of unanimity of the chambers is analogous to adopting a supermajority rule in a unicameral chamber. Second, fiscal policy decisions made across bicameral chambers ought to vary with constituent homogeneity. As chamber preferences become more similar, constituents are more likely to agree on government consumption choices and thereby increasing the amount of government spending in certain areas. Two studies have examined these empirical predictions.

Bradbury and Crain (2001) use the "law of $1/n$" to analyze the influence of bicameral chambers on fiscal policy. The law of $1/n$, developed by Weingast, Shepsle, and Johnsen (1981), suggest that government spending is positively associated with the number of seats in a legislative chamber.[6] The fiscal inefficiency of the law of $1/n$ results from the dispersion of the tax burden across many legislative districts. In the simplest form of the model, representatives allocate funds from a common tax base. Each representative district contributes an equal share to the tax base, and constituents demand district-specific spending where the benefits equal the costs. The benefits of a district-specific project are fully captured by the district. However, because the tax burden is evenly distributed across all districts, each district bears only a fraction of the cost of any parochial project equal to $1/n$, where n is the number of representative districts. As the number of representative seats in the legislature increases the constituent-specific cost burden of any project declines, thereby lowering the marginal cost of any parochial project to the district. As the cost falls with increasing legislative districts the demand for publicly funded projects will increase. Driven by the demand for reelection and assuming the norm of universalism, where representatives support each other's specific projects, the logrolling process generates spending on parochial goods above the efficient level. In sum, constituents receive parochial goods at a price greater than they value those goods. Attempts to oppose unilaterally a parochial project in any given district will fail, because constituents will still have to pay for the parochial projects in other districts.

Theoretically, the law of $1/n$ applies to a unicameral legislature. Representatives must only logroll among the members of a single chamber to allocate these parochial goods. Adding a second chamber to the decision-making process can have an important effect. Two dissimilar groups of representatives in separate chambers must reach consensus for a fiscal policy goes into effect. As discussed above, differing electoral constituencies limits the area of agreement over which constituents to tax and subsidize. This suggests that spending in a bicameral structure will be less than the level that each chamber would prefer if it were the single chamber. As Perrson, Roland, and Tabellini (1997) note, bargaining across chambers is much more costly than bargaining within chambers. Using a sample of bicameral and unicameral countries Bradbury and Crain (2001) examine the $1/n$ effect in both types of legislatures. The results indicate that bicameralism dampens the marginal impact of seats in bicameral chambers relative to unicameral chambers by up to one-third. This is important considering that the spending generated by the law of $1/n$ is undesirable.

Bradbury and Crain (2001) also note that the presence of a divided legislative body changes the outcome from the unicameral setting for a second reason: asymmetries in legislative power. If one chamber has more political power than the other, outcomes may be asymmetrically favorable to the stronger house. In this case the policy preference of one chamber is more relevant than that of the other chamber. The bias in power between chambers results from the proximity of a chamber's median preference to the status quo, or fallback position, as figure 7.2 illustrates. U and L represent the median logrolling outcomes for two chambers of a bicameral legislature.[7] The model is one-dimensional, because, as Tsebelis and Money (1997) demonstrate, bicameralism reduces the locus of agreement in multidimensional policy space to a single dimension. S^*, S^U, and S^L represent the reversion, or status quo policy position, if the chambers cannot reach agreement under symmetric power (S^*), asymmetric power that favors chamber U (S^U), and asymmetric power that favors chamber L (S^L). The solid (L) and dashed (U) curves are indifference curves, indicating an increase in utility as the status quo fallback position approaches the chamber's median. Given S^U, failure to reach an agreement means that the upper chamber (U) suffers less regret than the lower chamber (L); reversion to the status quo results in a smaller deviation from U's preferred outcome than from L's preferred outcome. This allows the upper chamber to best the lower chamber in inter-cameral negotiations, and the outcome moves closer to U than L on ray UL in figure 7.2. The closer S to the chamber median, the more power the chamber holds in inter-cameral negotiations.

As seen in this example, the location of the status quo policy position in relation to each chamber's preferred outcome determines the relative bargaining power of each chamber. If the fallback position is S^L, then the lower chamber has greater bargaining power than the upper chamber. Consistent bias toward one chamber is an exogenous function of institutional procedures or constitutional rules that bestow asymmetric power. In the absence of an institutional rule that grants greater advantage to one chamber over another, the power bias should vary randomly over time, as determined by the constituency preferences of the two chambers. This implies that under repeated, multiperiod inter-chamber bargaining, both chambers exert influence over the outcome in any single period. The chamber that has agenda-setting power in one period realizes that the other chamber will possess agenda setting power in a future period. In other words, absent any constitutional rule that yields agenda power, a cooperative strategy is appropriate in inter-chamber negotiations. Under such a situation the fallback position becomes S^*.

The institutional design of most national legislatures gives the greatest amount of power to the lower chamber (Tsebelis and Money 1997). Thus in the law of $1/n$ framework the marginal impact of a seat in the lower chamber should be greater than in the upper chamber. Consistent with this prediction Bradbury and Crain (2001) finds lower chambers to be more powerful than upper chambers in affecting $1/n$ spending.

In a second study Bradbury and Crain (2002) examine difference in fiscal policy choices across American state legislatures. Rather than viewing differences in fiscal policy choices between unicameral and bicameral legislatures, this study measures bicameralism as a measure of constituent homogeneity. That is, the similarity of constituent preferences between chambers facilitates agreement. As figure 7.1 demonstrates, increasing similarity among constituents across chambers will tend to facilitate agreements on redistributive policies, while dissimilar constituencies suppress such agreements. Using information about constituent preferences in each state the Bradbury and Crain (2002) study examines the effect of constituent differences between chambers on fiscal policy. States with less similar chamber preferences are de facto more "bicameral" than states that have more similar chamber preferences. This study uses chamber differences in the median representative in four demographic measures to proxy constituent differences: average household income, the percentage of households with incomes greater than $50,000, the percentage of households receiving social security benefits, and the percentage of constituents employed in the manufacturing sector. As the difference increases between the median representatives in the two chambers the preferences over fiscal policy will predictably increase. The results support the notion that more similar legislative chambers are more likely to prefer welfare spending and other fiscal policies that redistribute income than dissimilar chambers. Additionally legislatures with dissimilar chambers are more willing to spend for public good–type programs, such as education and highways. This finding indicates that the constituent homogeneity aspect of bicameralism does appear to affect legislative outcomes in a predictable manner. Separating differing interests between chambers is likely to reduce transfer spending and narrow government spending choices to public goods that are beneficial to all interests in the polity.

It is also important to note that the results are consistent and not distinct from Riker's stability hypothesis. It may be that some of the measured effects on fiscal policy outcomes result from increased stability of legislative decisions. But this is largely irrelevant from a policy standpoint. Regardless of the reason separating chambers into diverse interests has a beneficial impact on fiscal policy choices. And it is not clear if the constituent homogeneity and legislative stability effects are unrelated. They are clearly intertwined, as greater constituent homogeneity ought to strengthen legislative stability by limiting possible opportunities for cycling and its harmful effects.

7.4 Conclusion

Classical political economists such as the American Founding Fathers embraced the institution of bicameralism based on a powerful intuition about its ability to protect minority interests. Modern scholars using rigorous theoretical models and empirical techniques support their intuitive analysis. Separating the legislative body into two distinct chambers acts to constrain elected representatives and help them compromise on fiscal policy in a manner that benefits the "general welfare" of constituents. Having two houses composed of differing interests provides a check on majority exploitation of minorities similar to supermajority voting rules. By adding a veto player to the legislative process, the potential for redistributive policies falls. With the reduction of redistributive opportunities, legislators are then more likely to concentrate on the production of efficient public goods as opposed to transfers. Additionally bicameral legislatures offer stability in policy choices. As Riker (1992) postulates, democratic instability can lead to increased demand for transfers; hence adding a second legislative chamber enhances policy stability and, in turn, reduces the demand for transfers. While current studies have not distinguished clearly between the constituent homogeneity and the legislative stability effects of bicameralism, these studies have verified the predicted outcome of reduced transfer spending that is consistent with both theories.

Notes

1. Tsebelis and Rasch (1995) and Tsebelis and Money (1997) provide excellent histories of bicameralism in the United States.

2. Also see Brennan and Hamlin (1992), Cox and McKelvey (1984), Hammond and Miller (1987), and Tsebelis and Rasch (1995).

3. Some of the difficulties of getting agreement between two chambers is circumvented by the introduction of conference committees that have been given agenda control powers (up or down votes on conference reports). This issue is raised by Shepsle and Weingast (1989).

4. For an empirical examination legislators elected through proportional representation, see Bradbury (2000).

5. See the discussion in Alesina and Tabellini (1990).

6. For empirical tests of the model, see Gilligan and Matsusaka (1995, 2001), Baqir (2002), and Bradbury and Stephenson (2003).

7. Here "median" refers to the preference of the median legislator within a chamber, which is not to be confused with the preference on the median voter in the polity. Granted the existence of the law of $1/n$ and the existence of parochial logrolling, the median legislator will support an inefficiently high level of spending.

References

Alesina, A., and G. Tabellini. 1990. Voting on budget deficits. *American Economic Review* 80: 37–49.

Baqir, R. 2002. Districting and overspending. *Journal of Political Economy* 110: 1318–54.

Bradbury, J. C. 2000. The political economy of legislative organization: An empirical analysis. Ph.D. dissertation. George Mason University.

Bradbury, J. C., and W. M. Crain. 2001. Legislative organization and government spending: Cross-country evidence. *Journal of Public Economics* 82: 309–25.

Bradbury, J. C., and W. M. Crain. 2002. Bicameralism legislatures and fiscal policy. *Southern Economic Journal* 68: 646–59.

Bradbury, J. C., and E. F. Stephenson. 2003. Local government structure and public expenditures. *Public Choice* 115: 185–98.

Brennan, G., and A. Hamlin. 1992. Bicameralism and majoritarian equilibrium. *Public Choice* 74: 169–79.

Buchanan, J. M., and G. Tullock. 1962. *The Calculus of Consent*. Ann Arbor: University of Michigan Press.

Cox, G. W., and R. D. McKelvey. 1984. A ham sandwich theorem for general measures. *Social Choice and Welfare* 1: 75–83.

Crain, W. M. 1979. Cost and output in the legislative firm. *Journal of Legal Studies* 8: 607–21.

Diermeier, D., and R. B. Myerson. 1999. Bicameralism and its consequences for the internal organization of legislatures. *American Economic Review* 89: 1182–96.

Gilligan, T. W., and J. G. Matsusaka. 1995. Deviations from constituent interests: The role of legislative structure and political parties in the states. *Economic Inquiry* 33: 383–401.

Gilligan, T. W., and J. G. Matsusaka. 2001. Fiscal policy, legislature size, and political parties: Evidence from state and local governments in the first half of the 20th century. *National Tax Journal* 54: 57–82.

Hamilton, A., J. Madison, and J. Jay. 1992. *The Federalist Papers*. Cutchogue, NY: Buccaneer Books.

Hammond, T. H., and G. J. Miller. 1987. The core of the Constitution. *American Political Science Review* 81: 1155–74.

Hayek, F. A. 1979. *Law, Legislation, and Liberty, Vol. 3: The Political Order of a Free People*. Chicago: University of Chicago Press.

Montesquieu, C. de Secondat. 1989. *The Spirit of the Laws*. Cambridge: Cambridge University Press.

Perrson, T., G. Roland, and G. Tabellini. 1997. Separation of powers and political accountability. *Quarterly Journal of Economics* 112: 1163–1203.

Riker, W. H. 1992. The justification of bicameralism. *International Political Science Review* 13: 101–16.

Shepsle, K., and B. Weingast. 1989. Penultimate power: Conference committees in the legislative process. In M. Fiorina and D. Rohde, eds., *Home Style, Washington Work*. Ann Arbor: University of Michigan Press, pp. 199–219.

Stigler, G. J. 1976. The sizes of legislatures. *Journal of Legal Studies* 5: 17–34.

Tsebelis, G., and J. Money. 1997. *Bicameralism*. Cambridge: Cambridge University Press.

Tsebelis, G., and B. Rasch. 1995. Patterns of bicameralism. In H. Doering, ed., *Parliaments and Majority Rule in Western Europe*. New York: St. Martin's.

Tullock, G. 1959. Some problems of majority voting. *Journal of Political Economy* 67: 571–79.

Weingast, B., K. Shepsle, and C. Johnsen. 1981. The political economy of benefits and costs: A neoclassical approach to distributive politics. *Journal of Political Economy* 89: 642–64.

III Decentralization and Federalism

8 Federalism: A Constitutional Perspective

Dennis C. Mueller

One of the key decisions that a community must face when writing its constitution is whether or not to structure itself as a federation. Many benefits have been claimed for federalist institutions. Given these, it is somewhat paradoxical that we observe so few countries in the world that possess all of the attributes of a strong federalist structure. There are two possible explanations for this paradox. First, there could be many disadvantages associated with federalism, so many that for most countries the disadvantages outweigh the advantages. Thus full-blown federalism could be rare because in fact it is undesirable.

The second possible explanation for federalism's rarity is that it is somehow inherently unstable. When it is chosen, it fails to survive, not because of any fundamental difficulty in the outcomes it produces, but because of the existence of forces in a democracy that undermine it. In this chapter, I argue that it is the latter characteristic of federalism that accounts for its rarity.

The chapter proceeds as follows: It begins with a discussion of the advantages of federalist institutions in a democracy. Following in section 8.2 it takes up the issue of how to go about designing these institutions from a constitutional perspective. In section 8.3 the issue is the disadvantages of federalism. This discussion, like that of the advantages of federalism, confines itself to the theoretical objections that have been raised against federalism. As always, the question of whether the advantages of a set of institutions outweigh their disadvantages must be settled empirically. The empirical literature on federalism, as it pertains to this question, is discussed in section 8.4. In section 8.5, I attempt to make the point that direct democracy is a natural accompaniment to federalism, and that both are likely to function better if they are combined. In section 8.6, I address the issue of how to preserve federalist institutions from being absorbed and corrupted by the central government. The chapter closes with a brief set of conclusions.

8.1 Why Federalism?

The normative rationale for the state in the public choice literature is that it is a low transaction cost institution for eliminating certain market failures and thereby achieving Pareto optimality (Mueller 2003, ch. 2). The two main categories of market failures in the public economics literature are public goods and externalities. The definition of public goods can be interpreted broadly to include police protection and a judicial system to enforce the rule of law. Both types of market failures implicitly introduce a spatial dimension to the polity. Once a public good is provided to one member of the community, it must (may) be provided at zero marginal cost to all other members. Examples of public goods are police protection (where the verb "must" is appropriate), and a bridge (where the verb "may" is appropriate). A police force only protects the citizens within a circumscribed area, however, and a bridge is of value only to those living near enough to wish to cross it. Different public goods can be consumed by different geographically dispersed groups—national defense by the entire nation, fire protection only by those within a small radius of a fire station.

The same is true for externalities. The pollution spewed into a lake by a factory located on its shores harms only those with access to the lake. Global warming affects everyone on the face of the earth. Thus the geographic dimensions of the spillovers from public goods and externalities lead naturally to the recommendation that different sets of governmental institutions be charged with the responsibility for dealing with different sets of market failures (Oates 1972, 1999). In a democracy such an organizational structure can take one of three forms:

1. A unitary, decentralized state with regional and local departments responsible to the central government, which in turn is responsible to the citizens. Elections serve the purpose of deciding the identities of the officials in the central government, they in turn appoint officials lower down in the administrative bureaucracy.

2. A federalist structure. Several levels of government exist, say, central, regional, and local, with each level having its own separately elected democratic bodies, and with each responsible for the efficient resolution of a particular set of market failures.

3. A confederate structure. At the most central level of government, citizens are not represented directly but indirectly through *national*

governments. These national governments can in turn be organized as either unitary states or federations. In this chapter we will not consider the possibility of a confederation any further.[1]

In principle, a single, unitary state can provide all public goods and optimally deal with all other market failures even in a geographically very large and diverse country. This is quite easy, for example, if the preferences of individuals for regional and local public goods are the same in all parts of the country. The level of police protection and trash collection that is optimal in one local community will then be optimal in all, and the central government will have a fairly easy time determining the levels of regional and local government services that are optimal. Even with substantial preference heterogeneity across communities, a unitary state may be optimal *if* there are zero transaction costs to gathering information on individual preferences for regional and local public goods. In any situation that is not Pareto optimal, it is possible to make some voters somewhere in the country better off without making anyone else worse off. Vote-maximizing politicians in a unitary state would not pass up such a costless opportunity to win more votes. But the zero transaction costs assumption is untenable in a large and diverse country. The costs of determining the preferences of citizens in each local jurisdiction for trash collection, police protection, and so on, through a national election would be enormous, even in a country with a fairly small and homogeneous population like Sweden. Thus the normative justification for federalism—as for the state itself—becomes that of minimizing the transaction costs of gathering information on voter preferences for public services (Mueller 2003, ch. 10). Federalism becomes the optimal institutional structure for any country of moderate size and preference heterogeneity.[2]

8.2 How Federalism?

Once the decision is made to have a federalist system, the next question concerns its optimal design. How many levels of government should there be? What should be the boundaries at each lower level? What expenditure responsibilities should be assigned to each level? What revenue sources should be assigned to each level? What should be the form of representative government at each level? These are difficult and interrelated questions, and no single set of answers will be optimal for all countries. Again the answers will depend in part on the nature and scale of transaction costs.

Quite possibly no two market failures have exactly the same geographic spillovers. A playground serves a small neighborhood, a fire station a somewhat larger area, a police station a perhaps still larger area. Although defining a separate democratic government for each market failure would be a possible response to these differences in geographic spillovers, the number of governments needed would become intractably large. A compromise becomes optimal with several government services assigned to each level of government, no two of which having identically contiguous spillovers.[3] The result is usually a multitier structure with three, possibly four tiers being the norm (central, regional, and local). In some cases the lower levels of government have considerable autonomy as in the United States, where the regional governments (states) have their own constitutions and cities their own charters.

The assignment of expenditure responsibilities ought to be made on the basis of the dimensions of geographic spillovers of each market failure addressed by the state. Once responsibilities for expenditures have been assigned, the next step is to assign revenue sources. Since the main purpose for creating a federalist state is to facilitate the revelation of preferences for public services, the choice of revenue sources should be made with this same goal in mind. The most obvious way to do this is to establish the Wicksellian connection—each public expenditure should be coupled with a tax to finance it so that the voter knows exactly how much she is paying for it (Wicksell 1896). Establishing such a link will make it easier for the voter to decide whether the government is providing the optimal amount of the public service. Establishing such a link in a federalist system implies further that each level of government have the fiscal capacity to finance all of its expenditure obligations so that voters at every level of government can assess the performance of their elected representatives at the level in question with respect to the amounts and qualities of government services they are getting for the taxes that they are paying.

A yet further implication is that a federalist state should make limited use of intergovernmental grants. Such grants make it difficult for voters to assess the costs of different programs. If, for example, a third of a local government's budget is funded by a grant from the central government, a citizen may mistakenly believe that her taxes at the local level pay for all of its programs. Underestimating the true costs of the local programs, she may favor greater expenditures by the local government than are optimal. Even if she recognizes that some of the local budget is financed by the central government and thus that her taxes to the central government are paying for local programs, it will be difficult for her to assess how much of her tax payments to the central government are going to for the local government's expenditures. Thus, at a minimum, grants from the central government to local governments reduce citizens' ability to monitor and thus to control their representatives in government.[4]

Thus, in an ideal federalist system, every person who benefits from the programs of a given political unit will pay taxes to that unit to pay for the benefits, and will be a citizen of it, and able to select the persons or parties that decide on the government's tax and expenditure programs.

8.3 Problems of Federalism

Several problems can arise in a federalist state that must be taken into consideration in the design of such a state and in its operation. In this section these problems are briefly discussed. In the next section we examine the empirical literature that tries to measure just how serious each potential problem is.

Fiscal Inequality

If public goods are normal goods, then the quantity demanded of them increases with the income of the community. If the quantity demanded is determined by the median voter, then it increases with the income of this voter. Communities with high incomes will demand, and presumably be supplied, greater quantities of public goods than low-income communities. Such inequalities may be deemed unacceptable when they appear for public programs like education. That is, everyone in a nation may agree that every child should be able to obtain an education of a minimum quality. If some communities are too poor to provide such an education, a Pareto improvement may be forthcoming by transferring funds from members of rich communities to the poorer communities so as to increase the capacity of the poorer communities to finance these minimum levels of public services.[5]

Geographic Externalities

The consumption or production activities of one community may have positive or negative external effects on another. If, for example, an upstream community dumps sewage into a river, it may adversely affect a downstream community. Such externalities can in general be resolved in a Pareto-optimal fashion by Coasian bargaining between the communities. The downstream community offers the upstream community a bribe to reduce the amount of sewage dumped into the river. Intergovernmental grants are again required to achieve a Pareto-optimal allocation of resources, but now they are between governments at a local or regional level rather than from the central government to lower levels. Only in the case where the number of externalities across local communities becomes so large and complex as to make Coasian bargaining among communities prohibitively costly do intervention and grants from the central government become optimal.

Migration Externalities

When local governments offer different bundles of tax and expenditure combinations, individuals may respond to these differences by migrating to those communities that provide the best match for their preferences. Such migration can improve allocative efficiency à la Tiebout (1956) and is an important justification for creating a federalist system. But migration can also bring about certain externalities that lead to Pareto inefficiencies. These externalities are of three types: crowding, fiscal capacity, and redistributive externalities.

Crowding and Fiscal Capacity Externalities

When someone moves from community *A* to *B*, she considers only her level of utility in the two communities. She moves if the expected utility in *A* is higher than in *B*. Her movement can adversely affect the existing residents in *A*, however, by leading to overcrowding in that community. Her movement could, alternatively or in addition, have an adverse effect on the residents of *B* by lowering its tax base. There are two possible ways to avoid these negative externalities from migration. One option again relies on the central government's power to tax and transfer wealth. It can levy taxes on community *A* and transfer funds to *B* in sufficient quantities to produce the optimal distribution of population between the two communities. The alternative solution vests the power to tax and subsidize with the local communities. For example, community *A* could effectively tax immigration into it by making large charges for new water and sewage hookups, levying high taxes on new construction sites and so on.[6]

Redistributive Externalities

Assume that everyone in a community of nine has the same utility function defined over private goods and a single public good, *G*. Let the community of nine be divided into three smaller communities, *A*, *B*, and *C*, each of which contains three people. Assume further that three of the nine people have incomes of 100, three have incomes of 200, and the remaining three have incomes of 300. Now assume that the three smaller communities initially contain one person with an income of 100, another with an income of 200 and the third person has an income of 300. If the quantity of *G* in each community is chosen using the simple majority rule, then the same quantity will be chosen in each community, namely the quantity favored by the median voter with an income of 200. If the individuals are allowed to move among the communities, a re-sorting can be expected with all persons with an income of 300 in one community, all with an income of 200 in the second, and the three with an income of 100 in the remaining community. It can easily be shown that such a re-sorting will result in a Pareto improvement in the allocation of resources in the three communities (Mueller 2003, ch. 9). Nevertheless, the three individuals with incomes of 100 will be consuming less of the public good than before and are likely to be made worse off by the re-sorting. Thus a situation that was possibly deemed acceptable on equity grounds in the initial situation might become unacceptable because of sorting by income.

8.4 Empirical Evidence Related to Federalism

A considerable amount of research has tried to measure the extent to which the hypothetical problems listed above exist in practice. In this section we review this evidence.

Federalism and Allocative Efficiency

The Flypaper Effect

Perhaps no single hypothesis in the literature on federalism has more empirical support than the prediction that intergovernmental grants lead to an expansion of the public sector. In a literature dating back some forty years countless studies have established that a local government generally spends a far larger fraction of an unconditional grant from a higher level of government than its citizens would appear to consider optimal.[7] The additional amounts spent often exceed the optimal amounts by factors of three, four, and more. As always when a controversial hypothesis receives empirical support, the findings of the flypaper literature have been challenged.[8] But the overwhelming weight of the evidence still supports the conclusion that the use of block intergovernmental grants leads to an expansion of the size of local government budgets beyond that favored by citizens of the local community.

Government Size

Taking into account only the flypaper effect, we might predict that the size of the total government sector would be larger in a federalist system than in a centralized one. Offsetting the effects of intergovernmental grants that can conceal government expenditures from the view of citizens are the effects of greater overall transparency in a federalist system, competition across governments at a given level, and therefore greater overall accountability of elected officials in a federalist system. Once again, the question of whether the government sector should be larger or smaller in a federalist system requires an empirical answer.

In a recent study Gemmell, Morrissey, and Pinar (2002) showed how the creation of a close link between taxes and expenditures at the local level of government can increase voter awareness of the costs of government services and thereby greater government accountability. This happened in Great Britain in 1990 when the highly controversial poll (head) tax was introduced.

Unfortunately, empirically identifying a causal link between the full set of federalist institutions and governmental efficiency and accountability is difficult owing to the scant number of countries that are true federalisms. To my mind, there are only five true federalist states in the world—Australia, Brazil, Canada, Switzerland, and the United States. Given its different state of development, Brazil is difficult to compare with the others. Within the set of rich, developed countries of the world, Australia, Switzerland, and the United States have somewhat smaller government sectors—that is under 40 percent of GDP. Canada's government sector is about average in size (around 50 percent of GDP).

Most studies that claim to test for the impact of federalism on government size instead compute an index of decentralization and test to see whether government size is inversely related to decentralization. In general, government size has not been found to be significantly related to measures of decentralization.[9] Recent work by Jonathan Rodden, however, has established a significant relationship between the strength of a country's federalist institutions and various measures of government performance. His work clearly reveals that the full benefits from a federalist structure can only be obtained when all of the components of a strong federalist structure are present. In countries where lower level governments have the authority to set both the levels of their expenditures and their taxes, government deficits are smaller, as is total government spending. When local governments are heavily dependent on grants from the central government, they are more prone to run deficits, and the country has a higher rate of inflation.[10]

Rodden's results linking the size of intergovernmental grants to government deficits reinforce the findings from studies of the flypaper effect of intergovernmental grants. Not only are local governments prone to spend more money when they receive grants from higher levels of government, but they are also more prone to run deficits in the expectation that the central government will bail them out. Limiting intergovernmental grants to those necessary for achieving intergovernmental fiscal equivalence would produce both greater accountability of local governments and greater intergovernmental competition and thereby better local governmental outcomes.[11]

Effects of Migration

Migration in a federalist system should have the positive effect of bringing about a better match between citizen preferences for local public goods and taxes, but it may have the negative side effects of producing crowding in particularly attractive communities, and may worsen the effects of income inequality by resorting citizens by income. Casual observation suggests that migration into some communities exceeds the optimal level producing pollution, traffic congestion and related problems. Here the world's largest cities—Buenos Aires, London, Los Angeles, Mexico City—come readily to mind. In surveys of the best places in the world to live, these once great cities now generally are placed behind smaller cities like Zurich, Vancouver, and Vienna. More systematic evidence exists related to the other two consequences of migration.

For the Tiebout process to work, there must be an array of alternative communities from which a citizen can choose, and sufficiently low mobility costs to make a move to a "better community" welfare enhancing. These conditions are more likely to be fulfilled in large urban areas than in small rural ones, as a citizen can change local communities without changing jobs or moving a great distance from family and friends. One expects to find a greater alignment of preferences for local government programs in large urban communities, therefore. This prediction has been confirmed in several studies, which report lower levels of dispersion of voter demands for education and other local expenditures in large urban communities (Munley 1982; Gramlich and Rubinfeld 1982). Gramlich and Rubinfeld (1982) also report a higher percentage of citizens in the Detroit metropolitan area who were satisfied with the level of expenditures of their local government than for citizens in rural areas of Michigan.

Numerous studies have reported that citizens' decisions to move from a community are affected by the government expenditures and taxes in both the community that they are leaving and the community into which they are moving.[12] Perceptions of problems in a community—a signal of a governmental failure—also causes people to move (Orbell and Uno 1972). Thus the existence of unhappiness over expenditure/tax combinations at the local level, or over the results of these expenditures, does lead to migration to other communities when more desirable communities exist and can be entered at relatively low cost.

There is also considerable evidence that migration re-sorts people into communities of more homogeneous incomes. The most ambitious and convincing study of this phenomenon is Gary Miller's (1981) study of the effects of migration between 1950 and 1970 in Los Angeles County. Local communities were significantly more homogeneous in terms of both income and race in 1970 than in 1950, and this was particularly true for communities that came into existence over the 20-year period. Corroborative evidence for the Boston area has been supplied by Grubb (1982). Nechyba and Walsh (2004) provide an excellent discussion of Tiebout sorting with numerous references to the recent literature. Although this literature seems to provide overwhelming evidence of sorting by race, income, and other characteristics, Rhode and Strumpf (2003) have recently presented evidence of *increasing* heterogeneity across communities. They cite survey evidence indicating that local public services and taxes are cited by only 5 percent of people changing residences as a reason for their moving. Location choices appear to be more influenced by the desire to be near where one works or friends and family. An additional factor affecting location choices in recent years is the spread of two-wage-earner families.

Mimicking Behavior

A closer alignment between citizen preferences and government tax/expenditure programs can evolve over time even when citizens do not migrate from one community to another, if local governments *imitate* the policies of their neighbors. Ladd (1992), Case, Rosen, and Hines (1993), and Besley and Case (1995) provide evidence implying local governmental imitating of neighboring governments' policies in the United States. Similar findings for Belgium have been reported by Heyndels and Vuchelen (1998), for Germany by Büttner (1999, 2001), and for Switzerland by Schaltegger and Küttel (2002). This evidence of imitation can be interpreted in two ways. First, it can imply that a successful innovation in the public sector by one local government is copied by others, for example, as a new source of tax revenue. The competitive pressure to win elections within each polity leads politicians to imitate the successful policies of their neighboring governments. The second interpretation is that the citizens observe the policies of neighboring communities and demand similar policies from their elected representatives. These two interpretations obviously complement one another and suggest that the multitude of different governments and different sets of governmental outcomes in a federalist state leads to the same benefits from competition that one expects in markets with large numbers of sellers.

8.5 Federalism and Direct Democracy

One expects that the kinds of benefits from competition across governments described in the previous subsection will be greater, the more effective the democratic institutions of a country are. The easier it is for voters to express their preferences and thereby influence their government, the closer the correspondence between a citizen's preferences and government policies. This reasoning suggests that democracy will function best when voters can express their preferences directly. Direct democracy is the oldest form of democratic government, and by some is still regarded as the *best* form of government.[13]

Direct democracy of the type where all citizens meet to debate and decide the issues can only take place in communities of small size. Thus there is a link between direct democracy and federalism. The town-meeting form of direct democracy is *only possible* if the polity has been broken up into politically autonomous units with some being of, say, no more than five or ten thousand inhabitants, so that all citizens physically can assemble together. Thus town-meeting democracy is only feasible in a federalist system.

When most people speak of direct democracy today, they do not mean town-meetings but rather citizen initiatives and referenda.[14] Although these can in principle be held in countries of any size, to place an initiative on a ballot requires gathering the signatures of a substantial fraction of the population, say, 10 percent, as it is in general infeasible to successfully organize signature drives in very large polities. Thus this form of direct democracy is more likely to be effective in a federalist system.

The number of truly federalist countries in the world is small, and the number that makes much use of institutions of direct democracy is smaller still. In this section we briefly review the evidence for the two countries making the most use of direct democracy—Switzerland and the United States.

Direct Democracy in Switzerland

Much of the public choice literature suggests that the government sector in a democracy will be bigger than is optimal from the perspective of the citizenry. Thus the more responsive governments are to the preferences of the citizens, the smaller the expected size of the government sector. Evidence from the public choice literature implies both a closer fit of government policies to citizens' preferences and overall smaller sized governments when institutions of direct democracy are present. Several studies have confirmed this result. One of the earliest was that of Pommerehne and Schneider (1982). They first estimated the parameters of a standard median-voter model of the demand for government services. They then used the estimated parameters from this model to predict the levels of government in several categories in communities that elected representatives. They found actual expenditures in communities with representative democracy exceeded predicted expenditures based on the estimates from communities with town-meeting forms of direct democracy in *every* category. Total government spending was 28 percent higher than predicted. Moreover, within the group of communities using representative democracy, spending was lower where citizen initiatives were possible than where they were not possible. Several other studies for Switzerland have confirmed the Pommerehne and Schneider findings.[15]

Using data for Switzerland, Schaltegger and Küttel (2002) find that the strength of democratic institutions in a local community, as measured by the degree of direct democracy, is inversely related to the proclivity of its government imitating the policies of neighboring governments. When citizens can effectively express their preferences directly, their governments do not have to take their signals from neighboring governments. Other indexes of government performance like GDP per capita also indicate superior performance (i.e., higher incomes) in communities with direct democracy (Feld and Savioz 1997; Freitag and Vatter 2000). Swiss citizens also report being *happier* in communities that make greater use of the institutions of direct democracy (Frey and Stutzer 2000).

The United States

Twenty states and more than 80 cities in the United States allow citizens to call initiatives. Initiatives have been used in some states for more than a century. These data have recently been utilized by Matsusaka (2003) to examine the effects of citizen initiatives on democratic outcomes. His study confirms the findings of the studies for Switzerland. The availability and use of citizen initiatives leads to a closer alignment of governmental policies to citizen preferences. In this section we briefly describe and comment on his main findings.

Finding 1. Over the period 1970 to 1999 state and local government expenditures in the United States were lower in states that allowed citizens to call initiatives than in other states. The availability of the initiative option reduced state and local government expenditures by 4 percent, roughly $468 for a family of four (Matsusaka 2003, ch. 3).

Finding 2. Initiatives lead to a greater decentralization of government expenditures. Local governments account for a greater fraction of total expenditures in states with initiatives. Cities that can call initiatives spend *more* money than cities without this option. Thus citizen initiatives change the composition of government spending as well as its size. Indeed, the decentralization effect of initiatives is greater than their effect on the size of the budget (Matsusaka 2003, ch. 4).

Finding 3. Initiatives alter the composition of revenue sources for state and local governments. Cities that allow initiatives make greater use of fees for government services and less use of taxes (Matsusaka 2003, ch. 5). For me, this is a most interesting finding, since I have recently advocated, in the context of a constitutional reform in Sweden, coupling the introduction of a federalist system with a greater use of user fees to finance local governmental expenditures (Mueller 2004; Mueller and Uddhammar 2004). My argument for doing so was that user fees made it easier for a citizen to judge the costs of a public service and thus lead to better informed citizens and consequently to a better match between citizen preferences and governmental polices. Matsusaka's findings imply that citizens themselves favor the greater transparency of user fees over taxes, and opt for them, if given the opportunity.

Finding 4. The results of polls indicate that the differences in outcomes between states with initiatives and those without are in the direction of what citizens want. During the period 1972 to 1995 citizens in the United Sates favored reductions in government expenditures and a greater reliance on user fees (Matsusaka 2003, ch. 6). Initiatives have moved governmental policies toward those favored by the majority of citizens.

Additional support for this finding is provided Gerber (1999) in her study of referenda and initiatives. She finds that *citizen groups* have some success in getting new legislation through the initiative process, but not *economic* interest groups, which presumably are less representative of the majority of citizens' views. Economic interest groups are successful only in sometimes blocking new legislation through initiatives.[16]

Of particular interest also is the finding that citizens are most content with the policies provided by their local governments, and least satisfied by what the central government does. I doubt very much that one can come up with a similar finding from polls conducted in, say, Sweden or Austria—countries where authority for decision-making or taxation are concentrated at the central level. Citizens in these countries do not perceive of their local governments as the main determinants of the bundles of expenditures and taxes that they experience. Satisfaction or dissatisfaction must be directed to the highest level of government. That the highest level of government is the one least liked in America is in itself a great endorsement for federalism.

Finding 5. In the period from 1902 to 1942, states with an initiative option spent 8 percent *more* on government goods and service than did states without the initiative (Matsusaka 2003, ch. 7). The massive shift in population from rural areas into the cities led to an increase in the demand for government services such as education, sanitation, and other public goods supplied to urban dwellers. In part, because of overrepresentation of rural areas in state legislatures, state and local governments were slow to respond to the shift in demand for government services over the first half of the twentieth century. In states where citizens could call initiatives, citizens were able to correct the mistakes of their representatives. This finding of Matsusaka indicates that initiatives do not necessarily result in smaller public sectors. The primary effect of initiatives is to bring governmental policies into closer alignment with citizen preferences. To the extent that representative democracy leads to government sectors that are too large from the perspective of citizens—as much of the public choice literature implies—initiatives will reduce government size. When, however, government budgets are too small from the perspective of a majority of voters, the initiative will increase the size of the government sector, as occurred in the United States during the first half of the twentieth century.

The literature on the effects of direct democracy in Switzerland (see chapter 2) and the United States reviewed in this section paints a remarkably consistent picture. When citizens can decide governmental policies directly, these policies shift in the direction of those favored by a majority of the electorate. Direct democracy leads to a closer alignment of government policies and citizen preferences. Since initiatives are easier to call in small polities than in large ones, and town-meeting democracy is only feasible in small communities, the literature on direct democracy's effects indirectly also argues for the introduction of a federalist system. The ideal governmental structure for representing citizen preferences would appear to be a federalist system with healthy doses of direct democracy.

8.6 The Problem of Centralization

In 1929, the federal government accounted for 30 percent of total government expenditures in the United States; today it accounts for some 60 percent of revenues and expenditures (*Statistical Abstract* 2002, tables 414, 449). In 1950, the central government raised roughly 60 percent of all tax revenue in *Federal* Republic of Germany; today it raises over 90 percent (Blankart 2000, p. 31). Similar processes of centralization occurred during the twentieth centuries in the federal states of Australia and Canada (Head 1983; Grossman and West 1994). So pervasive is the process of centralization even within federalist states that it has come to be referred to as *Popitz's law*, named after the German economist who in the early part of the twentieth century already remarked on the tendency toward centralization in state revenue sources and expenditures (Blankart 2000). Thus any country that opts for a federalist structure to benefit from the advantages of decentralization must also determine how it intends to protect any degree of decentralization originally defined in the constitution from the workings of Popitz's law.[17]

One strategy for preventing the central government from usurping the tax and expenditure authorities of lower levels of government is to assign explicitly in the constitution specific responsibilities for certain activities to each level of government, and charge either a specially created federalist court or the regular courts with ensuring that each level of government restricts itself to the set of activities assigned to it (Mueller 1996, ch. 6). The US constitution contains such language, and its presence in the constitution plus the Supreme Court's willingness to enforce this provision undoubtedly helps to explain why the central government's share of total government expenditures was so small in 1929. The Supreme Court's capitulation in the 1930s to Franklin Roosevelt's pressure to allow the federal government to expand its domain explains the relative growth of the central government in the United States since that time. The US experience indicates that the assignment of specific functions in the constitution can help avoid the enforcement of Popitz's law—*if the language of the law is defended by the judicial system*. The US experience further illustrates that without the support of the judiciary, the language of the constitution alone will not deter a central government bent on expanding its domain.

Italy's experience over the latter part of the twentieth century provides an additional example of how constitutional and legal restrictions on the central government can prevent it from encroaching on the authority of lower levels of government, when backed up by the judiciary. Despite the fact that Italy is more of an example of a unitary state than a true federalism, the assignment of specific authorities to regional governments in the constitution in combination with the willingness of Italy's Constitutional Court to enforce this article, and subsequent acts of the parliament guaranteeing the regional governments' authority, have succeeded in maintaining a certain degree of decentralization in Italy's fiscal structure.[18]

In Austria, Germany, and Switzerland, the legislature's second chamber is filled by representatives of the regional governments, the Länder. The claim has been sometimes made that this system of representation helps preserve the federalist integrity of these states, since the representatives of the regional governments can resist any efforts by the central government to encroach upon their expenditure or tax authorities. The history of Germany over the last fifty years clearly contradicts this claim, and the same can be said for Austria (Blankart 2000).

All citizens dislike taxes and appreciate the benefits that flow from government outlays. All vote-maximizing politicians would rather raise expenditures than taxes. This set of preferences explains why government deficits are far more common than government surpluses, and the growth in the centralization of tax revenues that took place in Germany over the last half century. The Länder governments were willing to hand over taxation powers to the central government so as to avoid having to raise taxes to finance the substantial growth in state expenditures that occurred over this period. The Länder governments effectively formed a cartel among themselves and the central government to hand over taxation authority and expand expenditures (Blankart 2000). Grossman and West (1994) explain the growth in size of the state sector in Canada over the last century as a result of the same sort of cartel behavior among its regional governments, the ten provinces.

Why has the same sort of centralization of government expenditures not taken place also in Switzerland? Indeed, the fraction of total tax revenue raised by the central government in Switzerland actually *fell* from roughly 60 percent as in Germany in 1950 to under 50 percent by 1995 (Blankart 2000, p. 31). Switzerland's federalist structure appears to have been protected not so much by its judiciary, but by its citizens exercising their constitutional right to call referenda on governmental actions. Once again, we observe the important symbiosis between federalism and direct democracy. One additional way to try to protect the decentralized nature of a federalist state is to combine it with institutions of direct democracy.

The case of Switzerland provides further evidence in support of Weingast's (1995) theory of "market-preserving federalism." According to Weingast, the necessary conditions to preserve federalism are not simply a well-designed set of institutions imbedded in a constitution. "Limited government ... depends on how citizens react to a potential violation of that constraint. The ultimate sanction on a government is the withdrawal of support by a sufficient proportion of its citizens so that the government cannot survive" (Weingast 1995, p. 26). Weingast illustrates his thesis with the examples of eighteenth-century Britain and nineteenth-century United States. In both cases the citizens were united in wishing to constrain the activities of the central government, and acted to do so. Referenda lower the transaction costs of constraining government and thereby facilitate achieving this goal—if the citizens want it.[19]

Preventing over centralization is one of the most difficult challenges facing the writers of a constitution. In this section I have suggested two institutional protections against Popitz's law—language in the constitution assigning authorities to each level of government backed by judicial enforcement, and referenda and citizen initiatives. I am more optimistic than Filippov, Ordeshook, and Shvestova (2003) about such constitutional devices for avoiding Popitz's law. One should not underestimate the difficulty of maintaining a strong federal structure. This goal must be uppermost in the minds of those who delineate a federalist system in a new constitution.

8.7 Conclusions

A federalist governmental structure can make governments more responsive to citizens' wishes and thereby bring about a close alignment between citizens' preferences and government policies. The empirical literature suggests that this alignment is particularly close when the institutions of federalism are combined with those of direct democracy. Only a handful of countries in the world have strong federalist systems in which the elected governments at each level can determine both the size and composition of their expenditures and the constellation of taxes and fees that finances them. Only two of these countries—Switzerland and the United States—combine federalism with direct democracy, and in the case of the United States this occurs in less than one half of the states. The potential benefits from federalism go unrealized in most countries, including those like Austria and Germany that call themselves federal republics.

The literature reviewed in this chapter indicates that federalism comes at a price. Perhaps its largest cost is borne by the citizenry who have to participate in elections at several levels of government. This burden becomes particularly large where federalism is combined with direct democracy. But the evidence from numerous studies from Switzerland and the United Sates indicates that the benefits from a greater alignment of citizen preferences and government policies outweigh the costs.

Federalism can impose additional costs on communities where the migration of citizens creates negative externalities or tax competition erodes government revenue sources. There is no evidence, however, that these costs outweigh the benefits from mobility and tax competition. The benefits from mobility come from increasing the degree of homogeneity of preferences in local communities, thereby narrowing the gap between what voters want from government and what they get. The benefits from tax competition come through the greater efficiency in the provision of government services that competition produces.

Thus the empirical literature suggests that federalism can be an attractive option for most countries seeking more responsive and efficient democratic institutions. The challenge these countries face is to design these institutions in such a way so as to achieve their maximum potential benefits, and to ensure that they resist the tendency toward centralization that exists in all countries.

Notes

1. See, however, Mueller (1996, ch. 21), and Blankart and Mueller (2004).

2. Bolton and Roland (1997) provide an analysis for why states with heterogeneous populations might subdivide or even break up.

3. See Tullock (1969), Oates (1972, 1999), Mueller (1996, ch. 7, 2003, ch. 10), and Inman and Rubinfeld (1997).

4. Knight in chapter 9 of this volume explores the effects of federalism on central government decision making.

5. The classic reference on this is Buchanan (1950). See also Chernick (1979).

6. For further discussion, see Mueller (2003, ch. 9).

7. Even the number of surveys of this literature is by now large, for example, see Gramlich (1977), Inman (1979), Fisher (1982), Heyndels and Smolders (1994, 1995), Hines and Thaler (1995), Becker (1996), and Bailey and Connolly (1998). For a recent study identifying a substantial flypaper effect in Taiwan, see Chu (2003). Gemmell, Morrissey, and Pinar (2002) also present recent evidence on the flypaper effect for the United Kingdom.

8. For two recent challenges, see Becker (1996) and Worthington and Dellery (1999).

9. See Oates's (1988) survey.

10. See Rodden (2001, 2002, 2003) and Rodden and Wibbels (2002). For additional recent evidence of an inverse relationship between federalist institutions and government size, see Vaubel (1996) and Persson and Tabellini (2003, tab. 3.1, p. 40).

11. For additional discussion of the problem of soft budget constraints and local government bailouts, see von Hagen and Eichengreen (1996), and von Hagen and Dahlberg (2004). Careaga and Weingast (2003) provide a case study of Mexico illustrating

how intergovernmental grants and soft budget constraints produce fiscal laxity by local governments.

12. See Gramlich and Laren (1984), Blank (1988), Cebula and Koch (1989), and Cebula (1990, 1991). The literature has been surveyed by Cebula (1979), Cebula and Kafoglis (1986) and Dowding, John, and Biggs (1994).

13. See chapter 2 of this volume.

14. For a discussion of the various forms of referenda and initiatives that are possible, see Mueller (1996, ch. 12).

15. See Pommerehne (1978), Pommerehne and Schneider (1983), Feld and Kirchgässner (1999), and Feld and Matsusaka (2000).

16. For further evidence that institutions of direct democracy in the United States have moved government policies closer to those favored the citizens, and reduced the sizes of government budgets, see Santerre (1986, 1989) and Kiewiet and Szakaly (1996).

17. The extent of this challenge has been stressed by many writers; in particular, see Riker (1964), Weingast (1995, 2004), and Filippov, Ordeshook, and Shvetsova (2003).

18. See the discussion by Breton and Fraschini (2003).

19. Both Weingast and Filippov, Ordeshook, and Shvetsova (2003) emphasize the role of a constitution as a "coordinating device" in preserving the integrity of a federalist system.

References

Bailey, S. J., and S. Connolly. 1998. The flypaper effect: Identifying areas for further research. *Public Choice* 95: 335–61.

Becker, E. 1996. The illusion of fiscal illusion: Unsticking the flypaper effect. *Public Choice* 86: 85–102.

Besley, T., and A. Case. 1995. Incumbent behavior: Vote-seeking, tax-setting, and yardstick competition. *American Economic Review* 85: 25–45.

Blank, R. M. 1988. The impact of state economic differentials on household welfare and labor force behavior. *Journal of Urban Economics* 24: 186–211.

Blankart, Ch. B. 2000. The process of government centralization: A constitutional view. *Constitutional Political Economy* 11: 27–39.

Blankart, Ch. B., and D. C. Mueller, eds. 2004. *A Constitution for the European Union*. Cambridge: MIT Press.

Bolton, P., and G. Roland. 1997. The breakup of nations: A political economy analysis. *Quarterly Journal of Economics* 112: 1057–90.

Breton, A., and A. Fraschini. 2003. Vertical competition in unitary states: The case of Italy. *Public Choice* 144: 57–77.

Buchanan, J. M. 1950. Federalism and fiscal equity. *American Economic Review* 40: 538–600.

Büttner, T. 1999. Determinants of tax rates in local capital income taxation: A theoretical model and evidence from Germany. *Finanzarchiv* 56: 363–88.

Büttner, T. 2001. Local business taxation and competition for capital: The choice of the tax rate. *Regional Science and Urban Economics* 31: 215–45.

Careaga, M., and B. R. Weingast. 2003. Fiscal federalism, good governance, and economic growth in Mexico. In D. Rodrik, ed., *In Search of Prosperity: Analytic Narratives on Economic Growth*. Princeton: Princeton University Press, pp. 399–435.

Case, A. C., H. S. Rosen, and J. R. Hines. 1993. Budget spillovers and fiscal policy interdependence: Evidence from the states. *Journal of Public Economics* 52: 285–307.

Cebula, R. J. 1979. *The Determinants of Human Migration*. Lexington, MA: Lexington Books.

Cebula, R. J. 1990. A brief empirical note on the tiebout hypothesis and state income tax policies. *Public Choice* 67: 87–89.

Cebula, R. J. 1991. A brief note on welfare benefits and human migration. *Public Choice* 69: 345–49.

Cebula, R. J., and J. V. Koch. 1989. Welfare policies and migration of the poor in the United States: An empirical note. *Public Choice* 61: 171–76.

Cebula, R. J., and M. Z. Kafoglis. 1986. A note on the Tiebout-Tullock hypothesis: The period 1975–1980. *Public Choice* 48 (1): 65–69.

Chernick, H. A. 1979. An economic model of the distribution of public grants. In P. Mieszkowski and W. H. Oakland, eds., *Fiscal Federalism and Grants-in-Aid*. Washington, DC: Urban Institute, pp. 81–103.

Chu, H.-Y. 2003. The dual-illusion of grants-in-aid on central and local expenditures. *Public Choice* 144: 349–59.

Dowding, K., P. John, and S. Biggs. 1994. Tiebout: A survey of the empirical literature. *Urban Studies* 31: 767–97.

Feld, L. P., and G. Kirchgässner. 1999. Public debt and budgetary procedures: Top down or bottom up? Some evidence from Swiss municipalities. In J. M. Poterba and J. von Hagen, eds., *Fiscal Institutions and Fiscal Performance*. Chicago: NBER, pp. 151–79.

Feld, L. P., and J. G. Matsusaka. 2000. Budget referendums and government spending: Evidence from Swiss cantons. Mimeo. University of St. Gallen.

Feld, L. P., and M. R. Savioz. 1997. Direct democracy matters for economic performance: An empirical investigation. *Kyklos* 50: 507–38.

Filippov, M., P. C. Ordeshook, and O. Shvestova. 2003. *Designing Federalism: A Theory of Self-Sustainable Federal Institutions*. Cambridge: Cambridge University Press.

Fisher, R. C. 1982. Income and grant effects on local expenditure: The flypaper effect and other difficulties. *Journal of Urban Economics* 12: 324–45.

Freitag, M., and A. Vatter. 2000. Direkte Demokratie, Konkordanz und Wirtschaftsleistung: Ein Vergleich der Schweizer Kantone. *Swiss Journal of Economics and Statistics* 136: 579–606.

Frey, B. S., and A. Stutzer. 2000. Happiness prospers in democracy. *Journal of Happiness Studies* 1 (1): 79–102.

Gemmel, N., O. Morrissey, and A. Pinar. 2002. Fiscal illusion and political accountability: Theory and evidence from two tax regimes in Britain. *Public Choice* 110: 199–224.

Gerber, E. R. 1999. *The Populist Paradox*. Princeton: Princeton University Press.

Gramlich, E. M. 1977. Intergovernmental grants: A review of the empirical literature. In W. Oates, ed., *The Political Economy of Fiscal Federalism*. Lexington, MA: Lexington Books, pp. 219–39.

Gramlich, E. M., and D. Laren. 1984. Migration and income redistribution responsibilities. *Journal of Human Resources* 19: 489–511.

Gramlich, E. M., and D. L. Rubinfeld. 1982. Micro estimates of public spending demand functions and tests of the Tiebout and median-voter hypothesis. *Journal of Political Economy* 90: 536–60.

Grossman, P. J., and E. G. West. 1994. Federalism and the growth of government revisited. *Public Choice* 79: 19–32.

Grubb, W. N. 1982. The dynamic implications of the Tiebout model—The changing composition of Boston communities, 1960–1970. *Public Finance Quarterly* 10: 17–38.

Hagen, J. von, and M. Dahlberg. 2004. Is there a bailout problem in Sweden. In P. Molander, ed., *Fiscal Federalism in Unitary States*. Dordrecht: Kluwer, pp. 47–76.

Hagen, J. von, and B. Eichengreen. 1996. Federalism, fiscal restraints, and European monetary union. *American Economic Review* 86: 134–38.

Head, J. G. 1983. Intergovernmental fiscal relations in Australia, Canada and the United States since World War II. In N. Adel, ed., *Handbuch der Finanzwissenschaft*, 3rd. ed. Tübingen: Mohr Siebezi, pp. 187–216.

Heyndels, B., and C. Smolders. 1994. Fiscal illusion at the local level: Empirical evidence for the Flemish municipalities. *Public Choice* 80: 325–38.

Heyndels, B., and C. Smolders. 1995. Tax complexity and fiscal illusion. *Public Choice* 85: 127–41.

Heyndels, B., and J. Vuchelen. 1998. Tax mimicking among Belgian municipalities. *National Tax Journal* 51: 89–101.

Hines, J. R., Jr., and R. H. Thaler. 1995. Anomolies: The flypaper effect. *Journal of Economic Perspectives* 9: 217–26.

Inman, R. P. 1979. The fiscal performance of local governments: An interpretative review. In P. Mieszkowski and M. Straszheim, eds., *Current Issues in Urban Economics*. Baltimore: Johns Hopkins University Press, pp. 270–321.

Inman, R. P., and D. L. Rubinfeld. 1997. The political economy of federalism. In D. C. Mueller, ed., *Perspectives on Public Choice*. Cambridge: Cambridge University Press, pp. 73–105.

Kiewiet, R. D., and K. Szakaly. 1996. Constitutional limitations on borrowing: An analysis of state bonded indebtness. *Journal of Law, Economics and Organization* 12: 62–97.

Ladd, H. F. 1992. Mimicking of local tax burdens among neighboring countries. *Public Finance Quarterly* 20: 450–67.

Matsusaka, J. G. 2003. For the many or the few. Mimeo. University of Southern California.

Miller, G. J. 1981. *Cities by Contract*. Cambridge: MIT Press.

Mueller, D. C. 1996. *Constitutional Democracy*. Oxford: Oxford University Press.

Mueller, D. C. 2003. *Public Choice III*. Cambridge: Cambridge University Press.

Mueller, D. C. 2004. Why federalism? In P. Molander, ed., *Fiscal Federalism in Unitary States*. Dordrecht: Kluwer, pp. 131–44.

Mueller, D. C., and E. Uddhammar. 2004. Strengthening federalism in Sweden. In P. Molander, ed., *Fiscal Federalism in Unitary States*. Dordrecht: Kluwer, pp. 145–67.

Munley, V. G. 1982. An alternative test of the Tiebout hypothesis. *Public Choice* 38 (2): 211–17.

Nechyba, T. J., and R. P. Walsh. 2004. Urban sprawl. *Journal of Economic Perspectives* 18 (4): 177–200.

Oates, W. E. 1972. *Fiscal Federalism*. London: Harcourt Brace.

Oates, W. E. 1988. On the nature and measurement of fiscal illusion: A survey. In G. Brennan et al., eds., *Taxation and Fiscal Federalism: Essays in Honour of Russell Mathews*. Canberra: Australian National University Press, pp. 65–82.

Oates, W. E. 1999. An essay on fiscal federalism. *Journal of Economic Literature* 37: 1120–49.

Orbell, J. M., and T. Uno. 1972. A theory of neighborhood problem solving: Political action vs. residential mobility. *American Political Science Review* 66: 471–89.

Persson, T., and G. Tabellini. 2003. *The Economic Effects of Constitutions*. Cambridge: MIT Press.

Pommerehne, W. W. 1978. Institutional approaches to public expenditures: Empirical evidence from Swiss municipalities. *Journal of Public Economics* 9: 163–201.

Pommerehne, W. W., and F. Schneider. 1982. Unbalanced growth between public and private sectors: An empirical examination. In R. H. Haveman, ed., *Public Finance and Public Employment*. Detroit MI: Wayne State University Press, pp. 309–26.

Pommerehne, W. W., and F. Schneider. 1983. Does government in a representative democracy follow a majority of voters' preferences? An empirical examination. In H. Hanusch, ed., *Anatomy of Government Deficiencies*. Berlin: Springer, pp. 61–84.

Rhode, P. W., and K. S. Strumpf. 2003. Assessing the importance of Tiebout sorting: Local heterogeneity from 1850 to 1990. *American Economic Review* 93: 1648–77.

Riker, W. H. 1964. *Federalism: Origins, Operations, and Significance*. Boston: Little, Brown.

Rodden, J. 2001. And the last shall be first: Federalism and fiscal outcomes in Germany. Mimeo. Harvard University, Cambridge, MA.

Rodden, J. 2002. The dilemma of fiscal federalism: Grants and fiscal performance around the world. *American Journal of Political Science* 46: 670–87.

Rodden, J. 2003. Reviving leviathan: Fiscal federalism and the growth of government. *International Organization* 57: 695–729.

Rodden, J., and E. Wibbels. 2002. Beyond the fiction of federalism. *World Politics* 54: 494–531.

Santerre, R. E. 1986. Representative versus direct democracy: A Tiebout test of relative performance. *Public Choice* 48: 55–63.

Santerre, R. E. 1989. Representative versus direct democracy: Are there any expenditure differences? *Public Choice* 60: 145–54.

Schaltegger, C. A., and D. Küttel. 2002. Exit, voice, and mimicking behavior: Evidence from Swiss cantons. *Public Choice* 113: 1–23.

Tiebout, Ch. M. 1956. A pure theory of local expenditures. *Journal of Political Economics* 64: 416–24.

Tullock, G. 1969. Federalism: Problems of scale. *Public Choice* 6: 19–30.

US Department of Commerce. 2002. *Statistical Abstract of the United States, 2002*. Washington, DC: US Government Printing Office.

Vaubel, R. 1996. Constitutional safeguards against centralization in federal states: An international cross-section analysis. *Constitutional Political Economy* 7: 79–102.

Weingast, B. R. 1995. The economic role of political institutions: Market-preserving federalism and economic development. *Journal of Law, Economics and Organization* 11: 1–31.

Weingast, B. R. 2004. The performance and stability of federalism: An institutional perspective. In C. Menard and M. Shirley, eds., *Handbook of New Institutional Economics*. Dordrecht: Kluwer.

Wicksell, K. 1896. *A New Principle of Just Taxation*. Finanztheoretische Untersuchungen. Jena. Reprinted in Musgrave and Peacock, 1967, 72–118.

Worthington, A. C., and B. E. Dellery. 1999. Fiscal illusion and the Australian local government grants process: How sticky is the flypaper effect. *Public Choice* 99: 1–13.

9 Common Tax Pool Problems in Federal Systems

Brian Knight

9.1 Introduction

Many countries are currently debating, or have recently debated, the proper assignment of taxation and public spending powers between levels of government within a federation. During the 1990s the United States devolved significant control over welfare policy to state and local governments; a current Bush administration proposal calls for the devolution of passenger rail service, which is heavily subsidized by the federal government at current. In developing new political institutions within Iraq, many have argued for a more prominent role for local governments. The countries of Europe have recently moved toward greater centralization at the supra-national level through expansions in the powers, including authority over monetary policy, of the European Union. Within the countries of Europe, by contrast, there have been movements toward greater regional autonomy as the economic benefits of political integration, such as the free movement of goods, labor, and capital, are guaranteed by membership in the European Union and are thus independent of country size. This movement toward greater fractionalization has been most pronounced in richer regions, such as northern Italy, presumably due to opposition to any redistribution benefiting poorer regions.

Economists and political scientists have long debated this exact normative question: What is the proper vertical assignment of fiscal responsibilities across governments within a federation?[1] According to the decentralization theorem (Oates 1972), decentralized provision of public goods is preferred to uniform centralized provision in the absence of both interjurisdictional spillovers and economies of scale under centralized provision. Inman and Rubinfeld (1997) focus on the trade-off between the disadvantages of political inefficiencies in the centralized provision of local public goods and the advantages of internalizing cross-jurisdiction externalities. These and other advantages of centralization, along with supporting empirical evidence, are summarized below:

Internalizing Expenditure Externalities

Cross-jurisdiction spillovers may lead to an inefficiently low provision of public goods under decentralization given that the benefits to neighboring jurisdictions are not internalized by local decision-makers. Centralized governments, by contrast, may better internalize such externalities through political bargaining among elected representatives or the budgetary powers of a nationally elected executive. While this argument has intuitive appeal, there is little in the way of direct empirical evidence on the existence of such spillovers. Holtz-Eakin and Schwartz (1995) find little evidence of productivity spillovers from US state highways and Knight (2004a) finds that congressional representative voting decisions do not reflect possible spillovers associated with spending on transportation projects in neighboring districts.

Lack of Tax Competition

Taxation of mobile factors may lead to the adoption of inefficient policies under decentralization. Goolsbee and Maydew (2000) find that state attempts to increase manufacturing employment by reducing payroll's weight in the corporate income tax apportionment formulae (and hence increasing the burden on sales and property) are associated with increases in manufacturing employment within the state but a reduction in employment in other states. The presence of this fiscal externality under decentralized taxation suggests that the apportionment formula may be more efficiently determined at the federal level.

Redistribution of Income

Related to this tax competition disadvantage under decentralization, some have argued that the federal government can better redistribute resources from rich to poor through progressive income taxation. Feldstein and Vaillant (1998) find that since high-income individuals can avoid progressive state income taxation by migrating to other states, an increase in the progressivity of state income taxes leads to an offsetting increase in gross wages for high-skilled workers and thus no change in net wages. Federal income taxes, by contrast, are less prone to this migration effect given the relatively low mobility of individuals across international borders.

Risk Sharing

Given that business cycles are often regional in nature, the federal government may help to smooth patterns of consumption and income through progressive income taxes, transfers to low-income individuals, and federal grants to state and local governments. Asdrubali, Sorensen, and Yosha (1996) and Bayoumi and Masson (1995) both find strong evidence that the federal government in the United States helps states to smooth through regional downturns in economic activity. This benefit of centralization may be somewhat specific to the United States given the strict balanced budget requirements in place in most US states and the significant budget of the central government. In Europe, by contrast, balanced budget rules are less binding in member counties, and the fiscal capacity of the European Union is small.

Opponents of centralization counter these arguments with justifications for greater decentralization. Chief among the proposed disadvantages of centralization are the following:

Policy Uniformity

Oates (1972) argues that centralized governments tend to adopt geographically uniform policies, which necessarily do not reflect heterogeneity in preferences across jurisdictions; policies adopted by decentralized governments, which may have better information regarding constituent preferences, are arguably more reflective of preference heterogeneity across jurisdictions. This benefit of decentralization is further reinforced by cross-jurisdiction mobility; under decentralization, constituents will sort themselves according to preferences for heterogeneously provided public goods (Tiebout 1956). Strumpf and Oberholzer-Gee (2002) provide evidence in support of Oates's central tenet of federalism: states with more heterogeneous preferences are more likely to decentralize liquor control and allow for local government decision-making.

Lack of Experimentation and Innovation

Given their sheer advantage in numbers, decentralized governments may have an advantage in the areas of experimentation and innovation;

successful innovations can be subsequently adopted by other jurisdictions.[2] This notion of increased experimentation and innovation by state and local governments was one of the prominent rationales for the recent devolution of welfare in the United States.

Common Tax Pool Problems

Inman and Rubinfeld (1997), Besley and Coate (2003), and Lockwood (2002) have argued that centralization may lead to the inefficient adoption of policies due to common tax pool problems; this drawback of centralization is the focus of this chapter. In particular, local public goods financed through central taxation provide geographically concentrated benefits to recipient jurisdictions but disperse costs due to a national, or common pool, tax base. In central legislatures with locally elected representatives, such as the US Congress, the geographic disconnect between program benefits and costs creates incentives for legislators to increase own-district spending because the district bears only a small share of the associated tax costs. Countering this bias toward higher spending, each legislator has an incentive to restrain spending in other districts due to the associated tax costs.

In this chapter, I survey the empirical literature on this final disadvantage of centralization, common tax pool problems. Through the focus on the appropriate degree of centralization of political authority, this survey is related to a broader literature on the role of political institutions in government finance. Buchanan (1949) distinguishes between an organismic framework, which conceptualizes the state as a single unitary actor, and the individualistic framework, in which the state is conceptualized as a collection of individuals and "cannot be considered the originator of action." More recently Hettich and Winer (1999) provide a theoretical and empirical analysis of tax systems from positive political economy perspective. Persson and Tabellini (2002) survey the recent game-theoretic literature on political economics and public finance. From an empirical perspective, Poterba (1996) and Besley and Case (2003) investigate the role of specific political institutions in explaining fiscal outcomes.

The following section discusses empirical studies testing for behavioral responses by legislators and legislatures to common pool incentives. Section 9.3 examines the redistributive consequences of common pool problems; in particular, small jurisdictions, which contribute little to the common tax pool and are typically overrepresented in central legislatures, are hypothesized to gain from common pool situations, while larger jurisdictions are net losers. Section 9.4 provides some policy implications and concludes.

9.2 Evidence on Responses to Common Pool Incentives

In order to provide a theoretical context for the empirical studies to be discussed, consider a model with a collection of J jurisdictions and a combined national population of N.[3] In a given jurisdiction (j), each of N_j residents is assumed to have quasi-linear preferences over consumption of a local public good (G_j) and consumption of a private good (z_j):

$$U(g_j, z_j) = h\left(\frac{G_j}{N_j^{\gamma}}\right) + z_j. \tag{1}$$

Preferences over public goods $[h(G_j/N_j^{\gamma})]$ are assumed to be increasing and concave and are normalized such that zero utility is obtained from zero spending $[h(0) = 0]$. The congestion parameter $[\gamma \in [0, 1]]$ captures the degree of rivalry in consumption; this specification nests the case of private goods $(\gamma = 1)$ as well as the case of pure public goods $(\gamma = 0)$. Each resident in jurisdiction j is endowed with m_j units of the private good, which can be converted into public goods at a dollar-for-dollar rate.

A central legislature determines both the available budget (G) and the geographic distribution of local public goods. In the legislature, delegation sizes of jurisdictions are given by V_j, and the total number of delegates (V) is given by $V = \sum_j V_j$. Public goods are financed from a national, or common pool, tax base, and per capita tax prices (p_j) are assumed to be equal across the nation $(p_j = 1/N)$. Finally, private consumption is determined residually $(z_j = m_j - G/N)$. Next, two commonly studied legislative processes, universalism and legislative bargaining, are considered.

Studies in Universalism Context

Many empirical studies have examined common tax pool problems in the context of the universalism model of Weingast, Shepsle, and Johnsen (1981). In this framework, state delegations, acting independently, increase spending on the local public good until marginal benefits are equal to marginal costs:

Table 9.1
Evidence on common pool problems using variation in legislature size

Author(s)	Sample	Endogeneity corrections	Legislature size and spending
Gilligan and Matsusaka	US states	Fixed effects	Positive effect
Bradbury and Crain	Countries	Fixed effects	Positive effect
Baqir	US municipalies	Historical instruments	Positive effect
Per Pettersson-Lidbom	Swedish municipalities	Natural experiment	Negative effect

$$\frac{h'(G_j/N_j^{\gamma})}{N_j^{\gamma}} = \frac{1}{N}. \tag{2}$$

Solving this equation for G_j yields the following expression:

$$G_j = N_j^{\gamma} f\left(\frac{N_j^{\gamma}}{N}\right), \tag{3}$$

where $f(x) = [h'(x)]^{-1}$. Note the two key properties of this inverse function: $f(x) > 0$ and $f'(x) = 1/h''(f(x)) < 0$.

In a test for behavioral responses to common pool incentives, DelRossi and Inman (1999) introduce variation in federal tax prices (p_j), which were assumed to be homogenous above. In this case jurisdiction spending is given as follows:

$$G_j = N_j^{\gamma} f(p_j N_j^{\gamma}). \tag{4}$$

With this equation it is easy to show that the universalism model predicts that delegation demand for local public goods is declining in tax prices $(\partial G_j/\partial p_j < 0)$. As the district's constituents bear a larger share of the tax burdens, the common pool problem becomes less severe, leading to a reduction in spending implied by legislator demands for local public goods.

DelRossi and Inman (1999) use legislator-level data to directly test this price sensitivity implication of the universalism model. In order to generate exogenous variation in local tax prices, the authors examine water project sizes chosen by representatives in the US House before and after passage of the Water Resources Development Act of 1986 (WRDA'86), which (for most projects) increased the fraction of project costs financed by local governments. As predicted, water project sizes generally fell following this exogenous increase in tax prices. As shown

Table 9.2
Price elasticity estimates

Project type	Price elasticity of demand
Flood control/shoreline	−1.273
Deep-draft navigation	−2.554
Shall-draft navigation	−1.207
River channel	0.374

Source: From DelRossi and Inmnan (1999).

in table 9.1, there was significant heterogeneity in estimated price elasticities of demand, ranging from 0.374 for river channel projects to −2.554 for deep-draft navigation projects. The authors conclude that the increases in tax prices associated with this legislation led to a 35 percent reduction in overall project spending on water projects.

A related empirical literature has used legislature-level data in order to examine the effects of the number of districts (J) on aggregate public spending (G). Given the focus on aggregate outcomes, consider next the special case of equal population states ($N_j = N/J$). In this case jurisdiction demands are identical, and the total provision of public goods in the legislature can be expressed as follows:

$$G = JG_j = J^{1-\gamma}N^{\gamma}f(J^{-\gamma}N^{\gamma-1}). \qquad (5)$$

Equation (5) leads directly to a second implication of the universalism model: aggregate public spending is increasing in the number of jurisdictions, or districts; that is, $\partial G/\partial J > 0$. As the number of districts increases, the common pool problem becomes more severe, increasing aggregate spending.

As summarized in table 9.2, empirical evidence has generally supported this prediction of a positive relationship between government spending and legislature size. The first test of which I am aware is by Gilligan and Matsusaka (1995), who use variation in the size of state legislatures in the United States. Their key finding is that state government expenditures per capita between 1960 and 1990 were increasing in the number of seats in the state legislature; this result is stronger for the upper chamber than for the lower chamber. Using cross-country evidence, Crain and Bradbury (1999) find that an increase in the size of legislature is associated with an increase in government spending but bicameralism dampens this effect. Baqir (2002) finds that an increase in the size of city councils in US municipalities leads to an increase in government spending. Broadly elected executives, in this case mayors, with greater veto power are able to mitigate common pool problems. Pettersson-Lidbom (2003) addresses potential endogeneity problems in this literature; in particular, states with high spending likely provide more constituent services and thus have a more complex public sector. This complexity may require larger legislatures in order to have specialists in each policy area. To address this issue of endogeneity, or reverse causation, Petterson-Lidbom uses a natural experiment induced by a statutory law linking council size to the number of voters in Swedish local governments. Evidence from this natural experiment provides a counterintuitive result: an increase in council size is associated with a reduction, rather than an increase, in government spending.

One limitation of this literature involves the measure of legislature size; in particular, most studies use the number of representatives (V) as a proxy for the number of jurisdictions (J). Baqir, for example, uses city council sizes as the measure of legislature size even though the majority of municipalities in the sample use at-large voting systems. As shown in equation (5), however, there is no predicted relationship between government spending and the number of representatives ($\partial G/\partial V = 0$). One possible reconciliation, as examined empirically in Baqir, involves core constituencies; in particular, to the extent that politicians represent the interests of subsets of voters, such as those affiliated with the politician's party, common pool problems may reemerge even in at-large voting systems.

Studies in Legislative Bargaining Context

Consider next a simple version of the legislative bargaining model due to Baron and Ferejohn (1987, 1989). Relative to the universalism model, in which political power was diffuse, such power is concentrated in legislative bargaining models. In particular, in the first stage, a single delegate is chosen, each with equal probability $1/V$, to be the agenda-setter. Denote the home state of the agenda setter as $j = a$. This agenda-setter then proposes a geographic distribution of the federal budget, subject to a balanced budget condition ($\sum_j G_j \leq G$); for simplicity, we take the aggregate budget size G as given. In the second stage, each delegate votes over whether to accept or reject the proposed budget. If the proposal receives a majority of votes from delegates in support, it is implemented; otherwise, a reversion distribution of zero spending is implemented.

Using the normalization that a zero budget provides zero utility $[h(0) = 0]$, each delegate will support proposals in which the total benefits accruing to a representative constituent exceed the tax costs associated with aggregate provision:

$$h\left(\frac{G_j}{N_j^{\gamma}}\right) \geq \frac{G}{N}. \tag{6}$$

The minimum cost (C_j) to the proposer of securing votes from all of the delegates of jurisdiction j can be expressed as follows:

$$C_j = \beta N_j^{\gamma}, \tag{7}$$

where $\beta = h^{-1}(G/N)$. In forming a majority coalition (M_a), the agenda-setter, taking voting rules as given, has an incentive to select delegates from those states with the highest vote yield, which is defined as the ratio of delegation sizes to the cost of securing the votes from a given delegation:

$$\frac{V_j}{C_j} = \frac{V_j}{\beta N_j^{\gamma}}. \tag{8}$$

As shown, vote yields are increasing in the number of delegates and decreasing in population so long as some congestion is present $(\gamma > 0)$. Under the special case of perfectly congestible public goods $(\gamma = 1)$, vote yields are proportional to delegates per capita. Using the expressions above, the agenda-setter's optimal allocation can be expressed as follows:

$$G_j = \beta N_j^{\gamma}, \qquad j \in M_a, \tag{9}$$

$$G_j = G - \sum_{k \in M_a} \beta N_k^{\gamma}, \qquad j = a, \tag{10}$$

$$G_j = 0, \qquad j \neq a,\ j \notin M_a. \tag{11}$$

Thus public spending is concentrated in politically powerful jurisdictions, those represented by the agenda-setter and those with the highest vote yields. We will return to these redistributive consequences of common pool problems later in the chapter.

To test for reactions to common pool incentives, Knight (2004a) introduces variation in tax prices (in a similar fashion to DelRossi and Inman) and analyzes 1998 congressional votes over funding for 1,653 transportation projects. With variation in federal tax prices, legislators will support proposals for which the benefits accruing to a representative constituent exceed the tax costs associated with aggregate provision:

$$h\left(\frac{G_j}{N_j^{\gamma}}\right) \geq p_j G. \tag{12}$$

Consider next a Cobb-Douglas parameterization for preferences over public goods:

$$h\left(\frac{G_j}{N_j^{\gamma}}\right) = \eta\left(\frac{G_j}{N_j^{\gamma}}\right)^{\alpha}, \tag{13}$$

where $\alpha \in (0,1)$ captures the marginal utility in own-jurisdiction project spending. The utility parameter η captures preferences for public goods and, while assumed homogeneous above, is permitted to vary empirically:

$$\eta_j = \exp(\theta X_j + \sigma \xi_j), \tag{14}$$

where the vector X_j and scalar ξ_j represent observed and unobserved preferences for public spending. If these two parameterizations are inserted into equation (12), representatives from delegation j will support the proposal if the utility benefits accruing to the district exceed its share of the total tax cost:

$$\exp(\theta X_j + \sigma \xi_j) G_j^{\alpha} N_j^{-\alpha\gamma} \geq p_j G. \tag{15}$$

Next, assume that conditional on observed preferences, population, own-district spending and tax prices, unobserved preferences are distributed standard normal $[\xi_j | X_j, N_j, G_j, p_j \sim N(0,1)]$. Using expressions (12) through (15), we can write, representative voting decisions as a familiar probit model:

$$\Pr(\text{support}) = \Phi\left[\text{Constant} + \frac{\theta}{\sigma} X_j + \frac{\alpha}{\sigma}\log(G_j) - \frac{1}{\sigma}\log(p_j)\right], \tag{16}$$

where Φ is the standard normal distribution function and the constant term includes log population $(\log(N_j))$, which varies only slightly across congressional districts in the United States (and thus does not allow for identification of the congestion parameter).

This empirical voting rule highlights the two common pool incentives facing legislators. The probability of supporting the proposal is increasing in own-jurisdiction spending (G_j) but is declining in the tax

Table 9.3
Evidence on common tax pool problems from congressional voting decisions: Profit marginal effects

Variable	Marginal effect	Marginal effect	Standard deviation
Log own-spending	0.0248**	0.0245**	6.3754
Log tax price	−0.1937**	−0.1857**	0.3776
District characteristics	No	Yes	
Observations	416	416	

Source: From Knight (2004a).
Notes: Dependent variable indicates whether or not the representative supported funding the projects; ** denotes 95% significance; * denotes 90%.

costs (p_j) associated with spending in other jurisdictions. While studies in the universalism context focus on the first incentive created by a common tax pool, namely a preference to expand own-district spending, Knight (2004a) incorporates both this first incentive as well as a second key incentive, a preference to restrain spending in other jurisdictions due to the associated tax liabilities.

As shown in table 9.3, the baseline results from this study provide strong evidence that individual legislators respond to common pool incentives inherent in the funding of transportation projects from a national gasoline tax. Districts with higher spending are more likely to support funding for the projects, while districts with high tax prices, as measured by estimated gasoline tax liabilities, were less likely to support funding. In addition to being statistically significant, the estimated effects are economically significant; a one-point standard deviation increase in log own-spending is associated with a 16 percentage point increase in the probability of supporting funding for the projects, while a one-point standard deviation increase in log tax costs is associated with a 7 percentage point reduction in the probability of support. These findings are robust to a series of alternative specifications, including controls for district characteristics, constituent characteristics, representative characteristics, and unobserved state characteristics.

9.3 Redistributive Consequences

Given strong evidence that legislatures and legislators respond to common tax pool problems, a natural follow-up question involves redistribution. In particular, which jurisdictions are most likely to benefit from and which are most likely to harmed by common pool situations?

Many studies have hypothesized that small jurisdictions are most likely to benefit; this advantage is manifested in a negative relationship between population and federal spending per capita. There are at least two underlying reasons for this hypothesized small jurisdiction bias. First, small jurisdictions are often overrepresented on a per capita basis in central legislatures, such as in the US Senate, and are thus often overrepresented on committees with key agenda setting powers. Second, small jurisdictions pay relatively low federal taxes, making them cheap and thus attractive coalition partners. As a formalization of this hypothesis, we next show that a small state bias is consistent with both theoretical models of legislative behavior.

Universalism

For simplicity, consider a representative system, such as the US Senate, in which each jurisdiction has the same number of delegates ($V_j = V/J$). While the number of delegates is constant across jurisdictions, the measure of delegates per capita ($v_j = V_j/N_j$) continues to vary across jurisdictions and is increasing in population size. Using the universalism allocations in equation (3), we can express the population-adjusted budget shares ($g_j = G_j/GN_j$) as a function of delegates per capita:

$$g_j = G^{-1}\left(\frac{Jv_j}{V}\right)^{1-\gamma} f\left(\left(\frac{Jv_j}{V}\right)^{-\gamma} N^{-1}\right). \tag{17}$$

The implication of this model is very simple: population-adjusted budget shares are declining in population and are thus increasing in delegates per capita ($\partial g_j/\partial v_j > 0$). Note that in this model, which has no political process, the result is driven purely by differences in population, as opposed to differences in representation; in aggregate, small states have lower federal tax liabilities and thus are more responsive to common pool incentives.

Legislative Bargaining

The legislative bargaining model has a qualitative prediction similar to that of the universalism model, although the underlying mechanism is somewhat different. At the agenda setter's optimal proposal, as expressed by equations (8) through (11), expected per capita budget shares can be summarized as follows:

$$E(g_j) = \underbrace{\frac{V_j}{V}}_{\Pr(j=a)} \underbrace{\frac{\delta}{N_j}}_{E(g_j|j=a)} + \underbrace{\left(1 - \frac{V_j}{V}\right)}_{\Pr(j \neq a)} \times \underbrace{(\beta/G)N_j^{\gamma-1}1[V_j/\beta N_j^{\gamma} > \text{Median}(V_k/\beta N_k^{\gamma})]}_{E(g_j|j \neq a)}, \tag{18}$$

where the payment to the agenda-setter's state is given by $\delta = 1 - \sum_{k \in M_j}(\beta/G)N_k^{\gamma}$, and the median is taken across all jurisdictions. Next, by the fact that $V_j = V/J$, $N_j = V/Jv_j$, and $\text{median}(f(x)) = f(\text{median}(x))$ of the function f is monotonic, per capita federal spending can be expressed solely as a function of delegates per capita:

$$E(g_j) = \underbrace{\frac{\delta v_j}{V}}_{\text{Proposal-power channel}} + \underbrace{[(J-1)/J](\beta/G)(V/J)^{\gamma-1}v_j^{1-\gamma}1[v_j > \text{Median}(v_k)]}_{\text{Vote-cost channel}} \tag{19}$$

As shown in equation (19), the legislative bargaining model also predicts that disproportionate representation by small states confers a small-jurisdiction bargaining advantage as per capita federal spending is strictly increasing in per capita representation. This relationship reflects two underlying channels. Through the proposal-power channel, small states are more likely to be represented as the agenda-setter after adjusting for population differences. Through the vote-cost channel, small states are more attractive coalition partners given their relatively low federal tax contributions into the common pool.

9.4 Evidence from the US Senate

Several studies have tested the hypothesis of a small jurisdiction bias using evidence from the US Senate, which has two delegates from each state regardless of state population. Atlas et al. (1995) report a statistically significant relationship between per capita representation in the US Senate and per capita federal spending in an econometric analysis of aggregate census data between 1972 and 1990. Lee (1998) tests for a small state advantage using data from the US Domestic Assistance Programs Database, as compiled by Bickers and Stein (1991). These data contain federal spending by Congressional districts, although the author aggregates up to the state level in order to focus on

Table 9.4
Evidence on small state bias in the US Senate

Data description spending included	Census all (1)	CAGW all projects (2)	CAGW Senate projects (3)	CAGW House/ Senate projects (4)
Senators per million residents	0.0002** (0.0000)	0.0044** (0.0004)	0.0097** (0.0009)	
Representatives per million residents	0.0023** (0.0008)	−0.0101 (0.0115)		
Delegates per million residents				0.0106** (0.0007)
Implied Senate elasticity	0.05	0.54	0.95	1.04
Observations	400	450	450	900
Fiscal years	1995–2002	1995–2003	1995–2003	1995–2003
State fixed effects	No	No	No	Yes
R-squared	0.1107	0.1522	0.1897	0.5024

Source: From Knight (2004b).
Notes: Dependent variable is per capita budget shares in 2003 dollars, standard errors in parentheses; ** denotes 95% significance; * denotes 90% significance. Census data refer to Consolidated Federal Funds Report, CAGW to Citizen against Government Waste, constant not reported. House delegation sizes normalized to Senate delegation sizes (i.e., divided by 4.35).

differences in per capita Senate representation. Similarly to Atlas et al. (1995), the author finds statistically significant evidence of a small state advantage in the US Senate.

Table 9.4 summarizes preliminary results from Knight (2004b) regarding the small-state bargaining advantage in the US Senate between 1995 and 2003. For comparability with the existing literature, column 1 provides results using aggregated census data. The following model, which relates per capita federal spending to per capita representation, is estimated:

$$g_{st} = \alpha + \beta_1 v_{st}^{SENATE} + \beta_2 v_{st}^{HOUSE} + u_{st}, \tag{20}$$

where s indexes states, t indexes time, and u_{st} represents unobserved determinants of the geographic distribution of per capita federal spending. As shown in column 1, an extra senator is associated with an extra 0.02 percent share of spending. Although statistically significant, this relationship is economically weak; the implied elasticity of federal spending with respect to Senate representation is just 0.05.

There are several possible explanations for the economically weak relationship between per capita federal spending and senators per capita. Knight (2004b) addresses and attempts to empirically account for three such explanations. First, for institutional reasons, it may be difficult to geographically manipulate many types of federal spending, such as social security, in the census data. Column 2 addresses this concern by focusing on projects earmarked in congressional appropriations bills, as catalogued by a watchdog organization known as the Citizens Against Government Waste (CAGW). Relative to the highly aggregated census data, the geography of these CAGW projects was more easily manipulated by congressional delegations. As shown, an extra senator is associated with an extra 0.4 percent share of federal spending, and this relationship is statistically significant. Moreover these results imply an elasticity of spending per capita with respect to Senate representation of 0.54, a significantly stronger result than that using the census data in column 1.

Even with these data on highly manipulable project spending, it may prove difficult to isolate the effect of Senate representation from other factors. In addition to the US Senate, several other political agents, such as the US House and the executive branch, play a role in the geographic distribution of funds associated with federal projects. To isolate the effects of representation in the US Senate, Knight (2004b) focuses on those projects that were identified by the CAGW as sponsored by the Senate. As shown in column 3, an extra Senator again has a statistically significant effect and the implied elasticity is 0.95, up significantly from that in column 2.

The final innovation of Knight (2004b) involves the role of unobserved state characteristics. States with high per capita representation in the Senate are considered outliers across many dimensions. Without controlling for unobserved characteristics of these states, any measured relationship between Senate representation and the distribution of federal funds may reflect the role of these unobserved factors. To address this omitted variable bias, the specification associated with column 4 includes observations on both Senate-sponsored projects and House-sponsored projects, allowing for the inclusion of state fixed effects. The estimating equation in this instance is given as follows:

$$g_{stc} = \alpha_s + \beta_1 v_{sct} + u_{stc}, \tag{21}$$

where c indexes chambers and α_s captures the state fixed effects. By including state-fixed effects, the small state bias is identified from within-state variation in both federal spending and representation. Part of this variation is due to differential growth rates in state population, as captured by annual population estimates available from the Census Bureau. More important, however, is the within-state variation across chambers. In particular, we attribute any differences between Senate and House appropriations in small population states, relative to those differences in large population states, to the overrepresentation of these small states in the US Senate.

As shown, after controlling for these unobserved state factors, we find that delegates per capita have a strong and statistically significant effect on the distribution of per capita federal spending, and the economic relationship becomes even stronger, as the implied elasticity rises to 1.04. Taken together, the regression results in Knight (2004b) provide strong evidence of a statistically and economically significant relationship between per capita delegation sizes and federal spending per capita.

9.5 Conclusion

In summary, the studies surveyed in this chapter provide consistent evidence that individual legislators and legislatures in the aggregate respond to common pool incentives. In turn, common pool situations, in conjunction with the overrepresentation of small states in central legislatures, lead to a redistribution of public spending from large to small jurisdictions. These findings raise a natural question: How should constitutional and political institutions be designed in order to minimize the inefficiencies associated with common pool problems under the centralized provision of local public goods? While much research remains to be done in this area, there are two clear areas in which institutions could be changed. First, public goods could be provided in a more decentralized fashion. Second, in addition to centralization in the provision of public goods, political institutions in central governments could be altered.

Decentralized provision of public goods should keep local governments from exploiting national common tax pools, since they must then fully internalize the costs associated with the provision of local public goods. As discussed by Mueller in chapter 8 of this volume, constitutional and legal institutions must be created to keep the central government from encroaching on the powers of decentralized governments. Where such institutions can be created, the disadvantages of centralization must, of course, be balanced against the potential benefits of centralization, as discussed in the introduction of this chapter. The benefits should include the internalization of cross-jurisdiction externalities, elimination of competition for tax revenues, better redistribution of income, and more risk sharing. Less than full decentralization should include at least an increase of local cost sharing aimed at minimizing the inefficiencies associated with common pool problems. As this chapter showed, the compelling evidence comes from DelRossi and Inman's (1999) study of representatives in the US Congress and their responsiveness to increases in local cost shares.

Within a federation, the political institutions in central governments are useful in ensuring that federal spending provides net benefits to a majority of taxpayers, not just those in small states. Political institutions under centralization increase the power of nationally elected executives who can serve to counterbalance the common pool incentives faced by locally elected representatives. In the US states Baqir (2002) provides evidence that mayors with strong veto power are able to mitigate common pool problems, and Holtz-Eakin (1988) demonstrates that politically powerful governors, executives use their veto powers to hold down aggregate state government spending. In the US states, minimizing common pool problems also means decreasing the powers of small states, which are often overrepresented in central legislatures such as the US Senate.[4] As shown in Knight (2004b), small states, which contribute little into the federal tax pool and are overrepresented on committees with key agenda-setting powers, are quite responsive to common pool incentives in the US Senate. By contrast, in the US House, which is apportioned according to population, small and large states receive similar funding on a per capita basis. From a positive perspective, changes in Senate representation are unlikely as Article V of the US constitution states that "no state, without its Consent, shall be deprived of its equal Suffrage in the Senate," effectively providing veto power to small states over any changes in Senate representation. Some legal scholars, however, have argued that abolishing the Senate may not violate this article, although such a change would still require support of two-thirds of both chambers and three-quarters of the states (Lee 1930). In the European Union, by contrast, the representation of countries is still being negotiated, and the results in this chapter suggest that the outcome of these negotiations may have an important effect on the cross-country distribution of EU spending.

Notes

1. Riker (1964) takes a more positive perspective. He argues that for a federation to form, the politicians must be motivated by both a desire to expand their territory and a military threat or opportunity.

2. For a opposing view, see Stumpf (2002), who argues that experimentation under decentralization introduces a free-rider problem; that is, jurisdictions fail to internalize.

3. This theoretical framework follows Persson and Tabellini (2002) and Knight (2004a, 2003b).

4. Other political institutions, such as supermajority voting rules, could be adopted in order to protect small states from being exploited in central legislatures by large states; this protection was one of the original motivations for equal representation in the US Senate.

References

Asdrubali, P., B. Sorenson, and O. Yosha. 1996. Channels of interstate risk sharing: United States 1963–1990. *Quarterly Journal of Economics* 111: 1081–1110.

Atlas, C., T. Gilligan, R. Hendershott, and M. Zupan. 1995. Slicing the federal government net spending pie: Who wins, who loses, and why. *American Economic Review* 85: 624–29.

Baqir, R. 2002. Districting and government overspending. *Journal of Political Economy* 110: 1318–54.

Baron, D., and J. Ferejohn. 1987. Bargaining and agenda formation in legislatures. *American Economic Review* 77: 303–309.

Baron, D., and J. Ferejohn. 1989. Bargaining in legislatures. *American Political Science Review* 83: 1181–1206.

Bayoumi, T., and P. Masson. 1995. Fiscal flows in the United States and Canada: Lessons for monetary union in Europe. *European Economic Review* 39: 253–74.

Besley, T., and A. Case. 2003. Political institutions and policy choices: Evidence from the United States. *Journal of Economic Literature* 41: 7–73.

Besley, T., and S. Coate. 2003. Centralized versus decentralized provision of local public goods: A political economy analysis. *Journal of Public Economics* 87 (12): 2611–37.

Bickers, K., and R. Stein. 1991. *Federal Domestic Outlays, 1983–1990: A Data Book.* M.E. Sharpe.

Bradbury, J., and M. Crain. 2001. Legislative organization and government spending: crosscountry evidence. *Journal of Public Economics* 82: 309–25.

Buchanan, J. M. 1949. The pure theory of government finance: A suggested approach. *Journal of Political Economy* 57: 496–505.

DelRossi, A., and R. Inman. 1999. Changing the price of pork: The impact of local cost sharing on legislators' demands for distributive public goods. *Journal of Public Economics* 71: 247–73.

Feldstein, M., and M. Vaillant. 1998. Can state taxes redistribute income? *Journal of Public Economics* 68: 369–96.

Gilligan, T., and J. Matsusaka. 1995. Deviations from constituent interests: The role of legislative structure and political parties in the states. *Economic Inquiry* 33: 383–401.

Goolsbee, A., and E. Maydew. 2000. Coveting thy neighbor's manufacturing: The dilemna of state income apportionment. *Journal of Public Economics* 55: 125–43.

Hettich, W., and S. Winer. 1999. *Democratic Choice and Taxation*. Cambridge: Cambridge University Press.

Holtz-Eakin, D. 1997. The line item veto and public sector budgets: Evidence from the states. *Journal of Public Economics* 36: 269–92.

Holtz-Eakin, D., and A. Schwartz. 1995. Spatial productivity spillovers from public infrastructure: Evidence from state highways. *International Tax and Public Finance* 2: 459–68.

Inman, R., and Rubinfeld, D. 1997. Rethinking federalism. Journal of Economic Perspectives, 11.

Knight, B. 2004a. Parochial interests and the centralized provision of local public goods: Evidence from congressional voting on transportation projects. *Journal of Public Economics* 88: 845–66.

Knight, B. 2004b. Legislative representation, bargaining power, and the distribution of federal funds: Evidence from the U.S. senate. NBER working paper 10385.

Lee, B. 1930. Abolishing the Senate by amendment. *Virginia Law Review* 16: 364–69.

Lee, F. 1998. Representation and public policy: The consequences of Senate apportionment for the geographic distribution of federal funds. *Journal of Politics* 60: 34–62.

Lockwood, B. 2002. Distributive politics and the benefits of decentralization. *Review of Economic Studies* 69: 313–38.

Oates, W. 1972. *Fiscal Federalism*. New York: Harcourt Brace.

Persson, T., and G. Tabellini. 2002. Political economics and public finance. In A. Auerbach and M. Feldstein, eds., *Handbook of Public Economics*, Vol III. Amstredam: New Holland.

Pettersson-Lidbom, P. 2003. Does the size of legislature a.ect the size of government? Evidence from a natural experiment. Working paper.

Poterba, J. 1996. Budget institutions and fiscal policy in the U.S. states. *American Economic Review* 86: 395–400.

Riker, W. 1964. Federalism: Origin, Operation, Significance. Boston: Little, Brown.

Strumpf, K. 2002. Does decentralization increase policy innovation. *Journal of Public Economic Theory* 4: 207–41.

Strumpf, K., and F. Oberholzer-Gee. 2002. Endogenous policy decentralization: Testing the central tenet of economic federalism. *Journal of Political Economy* 110: 1–36.

Weingast, B., K. Shepsle, and C. Johnsen. 1991. The political economy of benefits and costs: A neoclassical approach to distributive politics. *Journal of Political Economy* 89: 642–64.

IV Legal Institutions, Regulation, and Economic Growth

10 Judicial Independence and Economic Growth: Some Proposals Regarding the Judiciary

Lars P. Feld and Stefan Voigt

10.1 Introduction

Hamilton called the judiciary "the least dangerous branch" (1787, Federalist Paper 78). This evaluation has frequently been invoked, and it might be one reason why the judiciary has rarely moved to center stage during discussions concerning issues of constitutional design. To give just one example: in his treatise on "Comparative Constitutional Engineering," Sartori (1994) deals extensively with electoral systems (majoritarian vs. proportional) as well as with the modus of electing the executive (presidential vs. parliamentary systems) but the term "judiciary" does not even appear in the index.

It has, however, been hypothesized that judicial independence (JI) is one central aspect in the proper functioning of the judiciary as part of the concept of separation of powers as it has been developed by Montesquieu and further concretized by Hamilton, Madison, and Jay, the authors of the Federalist Papers. Feld and Voigt (2003) have recently presented two indicators that aim at making judicial independence measurable. Their first indicator deals with de jure independence, meaning the independence of the superior courts as it can be deduced from legal documents. Their second indicator deals with de facto independence, meaning the degree of independence that the superior courts factually enjoy. Estimating the impact of judicial independence on economic growth, Feld and Voigt (2003) find that while de jure judicial independence does not have an impact on economic growth, de facto judicial independence has positively influenced real GDP per capita growth in a sample of 56 countries. The impact of de facto judicial independence on economic growth is robust to outliers, to the inclusion of several additional economic, legal, and political control variables and to the construction of the index. The clear conclusion is that judicial independence matters for economic growth.

If judicial independence matters for growth, economists ought to reconsider its role when discussing issues of constitutional design. Accordingly, the main question of this chapter is to ask what components of de jure and de facto judicial independence are particularly conducive to economic growth and how they interact with the constitutional and legal environment in the different countries.[1] This investigation is based on a cross section of 73 countries, extending the Feld and Voigt (2003) data set. In a first step, we replicate the result of the former paper—namely that the independence of superior courts matters for economic growth—for the extended data set. In a second step, we inquire into the effects of the organizational structure of the judiciary. In a third step, it is asked whether institutional arrangements that are not part of the judiciary themselves have an impact on economic growth and whether there is an interaction of other constitutional and legal provisions with JI. We find that de facto JI has a robust and highly significant positive impact on economic growth.

Looking at the components of de jure JI, the specification of the procedures, of the accessibility, and of the term length of highest court judges in the constitution show a modestly significant positive impact on economic growth, while a wide accessibility of the highest court as well as the highest court's power for constitutional review are negatively affecting economic growth. The other components of de jure JI do not appear to have an impact. With respect to de facto JI, no deviations from "normal" average term length, low numbers of changes of the number of judges since 1960, and a competitive income of judges are the main factors influencing growth. With regard to the impact of the organizational structure of the courts on economic growth, we find no significant differences between courts organized as constitutional courts and courts organized differently. Concerning the additional constitutional and legal environment, our results indicate that the positive impact of de facto JI on economic growth is stronger in presidential than in parliamentary systems as well as in systems with a high degree of checks and balances. De facto JI appears to be effective regardless of the age of a constitution. However, where countries are able to implement de facto JI, those with older constitutions have a growth disadvantage.

To noneconomists, the approach taken in this chapter might seem odd: according to many, the primary function of the judiciary would be to enhance justice, fairness, and equity. Yet, these goals do not necessarily conflict with economic growth. If the degree to which these goals are realized can be kept constant and with different institutional arrangements promote different levels of growth (or per capita income), it makes sense to argue in favor of the implementation of institutional arrangements that are most conducive to economic growth.

In this chapter we are concerned with the economic consequences of institutional choices regarding the judiciary broadly conceived. It is thus a positive analysis. As long as the underlying goal—economic growth—is shared, it can easily be turned into constitutional advice. The choice of institutional arrangements, however, will not be endogenized. We are thus not concerned with possible reasons of constitution-makers to choose different institutional arrangements with regard to the judiciary (for this question, see Landes and Posner 1975; Ramseyer 1994; Ginsburg 2002). The chapter is organized as follows: In section 10.2, there is a short review of the existing literature. Section 10.3 presents a number of hypotheses concerning the effects of JI, judicial structure, and the structure of state organization on economic growth. Section 10.4 contains the description of our data set as well as our estimations. In section 10.5 we make some preliminary conclusions regarding constitutional design and in section 10.6 we offer some closing remarks.

10.2 Survey of the Literature

We will simply assume that the goal of constitutional design, concerning propositions on how the constitution should be designed, is a high growth rate of per capita income. We conjecture—and set out to test—that judicial independence is conducive to economic growth. If this effect can be proved, we consider it sufficient reason to establish an independent judiciary at the constitution-making stage (for a contractarian argument in favor of judicial independence, see Congleton 2003).

A diagrammatic description of the impact of judicial independence on economic growth is given in figure 10.1. As the figure shows, in a sense, JI is both a dependent and an independent variable: once the constitutional convention has made its choice, JI can be used as an independent variable to explain economic growth. But, if the analysis of the choices of the constitutional convention are the target, JI is instead a dependent variable. There have been attempts to deal with the judiciary from both angles. Persson and Tabellini (2003) have

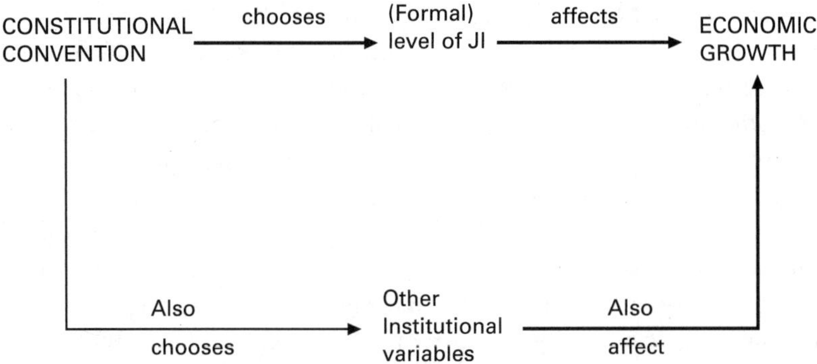

Figure 10.1
Impact of judicial independence on economic growth

shown that other constitutional arrangements such as the degree of checks and balances can—jointly with JI—also have an impact on economic growth. We thus test for other interaction effects.

Judicial independence has been analyzed as the amount of discretion that judges have at their disposal vis-à-vis representatives of other government branches by a research program dubbed "positive political theory" (for a survey see Weingast 1996). Papers originating from this program usually apply spatial voting models that identify the ideal points of all relevant actors in issue space.[2] The amount of discretion that the judiciary has at its disposal then depends on the exact location of the ideal points of the other actors. If one actor anticipates the locations of other actors correctly, he can make a decision that maximizes his own utility subject to two constraints: (1) the danger of being overridden by fresh legislation passed through the legislature or (2) the danger of having its dicta ignored by the executive. These models particularly center on the power games played among representatives of the various government branches.

The degree of independence is not completely determined by institutional provisions (number of chambers needed to press fresh legislation, required supermajorities, etc.) but also by the current preferences of politicians holding office. This is why empirical studies based on the positive political theory approach have focused on change of the level of judicial independence within a single country over time (Chavez, Ferejohn, and Weingast 2003 apply such a model to the United States and to Argentina over long periods of time). Empirical use of these models is, however, a tricky business because the relevant dimensions of many issues are anything but obvious and the ideal points of many actors are difficult to identify.

In her paper on "the budget as a signaling device," Toma (1991) analyzed one channel through which the other branches can communicate their (dis-)content with the decisions of the Supreme Court, namely by increasing or decreasing the Court's budget. Judicial independence can here be interpreted as the dependent variable, since the functioning of the Court depends on how the budget it gets allocated.

Hanssen (2002) recently tested two predictions first generated by Ramseyer (1994), namely that judicial independence will be higher (1) if politicians fear loss of power and (2) the more the ideal points of the rival parties are set apart. Using judicial retention procedures as the proxy for judicial independence, he finds empirical support for both hypotheses in his analysis of panel data on the US states between 1950 and 1990. In a number of papers, Ramseyer and Rasmusen have investigated the independence of the Japanese judiciary. Using personnel data on 276 judges, Ramseyer and Rasmusen (1997) present evidence that judges who decided a case against the government incurred the risk of being punished with less attractive posts. Ramseyer and Rasmusen (1999) extend that analysis by showing that Japanese judges who decide cases in favor of the government do better than those who favor taxpayers in two samples of 179 tax trial and 284 tax appeal cases.

Obviously judicial independence is endangered if the government is solely responsible for career developments of judges. This should particularly hold with respect to judges' re-election possibilities. With new and more detailed data, Ramseyer and Rasmusen (2001a) do, however, find evidence that judges who enjoin the national government jeopardize their career: Judges who enjoined the national government received fewer administrative responsibilities. Finally, Ramseyer and Rasmusen (2001b) provide evidence for the hypothesis that the high Japanese conviction rates (over 99 percent) reflect case selection and low prosecutorial budgets instead of any pro-conviction bias at the judicial administrative office.

Besley and Payne (2003) have recently used a similar approach to explain differences in judicial behavior: they find that judges bring about decisions that favor important parts of the electorate as this might increase their chances of being re-elected. Differences in the institutional arrangements of JI are used to explain differences in judicial decision-making. This is thus a study in which JI is indeed an independent variable. La Porta et al. (2004) have recently developed a measure that distinguishes the British and American concepts of JI and have found that the British concept is a good predictor for economic freedom whereas the American one is a good predictor for political freedom. Yet they have not tried to distinguish between JI as it is written in the books and as it is factually implemented. Neither of these papers, however, estimates the effects of JI on economic growth.

As figure 10.1 indicates, it might further be useful to think about possible impacts of other institutional variables such as the separation of powers on economic growth. Separation of powers is believed to constrain government and to make citizens better off. Yet its economic analysis has only recently begun. Brennan and Hamlin (1994) show that a strict separation of powers—as opposed to checks and balances, where the various branches check each other—can make citizens even worse off. Persson, Roland, and Tabellini (1997) find that the separation of powers can increase accountability of politicians vis-à-vis citizens. They also find that presidential systems can have an advantage over parliamentary ones with regard to accountability because the president is elected directly. The executive in parliamentary systems does not have to step down after legislative elections. So there is an incentive for the two branches to collude, which enables the executive to realize rents after election day.

Both models deal with the relationship among executive, legislature, and voters. Neither model treats the judiciary as an agent that functions as a constraint on the executive or the legislature. Padovano, Sgarra, and Fiorino (2003) extend the Persson et al. model to incorporate the judiciary as a fourth actor. They find that an independent judiciary improves accountability but that this is not the case for an accommodating judiciary. They conjecture that the likelihood that the three branches will collude (and that accountability will suffer) depends on the term lengths of the three branches. With regard to the judiciary, they expect longer term lengths to lead to lower accountability—and less welfare. Judicial independence as independence from pressure by representatives of the other government branches is not only a necessary condition for the implementation of the policies announced by the legislature, it also constitutes a danger: judges that are independent have incentives to remain uninformed, become lazy, and even corrupt.

Ferejohn (1999; see also Ferejohn and Kramer 2002) has argued that many judges are interested in the reputation of the judiciary because the other branches will be more likely to reduce JI if the judiciary does not maintain a high reputation. In other words, individual judges who do not live up to judicial standards can inflict costs on the branch as a whole. Voigt (2005) argues that independence from other government branches and accountability to the law need not compete with each other, as is often argued, but can, in fact, complement each other.

Another way to approach the judiciary is to view it as a technical institution to which a limited range of competence is delegated. Although the rational choice analysis of delegation has recently boomed (e.g., Majone 1996; Epstein and O'Halloran 1999; Voigt and Salzberger 2002 provide an overview), path-breaking theoretical insights concerning the judiciary have not yet emerged. In a paper concerned with the accountability of both politicians and judges, Maskin and Tirole (2001) confirm conventional wisdom that technical issues are ill-suited for the political process and that nonaccountable officials should be given less discretion than their elected counterparts.

Although research into causes and effects of the judiciary are of rather recent vintage, constitution-makers have, of course, always dealt with the issue. The *locus classicus* for issues regarding the institutional structure of the judiciary is still the Federalist Papers. Federalist 78 and 79, both penned by Hamilton, contain a number of institutional provisions that are to safeguard the independence of (federal) judges. In Federalist 78, Hamilton argues for life tenure, discusses the competence of nominating and appointing judges and makes a point in favor of giving the courts the competence of judicial review.[3] Mueller (1996) has recently reiterated that point stressing that the competence of judicial review is logically necessary if the judiciary is to safeguard citizens from the other government branches. In Federalist 79, Hamilton pleads in favor of guaranteeing judges a nondecreasing income and of introducing a highly regulated—and thus difficult to misuse—impeachment procedure.

It is interesting to note that Mueller (1996) does not think that institutional structure is sufficient to ensure a judiciary that is independent and accountable to its principals, namely the citizens: "For these, one has to rely on the 'culture of the judiciary' and the great status (and possibly financial rewards) that surround it." In other words, formal constitutional rules might not be sufficient to ensure an independent judiciary.

10.3 Hypotheses on the Impact of Judicial Independence on Economic Growth

A Very General Argument

JI assumes that judges can expect their decisions to be implemented regardless of whether they are in the (short-term) interest of other government branches on which implementation depends. It further assumes that judges—apart from their decisions not being implemented—do not have to anticipate negative consequences as the result of their decisions, such as (1) being expelled, (2) being paid less, or (3) being made less influential.

Three archetypical situations in which the independent judiciary plays a crucial role can be distinguished:

1. Cases of conflict between private parties. If two parties have voluntarily entered into a contract and one of the contracting parties believes that the other side has not lived up to the contract, impartial dispute resolution may be necessary. As long as both sides expect the judiciary to be impartial and hence independent from pressure emanating from either of the contract partners or any third party, they can save on transaction costs while negotiating their contract. On average, lower transaction costs will lead to more welfare-enhancing transactions taking place.
2. Cases of conflict between government and the citizens, where the citizens are in need of an organization that can adjudicate who is right (who has acted according to the law). The judiciary performs this task. The task is not only to ascertain the constitutionality of newly passed legislation but also to check whether the representatives of the state have followed the procedural devices that are to safeguard the rule of law. The judiciary helps ensure that the government acts under the rule of law.
3. Cases of conflict between various government branches. In the absence of an impartial arbiter, conflicts between government branches are most likely to develop into simple power games. An independent judiciary can keep them within the rules laid out in the constitution.

Among the many functions of government the reduction of uncertainty is most important. However, a law will only reduce uncertainty if the citizens can expect the letter of the law to be followed by government representatives. An independent judiciary can thus also be interpreted as a device to turn promises into credible commitments—for example, to respect property rights and abstain from expropriation. Where government abides by judiciary functions, citizens can develop longer time horizons that lead to investment in physical capital and higher specializations corresponding to different levels of human capital. In this case a high degree of JI can be conducive to economic growth.

Constitutional Provisions to Safeguard Judicial Independence

Suppose that JI does induce economic growth, how can constitutional provisions safeguard it? The independence of judges is dependent on the *stability* of the set of constitutional provisions within which they operate. Formally, the stability of the powers and procedures of the court depend on how difficult it is to change them. If they are specified in the constitution, we can expect a greater degree of independence than if they are simply fixed by law. This presupposes that constitutional law is more difficult to change than ordinary legislation.

The *appointment procedure* of the judges can have a big effect on the independence of the court. As it is inter alia supposed to protect citizens from illegitimate use of power by other government branches as well as to settle disputes between the branches of government, the judiciary ought to be as independent as possible from the other branches. We hypothesize that the most independent procedure for judicial appointment is by professionals (other judges or jurists).[4] The least independent method is appointment by one powerful politician (e.g., by a prime minister or a minister of justice).

Judicial tenure is also crucial for the independence of the judiciary. We assume that judges are most independent if they are appointed for life (or up to a mandatory retirement age) and cannot be removed from office, save by legal procedure. Judges are less independent if terms are renewable because they have an incentive to please those who can reappoint them. Further, if their *salaries* are determined by the members of one of the other government branches, this raises incentives to take the preferences of these members explicitly into account. General rules that their salary cannot be reduced increase, in turn, the independence of the judiciary.

Another component of judicial independence is the *accessibility* of the Court and its ability to initiate proceedings. A court that is accessible only to certain members of parliament or other officials will be less effective in constraining government than a court that is accessible to every citizen who claims that their rights are violated.

If the *allocation of cases* to the various members of the court is at the discretion of the chief justice, the chief justice's influence will be substantially greater than that of the other members of the court. It follows that in such an institutional environment, there may be interest to try to "buy" just the chief justice. We expect independence to be larger if there is a general rule according to which cases are allocated to the responsibility of single members of the court.

The competencies assigned to the constitutional court do not bear directly on its independence. Yet highest courts must have certain competencies in order to be able to check the behavior of the other government branches. If the constitution is interpreted as the most basic formal layer of rules that is to restrain (and to enable) government, then the competence of the court to check whether legislation is in conformity with the constitution is crucial. This is also known as the competence to constitutional or *judicial review*.

If courts have to *publish their decisions*, others can scrutinize them, and the reasoning can become subject to public debate. This can be interpreted as making it more difficult for representatives of the other government branches to have irrelevant considerations influence their decisions. The transparency will be even higher if the courts publish dissenting opinions.

All these issues can be taken up by corresponding constitutional provisions. In order to find out whether these have the expected effect on economic growth, we will test for their respective impacts in section 10.4.

Organizational Structure of the Judiciary

The variables discussed in the last section were all conjectured to affect judicial independence. There are a number of potentially relevant variables that might also determine the capacity of the judiciary to act as a constraint on the other government branches. If a strong and independent judiciary enhances economic growth, then the issues of judicial organization and structure can have an indirect effect on growth.

There are various possibilities to design constitutional review. (1) The review may be allocated to each and every court of a country, as it is the case in the United States, where there is no specialized court. In this case constitutional review is a posteriori, and the uniformity of jurisdiction is secured by the highest court of the country (as in the US Supreme Court). (2) The Austrian model as proposed by Kelsen (1920) creates a specialized constitutional court to deal with constitutional matters. It can undertake both abstract and concrete reviews, as well as ex ante and ex post reviews. (3) The French model assigns constitutional matters to a special body (the *Conseil Constitutionnel* in France) that is constrained to ex ante review (Harutyunayn and Mavcic 1999).[5]

There is no clear-cut hypothesis concerning the effects of the various systems. It can, however, be argued that judicial influence is broadest where the judiciary has the competence to check upon the constitutionality of laws both ex ante and ex post and where constitutional review can be both abstract and concrete. In the US model, constitutional review is restricted to ex post and concrete review. Formal competencies of judiciaries organized along the lines of the Austrian model are often broader, since they can encompass ex ante and abstract constitutional review. The French model is more restricted from the other side of the spectrum. In France constitutional review is only possible before a law has come into force. If laws are recognized to be incompatible with the constitution after they have been in force, there is little that the *Conseil Constitutionnel* can do.

Assuming that legislators prefer not to be called back by the judiciary and that judicial decisions can be anticipated perfectly by the members of the legislature, it is difficult to see why there should be any systematic difference between ex ante and ex post reviews. If the only difference is the timing, then government would never announce an unconstitutional law. Given these restrictive assumptions, no law will ever end up contested in court.

Relaxing the assumptions can change the results, however. If we introduce imperfect foresight in the effects of fresh legislation both with regard to legislators and to judges, the equilibria under ex ante review can be different from those under ex post review. If some of the effects of newly announced legislation are not anticipated, ex ante review will find the law in accordance with the constitution, whereas ex post review, taking into account some of the experiences already due to the new law, will lead the judges to declare it unconstitutional.[6]

In this case we would expect the Austrian model to have some advantages over that of the United States and also that of France. Between the latter, the French system seems to be the one conferring least competence to the judiciary.

Effects of Constitutional Provisions Not Dealing with the Judiciary

Constitutional provisions not directly dealing with the judiciary can also have an impact on the influence of the judiciary. For example, if the system of checks and balances puts tight constraints on the executive and the legislature, this could translate into relatively more influence for the judiciary. Henisz (2000) has proposed an indicator for measuring the degree of checks and balances that is based on the number of veto players found in a political system. Beck et al. (2000) have proposed a similar measure on which we concentrate here.[7]

Closely related to the number of veto players is the question whether the political system is a parliamentary or a presidential one. Presidential systems are characterized by a more stringent separation of powers. This could lead one to conjecture that the role of the judiciary should be more important in presidential systems. Yet there are a number of counterarguments: the effectiveness of the judiciary does not depend on legal provisions alone, it depends more on the ways the provisions are enforced. Factual judicial independence is a result of the incentives of the members of the other government branches to comply with rules regarding the judiciary as laid down in the constitution. It will therefore be asked whether the incentives to renege on the relevant constitutional rules depend on whether the system is presidential or parliamentary. We include a variable here that distinguishes between presidential and parliamentary systems based on the Database on Political Institutions (DPI), which was provided by Beck et al. (2000).

A third possible determinant, also closely related to the first one, is the question of whether one is dealing with a unitary or a federal system. Federal systems have a larger number of veto players than unitary ones and we would, ceteris paribus, expect a higher degree of de facto JI in federal than in unitary states. Unfortunately, it is notoriously difficult to "measure" the degree of federalism of a given political system. Treisman (2000) uses a dummy variable to account for federalism based on the work of Elazar (1995) and Riker (1964). This variable is adopted here.

Yet another aspect of the issue of veto players is the possibility to constrain the judiciary itself. If the judiciary has the competence to constrain the legislature and the executive but no branch has the (legal) competence to constrain the judiciary, its members might have incentives to become overly active, overly passive, or to follow their own agenda, whatever that may be. This danger was precisely described by Brutus in the Anti-Federalist Paper 11 (Ketcham 1986): "It is, moreover, of great importance, to examine with care the nature and extent of the judicial power, because those who are to be vested with it, are to be placed in a situation altogether unprecedented in a free country. They are to be rendered totally independent, both of the people and the legislature.... No errors they may commit can be corrected by any power above them... nor can they be removed from office for making ever so many erroneous adjudications." Another possible constitutional constraint on judicial behavior is the popular referendum. Hayek (1960, p. 192), for example, suggests this possibility: "the practice of restraining government's pursuit of immediate aims by general principles is partly a precaution against drift; for this, judicial review requires as its complement the normal use of something like the referendum, an appeal to the people at large, to decide on the question of general principle." It can thus be argued that the use of referenda acts as a constraint on the judiciary and makes it more accountable.[8] Whether referenda can induce additional economic growth cannot be tested due to the lack of internationally comparable data, but it is a mechanism to keep in mind for future research.

The design of basic rights also shapes the decisions of an independent judiciary. For example, a free press is hypothesized to be conducive to a high degree of de facto JI. If politicians consider tinkering with the independence of the judiciary, a press that is largely free from government interference can make such attempts costly—and hence less attractive—for politicians by widely reporting them. In such cases a free press can help those opposed to undermining the independence of the judiciary to overcome their collective action problems. The indicator used here is provided by Freedom House on an annual basis and takes into account aspects such as whether or not dissent is allowed, whether there is political pressure on the content of the media no matter whether state run or privately owned, whether there is economic influence on media content that can distort the quality of reporting, and whether there have been any incidents in which press freedom was violated, in murders, arrests, suspensions, and the like.

10.4 Data Description, Estimation Approach, and Results

Recently two new indicators measuring de jure as well as de facto JI were introduced (Feld and Voigt 2003). For reason of simplicity, these indicators measure the independence of only the highest court of a country, be it a appellate court or a constitutional court. Because the judiciary within many states is made up of thousands of decision-makers, radical simplification was necessary. The focus on the highest court seems warranted because the ultimate control of court decisions lies with the highest court. The highest court reviews—on the initiative of the parties involved—the lower court decisions. The independence of the highest court thus is crucial for constitutional design.

The two indicators are constructed to be objective. This avoids measurement problems associated with independence data obtained by polls. People who live under different rules are sure to have their perceptions of their judiciary systems determine their behavior. Thus the norm of what is an ideally independent judiciary will most likely be different in different parts of the world and yield data that are not easily comparable. By basing the two new indicators on factual information, we obtain a uniform measure of judicial independence.

The indicator measuring de jure JI contains sixteen variables, the indicator measuring de facto JI includes ten. The de jure indicator is made up of the variables already described in section 10.2 and includes the method of nominating or appointing the highest judges, their term lengths, the possibility of reappointment, the procedure of removing them from office, their pay and possible measures against reduction of their income, the accessibility of the court, the question of whether there is a general rule allocating cases to specific judges, and publication requirements concerning the decisions of the court. The de facto indicator includes variables such as the effective average term length, the number of times judges have been removed from office since 1960, whether their income has remained at least constant in real terms since 1960, whether the size of the budget of the court has remained at least constant in real terms since 1960, and the number of cases in which judicial articles of the constitution were changed as well as the number of times in which other government branches remained inactive when their action was necessary in order to implement a court ruling.[9] All variables take values between 0 and 1. The sum of the variables is then divided by the number of variables for which information is available. The result is two indexes (de jure and de facto JI) that lie between 0 and 1. Currently data are available for about 80 countries (the data can be obtained from the authors upon request).

The estimation approach is straightforward and follows the method used in modern empirical growth studies (e.g., see de Haan and Sturm 2000). The following equation is estimated:

$$\Delta Y_i = \alpha M_i + \beta JI_i + \gamma Z_i + \varepsilon_i, \quad (1)$$

where ΔY_i is average real GDP growth per capita of country i between the years 1980 and 1998, M_i is a vector of standard explanatory variables of country i, JI_i are the de jure and de facto indexes of judicial independence in country i, Z_i is a vector of additional explanatory variables in country i that are introduced to check the robustness of the baseline model and to consider the interaction with the constitutional, legal and political environment of a country, and ε_i is an error term.

Average real GDP growth per capita is obtained from the new Penn World Tables Version 6.0 (Heston, Summers, and Aten 2001). The data set has various problems with respect to eastern European countries. The 1990s data for these countries are not comparable to the 1980s data or do not even exist for the 1980s in some newly created states. Thus real GDP growth per capita had to be averaged for these countries, starting with the first year GDP data are available instead of averaging it for the time period 1980 to 1998.[10] To ensure that the eastern European countries do not drive the results, a dummy variable is introduced that takes on the value of one if the country is a transition country and is zero otherwise.

The vector M_i consists of three variables that are robustly linked to economic growth according to previous studies (de Haan and Sturm 2000). These variables are the level of initial real GDP per capita (in our sample, "initial" is 1980), investment in percent of GDP averaged over the period 1980 to 1998, and the percentage of secondary school attained in the total population aged 15 and older in 1980. With the exception of the latter variable, which is from the Barro and Lee data set, these data are from the PWT 6.0.

The additional economic variables making up the vector Z_i are average government consumption in percentage of GDP between 1980 and 1996, openness measured by the sum of exports and imports in percent of GDP, average population growth between 1980 and 1998, and the average inflation rate, all from the PWT 6.0 data set. The reason for including these variables for testing the impact of judicial independence stems from empirical growth studies. We use continent dummies to check for robustness of the estimation results. In addition to these standard variables, the data by La Porta et al. (1999) on the legal origin of countries are used to test robustness of the growth impact of JI. Finally, a number of additional constitutional, legal, and political variables are included, such as the age of the constitution, whether or not the court system follows the Austrian model, the extent of checks and balances in the constitution, and the distinction between presidential and parliamentary systems—the latter two based on the Database on Political Institutions (DPI) provided by Beck et al. (2000) —a dummy variable on federalism reported by Treisman (2000), and an indicator for a free press provided by Freedom House.

The empirical strategy is the following: First, baseline regressions are performed adding the two JI indicators in turn. Second, the additional economic variables and continent dummies are included in the regression in order to check the robustness of the results. Third, the JI indexes are differentiated into their single components. Fourth, the additional constitutional, legal, and political variables are included in the regression and are interacted with de facto JI in order to investigate the differential effects. We present only a selection of robustness checks in order to keep the chapter readable. Several other variations of these regressions, not reported here, were also performed in order to check robustness. The cross-sectional analysis is performed by the simple OLS technique, while inference is based on *t*-statistics computed on the basis of White heteroscedasticity consistent standard errors.[11]

Baseline Results

The estimation results of the baseline specification are presented in table 10.1. The three basic economic variables in column 1 explain the average real economic growth per capita quite well. These variables have the expected signs and high explanatory power. Note that the initial real GDP per capita has a negative impact on economic growth that is significant at the 1 percent significance level. Thus a catch-up effect can be observed in the cross-country sample. The real investment share has the expected positive impact on economic growth and is significant on the 1 percent level, while the secondary school attainment rate has the expected positive impact and is significant on the 5 percent significance level. The dummy variable for transition countries indicates a significant negative impact on economic growth. This simple

Table 10.1
OLS regressions of GDP growth per capita from 1980 to 1998 on judicial independence and controls, baseline specifications

Variables	(1)	(2)	(3)	(4)	(5)	(6)
De jure judicial independence	—	0.635 (0.42)	—	−0.463 (0.29)	0.081 (0.05)	0.280 (0.18)
De facto judicial independence	—	—	1.885*** (3.20)	1.914*** (3.08)	1.511** (2.34)	1.673** (2.49)
Real GDP per capita in 1980 ($1,000s)	−0.177*** (4.04)	−0.180*** (4.06)	−0.200*** (4.19)	−0.200*** (4.15)	−0.205*** (3.42)	−0.264*** (4.40)
Secondary school attainment rate in 1980 (%)	0.047** (2.47)	0.048** (2.48)	0.037* (1.95)	0.036* (1.84)	0.032 (1.58)	0.037* (1.74)
Real gross domestic investment (% of GDP), average in 1980–98	0.170*** (5.63)	0.169*** (5.61)	0.178*** (6.81)	0.180*** (7.04)	0.159*** (5.43)	0.144*** (3.63)
Dummy for transition countries	−1.805** (2.19)	−1.798** (2.19)	−1.085 (1.23)	−1.065 (1.20)	−1.549* (1.70)	−2.202** (2.14)
Dummy for Africa	—	—	—	—	−0.890 (1.30)	—
Dummy for Asia	—	—	—	—	−0.060 (0.10)	—
Dummy for South America	—	—	—	—	−1.196** (2.38)	—
Average population growth, 1980–98	—	—	—	—	—	−0.821*** (2.82)
Openness (% of GDP)	—	—	—	—	—	0.006 (1.03)
Government consumption (% of GDP)	—	—	—	—	—	−0.011 (0.45)
Inflation	—	—	—	—	—	−0.020 (1.10)
Constant	−1.352	−1.646	−2.136	−1.920	−1.004	−0.038
$\bar{R}^2$	0.508	0.503	0.641	0.636	0.476	0.657
SER	1.800	1.808	1.571	1.582	1.565	1.537
J-B	4.206	4.975	2.327	1.719	5.226	5.191
Observations	87	87	73	73	73	73

Notes: The numbers in parentheses are the absolute values of the estimated *t*-statistics, based on the White heteroscedasticity-consistent standard errors. ***, **, or * show that the estimated parameter is significantly different from zero on the 1, 5, or 10% level, respectively. SER is the standard error of the regression, and J-B the value of the Jarque-Bera test on normality of the residuals.

growth model explains about 50 percent of the variance of the real growth rate per capita, and the hypothesis of normality of the residuals cannot be rejected according to the Jarque-Bera test statistics.

Explanatory power is not improved if the de jure JI indicator is introduced in the model (column 2). The adjusted R^2 slightly declines from 51 to 50 percent. Adding the de jure JI indicator to the baseline regression does not affect those estimation results. De jure JI has the expected positive impact on average real GDP growth per capita, but it is not significantly different from zero. Introducing de facto JI instead of de jure JI (column 3) noticeably changes the estimation results however.[12] It increases the explanatory power of the empirical model measured in the adjusted R^2 from 51 to 64 percent. Moreover, and as expected, de facto JI has a positive impact on real economic growth per capita and is significantly different from zero on the 1 percent significance level. The impact of the variables of the baseline regression remains robust, although the significance of the impact of the secondary school attainment rate is reduced to the 10 percent level and the dummy variable for transition countries is not significant anymore.

These overall results do not change if both indicators of JI are introduced in one equation (column 4). De facto JI has a significantly positive impact on economic growth, while the impact of de jure JI changes its sign but is far from any significance level. The impact of de facto JI is robust to the inclusion of continental dummies (column 5) and additional economic variables (column 6), both groups of variables only reduce the significance of the impact of de facto JI to the 5 percent level. The overall performance of the estimated model is reduced when the continent dummies are included. It increases compared to the specification reported in column 4 when the additional economic variables are introduced. In all the specifications reported in table 10.1 the hypothesis of normal distribution of the residuals cannot be rejected at any conventional significance level. The latter holds for nearly all further estimations and is thus not mentioned below. This result is important to be kept in mind, however, because it indicates the absence of outliers.

Results on Single Indicators

It is easy to recommend the implementation of higher levels of JI in general, but specifying how this can be achieved and what the crucial elements of JI are appears to be more challenging. For questions of constitutional design, the effects of the different components of de jure and de facto JI are of great interest.

In order to ascertain the impact of different components of both JI indicators, we include the single indicators separately. Because the indexes are not complete for each question, the missing values are set to the median of each variable. This is a method that is often used in survey studies. Although this might appear to be a questionable method, it does provide insight as to whether there are specific components of JI that exert particular impacts on economic growth.

The results for the de jure JI components, as reported in table 10.2, column 1, support those from the baseline specifications. Since some variables are positively and others negatively correlated with GDP growth, it is no surprise that the index as an aggregate of those countervailing influences does not have a significant impact. Moreover almost none of the single indicators exhibit a statistically significant individual impact on GDP growth. The one exception is the anchoring of the procedures of the highest courts in the constitution, which is significant on the 5 percent level and exhibits a positive sign. However, several variables have t-statistics that are higher than 1, and the hypothesis that all indicators of de jure JI together have no impact on real GDP growth per capita can be rejected on the 10 percent level (F-statistic $= 1.611$).

In a next step we drop individual variables by testing for redundancy and keep those variables for which redundancy is rejected. The results of this procedure are reported in column 2. Seven single components of de jure JI appear to have a common impact on economic growth. At least, the hypothesis that they have no impact is rejected on the 5 percent significance level ($F = 2.803$). Again, the anchoring of the procedures of the highest courts in the constitution exhibits a positive sign, which is significant at the 5 percent level. In addition the broad accessibility of courts and the court's power for constitutional review are both significant at the 10 percent level and have a negative impact on economic growth.

The drawback of the estimation results in column 2 of table 10.2 on single components of de jure JI is that the impact of de facto JI is not controlled for. Including the index of de facto JI (column 3) notably affects the results. We thus repeat the test for redundancy on different groups of variables and exclude those for which redundancy cannot be rejected, a procedure that finally leaves us with the estimated equation in column 4.

Table 10.2
OLS regressions of GDP growth per capita from 1980 to 1998 on de jure judicial independence and controls, single indicators

Variables	(1)	(2)	(3)	(4)
Highest court mentioned in the constitution	−1.061 (0.68)	—	—	—
Competences of highest court enumerated	−3.120 (0.61)	—	—	—
Procedures specified	9.169** (2.22)	8.062** (2.08)	4.085 (0.92)	4.829 (1.30)
Accessibility specified	4.694 (1.44)	3.940 (1.17)	4.986 (1.35)	5.152 (1.44)
Term length specified	9.656 (1.02)	10.003 (1.37)	10.068 (1.36)	9.497 (1.32)
Number of judges specified	−0.945 (0.11)	—	—	—
Constitutional rigidity	0.479 (0.56)	—	—	—
Agreement requirement of branches of government	−0.929 (0.68)	—	—	—
Majorities at different points in time requirement	2.509 (0.95)	—	—	—
Election methods of the members of the highest court	0.291 (0.42)	—	—	—
Ratio of term of office and parliament election period	−2.679 (0.63)	—	—	—
Reelection possibility of judges	0.653 (1.21)	0.555 (1.22)	0.632 (1.16)	—
Removal of judges from office	−0.099 (0.21)	—	—	—
Accessibility to highest court	−1.145 (1.44)	−1.398* (1.78)	−1.444* (1.80)	−1.003 (1.46)
Rule for allocation of cases	−0.192 (0.43)	—	—	—
Discretion for allocation of cases	−0.936 (1.53)	−0.640 (1.36)	−0.281 (0.62)	—
Constitutional review part of constitution	−0.890 (1.52)	−0.986* (1.85)	−0.910* (2.14)	−0.702 (1.48)
Publication requirements	0.021 (0.03)	—	—	—
De facto judicial independence	—	—	1.297** (2.24)	1.177** (2.13)
F-statistics	1.611*	2.803**	2.709**	3.025**
Standard controls	Robust	Robust	Robust	Robust
$\bar{R}^2$	0.536	0.579	0.683	0.683
SER	1.756	1.672	1.485	1.476
J-B	0.129	0.474	0.567	2.546
Observations	87	87	73	73

Notes: See table 10.1.

The hypothesis that reelection possibilities of judges and discretion in the allocation of cases do not have a joint impact on real GDP growth per capita cannot be rejected at any conventional significance level ($F = 0.816$). The anchoring in the constitution of procedures, of the accessibility of the highest courts and also the term length of its judges, as well as the broad accessibility to the highest court and the power for constitutional review does, however, have a joint impact on economic growth ($F = 3.025$). According to these results, the specifications of the powers and procedures of the court have a (modest in statistical terms) positive impact on economic growth. If the procedures are specified in the constitution there is a greater degree of independence than if they are simply fixed by ordinary law. However, the broad accessibility to highest courts and the power for constitutional review exert a negative impact on economic growth. Neither the appointment procedure, nor judicial tenure, the legal term length or publication requirements appear to play an additional role.

Following the same procedure of exclusion of variables, we obtain the main components of de facto JI that have an impact on economic growth.[13] According to the results in column 5 of table 10.3, the positive impact of de facto JI on economic growth is mainly obtained for countries with no or only slight deviations from the "normal" average term length of judges, those with a small number of changes of the number of judges and those countries that secure at least a real constancy of judges' salaries. These three variables each have a positive impact on economic growth that is significant on the 5 percent level. Excluding one of these variables in turn leaves the impact of the remaining two variables unaffected.

Interaction of Judicial Independence with Organizational, Constitutional, Legal, and Political Environment

As noted above, judicial independence might work differently in different environments. Three measures of organizational environment are analyzed in this section. First, the legal origin of a country as a kind of legal tradition is included as an explanatory variable. La Porta et al. (1999) distinguish among English, Socialist, French, Scandinavian, and German legal origins.[14] Column 1 in table 10.4a contains the estimation results of the baseline specification, including the two JI indicators and the legal origin dummies of which we chose to exclude the Scandinavian legal origin dummy in place of the constant term. The inclusion

Table 10.3
OLS regressions of GDP growth per capita from 1980 to 1998 on de facto judicial independence and controls, single indicators

Variables	(1)	(2)	(3)	(4)	(5)
Measures against income reductions of judges	0.207 (0.49)	—	—	—	—
Adequate payment of judges legally fixed	−0.165 (0.22)	—	—	—	—
Effective average term length of judges	0.351 (0.35)	0.389 (0.41)	—	—	—
No or small deviations from "normal" average term length	1.033* (1.71)	1.180** (2.23)	1.205** (2.33)	1.178** (2.24)	1.148** (2.10)
Small numbers of effective removals before end of term	0.505 (1.05)	0.570 (1.22)	0.577 (1.24)	0.584 (1.26)	—
No or small changes of the number of judges	1.378** (2.02)	1.437** (2.14)	1.428** (2.14)	1.414** (2.13)	1.483** (2.06)
Real income at least constant	1.508*** (2.78)	1.458*** (3.14)	1.467*** (3.12)	1.052** (2.57)	1.045** (2.54)
Budget of the highest court at least constant	−0.629 (1.11)	−0.548 (1.18)	−0.550 (1.18)	—	—
No or small number of changes of relevant articles of the constitution	0.672 (0.70)	—	—	—	—
No or small implementation deficit of court's rulings	0.485 (0.73)	—	—	—	—
F-statistics	3.112***	4.287***	5.056***	4.390***	5.280***
Standard controls	Robust	Robust	Robust	Robust	Robust
$\bar{R}^2$	0.561	0.575	0.580	0.582	0.580
SER	1.700	1.672	1.662	1.658	1.663
J-B	0.909	1.965	1.845	1.426	1.499
Observations	73	73	73	73	73

Notes: See table 10.1. The estimation results for the dummy for transition countries are not reported.

of the legal origin variables does not have an impact on the estimation results of the two JI variables. As before, de facto JI is significant at the 1 percent level and has a positive impact on economic growth, whereas de jure JI does not reach any significance level. Of the legal origin variables, only socialist legal origin has a significant positive impact, although the hypothesis that the legal origin variables has no impact on economic growth is rejected on the 1 percent significance level ($F = 17.811$).[15]

Table 10.4a
Regressions of GDP growth per capita from 1980 to 1998 on judicial independence and controls, interactions with legal and constitutional environment

Variables	(1)	(2)	(3)	(4)	(5)
De jure judicial independence	−0.032 (0.02)	−0.476 (0.29)	−0.852 (0.53)	−0.357 (0.22)	−0.373 (0.23)
De facto judicial independence	1.970*** (2.98)	1.959*** (3.20)	2.922*** (3.41)	2.041*** (3.12)	1.969*** (2.71)
Additional variables					
English legal origin	0.017 (0.03)	—	—	—	—
Socialist legal origin	3.140*** (4.52)	—	—	—	—
French legal origin	−0.589 (1.21)	—	—	—	—
German legal origin	−0.528 (0.78)	—	—	—	—
F-statistic: Legal origin	17.811***	—	—	—	—
Age of the constitution	—	0.004** (2.12)	0.019*** (3.11)	—	—
Age of the constitution * de facto judicial independence	—	—	−0.022** (2.59)	—	—
Constitutional court	—	—	—	−0.537 (1.22)	−0.624 (0.70)
Constitutional court * de facto judicial independence	—	—	—	—	0.150 (0.13)
Dummy for transition countries	−4.356*** (4.50)	−0.775 (0.87)	−0.637 (0.74)	−0.722 (0.77)	−0.700 (0.74)
Standard controls	Robust	Robust	Robust	Robust	Robust
F-statistics: De facto judicial independence	—	—	5.838***	—	6.498***
F-statistics: Age of the constitution	—	—	4.830***	—	—
F-statistics: Constitutional court	—	—	—	—	0.835
$\bar{R}^2$	0.648	0.649	0.664	0.639	0.634
SER	1.554	1.572	1.540	1.574	1.586
J-B	4.758*	1.876	0.763	1.130	0.963
Observations	73	71	71	73	73

Notes: See table 10.1. Results for the standard controls and constant are not reported.

Table 10.4b

Regressions of GDP growth per capita from 1980 to 1998 on judicial independence and controls, interactions with legal and constitutional environment

Variables	(1)	(2)	(3)	(4)	(5)	(6)
De jure judicial independence	−0.418 (0.26)	−0.379 (0.23)	−0.116 (0.08)	−0.632 (0.43)	−0.991 (0.58)	−0.954 (0.54)
De facto judicial independence	1.904*** (3.17)	0.909 (1.06)	1.580*** (3.04)	2.581*** (2.84)	2.117*** (3.16)	1.817*** (2.68)
Additional variables						
Checks and balances	0.119** (2.07)	−0.120 (0.61)	—	—	—	—
Checks and balances ∗ de facto judicial independence	—	0.298 (1.49)	—	—	—	—
Parliamentary system	—	—	0.729*** (3.26)	1.190*** (3.46)	—	—
Parliamentary system ∗ de facto judicial independence	—	—	—	−0.996* (1.75)	—	—
Federalism	—	—	—	—	−0.235 (0.51)	−0.995 (1.02)
Federalism ∗ de facto judicial independence	—	—	—	—	—	1.330 (1.04)
Dummy for transition countries	−1.091 (1.25)	−1.013 (1.15)	−1.374 (1.60)	−1.441* (1.72)	−1.641 (1.48)	−1.567 (1.46)
Standard controls	Robust	Robust	Robust	Robust	Robust	Robust
F-statistics: De facto judicial independence	—	5.688***	—	4.806**	—	5.595***
F-statistics: Checks and balances	—	6.718***	—	—	—	—
F-statistics: Parliamentary system	—	—	—	6.881***	—	—
F-statistics: Federalism	—	—	—	—	—	0.559
$\bar{R}^2$	0.468	0.467	0.678	0.688	0.459	0.459
SER	1.577	1.578	1.488	1.463	1.625	1.625
J-B	2.758	2.261	1.903	1.285	0.177	0.028
Observations	73	73	73	73	63	63

Notes: See table 10.1. Results for the standard controls and constant are not reported.

Table 10.4c
Regressions of GDP growth per capita from 1980 to 1998 on judicial independence and controls, interactions with legal and constitutional environment

Variables	(1)	(2)	(3)	(4)
De jure judicial independence	−0.443	−0.580	−0.127	−0.627
	(0.27)	(0.34)	(0.09)	(0.41)
De facto judicial independence	1.870***	1.108	1.669**	2.999***
	(3.31)	(0.80)	(2.63)	(2.91)
Additional variables				
Age of the constitution	—	—	0.010**	0.015*
			(2.39)	(1.94)
Age of the constitution ∗ de facto judicial independence	—	—	—	−0.013
				(1.22)
Constitutional court	—	—	−0.201	−0.231
			(0.38)	(0.45)
Parliamentary system	—	—	0.936***	1.114***
			(3.71)	(3.11)
Parliamentary system ∗ de facto judicial independence	—	—	—	−0.563
				(0.94)
Checks and balances	—	—	0.018	0.018
			(0.21)	(0.20)
Federalism	—	—	−0.453	−0.297
			(0.98)	(0.65)
Free press	−0.003	−0.010	−0.005	−0.002
	(0.16)	(0.44)	(0.31)	(0.14)
Free press ∗ de facto judicial independence	—	0.022	—	—
		(0.60)		
Dummy for transition countries	−1.073	−1.139	−1.753*	−1.575
	(1.21)	(1.23)	(1.70)	(1.54)
Standard controls	Robust	Robust	Robust	Robust
F-statistics: De facto judicial independence	—	5.623***	—	3.047**
F-statistics: Free press	—	0.178	—	—
F-statistics: Age of the constitution	—	—	—	2.321
F-statistics: Parliamentary system	—	—	—	6.215***
$\bar{R}^2$	0.630	0.628	0.572	0.578
SER	1.594	1.599	1.468	1.457
J-B	1.529	1.300	1.389	1.521
Observations	73	73	61	61

Notes: See table 10.1. Results for the standard controls and constant are not reported.

Second, the organizational environment is represented by the age of the constitution.[16] It could be argued that de facto JI is higher in countries that have not had many changes in their constitutions for the last 40 years. This argument stems from the construction of the de facto index that includes information on changes in the number of judges since 1960, real constancy of income and budget of judges since 1960, and so on. If the argument holds, newly created countries with new constitutions would have a clear disadvantage by construction. Column 2 of table 10.4a presents the results of the JI augmented baseline model to which the age of the constitution is included. The higher the age of the constitution, the higher is economic growth of the respective country, ceteris paribus. The impact of the age of the constitution is significant at the 5 percent significance level. The JI augmented baseline model is, however, not affected by the inclusion of that variable. In particular, the significant positive impact of de facto JI remains robust.

Interacting de facto JI with the age of the constitution produces an interesting result. While separately de facto JI and the age of the constitution remain robust and conducive toward economic growth, their interaction has a significantly negative impact. Countries with old constitutions experience significantly lower real GDP growth per capita given that they have a high degree of de facto JI. Turning this result around, it can be inferred that countries with new constitutions will experience higher growth rates given that they have a high degree of de facto JI. Unfortunately, the partial correlation coefficient between the variable "age of constitution" and de facto JI is −0.31, implying that the probability that a country with a young constitution manages to have a high degree of de facto JI is rather low.

The results are slightly different if real per capita GDP is used as the dependent variable. De facto judicial independence has a positive impact on real GDP per capita with an estimated coefficient of 3561.23 that is significant at the 5 percent level (t-statistic $= 2.20$), while the age of the constitution also exerts a positive influence of 58.75 that is significant at the 1 percent level (t-statistic $= 5.18$). An analysis of the interaction between both variables reveals an insignificant positive effect for the interaction term, while the significance of de facto JI is reduced to the 10 percent level ($F = 2.788$).[17] Hence the effect of age of the constitution in economic performance is independent of judicial independence.

Third, and most important, the consequences of JI could depend on the underlying court model. As argued above, constitutional review could be allocated to each court of a country as in the United States, to a specialized constitutional court that deals with constitutional matters as in Germany, or to a special body that is constrained to ex ante review as in France. With regard to the efficacy of JI, the constitutional court model has an advantage over the other two because it entails the power for ex ante and ex post as well as abstract and concrete review. Hence a dummy variable being one for a constitutional court according to the Austrian model and zero otherwise is included in the estimated equation. As reported in columns 3 and 4, neither the constitutional court variable nor its interaction with de facto JI has any significant impact on economic growth, while the impact of de facto JI remains robust with a significant positive effect.[18]

In addition to the organizational environment, other constitutional provisions can work together with JI to raise economic growth. Again, we focus on three variables. First, the extent of checks and balances is included in the model by drawing on an ordinally scaled variable provided by Beck et al. (2000). The more checks and balances in a constitution, the higher are the values of that variable, and thus economic growth. According to the results in column 1 of table 10.4b, this variable is significant at the 5 percent significance level but leaves the significant positive value of de facto JI unaffected. The interaction of de facto JI with the checks and balances variable does not entail clear-cut results. The overall effect of both de facto variables remains significant ($F = 5.688$), just as the overall effect of checks and balances remains significantly different from zero ($F = 6.718$). While the interaction term is not significant, the presence of strong checks and balances reinforces the impact of de facto JI on economic growth.

Closely connected to the checks and balances discussion is the political economics analysis of presidential versus parliamentary systems. In order to control for the differences in these systems, a variable by Beck et al. (2000) is used that adopts values of 0 for direct elections of the president, 1 for a strong president elected by an assembly, and 2 for elections of the head of state by the parliament. The results in columns 3 and 4 of table 10.4b indicate that parliamentary systems had much higher growth rates between 1980 and 1998 than presidential systems. These results corroborate the findings by Persson and Tabellini (2003, ch. 7) who find that presidential systems have lower labor productivity. While the significantly positive impact of de facto JI remains robust in both equations, it is most interesting that the interaction term of de facto JI and the parliamentary system variable has a significant negative impact indicating that the growth enhancing effect of de facto JI in particular exists in presidential systems.[19] Including a dummy variable for federalism as an indicator for the extent of vertical checks and balances does not have any significant impact on economic growth as columns 5 and 6 in table 10.4b reveal.

With respect to the political environment of JI, only the results of the free press are shown in the first two columns of table 10.4c. Neither the free press, nor the interaction term has any significant impact on economic growth while de facto JI remains robust. In addition we analyzed the impact of ethnic fractionalization and political stability in this model of economic growth. Since the results are similar to those reported by Feld and Voigt (2003), we abstain from reporting them here. Finally, the different organizational, constitutional, and political variables are included in the model jointly with the two JI indicators. The results are reported in columns 3 and 4 of table 10.4c. De facto JI keeps its remarkably robust impact on economic growth while the age of the constitution and the parliamentary system variable keep their impact from the analysis above, ceteris paribus. The single interaction terms are no longer significant. We show them only for the two variables mentioned before. The two de facto JI variables ($F = 3.047$) and the two parliamentary system variables ($F = 6.215$) are jointly significant, while the two age of constitution variables ($F = 2.321$) are not. Still these two reported interaction terms keep their signs from the preceding analysis such that some modest support for these hypotheses is possible.

10.5 Consequences for Constitutional Design

So far we have only reported the statistical significance of JI on economic growth. For issues of constitutional design this is, of course, insufficient. Advising constitutional designers to put great emphasis on creating the prerequisites for an independent judiciary can only be justified if its effects are also economically significant. A switch from a totally dependent to a totally independent judiciary would, ceteris paribus, lead to an increase in growth rates of between 1.5 to 2.1 percentage points according to our estimates.[20] This is an enormous increase in economic growth, which implies that real per capita GDP of a country with such an extreme constitutional switch will double in roughly 33 to 47 years.

Taken at face value, the consequences of our analysis for constitutional design are quite obvious: With respect to de jure JI, (1) the specification of the court procedures in the constitution, (2) the specification of the accessibility of the highest court, and (3) the specification of the term length of its judges have a (modest in statistical terms) positive impact on economic growth. It thus seems that special emphasis should be given to these three issues. Neither the appointment procedure, nor judicial tenure, the legal term length, or publication requirements appear to play an additional role.

It should be noted that it is the specification in the constitution that matters, and not the relative term length of judges, for example, vis-à-vis the other branches of government, as conjectured by Padovano, Sgarra, and Fiorino (2003). The key to understanding this result lies in the fact that constitutional revision is costly, so judges are more strongly insured against discretion of other branches of government. These results support the hypothesis that the foundation of JI in the constitution is desirable to its decree by simple legislation. *In turn, this leads to the advice to fix procedures and powers of the judiciary in the constitution.*

However, establishing broad access to the highest courts by individuals as well as enabling the court by constitutional means for constitutional review do not appear to be conducive to economic growth. At first sight this might contradict the separation of powers view, but close inspection underlines however the drawbacks of increasing JI too strongly. Both characteristics of independent courts have veto power that can bring on political stalemate. This is clearly counterproductive in economic terms, *so there is need to carefully consider the provisions that may reduce the effectiveness of JI by increasing courts' workload extensively either due to individual demand or to own initiative.*

With respect to de facto JI, our results show no or only slight deviations from the "normal" average term length of judges, infrequent changes of the number of judges, and judges' salaries kept at least constant in real terms account for the overall strong impact of de facto JI on economic growth. The first two components are a result of the constraints that the other branches of government have vis-à-vis the judiciary. The last component supports the notion that judicial independence is also a function of monetary rewards. If the members of one of the other government branches determine judges' salaries, this raises incentives to take the preferences of these members explicitly into account. *Here we have two suggestions: (1) reduce the actual use of dis-*

cretionary power of the other branches of government vis-à-vis the judiciary, and (2) provide judges with adequate pay.

An old and stable constitution is not a precondition for de facto JI to have a positive impact on economic growth. This is good news for countries willing to write a new constitution with full JI. Moreover the positive impact of de facto JI is independent of the legal structure of a country and the court type. Thus one size does not necessarily have to fit all. Other considerations in the choice of the court structure play a role without detering economic growth. According to our results, de facto JI interacts with the basic constitutional provisions. JI positively influences economic growth in presidential systems, and it appears to be a necessary component of checks and balances, or the separation of powers, in presidential systems. *A high degree of de facto JI is therefore advisable to restrict abuse of power by a president.*

But a few words of caution are in order. We have focused on one important part of the constitution—the judiciary—and ways to make it effective. Yet the introduction of judicial independence in an environment otherwise hostile to economic development does not have beneficial effects: What happens if formally judicial independence is introduced, but the legal rules that the judiciary is to decide on are inadequate for development? What happens if a newly established regime keeps its former corrupt judges and endows them with independence? Judicial independence is only part of a larger picture. Alone as a corrective measure, it is not sufficient to induce economic growth.

A recent issue of the World Development Report (2002, ch. 6) dealt with one part of the problem, namely judicial efficiency. The editors propose (1) increased accountability of judges, (2) simplification, and (3) increased resources. Increased accountability is supposed to be obtained by information on judicial performance, judges who work on individual calendars, and reporting of judicial statistics. Moreover open trials are expected to enable everyone to observe judges' conduct and keep them accountable. While we have not explicitly dealt with judicial accountability in this chapter, Hayek's (1960, p. 192) suggestion to supplement judicial independence by instruments of direct democracy in order to make judges accountable is well worth noting again. Curiously, it is often representatives of the legal science—the lawyers, law professors, and judges—who oppose the introduction of direct democracy.

We have not dealt with the political economy of establishing JI. From the empirical support for the hypothesis that JI is conducive to economic growth, we have inferred that it should be designed on the constitutional stage. Yet an independent judiciary can make the lives of government members more complicated because it acts as an additional constraint on their behavior. If members of the legislature and the executive are crucial for constitutional design, considerations such as these will often prevent them from installing an independent judiciary.

Finally, de facto judicial independence is what matters most. Despite the fact that the age of the constitution does not appear to be a precondition of de facto JI, it is not sufficient to write JI in new legal or constitutional documents without demonstrating that the state can live up to JI de facto. Reputation building is a time-consuming and costly exercise. Its dynamics are asymmetric in the sense that it is difficult to build up a replitation but easy to destroy it quickly. Both the political economy aspect and the importance of factual JI indicate the potential for time inconsistency in establishing an independent judiciary.

10.6 Conclusions and Outlook

In this chapter we investigated the impact of judicial independence (JI) on economic growth for a cross section of about eighty countries. We use two indicators of JI we introduced earlier (Feld and Voigt 2003), one measuring de jure and another measuring de facto JI. Basically our earlier results are reproduced for a larger sample, although they are stronger and more robust. De facto JI has a strong, significantly positive impact on economic growth whereas de jure JI does not. Some of our suggestions for constitutional design are obtained by estimating the impact of single components of both indicators and looking at their interaction with other organizational and constitutional factors. We summarize them here: First, the procedures and powers of the judiciary should be specified in the constitution instead of granting only legal independence. Second, the actual use of discretionary power of the other branches of government should be reduced vis-à-vis the judiciary and judges paid adequately. Third, high degrees of de facto JI in presidential systems can help restrict the abuse of power by presidents.

The most important issue for future research is to improve our knowledge of channels through which JI has an impact on economic growth. One way to approach this issue is to estimate the amount of additional (foreign direct) investment that is triggered by having a more independent judiciary and to estimate the growth in productivity of capital already in use that can be attributed to an independent judiciary. Another way to approach this issue is to go back to our scheme of three paradigmatic interaction situations that can be influenced by the existence of an independent judiciary, namely interactions among private citizens, interactions between citizens and the state, and interactions among government branches. The first interaction situation is within the realm of private law, whereas the other two situations are within the realm of public law. Knowing more about the channels through which JI has an impact on economic growth should enable us to give better constitutional advice.

Appendix

Descriptive statistics

Variable	Mean	Standard deviation	Minimum	Maximum
Real per capita GDP growth (%)	1.200	2.872	−9.997	14.058
Real GDP per capita 1998 ($1,000s)	9650.449	8354.589	493.00	31299.00
Real GDP per capita 1980 ($1,000s)	7299.250	5837.193	462.00	23350.00
Average real gross domestic investment 1980–98 (% of GDP)	15.182	7.501	1.987	44.168
Secondary school attainment rate in 1980 (%)	29.399	16.965	1.100	66.200
Average population growth (%), 1980–98	1.521	1.184	−1.103	4.185
Openness (% of GDP)	47.160	33.715	23.320	71.000
Government consumption (% of GDP)	21.418	8.033	8.213	60.154
Inflation (% relative to the US)	−3.362	17.846	−50.528	76.396
De jure JI	0.503	0.164	0.000	1.000
De facto JI	0.558	0.293	0.000	1.000
English legal origin	0.282	0.452	0.000	1.000
Socialist legal origin	0.204	0.405	0.000	1.000
French legal origin	0.408	0.494	0.000	1.000
German legal origin	0.058	0.235	0.000	1.000
Scandinavian legal origin	0.049	0.216	0.000	1.000
Age of the constitution	36.394	42.122	2.000	216.000
Court	0.899	0.798	0.000	3.000
Checks and balances	2.940	1.879	0.000	15.000
Parliamentary system	0.930	0.956	0.000	2.000
Federalism	0.210	0.410	0.000	1.000
Free press	37.760	21.040	8.000	83.000

Note: The variables are defined in the main text. Descriptive statistics for the single indicators of de jure and de facto JI can be obtained from the authors upon request.

Notes

The authors would like to thank the participants of the SNS Conference on Constitutional Design, in particular, Roger Congleton and Torsten Persson, for stimulating suggestions; the support of the Gesellschaft für Technische Zusammenarbeit (GTZ) in collecting data is gratefully acknowledged.

1. A number of programs of the World Bank deal with similar yet not identical goals. Our interest is in the independence of the judiciary from the other two government branches, whereas the World Bank often puts emphasis on the efficiency of the court system. Dakolias (1999) explained that efficiency-enhancing measures within the judiciary can be kicked off without having to wait for the consent of the other government branches. A more recent description of the World Bank's activities can be found in the World Development Report 2002 (especially chapter 7).

2. There are models on judicial discretion in statutory interpretation (e.g., Ferejohn and Weingast 1992) and on the reactions of the legislature (e.g., Gely and Spiller 1990). Others have analyzed the relationship between Congress and bureaucracy extensively (McCubbins and Schwartz 1984; McCubbins, Noll, and Weingast 1987, 1989; Moe 1990; Macey 1992; Zeppos 1993). There is plenty of institutional detail in these models, but one of their weaknesses is that they almost exclusively focus on the United States. A model in which the judiciary has some implicit scope for constitutional change is developed in Schnellenbach (2004).

3. On appointment, see also Federalist Paper 51 written by James Madison: "In order to lay a due foundation for that separate and distinct exercise of the different powers of government,..., it is evident that each department should have a will of its own; and consequently should be so constituted that the members of each should have as little agency as possible in the appointment of the members of the others."

4. In Federalist Paper 51, James Madison (Hamilton, Madison, and Jay 1788/1961, p. 321) writes: "In order to lay a due foundation for that separate and distinct exercise of the different powers of government,..., it is evident that each department should have a will of its own; and consequently should be so constituted that the members of each should have as little agency as possible in the appointment of the members of the others." On the same topic, Hamilton writes (Hamilton, Madison, and Jay 1788/1961, p. 470f.): "That inflexible and uniform adherence to the rights of the Constitution, and of individuals, which we perceive to be indispensable in the courts of justice, can certainly not be expected from judges who hold their offices by a temporary commission. Periodical appointments, however regulated or by whomever made, would, in some way or other, be fatal to their necessary independence. If the power of making them was committed either to the executive or legislature there would be danger of an improper complaisance to the branch which possessed it; if to both, there would be an unwillingness to hazard the displeasure of either; if to the people, or to persons chosen by them for the special purpose, there would be too great a disposition to consult popularity to justify a reliance that nothing would be consulted by the Constitution and the laws."

5. Most, but not all, constitutional systems can be grouped into one of the three models presented. Additionally Harutyanayn and Mavcic (1999) introduce a "new (British) Commonwealth model" implemented by Mauritius, and a "mixed (American continental) model," as can be found in a number of states, inter alia in Portugal, Columbia, Ecuador, Guatemala, and Peru.

6. Additionally it could be argued that the costs for government to be critically reviewed after a law has been passed are higher. So the opposition has the incentive to push to have laws evaluated as unconstitutional in ex post review. It would, of course, be desirable to separate the institutional effects of timing and to control for other differences such as the number of courts that have the power of constitutional review. This is not possible because the number of cases is often too small to subject to any econometric analyses.

7. Keefer and Stasavage (2003) find that the estimations of inflation rates based on (de jure) central bank independence significantly improve if the number of veto players is controlled for.

8. The instrument of referenda acts as an additional constraint on the other two government branches and against collusion between them. See, for example, chapter 2 by Frey and Stutzer in this volume and the references quoted there.

9. For a more detailed list of the different components of these indicators, see the appendix in Feld and Voigt (2003). Any questions concerning the data can be addressed to the authors.

10. Real GDP growth per capita is averaged in the following way: Slovak Republic 1987 to 1998, Ukraine 1989 to 1998, Czech Republic and Slovenia 1990 to 1998, Bulgaria and Russia 1991 to 1998, Armenia and Estonia 1992 to 1998, Lithuania 1993 to 1998, Azerbaijan and Kazakhstan 1994 to 1998, Croatia 1995 to 1998, and Georgia 1996 to 1998. Real GDP growth per capita thus corresponds less and less to long-term growth as supposed by the underlying growth theory. The structural shift between West German and unified German growth data is incorporated with in the following way: First, the average growth rate of GDP is computed for the period 1980 to 1990 for West Germany. Second, the average growth rate of GDP is computed for the period 1990 to 1998 for Unified Germany. Third, the mean is taken of both rates.

11. In order not to overburden the tables, standard errors are not reported without the White correction. These data can be obtained from the authors upon request.

12. Information on de facto JI is available for only 73 countries.

13. Comparison of the estimated equation in column 1 with that in column 5 of table 10.3 indicates that the hypothesis that the excluded variables are redundant cannot be rejected on any significance level (F-statistic $= 0.522$).

14. Note that the dummy variable for socialist legal origin and that for transition countries are not identical because the latter comprises the former USSR countries and the Eastern European countries only, but not China, Vietnam, Cambodia, and some African former socialist countries.

15. To account for the positive impact of the socialist legal origin east European transition countries are controlled for by the dummy for eastern European countries. Again, the socialist legal origin dummy mainly controls for China, Vietnam, Cambodia, and some African former socialist countries.

16. Including that variable reduces the number of observations by 2 because it is difficult to assess the age of a constitution in countries that do not possess a formal constitutional document like England.

17. Extending the analysis to real per capita GDP instead of growth is beyond the scope of this chapter. The full results can be obtained from the authors upon request. One of our next projects will be to analyze the impact of judicial independence on total factor productivity.

18. We estimated the same equation by re-coding the constitutional court variable to separate the French model from the American model. This way we measured the absence of a constitutional court in addition to the variable used in table 10.4a to capture the presence of a constitutional court. The results were virtually the same. A more precise analysis is left to our future research.

19. We offer here some words of caution. From earlier research (Hayo and Voigt 2003), we know that parliamentary systems are much more likely than presidential systems to realize high degrees of de facto JI. A few presidential systems have begun to do likewise, and the trend is likely to continue with other presidential systems adopting de facto JI.

20. The switch in judicial independence in the example is in the range of the de facto JI variable. The growth rates are derived from the minimum and maximum estimates in our regressions without interaction terms. In addition the net present value of additional growth should be compared to the costs of establishing a (more) independent judiciary. Only if the former is larger than the latter, does there exist a sufficient reason for trying to increase judicial independence.

References

Beck, Th., G. Clarke, A. Groff, Ph. Keefer, and P. Walsh. 2000. *New Tools and New Tests in Comparative Political Economy: The Database of Political Institutions*. Washington, DC: World Bank.

Besley, T., and A. Payne. 2003. Judicial accountability and economic policy outcomes: Evidence from employment discrimination charges. Mimeo, June.

Brennan, G., and A. Hamlin. 1994. A revisionist view of the separation of powers. *Journal of Theoretical Politics* 6: 345–68.

Brennan, G., and H. Kliemt. 1994. Finite lives and social institutions. *Kyklos* 47: 551–71.

Chavez, R., J. Ferejohn, and B. Weingast. 2003. A theory of the politically independent judiciary. Paper presented at the annual meeting of the American Political Science Association, Philadelphia, August.

Congleton, R. 2003. *Improving Democracy through Constitutional Reform: Some Swedish Lessons*. Dordrecht: Kluwer.

Dakolias, M. 1999. Court performance around the world: A comparative perspective. *Yale Human Rights and Development Law Journal*; downloadable from: http://www.yale.edu/yhrdlj/vol02/dakolias_maria_article.htm (June 22, 2003).

Duverger, M. 1980. A new political system model: Semi-presidential government. *European Journal of Political Research* 8: 165–87.

Elazar, D. 1995. From statism to federalism: A paradigm shift. *Publius* 25: 5–18.

Epstein, D., and S. O'Halloran. 1999. *Delegating Powers*. Cambridge: Cambridge University Press.

Feld, L. P., and S. Voigt. 2003. Economic growth and judicial independence: Cross-country evidence using a new set of indicators. *European Journal of Political Economy* 19: 497–527.

Ferejohn, J. 1999. Independent judges, dependent judiciary: Explaining judicial independence. *Southern California Law Review* 72: 353–72.

Ferejohn, J., and B. Weingast 1992. A positive theory of statutory interpretation. *International Review of Law and Economics* 12: 263–79.

Ferejohn, J., and L. Kramer. 2002. Independent judges, dependent judiciary—Institutionalizing judicial restraint. *New York University Law Review* 77: 962.

Gely, R., and P. Spiller. 1990. A rational theory of Supreme Court statutory decisions with applications to the State Farm and Grove City Cases. *Journal of Law, Economics, and Organization* 6: 263–300.

Ginsburg, T. 2002. Economic analysis and the design of constitutional courts. *Theoretical Inquiries in Law* 3: 49–85.

Haan, J. de, and J. E. Sturm. 2000. On the relationship between economic freedom and economic growth. *European Journal of Political Economy* 16: 215–41.

Hamilton, A., J. Madison, and J. Jay. [1788] 1961. *The Federalist Papers*, with an introduction by C. Rossiter. New York: Mentor.

Hanssen, A. 2002. Is there a politically optimal level of judicial independence? Mimeo.

Harutyunayn, G., and A. Mavcic. 1999. *Constitutional Review and Its Development in the Modern World: A Comparative Constitutional Analysis*. Yerevan and Ljubljana: Hayagitak.

Hayek, F. A. von. 1960. *The Constitution of Liberty*. Chicago: University of Chicago Press.

Hayo, B., and S. Voigt. 2003. Explaining de facto judicial independence. Volkswirtschaftliche Diskussionsbeiträge 46/03. Department of Economics, University of Kassel.

Henisz, W. 2000. The institutional environment for economic growth. *Economics and Politics* 12: 1–31.

Heston, A., R. Summers, and B. Aten. 2001. *Penn World Table, Version 6.0*. Center for International Comparisons at the University of Pennsylvania (CICUP).

Keefer, Ph., and D. Stasavage. 2003. The limits of delegation, veto players, central bank independence, and the credibility of monetary policy. *American Political Science Review* 97: 407–23.

Ketcham, R. ed. 1986. *The Anti-Federalist Papers and the Constitutional Convention Debates*. New York: Mentor.

La Porta, R., F. López-de-Silanes, Ch. Pop-Eleches, and A. Shleifer. 2004. Judicial checks and balances. *Journal of Political Economy* 112 (2): 445–70.

La Porta, R., F. Lopez-de-Silanes, A. Shleifer, and R. Vishny. 1999. The quality of government. *Journal of Law, Economics and Organization* 15: 222–79.

Landes, W., and R. Posner. 1975. The independent judiciary in an interest-group perspective. *Journal of Law and Economics* 18: 875–911.

Macey, J. R. 1992. Separated powers and positive political theory: The tug of war over administrative agencies. *Georgetown Law Journal* 80: 671–703.

Majone, G. 1996. Temporal consistency and policy credibility: Why democracies need non-majoritarian institutions. Working Paper RSC 96/57. European University Institute.

Maskin, E., and J. Tirole. 2001. The politician and the judge: Accountability in government. Working Paper.

McCubbins, M., and T. Schwartz. 1984. Congressional oversight overlooked: Police patrols versus fire alarms. *American Journal of Political Science* 28: 165–79.

McCubbins, M., R. Noll, and B. Weingast. 1987. Administrative procedures as instruments of political control. *Journal of Law, Economics, and Organization* 3: 243–77.

McCubbins, M., R. Noll, and B. Weingast. 1989. Structure and process, politics and policy: Administrative arrangements and the political control of agencies. *Virginia Law Review* 75: 431–82.

Moe, T. M. 1990. Political institutions: The neglected side of the story. *Journal of Law, Economics, and Organization* 6: 213–53.

Mueller, D. 1996. *Constitutional Democracy*. Oxford: Oxford University Press.

Padovano, F., G. Sgarra, and N. Fiorino. 2003. Judicial branch, checks and balances and political accountability. *Constitutional Political Economy* 14: 47–70.

Persson, T., and G. Tabellini. 2003. *The Economic Effects of Constitutions: What Do the Data Say?* Cambridge: MIT Press.

Persson, T., G. Roland, and G. Tabellini. 1997. Separation of powers and political accountability. *Quarterly Journal of Economics* 115: 1163–202.

Ramseyer, M. 1994. The puzzling (in)dependence of courts: A comparative approach. *Journal of Legal Studies* 23: 721–47.

Ramseyer, M., and E. B. Rasmusen. 1997. Judicial independence in a civil law regime: The evidence from Japan. *Journal of Law, Economics and Organization* 13: 259–86.

Ramseyer, M., and E. B. Rasmusen. 1999. Why the Japanese taxpayer always loses. *Southern California Law Review* 72: 571–95.

Ramseyer, M., and E. B. Rasmusen. 2001a. Why are Japanese judges so conservative in politically charged cases? *American Political Science Review* 95: 331–44.

Ramseyer, M., and E. B. Rasmusen. 2001b. Why is the Japanese conviction rate so high? *Journal of Legal Studies* 30: 53–88.

Riker, W. 1964. *Federalism: Origin, Operation, Significance*. Boston: Little Brown.

Sartori, G. 1994. *Comparative Constitutional Engineering*. New York: New York University Press.

Schnellenbach, J. 2004. The evolution of a fiscal constitution when individuals are theoretically uncertain. *European Journal of Law and Economics* 17: 97–115.

Toma, E. 1991. Congressional influence and the Supreme Court: The budget as a signaling device. *Journal of Legal Studies* 20: 131–46.

Treisman, D. 2000. The causes of corruption: A cross-national study. *Journal of Public Economics* 76: 399–457.

Voigt, S. 2005. The economic effects of judicial accountability—Some Preliminary insights. Mimeo. University of Kassel.

Voigt, S., and E. Salzberger. 2002. Choosing not to choose: When politicians choose to delegate powers. *Kyklos* 55: 247–68.

Weingast, B. 1996. Rational choice perspectives on institutions. In R. E. Goodin, and H. D. Klingemann, eds., *A New Handbook of Political Science*. New York: Oxford University Press.

World Development Report. 2002. Chapter 6: The Judicial System. Washington: World Bank.

Zeppos, N. S. 1993. Deference to political decisionmakers and the preferred scope of judicial review. *Northwestern University Law Review* 88: 296–371.

11 Constitutions and Prosperity: The Impact of Legal and Economic Institutions on the Wealth of Nations

Randall G. Holcombe, Robert A. Lawson, and James D. Gwartney

The relationship between constitutions and prosperity was seldom considered by economists through most of the twentieth century.[1] However, toward the end of that century economists increasingly recognized that prosperity requires institutions that protect property rights and freedom of exchange, and that allow people to be rewarded for their economic activities. The modern theory of economic growth, beginning with Solow (1956) and extended by Lucas (1988), Romer (1986, 1990), and others, focuses in the inputs of physical and human capital into the production process, and on technological advances, as the determinants of economic performance. In contrast to this production function approach, other scholars, such as Scully (1988, 1992), North (1990), Barro (1996), Landes (1998), Knack (1996, 2003), and Hall and Jones (1999), have emphasized the institutional foundations that are necessary for economic prosperity.[2] This chapter builds on the institutional approach by addressing two questions regarding constitutional design: What provisions should a constitution contain to promote prosperity? And how much of a difference does it make when those conditions are present?

11.1 Prosperity, Economic Freedom, and Constitutional Design

At the beginning of the twenty-first century, the idea that a market economy lays the foundation for prosperity, and that government interference with the market hinders economic progress, is generally accepted.[3] Yet there is less agreement on what the appropriate role for government is in a market economy. While some might argue that markets work best in the complete absence of government,[4] arguments from the market failure literature suggest that there is an extensive role for government to control the problems that would exist in an unfettered market. Mancur Olson (2000) argues for market-augmenting government, which is government activity that supports the operation of the market. Olson's market-augmenting government is not a middle ground between extreme laissez faire and central planning, but rather is a set of government institutions that lays a foundation for market activity and then steps out of the way to allow markets to function.[5] Olson's idea is appealing, but the question remains about what government institutions constitute market-augmenting government.

One answer to this question is given by the Economic Freedom of the World (EFW) index constructed by Gwartney and Lawson (2003). The EFW index is composed of 38 components that are designed to measure the degree to which a nation's institutions and policies support voluntary exchange, the protection of property rights, open markets, and minimal regulation of economic activity. There is solid empirical evidence that the EFW index is positively correlated with both the income levels of countries and their GDP growth rates. Gwartney, Holcombe, and Lawson (2004) show that the EFW index is positively correlated with income levels and growth rates for a set of 99 countries that range from developed nations to those that are poor and that have negative growth rates. Gwartney, Lawson, and Holcombe (1999) show similar results using an earlier version of the EFW index.[6] This suggests that the components of the EFW index can be used as a guide to the design of a constitution to promote prosperity.

The EFW Index as a Measure of Constitutional Design

The EFW index contains 38 individual components grouped into five broad areas. The details of its construction are explained in Gwartney and Lawson (2003). The raw data for each component were transformed into a zero to ten scale and then aggregated into five general areas to construct the index. The areas and individual components are listed in table 11.1. The broad areas are (1) size of government, (2) legal structure and security of property rights, (3) access to sound money, (4) exchange with foreigners, and (5) regulation of economic activity. The components of the EFW index were chosen because they are factors the economics literature has cited as facilitating market exchange. They are not intended to be used as instruments, for example, as Acemoglu and Robinson's (2001) use of malaria rates as an indicator of institutional quality, but rather as actual measures of institutional

Table 11.1
Areas and components of the EFW index

Area 1: Size of government expenditures, taxes, and enterprises

A. General government consumption spending as a percentage of total consumption.
B. Transfers and subsidies as a percentage of GDP.
C. Government enterprises and investment as a percentage of GDP.
D. Top marginal tax rate (and income threshold to which it applies).
   i. Top marginal income tax rate (and income threshold at which it applies).
   ii. Top marginal income and payroll tax rate (and income threshold at which it applies).

Area 2: Legal structure and security of property rights

A. Judicial independence: The judiciary is independent and not subject to interference by the government or parties in disputes.
B. Impartial courts: A trusted legal framework exists for private businesses to challenge the legality of government actions or regulation.
C. Protection of intellectual property.
D. Military interference in rule of law and the political process.
E. Integrity of the legal system.

Area 3: Access to sound money

A. Average annual growth of the money supply in the last five years minus average annual growth of real GDP in the last ten years.
B. Standard inflation variability in the last five years.
C. Recent inflation rate.
D. Freedom to own foreign currency bank accounts domestically and abroad.

Area 4: Freedom to exchange with foreigners

A. Taxes on international trade.
   i. Revenue from taxes on international trade as a percentage of exports plus imports.
   ii. Mean tariff rate.
   iii. Standard deviation of tariff rates.
B. Regulatory trade barriers.
   i. Hidden import barriers: No barriers other than published tariffs and quotas.
   ii. Costs of importing: The combined effect of import tariffs, license fees, bank fees, and the time required for administrative red tape raises costs of importing equipment by (10 = 10% or less; 0 = more than 50%).
C. Actual size of trade sector compared to expected size.
D. Difference between official exchange rate and black market rate.
E. International capital market controls.
   i. Access of citizens to foreign capital markets and foreign access to domestic capital markets.
   ii. Restrictions on the freedom of citizens to engage in capital market exchange with foreigners: Index of capital controls among 13 IMF categories.

Area 5: Regulation of credit, labor, and business

A. Credit market regulations.
   i. Ownership of banks: Percentage of deposits held in privately owned banks.
   ii. Competition: Domestic banks face competition from foreign banks.
   iii. Extension of credit: Percentage of credit extended to private sector.
   iv. Avoidance of interest rate controls and regulations that lead to negative real interest rates.

Table 11.1
(continued)

- v. Interest rate controls: Interest rate controls on bank deposits and/or loans are freely determined by the market.

B. Labor market regulations.
- i. Impact of minimum wage: The minimum wage, set by law, has little impact on wages because it is too low or not obeyed.
- ii. Hiring and firing practices: Hiring and firing practices of companies are determined by private contract.
- iii. Share of labor force whose wages are set by centralized collective bargaining.
- iv. Unemployment benefits: The unemployment benefits system preserves the incentive to work.
- v. Use of conscripts to obtain military personnel.

C. Business regulations.
- i. Price controls: Extent to which businesses are free to set their own prices.
- ii. Administrative conditions and new businesses: Administrative procedures are an important obstacle to starting a new business.
- iii. Time with government bureaucracy: Senior management spends a substantial amount of time dealing with government bureaucracy.
- iv. Starting a new business: Starting a new business is generally easy.
- v. Irregular payments: Irregular, additional payments connected with import and export permits, business licenses, exchange controls, tax assessments, police protection, or loan applications are very rare.

factors. Because of this connection with the literature, the components of the EFW index are good measures for drawing policy conclusions about specific institutional changes that can actually be implemented.[7]

Consistent with Olson's (2000) idea of market-augmenting government, in order to achieve a high EFW rating, a country must do some things while refraining from doing others. The country's legal institutions must protect the property rights of owners and enforce contracts. The country must also provide access to sound money. Governments must refrain from activities that interfere with voluntary exchange and the freedom to compete in labor, capital, and product markets. As measured by the EFW index, economic freedom is reduced when taxes, government expenditures, and regulations are substituted for personal choice, voluntary exchange, private contracts, and market coordination.

The use of the EFW index as a measure of institutional quality is attractive for several reasons. First, it is comprehensive; it measures a wide range of institutional factors that the literature on growth and development suggests should lay a foundation for prosperity. Second, as the results from a broad literature show, there is a strong correlation between the EFW index and both the level of income and growth of income. While the idea that market institutions lead to economic prosperity is widely accepted, there is not as general an acceptance of what the role of government should be in a market economy. Because of the correlation between economic performance and the EFW index, one can argue that the components of the EFW index provide a good list of institutional factors that affect prosperity.

In reviewing the broad areas of the EFW index, some areas appear more directly related to constitutional design than others, which relate more to institutions than policies. Area 1, Size of government, might be viewed more as an issue of collective preference rather than constitutional design,[8] and area 3, Access to sound money, also might be viewed as an issue of public finance or monetary policy rather than a constitutional issue. The question of whether these areas reflect constitutional or merely institutional issues will be considered further below. Meanwhile, in the empirical work that follows, an abridged EFW index containing only areas 2, 4, and 5 (Legal structure and property rights, Freedom to exchange with foreigners, Regulation) will be used as measures of constitutional quality in addition to the complete EFW index. This way an empirical examination can be made of constitutional design issues using both a broader and a narrower measure of constitutional quality.

Related Literature

A number of studies have used the EFW index to examine the impact of economic institutions on income and growth, while other studies have looked at the correlation between some specific institutional characteristic and economic prosperity, or have used some narrower measure as a proxy for the broader concept of institutional quality.[9] Berggren (2003) gives a good review of the EFW index and an extensive literature that has used it in empirical work. Berggren (2003, p. 202) presents a table showing that studies using the EFW index have consistently found that the level of the index is positively correlated with the level of income, and that a change in the index is positively correlated with income growth. Carlsson and Lundstrom (2002) look at components of the EFW index and find that while the index as a whole is positively correlated with higher income levels, some components have a weak—or even negative—relationship. For example, the size of government component tends to be negatively correlated.[10] Nevertheless, the index overall shows a strong positive correlation with income. Thus it appears that better institutions, as measured by the EFW index, result in higher income, and an improvement in institutions leads to higher income growth.

In contrast to the consistent results that higher institutional quality, as measured by the EFW index, produces a higher level of income, and a change in institutional quality produces a change in the growth rate of income, some studies find that the level of the index is positively correlated with income growth, while others find an insignificant relationship. If higher EFW indexes did not produce permanently higher rates of income growth, this would be consistent with the Solow (1956) growth model in which all economies have the same long-run steady-state growth rates. This interpretation suggests that once a country reaches a level of income consistent with its EFW index, better institutions yield higher income but may not produce higher growth rates over the long run. Readers interested in more detail about how the EFW index has been used in the empirical literature on economic growth should consult Berggren (2003) for a thorough review.

The idea that institutions lay a crucial foundation for economic prosperity is not new, but only recently has the importance of institutions been emphasized. When Bauer (1957) focused on the importance of market institutions to economic development, his view ran counter to most development economists. The conventional wisdom in development at that time was that, following Solow (1956), inputs into the production process and technological advancement were the keys to growth, and that government planning showed more promise than a reliance on market institutions. While development economists do not advocate government planning in place of markets, the more recent contributions to the growth literature that build on Solow (1956), such as Lucas (1988) and Romer (1986, 1990), typify the literature emphasizing this production function approach to growth, where institutions are largely ignored and the focus is on inputs and technology. In this context the empirical work below tries to disentangle the effects of institutions from the effects of inputs.

North (1990) is another economist who has consistently argued the role of institutions in economic development, and Landes (1998) has followed North's historical emphasis by describing in detail the role of institutions in the creation of prosperity. Olson (1982, 1996, 2000) has also consistently argued the importance of institutions to prosperity. Despite a number of prominent economists who made such arguments, one factor that has hampered those who have argued the importance of institutions is that institutional quality is difficult to quantify. In contrast, taking a production function approach, capital and labor are relatively easy to measure, so quantifying the impact of inputs into the production process is easier than quantifying the effects of institutions. Scully (1988, 1992) was one of the early scholars who attempted such a quantification by using the Freedom House index appearing in Gastil (1978) and in subsequent volumes that quantified freedom in a cross section of countries. Scully's results showed the positive correlation between freedom and prosperity, but the Freedom House index explicitly measures political freedoms, not economic freedoms, and following the literature on institutions and prosperity, there may be significant differences between economic and political freedom.

Economic freedom and political freedom are closely correlated, as Gwartney, Lawson, and Holcombe (1999) show, but Barro (1996) argues, that democracy, a big component of political freedom, does not appear to be a causal factor in economic growth. Similarly Gwartney, Lawson, and Holcombe (1999) show that when economic freedom, as measured by the EFW index, is accounted for, political freedom is not correlated with higher income or greater income growth. Because of the correlation between economic and political freedoms, political freedom may work as a proxy for the quality of economic institutions, but the literature shows that economic institutions, not political institutions, lay the foundation for prosperity.[11] Of course, people desire political freedoms for other reasons, and perhaps even directly economic reasons. They may view democratic government as a form of insurance against uncertainties inherent in the market, and along the lines of Piketty (1995), they may have beliefs about political systems because of their backgrounds. This discussion is not intended to minimize the significance of democracy but rather to note that the empirical literature finds that prosperity is more highly correlated with economic freedoms than political freedoms.

Knack and Keefer (1995) examine several different measures of institutional quality, including the Gastil political freedom index and measures compiled by two private firms on international investment risk. These private risk guides rate countries according to the security of private contracts, corruption in government, and other factors more closely related to the economic environment. As such, they are good measures of the legal structure and security of property rights idea that appears as area 2 in the EFW index. They find that the political and civil liberties variables from Gastil are insufficient as measures of security of property rights, and that there is a strong correlation between security of property rights and both investment and economic growth. Similarly, Knack (1996) looks at security of property rights and growth within the context of the convergence hypothesis and finds a close correlation between property rights protection and prosperity. A number of related papers are collected by Knack (2003).

Measures of property rights protection and rule of law go a long way toward quantifying the quality of economic institutions, but other proxies have appeared in the literature. Acemoglu, Johnson, and Robinson (2001) use mortality rates of colonial settlers as an instrument to proxy for institutional quality in colonized areas. They argue that where colonizers encountered relatively few health hazards, they erected solid institutions to protect property rights and establish rule of law, whereas in other areas they concentrated on extracting resources quickly, and left behind relatively poor institutions. Using this proxy for institutional quality, they conclude that better institutions lead to higher income. Hall and Jones (1999) use the fraction of the population speaking English and western European languages as a proxy for institutional quality. Like Acemoglu, Johnson, and Robinson (2001), they find that better institutions as measured by their language proxy result in higher income. Comparable results are also found in Bueno de Mesquite et al. (2003, pp. 156–57) using an entirely different measure of institutional improvement.

The results of these studies are consistent with the hypothesis that institutions matter, but they also raise a number of questions. One issue is the possibility that the direction of causation goes the other way. Another is that the proxies measured in these studies capture some geographic factors that may affect prosperity. Diamond (1997) has a detailed discussion of the impact of geography on development, and Gallup, Sachs, and Mellinger (1998) and Sachs (2001) also argue that geography is a crucial determinant. People who live in the tropics may be more exposed to productivity-sapping diseases, and tropical weather may have a negative impact simply because tropical heat may reduce worker productivity. Access to ports, and proximity to major commercial centers, may also impact development. This makes it important to separate out factors due to geography from those that are due to institutions independently of a country's location. These potential problems can be overcome by using an institutional measure like the EFW index that more directly measures institutional quality rather than merely being a proxy.

Within the context of this chapter it is worth remarking that none of these studies look at issues of constitutional design specifically. Rather, they offer more general measures—or proxies—for institutional quality, of which constitutional issues would be a subset. From an empirical standpoint there are three major hypotheses regarding factors that generate economic prosperity. The production function approach to the issue focuses on inputs into the production process, and on technology, as factors that generate economic growth and that lead to high incomes. The geography hypothesis argues that geographic factors are the most important determinants of prosperity. The institutional approach focuses on institutions as the main determinant.

The institutional approach has used a number of different measures and proxies to quantify institutional quality. One advantage of the EFW index as a measure of institutional quality is that it is a comprehensive measure, and its components are factors that the institutional literature suggests should lay the foundation for prosperity. Its components are derived from and supported by economic theory. Thus, if the EFW index is correlated with prosperity, as the literature suggests, its components can be used as a road map for constitutional design. The evidence is persuasive in studies that look at a wide range of countries, suggesting that the components of the EFW index are good indicators for what institutions lay the foundation for prosperity.

Countries to Be Studied: Is There a Threshold Effect?

Past studies using the EFW index, and more generally, empirical studies that have examined the impact of institutions on prosperity, have covered a wide range of countries, from developed nations to those that are poor and have slow or negative rates of growth. The use of a data set with many different types of countries is useful for showing that poor countries and slow-growth or no-growth countries are hindered by institutional deficiencies. The clear indication is that if poorer countries adopted the institutions found in developed countries, their rates of income growth would increase and they would close the income gap between themselves and developed economies.[12] A cross-sectional study of a wide range of countries obscures some of the relationship between institutions and prosperity, however.

It is apparent from looking at the data that there is a bimodal distribution of GDP growth rates across countries (Quah 1996). Countries with good institutions grow faster, while those with poor institutions experience slower growth, or none at all. This bimodal distribution suggests the possibility that there is some threshold for institutional quality, and that once countries meet that threshold, their institutions will promote economic growth. The question arises as to whether developed nations with good institutions in place will see any additional benefit from institutional improvements. A related issue is, if institutional differences among developed economies do have a measurable impact, whether the impact is large enough to make it worthwhile to incur the political costs to make those changes. If, within a fairly homogeneous set of developed nations, institutional differences appear to have little impact, then the issue of institutional quality is more an issue of what institutions can increase the prosperity of less-developed nations. If institutional differences have measurable and sizable impacts even among developed nations, then there are clear policy implications for developed as well as developing nations. Thus it is worthwhile to look at a smaller set of developed nations to gauge the relationship between institutional differences and prosperity.

Many previous studies have used the EFW index and other institutional measures to show that institutions have a substantial impact on prosperity when looking at a wide range of countries. This study looks at a considerably narrower set of developed nations to see whether there is still a measurable effect of institutions on prosperity in countries that already have relatively good institutions.

11.2 Institutions and Prosperity in a Set of Developed Countries

The EFW ratings that are used as a measure of institutional quality have been computed for 123 countries and are described in Gwartney and Lawson (2003). The EFW index rates countries on a scale of from 0 to 10. For the 99 countries used in Gwartney, Holcombe, and Lawson (2003), the average EFW ratings for 1980 to 2000 vary from 3.51 for the Democratic Republic of the Congo to 8.61 for Hong Kong, and it is clear that with this range of variation, higher EFW ratings are positively correlated with higher levels of income and higher rates of income growth. The empirical work presented here narrows the list of countries to 18 OECD countries with EFW ratings that vary from 7.98 for the United States and Switzerland to 6.13 for Italy. An examination of this narrower set of countries brings with it two important differences in the EFW variable that measures institutional quality. First, it considerably narrows the range of institutional differences among

Table 11.2
Institutions and investment in physical and human capital

	Dependent variable			
	Physical capital per worker		Human capital per worker	
	(1)	(2)	(3)	(4)
EFW	8,409 (3.10)		1.167 (5.28)	
Constitution		8,484 (3.08)		1.334 (6.74)
Constant	11,151 (0.59)	9,778 (0.50)	0.324 (0.21)	−0.975 (0.69)
Adjusted R^2	22.1	19.5	45.0	55.9

Note: *t*-values are in parentheses.

the countries being examined from a difference of 5.30 in EFW to a difference of 1.85. Thus it is possible to see the impact of a narrower range of institutional changes. Second, the lowest EFW rating in the narrower data set falls in the top half of countries from the larger data set, so the investigation is limited to countries that already have pretty good institutions by world standards.[13] This addresses the issue of whether substantial gains would be possible from improving the institutional quality in countries that already have pretty good institutions.

Institutions and Investment

One line of analysis regarding economic growth, based on the Solow (1956) growth model and developed further by Lucas (1988), Romer (1986, 1990), and others, takes a production function approach to income determination. Following this line of reasoning, output Q is a function of the inputs of capital K and labor L, so $Q = f(K, L)$. To generate economic growth, this approach focuses on the capital and labor inputs into the production process, and on technological advances that might affect the functional form of the production function to generate more output with the same inputs. An extensive literature shows that these inputs are essential to economic growth, but that literature has not recognized the influence of institutions on investment in human and physical capital. Table 11.2 presents results showing the effect of the EFW rating on physical and human capital in these 18 developed economies.

The first regression uses physical capital per worker as the dependent variable. The physical capital measure comes from Baier, Dwyer, and Tamura (2003). Use of EFW as the dependent variable explains about 22 percent of the difference in the level of physical capital per worker, and the coefficient on EFW shows that a one-unit difference in EFW is associated with a difference of $8,409 in physical capital per worker. The *t*-value of 3.10 shows that EFW is closely correlated with physical capital per worker, and the size of the coefficient shows that the impact of institutional quality, as measured by EFW, is substantial. Countries with more market-friendly institutions have more physical capital, and it makes sense that they would. Individuals who are making investment decisions will more readily invest when institutions make returns to their investment more secure. The impact of institutions on capital per worker is strong and substantial even in this limited data set of developed economies, showing that even among developed economies, improvements in institutions can yield sizable impacts.

The second regression replicates the first, but rather than using the complete EFW index, only areas 2, 4, and 5 are used to construct the index to produce the independent variable called Constitution. The logic of this, as discussed above, is that the size of government, area 1 of the EFW index, may be more a matter of policy than of constitutional design, and the same may be true of area 3, which measures access to sound money. A comparison of the second regression with the first shows that the results are similar when only areas 2, 4, and 5 are included in the index. The coefficients and *t*-values are close to the same magnitudes, although the adjusted R^2 is slightly lower. Regardless of which measure of constitutional quality is used, the higher the quality of institutions, the higher is the level of physical capital per worker.

The third regression looks at the relationship between human capital and EFW. The measure of human capital per worker comes from Baier, Dwyer, and Tamura (2003), and is a measure of years of schooling per worker adjusted for the demographic composition of the work force. Institutional quality, measured by EFW, accounts for about 45 percent of the difference across these 18 countries in human capital per worker, and the *t*-value of 5.28 shows a very close fit. The coefficient on EFW shows that a one-unit increase in EFW is associated with an increase of about 1.2 years of schooling, showing the impact of EFW on human capital. As with physical capital, the relationship is strong from a statistical standpoint and is quantitatively substantial.

When the more narrow measure of institutional quality, Constitution, is used instead of EFW in regression 4, the coefficient is about 14 percent greater, and both the *t*-value on Constitution and the adjusted R^2 are higher, indicating a stronger effect and a better fit. This reinforces the conclusion that better institutions lead to a greater investment in human capital per worker.

Inputs into the production process are an important determinant of income and economic growth, and the results in table 11.2 show that institutional quality, as measured by EFW or by the more narrow Constitution variable, has a substantial impact on the level of both physical and human capital. The production function approach to economic growth hypothesizes that a country's income is a function of the inputs into the production process, and that increases in the inputs of physical and human capital increase income and growth. The results presented here show that for developed economies, better institutions, as measured by both the full and the abbreviated EFW index, result in an increase in inputs into the production process. This makes sense because, if institutions are in place to protect property rights and allow people to retain ownership of the product of their economic activity, then individuals have a greater incentive to invest in physical and human capital to capture these returns. Institutions are an important determinant of the factors of production that generate prosperity. This is true not only in developing economies, as these results show. Even in developed economies, better institutions encourage more investment in human and physical capital.

Institutions and Per capita Income

Table 11.3 examines the relationship between institutions, as measured by the EFW index, and per capita income more directly. Regression 1 uses the EFW index as the only independent variable and the coefficient shows that a one-unit increase in EFW is associated with a $3,570 increase in per capita income. The EFW index by itself explains 47.6 percent of the variation in per capita income, and the *t*-value of 5.73 on the EFW coefficient shows a close relationship between EFW and per capita income.

Regression 2 depicts the production function approach to income determination, showing per capita income as a function of physical and human capital. Taken together, differences in human and physical capital explain 61 percent of the variation in per capita income across countries, and the *t*-values show that both have a strong relationship

Table 11.3
Institutions and per capita income

Independent variables	Dependent variable: Real GDP per capita (1)	(2)	(3)	(4)
EFW	3,570		1,448	3,570
	(5.73)		(1.94)	(6.91)
K per worker		0.126	0.104	
		(3.97)	(3.17)	
L per worker		1,555	1,072	
		(4.75)	(2.67)	
K res. per worker				0.103
				(3.17)
L res. per worker				1,072
				(2.67)
Constant	−3,924	−997	−5,427	−3,924
	(0.90)	(0.34)	(1.49)	(1.08)
Adjusted R^2	47.6	61.0	64.0	67.1

Note: *t*-values are in parentheses.

with per capita income. The coefficient on physical capital suggests that an additional dollar in physical capital per worker is associated with an increase of 12.6 cents in per capita income, and the coefficient on human capital indicates that an additional year of schooling is associated with a $1,555 higher level of per capita income. Regressions 1 and 2 show that both institutional variations and differences in physical and human capital by themselves explain a substantial amount of the variation in per capita income across this set of countries.

Regression 3 includes both the institutional variables and inputs as independent variables. All three remain closely correlated with per capita income, although the magnitudes of the coefficients are lower, and in the case of the coefficient on EFW, much lower. One reason for this is that, as table 11.1 shows, institutional differences as measured by EFW are strongly correlated with the levels of physical and human capital. Thus part of the variation in human and physical capital across countries in regression 3 is due to differences in institutions. Institutions, as measured by the EFW rating, have a direct effect on per capita income, which is captured in the coefficient on EFW in regression 3, but also have an indirect effect because a higher EFW rating is associated with higher levels of physical and human capital. This indirect effect of EFW through physical and human capital is not captured in the coefficient in regression 3.

To capture both the direct and indirect effect of EFW on per capita income, the residuals from the regressions in table 11.2 are substituted for the coefficients on human and physical capital. Looking back at table 11.2, the residuals from the first regression using physical capital per worker measure the variation in physical capital per worker that is not accounted for by the variation in EFW. Similarly the residuals in the second regression measure the variation in human capital per worker not accounted for by the variation in EFW. When these residuals for physical and human capital are substituted for their actual values, the coefficient on EFW measures both the direct and indirect impact of EFW on per capita income. Regression 4 shows the result.

The residuals from physical and human capital along with EFW explains more than two-thirds of the variation in per capita income across this set of countries, and a one-unit increase in the EFW rating is associated with a $3,570 increase in per capita income. The *t*-value of 6.91 shows that there is a strong correlation between EFW and per capita income, so the relationship is statistically strong in addition to being empirically meaningful. These results show that institutional differences, as measured by the EFW rating, make a substantial difference in per capita income levels even among the developed economies in this sample. One reason for looking at this small sample of developed economies was to see if there is any evidence that there is some threshold for institutional quality beyond which countries had a sufficient foundation for market a economy that further changes would not improve economic performance. These results show that there is no evidence of a threshold effect. Even for developed economies, better institutions result in better economic performance.

Table 11.4 replicates the regressions from table 11.3 but substitutes the abbreviated index, Constitution, for the full EFW index. Qualitatively, the results are the same. Compared with the coefficients on EFW in table 11.3, the coefficients on Constitution are higher in all three regressions in which they appear, and the *t*-values are higher in two of the three regressions. The higher coefficients using Constitution as an independent variable suggest that when this more narrow measure of institutional quality is used, institutions have even a larger effect on real GDP per capita. Also, when Constitution is substituted for EFW, the coefficients on the capital-related independent variables go up slightly, and the coefficients on the labor-related independent variables go down. In table 11.4 the labor variables are not statistically significant at generally accepted levels, although they are in table 11.3.

Table 11.4
Constitutions and per capita income

Independent variables	Dependent variable: Real GDP per capita (1)	(2)	(3)	(4)
Constitution	4,084		2,019	3,818
	(4.54)		(2.31)	(7.13)
K per worker		0.138	0.111	
		(4.17)	(3.33)	
L per worker		1,417	643	
		(4.15)	(1.38)	
K res. per worker				0.111
				(3.33)
L res. per worker				643
				(1.38)
Constant	−7,048	−595	−6,423	−5,965
	(1.10)	(0.19)	(1.67)	(1.57)
Adjusted R^2	33.4	58.5	63.3	63.3

Note: t-values are in parentheses.

The key point, though, is that regardless of which institutional variable is used, institutional quality has a strong positive impact on GDP per capita, even among countries that already have above-average institutional quality by world standards.

Institutions and Income Growth

Higher levels of income must be the result of more growth some time in the past, so if institutional quality is related to income level, it should also be related to income growth. Table 11.5 examines this issue by looking at the relationship between growth in per capita GDP and EFW as a measure of institutional quality. GDP growth was measured in five-year intervals for each country, from 1980 to 1985, 1985 to 1990, 1990 to 1995, and 1995 to 2000. Each country has four observations, for a total of 72 observations for the regressions in table 11.5. The first regression excludes investment as an independent variable, and the second includes it. However, as the results show, differences in investment do not explain differences in GDP growth for these countries over this period, and the adjusted R^2 is lower in the second regression that includes investment.

The first independent variable is the level of the EFW index at the beginning of the five-year period in question, which the t-value shows

Table 11.5
Institutions and income growth

Independent variables	Dependent variable: Growth in real GDP per capita (5-year intervals) (1)	(2)	(3)	(4)
EFW	0.074	0.106		
	(0.28)	(0.39)		
ChEFW	−0.313	−0.217		
	(0.60)	(0.38)		
ChEFW-5	1.042	1.046		
	(2.24)	(2.24)		
Constitution			0.162	0.176
			(0.57)	(0.59)
ChConstitution			−0.399	−0.375
			(0.71)	(0.65)
ChConstitution-5			0.942	1.150
			(1.92)	(2.19)
Investment		0.021		2.354
		(0.44)		(0.19)
1985	1.415	1.379	1.541	1.530
	(3.00)	(2.86)	(3.32)	(3.25)
1990	−0.829	−0.817	−0.579	−0.572
	(1.72)	(1.68)	(1.27)	(1.24)
1995	1.023	1.036	1.151	1.150
	(2.07)	(2.08)	(2.21)	(2.19)
Constant	0.808	0.091	0.103	−0.188
	(0.47)	(0.04)	(0.05)	(0.08)
Adjusted R^2	24.4	23.6	24.0	23.0

Note: *t*-values are in parentheses.

is not related to changes in GDP growth. This is consistent with the literature that has found that the level of institutional quality is not related to the *change* in income. The second independent variable is the change in the EFW rating during the five-year period. For example, it is the change in EFW from 1980 to 1985 when the dependent variable is GDP growth from 1980 to 1985; it also has little explanatory power. The third independent variable is the change in the EFW rating in the five years prior to the observation for GDP growth, so is the change in the EFW rating from 1975 to 1980 when the dependent variable is GDP growth from 1980 to 1985. In both specifications the *t*-value is 2.24, indicating a close relationship between the GDP growth rate and the change in the EFW rating five years prior to that GDP growth. Dummy variables were included for the five-year intervals, and show that compared with the 1980 to 1985 period, GDP growth in these countries was higher in 1985 to 1990 and 1995 to 2000, and lower in 1990 to 1995.

While the results in tables 11.3 and 11.4 showed that the level of the EFW rating is correlated with the level of income in these countries, table 11.5 shows that the level of EFW is not highly correlated with the GDP growth rates.[14] Similarly the contemporaneous change in the EFW rating is not highly correlated with GDP growth. However, the change in EFW in the five years prior to the measurement of GDP growth is correlated with GDP growth. This shows that improvements in institutional quality, as measured by the EFW rating, lead to higher GDP growth, but with a lag.

A commonsense explanation for this lag is that it takes some time for economic actors to assess the likelihood that institutional changes will be permanent, rather than quickly reversed, and it takes some time for economic actors to make plans based on the changed institutional environment. Because of this, policy makers should not expect immediate results from institutional improvements. Improvements in institutions will take five to ten years to show up in increased GDP growth.

Note that the magnitude of the coefficient on the EFW rating lagged five years is substantial when compared to typical rates of economic growth. The mean rate of real per capita GDP growth for these 18 countries is 2.09 percent, so the coefficient of 1.04 on the change on EFW five years prior suggests that countries in this group could increase their per capita GDP growth rates by about 50 percent if they improved their EFW rating by one point.

Regressions 3 and 4 in table 11.5 replicate regressions 1 and 2, but substitute Constitution and change in Constitution for the EFW and change in EFW variables. Qualitatively there is little difference in the results. The Constitution and ChConstitution coefficients are not statistically significant, paralleling the first two regressions, and ChConstitution-5 is statistically significant, albeit with slightly lower *t*-values in both regressions. In one regression the coefficient on ChConstitution-5 is slightly lower than in the parallel EFW regression, while in the other it is slightly higher. In both regressions 2 and 4 Investment is not statistically significant. Regardless of which measure of institutional quality is used, the results show that an improvement in institutional quality can have a large impact on real GDP growth, even within this set of developed economies.

The results in tables 11.3, 11.4, and 11.5 show that there is a substantial payoff in terms of economic performance from improving institutions by making them more market-friendly, even in countries that are already among the wealthiest in the world.

11.3 Implications for Constitutional Design

The preceding empirical results show that there is a close correlation between institutional quality, as measured by the EFW index, and prosperity. Better institutions lead to higher income levels, and improvements in institutional quality lead to faster rates of economic growth. The next several sections look at the components of the EFW index to examine the implications for constitutional design. The idea is that if one wants to establish a constitutional foundation for prosperity, the EFW index shows institutional features that are important sources of prosperity, so these features should be a part of a country's constitutional framework.

Size of Government

As table 11.1 shows, the first area of the EFW index is size of government. The general principle is that bigger government reduces the scope for market activity, reducing economic freedom. The components of this area include government consumption, transfers and subsidies, government enterprises, and marginal tax rates. Gwartney, Holcombe, and Lawson (1998) show that higher levels of government expenditures by themselves result in slower economic growth, and also show that when one looks at a group of developed economies, the percentage of GDP devoted to core functions of government such as education and infrastructure does not vary much across countries. Rather, variations in government expenditures in developed economies come from the levels of transfers, subsidies, and government enterprises. These in turn lead to higher taxes to finance the governmental activities. If one wants to constitutionally constrain government size, that means constraining the ability of the government to engage in transfers and subsidies, to shift production from government enterprises to the private sector, and to keep marginal tax rates low.

The major problem with controlling governmental activity in all of these areas is the rent-seeking activity of special interests, and as Olson (1982) argues, the problems of rent seeking are likely to get worse over time. In the regressions using the Constitution variable rather than EFW, this area was omitted from the index of institutional quality with the thought that perhaps size of government is a matter of political preference rather than constitutional design. On the matter of constitutional design, Mueller (2002) suggests that the differences between democratic institutions in the United States and Europe make redistributive activities less politically costly in Europe, so governments are bigger in Europe than in the United States. In the United States, where elected representatives are more independent of their parties and of their governments, it is difficult to create a majority in favor of creating transfers to interest groups. In Europe, where parliamentary democracies push representatives to vote with their parties, interest groups need only a relationship with the party to get support, and not with every representative. Not only are such relationships less costly to create in parliamentary systems, they also are more durable. In the United States, when a representative leaves office, that terminates any relationship between interest groups and the office, whereas in parliamentary systems, relationships can persist between interest groups and parties regardless of whether there is turnover in party membership. Thus Mueller's analysis suggests that size of government is a direct result of constitutional design, and that different constitutional structures can be used to affect the size of government.

Mueller's analysis (2002) offers a policy suggestion for designing a constitution for prosperity: create a representative democracy along the lines of the United States, where representatives are more independent of their parties and of their governments, rather than along the lines of European parliamentary democracies. Yet the empirical results of Gwartney, Holcombe, and Lawson (1998) suggest that even the US government, and every other government in a developed economy, is larger than is optimal for income growth, so even the US model can result in excessively large government. An argument might be made that there are other national policy goals besides income maximization, so governments are not too large. However, Mueller (2002) addresses this concern by showing that much of government expenditure amounts to rent seeking, with the attendant economic costs. The result is that transfers go to those with political power rather than to those who might be considered most worthy of them.

Building on Mueller (2002), one can argue against parliamentary systems as a method of controlling rent seeking in government, but clearly that is not enough. Other constitutional means of controlling government expenditures should be examined. Several states in the United States have enacted expenditure limitations that explicitly limit their state government expenditures to grow no faster than state income, or than population growth plus inflation. Most states in the United States also have a balanced budget requirement that prevents government from running deficits, and a balanced budget requirement for the national government in the United States has been discussed but never implemented. The requirement of supermajority votes on budgetary matters is another possible method of constraining spending, as is allowing the chief executive to have line-item veto over budgetary items. The empirical evidence shows that government expenditures are so large that they impede economic growth and reduce incomes, and the theoretical evidence shows that rent seeking activities from interest groups create excessive government expenditures. This provides the rationale for examining the possibilities for designing constitutional constraints on government spending. A number of tools are available.

Are differences in the size of government across countries a product of constitutional design, or do they reflect differences in preferences among different people for different sizes of government? The preferences argument is unsatisfying to an economist, because as Stigler and Becker (1977) argue, attributing different outcomes to differences in preferences really says that there is no economic explanation for the differences. There are, however, clear constitutional mechanisms that can affect the size of government. Mueller (2002) argues that the European parliamentary type of democracy leads to larger government because it facilitates rent seeking, and mechanisms such as balanced budget requirements and supermajority voting have been suggested as constitutional mechanisms that can affect government size. Perhaps preference differences across countries may account for differences in government size, but there are clear constitutional design issues that affect the size of government.

Legal Structure and Property Rights

The second area of the EFW index is legal structure and the security of property rights. While constitutional design fits most closely with what is likely to be in a written constitution, it is perhaps more challenging to implement a constitution successfully. Judicial independence is a key component here, as is having a rule of law that applies in the same way to everyone. In many countries around the world a big problem with the legal system is corruption. This is not as much of a problem in the developed nations examined here. Rather, the threat to property rights comes from a more sophisticated type of rent seeking where interest groups enter the political process to have rights transferred from some parties to others. Through environmental regulations, eminent domain (Berliner 2003), land use policies, and other methods justified by the economic theories of externalities and public goods, interest groups use the political process to weaken property rights. The result is that people cannot be assured that they will be able to maintain control of their property.

Olson (2000) suggests that a legal system that prevents mutually beneficial exchanges encourages corruption. When the law is limited to the protection of property rights and the prevention of fraud, violations of the law will impose clearly identifiable costs on some people, and those people have an incentive to follow through to try to enforce the laws' provisions. If there are price controls or regulatory barriers that stand in the way of mutually beneficial exchanges, every party to an illegal exchange benefits, so no one with knowledge of the violation has an incentive to report it. It then is easier to bribe government officials to look the other way or even facilitate violations. Laws that support market transactions discourage corruption, whereas laws that hinder market transactions encourage corruption. If corruption becomes established in some areas of government, it lays the foundation for more corruption. The legal system can be designed to discourage corruption so that government does not interfere with voluntary market exchange.

In developed economies, corruption and political interference with the judicial system is not as much of a problem as rent seeking and legislative abridgement of property rights. This implies that the constitution should be designed to prevent the political attenuation of property rights. Legal protections of property rights becomes more difficult in a political environment where the prevailing ideology is that one role of a democratic political system is to balance the economic power of the most wealthy by using the political power of government. This ideology is, as Hayek (1944) argued, the road to serfdom, but a democratic political system aims toward this road if citizens believe that democratic government should carry out the will of the majority that may want to attenuate property rights. Holcombe (2002) argues that there is an inherent tension between liberty and democracy. A democratic ideology works against the promotion of economic freedom because it suggests that property rights can be attenuated if the majority supports it. Constitutional constraints that protect people from the majority in a democratic government are essential to preserve rule of law and to protect property rights in developed economies.

11.4 Conclusion: Constitutions, Democracy, and Prosperity

The reasoning behind using the EFW index as a measure of institutional quality is that its components are all items that the literature has suggested should enhance economic performance, and empirically the EFW index shows a strong correlation between both income levels and growth. There are both theoretical and empirical reasons for using the components of the EFW index as a guide to designing a constitutional framework for prosperity.

The substantial literature that documents the relationship between institutional quality and economic performance has used a broad range of countries to show that relationship. Because the existing literature looks at both growing and developed economies along with stagnant and less-developed economies, and because the distribution of growth rates across countries is bimodal (Quah 1996), it may be that there is some threshold of institutional quality that creates a foundation for growth. Countries below the threshold will not grow, while those above will, creating the bimodal distribution of growth rates. Also, once the threshold is met, better institutions may not create more growth. By showing that the relationship holds even within a smaller set of high-income developed nations, the empirical work in this chapter demonstrates that this is not the case. Even in countries where institutions are already relatively good, and where incomes and growth rates are already high by world standards, institutional improvements will lead to improvements in economic performance.

Because the EFW index is closely correlated with economic performance, both in a large set of countries and in a smaller set of developed nations, its components provide a guide for designing a constitutional framework for prosperity. The basic ingredients are straightforward, and follow from the areas that make up the EFW index. A constitutional framework for prosperity will (1) limit the size of government and keep marginal tax rates low, (2) protect property rights and provide an impartial rule of law, (3) provide access to sound money, (4) minimize barriers to exchange with foreigners, and (5) minimize regulatory restrictions placed on credit markets, business, and labor. The challenge is designing the various constitutional provisions that implement these components.

Constitutional design must be regarded in two ways: as technical and as ideological. The technical aspect concerns the mechanisms that might be used to implement improvements in the five areas listed in the preceding paragraph. More general than that are the impediments to improvement in the individual EFW areas where the most serious threat is rent-seeking activities from special interests. Limiting rent-seeking activities might be considered from a technical standpoint as well, but a broader problem is that rent-seeking is often justified ideologically. While in the abstract people may oppose rent-seeking activities, the general acceptance of the activities of the welfare state poses a threat to institutional improvement, because many welfare state policies are in direct opposition to the institutions that support economic freedom. Because the ideology of the welfare state views one of the roles of government as protecting people's economic interests, the goals of rent-seekers have increasingly come to be accepted as a legitimate part of the political process.[15]

From a technical standpoint, rent seeking can be limited by constitutional constraints such as term limits, line-item veto, debt and expenditure caps, and a requirement of supermajority approval for expenditures. Yet constraints like these are likely to be ineffective in securing economic freedom if there is political support for a transfer state. Fukuyama (1992) has argued that democratic governments and market economies are the final step in the evolution of political and economic institutions, but Holcombe (2002) argues that there is an inherent tension between the two. Democratic ideology suggests that governments should carry out the will of the majority, which leads toward political allocation of resources, with increased rent-seeking and interest group politics. The ideology of democracy is in this way at odds with the institutions that support economic progress.

The inherent tension between democratic government and market institutions means that constitutional reform to promote prosperity requires more than just identifying those changes that enable markets to function better and implementing them. In a democracy the ideology that government is responsible for protecting the economic well-being of its citizens opens the door to rent seeking by special interests, and the population accepts this activity as a part of the democratic process. Without a shift in ideology, rent seeking and special interest activity will continue and grow, as Olson (1982) projected, leading to the decline of nations. In developed economies with democratic governments, the biggest challenge to the design of a constitution for prosperity is not a technical one of finding the most effective constitutional provisions, but an ideological one of generating popular support for the limiting of government interference with markets.

Notes

1. This may be the result of nineteenth-century political economy dividing into economics and political science. Certainly earlier economists, such as Smith (1776), Ricardo (1817), and Mill (1848), were very cognizant of the relationship between institutions and economic performance.

2. These works are cited in the context of modern growth theory, but see Bauer (1957) for a clear recognition of the importance of market institutions for economic development.

3. The idea is so generally accepted that it may be worth recalling that shortly before the collapse of the Berlin Wall in 1989, many reputable economists argued that centrally planned economies could allocate resources more efficiently than market economies, and thus would have faster economic growth. At one point Ludwig von Mises (1951) and Friedrich Hayek (1945) were almost alone in claiming that centrally planned economies could not allocate resources efficiently. Samuelson (1973, p. 883), in the year Ludwig von Mises died, argued that although per capita income in the Soviet Union was about half that in the United States, because of its superior economic system the Soviet Union would have faster economic growth, and would catch up to the United States in per capita income perhaps as early as 1990 and almost surely by 2010.

4. For one of the more persuasive defenses of the benefits of an orderly anarchy, see Rothbard (1973).

5. See also Azfar and Cadwell (2003) and Knack (2003) for a body of work that supports Olson's idea of market-augmenting government.

6. The earlier index was published in Gwartney, Lawson, and Block (1996), and contained 17 components.

7. One reason for using instrumental variables is concern about the direction of causation. Gwartney, Holcombe, and Lawson (1999 and in later unpublished work) have examined the direction of causation empirically and found that the direction of causality goes from institutional quality to economic prosperity (level of income and growth rate of income), and not in the other direction. The fact that other studies using instrumental variables, such as Acemoglu and Robinson (2001) and Bueno de Mesquita (2003, pp. 156–57), arrive at similar conclusions regarding institutional quality provides additional reassurance. We see merits in both approaches and view them as complementary, but the approach used here offers more direct policy implications.

8. However, see Mueller (2002) for a persuasive argument that size of government is directly related to issues of constitutional design.

9. See, for examples, Dawson (1998), Knack (1996), Knack and Keefer (1995), Gwartney, Holcombe, and Lawson (1998), Scully (1988, 1992), and Torstensson (1994).

10. The direction of causality was not investigated by Carlsson and Lundstrom (2002), and especially with the size of government area, it is likely that higher income leads to a larger public sector rather than the other way around.

11. This became an issue in the early 1990s with regard to former communist countries that are transitioning to market-oriented democracies. Some observers placed an overly heavy emphasis on democracy as the key to prosperity, while underemphasizing the market institutions that are absolutely essential to such a transition.

12. We present a more detailed case for this argument in Gwartney, Holcombe, and Lawson (2003).

13. The countries used in this study are Australia, Austria, Belgium, Canada, Denmark, Finland, France, Germany, Ireland, Italy, Japan, the Netherlands, New Zealand, Norway, Sweden, Switzerland, the United Kingdom, and the United States. Iceland and Luxembourg were not included because the data on human capital for those countries were not available.

14. In a larger sample of 91 countries, Gwartney, Holcombe, and Lawson (2003) find that the level of EFW is correlated with GDP growth. This smaller sample has a much narrower range of both EFW ratings and GDP growth rates.

15. Perhaps the best example is the use, in some countries, of currency boards to maintain their currency at parity with another currency. Even this is not a good example because the country with the currency board must rely on sound monetary policy from the country to which its currency is pegged.

16. Higgs (1987) offers an insightful discussion of the legitimization of this ideology in the United States.

References

Acemoglu, D., S. Johnson, and J. A. Robinson. 2001. The colonial origins of comparative development: An empirical investigation. *American Economic Review* 91: 1369–1401.

Azfar, O., and C. A. Cadwell. 2003. *Market-Augmenting Government.* Ann Arbor: University of Michigan Press.

Baier, S. L., G. P. Dwyer, and R. Tamura. 2003. How important are capital and total factor productivity for economic growth? Working Paper, Federal Reserve Bank of Atlanta Research Department.

Barro, R. J. 1996. Democracy and growth. *Journal of Economic Growth* 1: 1–27.

Bauer, P. T. 1957. *Economic Analysis and Policy in Underdeveloped Countries.* Durham, NC: Duke University Press.

Berliner, D. 2003. *Public Power, Private Gain.* Washington, DC: Institute for Justice.

Berggren, N. 2003. The benefits of economic freedom: A survey. *Independent Review* 8: 193–211.

Bueno de Mesquita, B., A. Smith, R. M. Siverson, and J. D. Morrow. 2003. *The Logic of Political Survival.* Cambridge: MIT Press.

Carlsson, F., and S. Lundstrom. 2002. Economic freedom and growth: Decomposing the effects. *Public Choice* 112: 335–44.

Dawson, J. W. 1998. Institutions, investment, and growth: New cross-country and panel data evidence. *Economic Inquiry* 36: 603–19.

Diamond, J. 1997. *Guns, Germs, and Steel.* New York: Norton.

Fukuyama, F. 1992. *The End of History and the Last Man.* New York: Free Press.

Gallup, J. L., J. D. Sachs, and A. D. Mellinger. 1998. Geography and environment. NBER Working Paper 6849.

Gastil, R. D. 1978. *Freedom in the World: Political Rights and Civil Liberties.* New York: Freedom House.

Gwartney, J., and R. Lawson. 2003. *Economic Freedom of the World Annual Report 2003.* Vancouver, BC: Fraser Institute.

Gwartney, J. D., R. G. Holcombe, and R. A. Lawson. 1998. The scope of government and the wealth of nations. *Cato Journal* 18: 163–90.

Gwartney, J. D., R. G. Holcombe, and R. A. Lawson. 2004. Economic freedom, institutional quality, and cross-country differences in income and growth. *Cato Journal* 24: 292–312.

Gwartney, J., R. Lawson, and W. Block. 1996. *Economic Freedom of the World: 1975–1995.* Vancouver, BC: Fraser Institute.

Gwartney, J. D., R. A. Lawson, and R. G. Holcombe. 1999. Economic freedom and the environment for economic growth. *Journal of Institutional and Theoretical Economics* 155: 643–63.

Hall, R. E., and C. I. Jones. 1999. Why do some countries produce so much more output per worker than others? *Quarterly Journal of Economics* 114: 83–116.

Hayek, F. 1944. *The Road to Serfdom.* London: Routledge.

Hayek, F. 1945. The use of knowledge in society. *American Economic Review* 35: 519–30.

Higgs, R. 1987. *Crisis and Leviathan: Critical Episodes in the Growth of American Government.* New York: Oxford University Press.

Holcombe, R. G. 2002. *From Liberty to Democracy: The Transformation of American Government.* Ann Arbor: University of Michigan Press.

Knack, S. 1996. Institutions and the convergence hypothesis: The cross-national evidence. *Public Choice* 87: 207–28.

Knack, S., ed. 2003. *Democracy, Governance, and Growth.* Ann Arbor: University of Michigan Press.

Knack, S., and P. Keefer. 1995. Institutions and economic performance: Cross-country tests using alternative institutional measures. *Economics and Politics* 7: 207–27.

Krueger, A. O. 1974. The political economy of the rent-seeking society. *American Economic Review* 64: 291–303.

Landes, D. S. 1998. *The Wealth and Poverty of Nations: Why Some Are So Rich, and Some So Poor.* New York: Norton.

Lucas, R. E., Jr. 1988. On the mechanics of economic development. *Journal of Monetary Economics* 22: 3–42.

Mill, J. S. [1848] 1884. *Principles of Political Economy.* New York: Appleton.

Mises, L. von. 1951. *Socialism.* New Haven: Yale University Press.

Mueller, D. C. 2002. Interest groups, redistribution, and the size of government. In S. L. Winer and H. Shibata, eds., *Political Economy and Public Finance.* Cheltenham, UK: Edward Elgar, pp. 123–44.

North, D. C. 1990. *Institutions, Institutional Change, and Economic Performance.* Cambridge: Cambridge University Press.

Olson, M. 1982. *The Rise and Decline of Nations.* New Haven: Yale University Press.

Olson, M. 1996. Big bills left on the sidewalk: Why some nations are rich, and others poor. *Journal of Economic Perspectives* 10: 3–24.

Olson, M. 2000. *Power and Prosperity: Outgrowing Communist and Capitalist Dictatorships.* New York: Basic Books.

Piketty, T. 1995. Social mobility and redistributive politics. *Quarterly Journal of Economics* 110: 551–84.

Quah, D. 1996. Convergence empirics across economies with (some) capital mobility. *Journal of Economic Growth* 1: 95–124.

Ricardo, D. 1817. *On the Principles of Political Economy and Taxation.* London: Murray.

Romer, P. M. 1986. Increasing returns and long-run growth. *Journal of Political Economy* 94: 1002–37.

Romer, P. M. 1990. Endogenous technological change. *Journal of Political Economy* 98: S71–S102.

Rothbard, M. N. 1973. *For a New Liberty.* New York: Macmillan.

Sachs, J. D. 2001. Tropical underdevelopment. NBER Working Paper 8119.

Samuelson, P. A. 1973. *Economics,* 9th ed. New York: McGraw-Hill.

Scully, G. W. 1988. The institutional framework and economic development. *Journal of Political Economy* 96: 652–62.

Scully, G. W. 1992. *Constitutional Environments and Economic Growth.* Princeton: Princeton University Press.

Smith, A. [1776] 1937. *The Wealth of Nations.* New York: Random House.

Solow, R. M. 1956. A contribution to the theory of economic growth. *Quarterly Journal of Economics* 70: 65–94.

Stigler, G. J., and G. S. Becker. 1977. De gustibus no est desputandum. *American Economic Review* 67: 76–90.

Torstensson, J. 1994. Property rights and economic growth: An empirical study. *Kyklos* 47: 231–47.

Tullock, G. 1967. The welfare cost of tariffs, monopolies, and theft. *Western Economic Journal* 5: 224–32.

V

Constitutional Design, Durability, and Stability

12 Amendment Procedures and Constitutional Stability

Bjørn Erik Rasch and Roger D. Congleton

12.1 Introduction

The study of constitutional design is of interest, in large part, because constitutions can be amended from time to time. Not every constitutional procedure or constraint will stand the test of time, and most constitutional designers take this into account by including constitutional procedures for changing the fundamental rules of the political game. Almost all national constitutions include articles that provide for partial or total change of their constitutions. Less than 4 percent of the world's constitutions lack articles on formal amendment procedures (Maarseveen and Van Der Tang 1978, p. 80). In this respect constitutions differ from rules governing parlor games, insofar as the latter do not include rules for changing the rules. Other less formal methods for reforming constitutional practice are also commonplace. Constitutional procedures and constraints may also be altered by judicial interpretation and political adaptation, and by irregular (nonlegal or unconstitutional) means. In democratic systems, constitutional developments are often gradual or incremental, although replacement of the entire document is also a possibility.[1]

Empirical work on the effects of amendment procedures is, however, a relatively recent and underinvestigated area of research. Contemporary empirical research begins with Lutz's (1994) pioneering investigation of the effects of amendment procedures and constitutional length on the frequency of amendment using data from state constitutions within the United States and a small international sample of constitutional democracies. Relatively few studies have extended his work. This chapter is consequently somewhat more descriptive and speculative than the preceding chapters.

The narrowness of this literature is not because amendment procedures are unimportant or a secondary matter in democratic constitutional design. If variations in the details of constitutional design have important effects on public policies and welfare within a polity, changes in the procedures by which constitutions may be changed are obviously important as well. Moreover amendment procedures may contribute to both the stability and durability of a constitutional regime, which may themselves have significant effects on welfare insofar as prosperity, health, and trust are promoted by stable institutions.

Indeed, the age of a particular constitution is often measured by the period in which its rules of amendment are followed, rather than by the period in which particular political procedures and constraints have been in place. By this measure, Norway has one of the oldest constitutions in the world, second only to the US constitution. It was signed and sealed by the Constituent Assembly at Eidsvoll (north of Oslo) on May 17, 1814, a few weeks after elected delegates from all parts of Norway had assembled. Since 1814, however, more than 200 amendments to the constitution have been adopted. During that time the balance of power within the Norwegian government and the nature of the electorate underwent substantial transformations. The authority to make public policies shifted from the king to the parliament. Suffrage was greatly expanded. The union between Norway and Sweden was broken in 1905.

Similarly the constitution of the United States is generally regarded to be more than 200 years old, although it has been amended 27 times, most recently in 1992. A bill of rights was passed soon after the constitution was adopted in 1787.[2] The manner in which the vice president is selected was changed in 1804. The manner in which representatives are selected for its federal chamber, the Senate, was changed by the 17th amendment in 1913 as direct election of senators replaced appointment by state governments. Suffrage rights for blacks and women were greatly expanded by the 15th and 19th amendments (1870 and 1920), and the term of office for American presidents was limited to two terms by the 22nd (1951).

Despite all these very substantial constitutional reforms, the constitutional regimes of Norway and the United States are normally dated to 1814 and 1789, respectively, rather than to the dates of their most recent amendments, 2004 and 1992.

If *durability* is measured by the existence of a stable amendment procedure rather than core features of political procedures and constraints, an important difference clearly exists between a constitution's durability and the stability of its associated pattern of governance. The fundamental rules and procedures of governance may change substantially—as they have in Norway, the United States, and many other countries—without changing amendment procedures.

This chapter investigates the extent to which formal amendment procedures affect the *stability* of a nation's written constitution. Changes in constitutional text can serve as a useful first approximation for constitutional stability, insofar as all formal changes in the constitution require changes in constitutional language, and all formal changes to a nation's written constitution change related unwritten parts of the constitution as well. It bears noting, however, that to the extent that unwritten parts of a nation's constitution change as a consequence of other factors, the true underlying stability of a polity's constitution will be somewhat understated by this approach.

Our analysis is organized into four sections. Section 12.2 discusses the demand for and the procedures of constitutional amendment. Section 12.3 compares formal amendment procedures, with an emphasis on OECD countries. Section 12.4 analyzes the relationship between the frequency of formal amendments and the stringency of the amendment process. Section 12.5 concludes the discussion. In general, we find that the stringency of amendment processes, specifically the number of veto points, affects the frequency of formal changes to modern democratic constitutions.

12.2 Constitutional Design and the Demand for Constitutional Reform

Formal constitutional documents describe the "law for making laws" (Congleton 2003, p. 11). Constitutions consequently include some of the most fundamental rules of the game in a society. Most constitutions include rules on the machinery of government as well as more or less extensive and general specifications of the rights of citizens. These procedure and constraints enable societies to make collective decisions to achieve outcomes that require coordination and joint action (Hardin 1989) while reducing the risks of collective action. Constitutional law differs from most other laws because it also normally includes procedures for changing its own required procedures and constraints.

Not all constitutions are democratic, but the present analysis is restricted to this subclass.[3] Four general objectives can be ascribed to democratic constitutions. First, there is the practical convenience of having standing collective decision-making routines to adjust the existing laws and services to better advance citizen interests as economic and political conditions change through time. The standing routines of modern democratic governments include competitive elections to select representatives, who in turn select among policy options, and a largely apolitical bureaucracy that implements the policies chosen.

Second, democratic constitutions attempt to ensure majority rule rather than minority rule. Representative democracy requires *delegation,* and there is always the risk that the *agents* employed will fail to act on the electorate's behalf.[4] An important task of a constitutional arrangement is to prevent delegation of authority from turning into abdication. Any agent may have an incentive to shirk, as long as the interests of principals and agents are not completely identical. The institutional problem then is to align the agent's interests with those of their principals. Democratic constitutions accomplish this alignment through provisions that assure competitive and open elections and through the power of the purse. Protections for the press and political speech also work to ensure open policy debates, which simultaneously improves the quality of policy choices and reduces opportunities for malfeasance among elected officials. Amendment procedures and similar rules also restrain a temporary majority from abusing its power by manipulating electoral rules and the management of elections. For example, constitutional provisions that establish maximal times between elections reduce legislative opportunities for governments that have outlived their majorities. The power of the purse allows elected representives to punish bureaucratic inefficiency and reward innovation.

Third, democratic constitutions address the classical "constitutionalist" concern of protecting individual and minority rights (e.g., Brennan and Buchanan 1985; Duchacek 1973). Democratic constitutions consequently include lists of fundamental rights that specify policy domains in which policies must or must not be made. Such constitutional constraints on the domain of government policy reduce the ability of simple majorities to transgress individual rights and the rights of permanent ethnic, religious, linguistic, or other identifiable minority groups. For example, "equal protection" clauses protect individuals and groups from discriminatory legislation, and "takings clauses" protect personal property by requiring compensation to be paid to those whose property is taken to advance public purposes.

Fourth, democratic constitutions address dynamic problems involving the stability and flexibility of the constitutional regime itself.

Modesty on the part of constitutional designers requires them to acknowledge that even their best efforts may need to be adjusted to take account of new circumstances, new ideas, or new information. However, a constitution that is too flexible ceases to serve as "rules of the game" for day-to-day politics, which can undermine a constitution's ability to advance the first three objectives. A democratic constitution's amendment process has to allow reforms that advance broad interests to be adopted, without undermining its practical value as a standing routine for advancing majority interests and protecting minorities.

The Demand for Constitutional Reform

Demands for constitutional reform may emerge whenever alternative procedures or constraints appear to advance the first three goals more effectively than existing ones—or whenever a more or less temporary majority believes that it can improve its own situation through constitutional reform. Political interests are not constant over time, nor are all institutional structures equally effective at advancing the shared interests of the electorates. A nation's citizenry may want to modify their system of governance as they learn about unintended, unexpected, and unwanted consequences of their present institutions. Voters may also wish to modify core procedures and constraints of governance as their values and goals change through time, as with women's suffrage and religious and racial tolerance, or as constitutional innovations are found to deliver more effective governance. Major realignments in the political arena may also generate relatively narrow partisan pressures for institutional reforms. Not every demand for constitutional reform attempts to advance broad interests.

General Methods of Constitutional Reform

Although there are always risks associated with constitutional reform because constitutional "mistakes" are more difficult to correct than ordinary policy mistakes, there are also risks associated with constitutional rigidity. A perfectly rigid constitution might not accommodate widespread demands for reform, and in limiting cases, a very costly civil or revolutionary war might be the only possible method of "amendment." An amendable constitution allows such changes to be made at a more reasonable cost. The trade-offs between constitutional rigidity and flexibility are complex and are, for the most part, beyond the scope of the present analysis. However, it is clear that

Table 12.1
Main types of constitutional changes

	Lawful constitutional reforms	Unlawful reforms
Explicit change: (change in constitutional text)	Formal amendment procedures	Irregular procedures
Implicit change	Judicial interpretation	Political adaption
(change in constitution without changing the text)	Durable legislation	Corruption

constitutional stability is partly determined by the requirements of ratification.

The four general methods of constitutional reform are shown in table 12.1 (Voigt 1999, p. 70; Giovannoni 2001). The simple matrix form has two dimensions. One focuses on the *formality* (whether or not to alter the text) of constitutional change, and the other on *lawfulness* of the process by which constitutional reforms are introduced (whether or not a reform is consistent with existing constitutional procedures and constraints). As indicated, this gives us four combinations. The text may or may not be changed through constitutional procedures. Constitutional practices may be changed informally through judicial review and quasi-constitutional legislation or through corruption and fiat.

Our analysis concentrates on formal and lawful reforms of constitutional documents, those in the upper left-hand corner in the table. However, first, a few words on the other methods of reform. Most constitutions, explicitly or implicitly, allow constitutional procedures and constraints to be altered without altering constitutional documents. For example, a constitutional framework may be substantially reformed by means of judicial interpretation. An example is the landmark Marbury v. Madison decision of the US Supreme Court in 1803, through which the principle of judicial review was established (Murphy 2000). Similarly the Norwegian constitution did not mention judicial review until the courts introduced it through interpretation during the first half of the nineteenth century (Smith 1993). Another lawful method of constitutional reform involves revision of the constitutional framework by means of political customs within the legislative and executive bodies. An important example in many other European constitutional monarchies was the gradual evolution of the procedures for government formation during the nineteenth century (Congleton 2001).[5]

It is also possible for a nation's constitutional practices to be revised by irregular means. This is illustrated by the 13th and 14th amendments to the US constitution in the 1860s, which emancipated the slaves and gave them suffrage (Mueller 1999). The amendments would not have been ratified if the formal process laid down in article V of the constitution had been strictly followed, as the southern states had enough votes to block the amendment, but in the circumstances following the Civil War the southern state governments were not fully operational. Similarly, when the wording of article 1 of the Norwegian constitution was changed in November 1814, reflecting the union with Sweden and in 1905 marking the dissolution of the union, the formal amendment procedure was not followed.

In addition constitutional procedures and constraints may simply be ignored or reconfigured without reference to constitutional documents. For example, constitutionally required election laws may be suspended, as the British government has occasionally done during periods of war, or permanently altered, as fascist Italy and Nazi Germany did prior to World War II. Indeed, major extra-legal reforms often mark the end of constitutional governance.

These three methods of constitutional change are alternatives to formal amendment procedures, and they may to some extent be used instead of formal procedures when formal procedures are too cumbersome. That is to say, as the marginal cost of formal constitutional reforms increase, the use of informal or illegal methods of reform will naturally tend to increase.

However, to the extent that formal documents continue to describe the fundamental processes and constraints of governance, informal reforms may be regarded to be of secondary importance. In cases where illegal methods are used, the principle of constitutionalism—politics by the rule of law—is undermined by illegal or extra-legal methods of reform. In such cases the term "constitutional government" clearly does not fully apply. For the purposes of this volume, we thus focus on formal methods of reform.

12.3 Formal Constitutional Amendment Procedures

Almost all constitutions specify procedures for rewriting or replacing the constitutional text, and they are almost always more stringent or demanding than ordinary legislative procedures.[6] However, a wide range of formal amendment procedures potentially satisfy this condition, and this allows the stringency of amendment processes to vary widely. More stringent amendment procedures help make constitutional commitments stable and thus credible. Such procedures consequently help create a higher legal system that can stand above and limit ordinary legislation (Ferejohn 1997). Less stringent amendment procedures allow constitutional mistakes to be readily corrected and institutional experimentation to be more readily conducted.

The stringency of a formal amendment process reflects a commitment by constitutional designers to *entrench* certain rules and procedures or specific programs and prohibitions. Often formal amendment procedures are complex, and most often different methods of amendment are stipulated for different provisions in the constitution or allowed in more or less urgent times. Finland, for example, has a main procedure requiring delay and decision by two-thirds of the members of parliament (MPs), as well as an urgency procedure in which the threshold is increased to a five-sixths majority for adoption of an amendment via a single vote. Estonia also has an urgency procedure. All the Baltic states have tried to protect the most important articles of their constitutions by saying that they cannot be amended unless the voters agree (referendum). In Lithuania no less than a qualified majority of three-fourths is needed to change the first article of the constitution.

Other constitutions rule out particular formal constitutional reforms altogether. For example, article V of the US constitution says that "no state, without its Consent, shall be deprived of its equal Suffrage in the Senate." In Germany, the federal system is protected against changes. Similarly amendments of the basic principles of articles 1 (on human dignity) and 20 (on basic principles of state order and the right to resist) are inadmissible (see article 79). A recent example to the same effect is found in the constitutional framework of Bosnia–Herzegovina, based on the Dayton Agreement. Paragraph 2 of article X states that "No amendment to this Constitution may eliminate or diminish any of the rights and freedoms referred to in Article II of this Constitution or alter the present paragraph."

Several authors have suggested simplified classification schemes to facilitate the comparison of constitutional amendment procedures. For example, Hylland (1994, p. 197) points to four main techniques: delays, confirmation by a second decision, qualified majorities, and participation of other actors than the national assembly. Lane (1996, p. 114) lists six mechanisms: no change, referendum, delay, confirmation by a second decision, qualified majorities, and confirmation by subnational government. Lutz (1994, p. 363) differentiates among four general amendment strategies: legislative supremacy, intervening election (double vote), legislative complexity (referendum threat), and required referendum or equivalent. Lijphart (1999, p. 219) reduces the great variety of methods of amendment to four basic types: ordinary majorities, between two-thirds and ordinary majorities, two-thirds majorities or equivalent, and supermajorities greater than two-thirds. In effect Lijphart disregards the procedural aspects of the amendment except the majority requirements. Elster (2000, p. 101) suggests the following categories: absolute entrenchment, adoption by a supermajority in parliament, requirement of a higher quorum than for ordinary legislation, delays, state ratification (in federal systems), and ratification by referendum.

In general, it becomes more difficult to change a constitution as the number of actors and decision points increase, and as the required degree of consensus increases. To put it differently, the stability of a constitution depends to some extent on the number of veto players, that is, actors whose agreement is necessary for amending the constitution (Tsebelis 2000).

Although amending processes are often strikingly complex, usually a relatively small set of devices are actually used in constitutions around the world (Maddex 1996). Table 12.2 characterizes amendment ratification processes for two dozen countries by tabulating veto players, decision points, and required majorities.

Table 12.2 suggests that constitutional stability is typically achieved in two ways. First, some form of *repeated decisions or a series of decisions by multiple actors* may be used. The purpose of these devices could simply be delay in order to ensure that society acts on well-founded and stable expectations about the consequences of reform and sufficient time is provided at the preparatory stages of the decision process. Second, ratification may require a broader consensus than ordinary legislation. Consensus can be broadened through supermajority rules or by including extra-parliamentary actors, such as the voters by means of a referendum or an intervening election, or subnational units of the state by means of a decentralized ratification method in federal systems. In most constitutional systems the elected representatives of the citizenry play a prominent, but not necessarily exclusive, role in amendment processes.

Table 12.2
Formal amendment rules (simplified) in selected countries

Country	Legislative decision(s)	Referendum and/or ratification	Comments
Norway	(Pre-election proposal) Post-election $\frac{2}{3}$		Delay, but single decision in parliament
Sweden	Pre-election $\frac{1}{2}$ Post-election $\frac{1}{2}$	(Referendum threat)	Referendum if claimed by more than $\frac{1}{3}$ of MPs
Denmark	Pre-election $\frac{1}{2}$ Post-election $\frac{1}{2}$	Majority ($\frac{1}{2}$+)	Majority more than 40 percent of electorate
Finland	Pre-election $\frac{1}{2}$ Post-election $\frac{2}{3}$		Urgency: Single decision with $\frac{5}{6}$ majority
Iceland	Pre-election $\frac{1}{2}$ Post-election $\frac{1}{2}$ Consent by president	(Selected articles only)	Referendum required to change the status of the church
Estonia	First vote $\frac{1}{2}$ Second vote $\frac{3}{5}$	(Selected articles only)	Referendum required to amend important articles (e.g., general provisions). $\frac{3}{5}$ in parliament to call referendum Urgency: Single decision with $\frac{4}{5}$ majority
Latvia	$\frac{2}{3}$ majority in *three* readings	(Selected articles only)	Referendum required to amend important articles (e.g., general provisions)
Lithuania	First vote $\frac{2}{3}$ Second vote $\frac{2}{3}$	(Selected articles only)	Referendum required to amend important articles (in which $\frac{3}{4}$ of electorate support the amendment). Delay of at least 3 months between decisions in parliament
Australia (federation)	Lower house $\frac{1}{2}$ Upper house $\frac{1}{2}$	Majority ($\frac{1}{2}$+)	Constitutional amendment must secure the support of a majority of the whole electorate and majorities in a majority of states (i.e., in four of six states)
Austria (federation)	Lower house $\frac{2}{3}$	(Referendum threat)	Referendum if claimed by more than $\frac{1}{3}$ of lower *or* upper house Separate procedure for "total revision" (referendum required)

Belgium (federation)	Pre-election declaration of revision (by federal legislative power) Post-election lower house $\frac{2}{3}$ Post-election upper house $\frac{2}{3}$		
France	Either (I) Lower house $\frac{1}{2}$ Upper house $\frac{1}{2}$ or (II) Parliament $\frac{3}{5}$	Majority (if procedure I)	No referendum if president decides to submit proposed amendment to parliament convened in Congress (i.e., procedure II) The republican form of government is not subject to amendment
Germany (federation)	Lower house $\frac{2}{3}$ Upper house $\frac{2}{3}$		Some articles of the constitution cannot be amended (e.g., division of federation into states)
Greece	Pre-election $\frac{3}{5}$ twice Post-election $\frac{1}{2}$		The pre-election decisions should be separated by at least one month. Reversed majority requirements possible (i.e., absolute majorities before election and $\frac{3}{5}$ majority after election) Some articles of the constitution cannot be amended (e.g., the basic form of government)
Ireland	Lower house $\frac{1}{2}$ Upper house $\frac{1}{2}$	Majority $\frac{1}{2}$	
Italy	Either (I) Lower house $\frac{1}{2}$ twice Upper house $\frac{1}{2}$ twice or (II) Lower house $\frac{1}{2}$ and $\frac{2}{3}$ Upper house $\frac{1}{2}$ and $\frac{2}{3}$	(Referendum threat if procedure I)	Referendum according to proedure I (absolute majority—but less than two-thirds—in second vote in the chambers) if claimed by (i) $\frac{1}{5}$ of members of either chamber, (ii) 500.000 electors, or (iii) at least five regional councils
Japan	Lower house $\frac{2}{3}$ Upper house $\frac{2}{3}$	Majority	Referendum requirement: "the affirmative vote of a majority of all votes cast thereon"
Luxembourg	Pre-election $\frac{1}{2}$ Post-election $\frac{2}{3}$		

Table 12.2
(continued)

Country	Legislative decision(s)	Referendum and/or ratification	Comments
Netherlands	Pre-election lower house $\frac{1}{2}$ Pre-election upper house $\frac{1}{2}$ Post-election lower house $\frac{2}{3}$ Post-election upper house $\frac{2}{3}$		Ratification by king required
New Zealand	Majority vote $(\frac{1}{2})$	(Majority)	Confirmation in referendum expected or customary if the amendment is considered sufficiently important
Portugal	Parliament $\frac{2}{3}$		Some limits on revision of substance of the constitution specified in article 288
Spain	Either (I) Lower house $\frac{3}{5}$ Upper house $\frac{3}{5}$ or (II) Lower house $\frac{2}{3}$ Upper house $\frac{1}{2}$	(Referendum threat)	Referendum if claimed by more than $\frac{1}{10}$ of the members of either chamber Separate procedure for total revision (i.e., $\frac{2}{3}$ majority in each chamber, dissolution, $\frac{2}{3}$ majority in both chambers, and ratification by referendum) Absolute majority required in the Senate according to procedure II
Switzerland (federation)	Lower house $\frac{1}{2}$ Upper house $\frac{1}{2}$	Majority $(\frac{1}{2}+)$	In referendum, majority of votes nationwide as well as majority support in a majority of cantons
United States (federation)	Either (I) Lower house $\frac{2}{3}$ Upper house $\frac{2}{3}$ or (II) Constitutional convention (called by $\frac{2}{3}$ of the states)	Ratification by $\frac{3}{4}$ of the states	Procedure II has never been used

Sources: Formal constitutions ⟨www.uni-wuerzburg.de/law⟩, Taube (2001) and Rasch (1995).
Key to table: Simple or absolute majority $= \frac{1}{2}$; qualified majorities indicated by $\frac{3}{5}$, $\frac{2}{3}$, $\frac{4}{5}$, etc.

With respect to the Nordic region, constitutional amendments require multiple decisions in parliament in all the countries but Norway. In Norway it is sufficient to submit the constitutional amendment to parliament one year before the next election, and it is the task of the next parliament to decide on the proposal after the election.[7] Denmark, Sweden, Finland, and Iceland require consent from two different parliaments, that is, those assembled before and after an election. The Baltic states require repeated decisions in parliament, but none of them demand that proposals must rest over an election (as in all the other countries of table 12.2). Denmark is the only Nordic country requiring direct voter involvement as part of any constitutional process, and not only with respect to the most important changes.

Bicameral and presidential systems normally require separate approvals by both chambers of the legislature and/or by an independently elected president. Germany illustrates this possibility. The consent of both the Bundestag and the Bundesrat is needed, but not an intervening election. In the Netherlands both chambers must agree to the constitutional amendment before and after an election, which requires a total of four separate decisions (or perhaps five, if the intervening election is counted).[8] In several countries separate constitutional referenda are also required, as in Denmark and Switzerland. In federal states consent of regional governments as in the United States, Canada, and Australia is also required for constitutional reform.

The degree of consensus can be increased through explicit supermajority requirements within legislatures, or implicitly through other institutional means. Bicameralism and presidential systems achieve a similar result insofar as the chambers are elected on a different basis and each chamber has veto power over constitutional reforms. In such cases the implicit electoral support for the constitutional reform is broader the more diverse the two legislative chambers are, and the greater are the supermajority requirements in the two chambers. Agreement after an intervening election may also implicitly increase the degree of consensus required insofar as the ideological composition of the new parliament is different from the previous one.[9]

In addition to protecting substantial minority interests, the use of qualified majorities creates constitutional inertia. Although simple majority rule ensures that alternative proposals are treated neutrally, a qualified majority introduces a bias against any constitutional amendment.

Majority *voter* interests are protected by requirements for an intervening election. The requirement of intervening elections and referenda

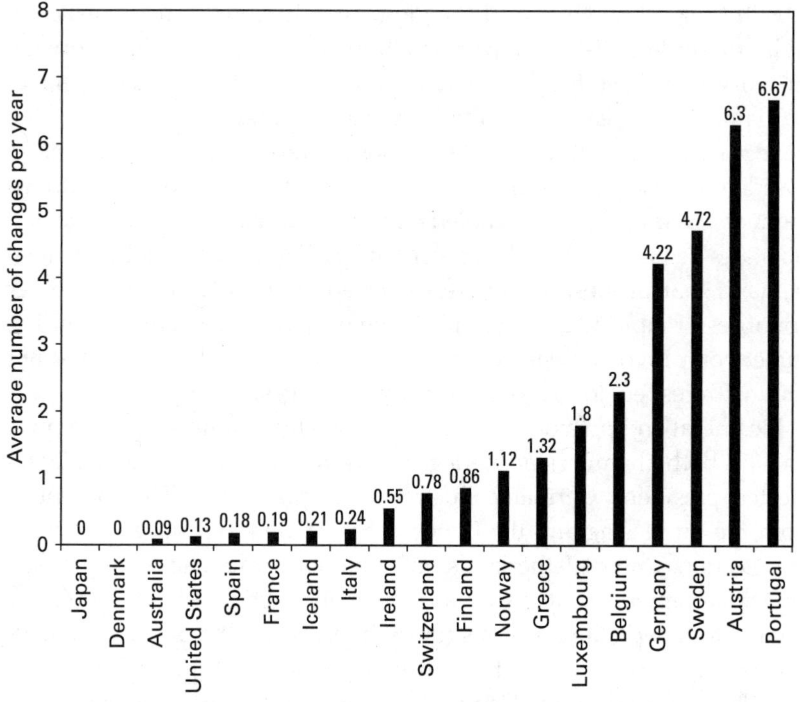

Figure 12.1
Amendment rates (yearly) in selected countries. Source: Lutz (1994, 1995); Denmark corrected and Norway (1814–2001), Sweden (instrument of government only, 1975–2000) and Germany (1949–1994) updated.

reduces prospects for elected leaders to adopt reforms that insulate them from electoral pressures. The referendum requirement in Denmark and Switzerland plays a similar role. However, by separating constitutional and ordinary political issues, constitutional referenda make the amendment procedures more directly responsive to voter opinion. (See chapter 2 for a lengthy discussion of the use of referenda in constitutional reforms.) The more restrictive the voting rule, the stronger is the bias in favor of the status quo or protection of the existing constitution.

12.4 Frequency of Constitutional Amendments

The stringency of a constitutional amendment process might be expected to have systematic effects on the frequency of formal changes to the constitutional text. Insofar as a stringent amendment process increases the "cost" of each constitutional reform, the number of reforms demanded by voters and their elected representatives would tend to decline. Moreover, as the time requirements of reform increase, fewer such reforms are feasible within a given time period, other things being equal. However, more demanding amendment procedures also imply that an amendment may be in place for a longer time, and consequently that the value of each amendment is increased somewhat. This value effect tends to increase the demand for constitutional amendments relative to ordinary legislation as the stringency of the amendment process increases. The overall effect of the difficulty of amendment on the frequency of amendment is thus ambiguous, and no systematic effect will be found unless the cost or value effect tends to dominate in most real-world settings.

Empirical evidence, to this point, suggests that the cost effect tends to dominate. Lutz (1994, 1995) demonstrates that the degree of rigidity of a constitution affects the amendment rate in a cross-national analysis. He builds a complex difficulty of ratification index, and his measure clearly correlates with formal changes to the constitution. After disaggregating the index, Ferejohn (1997, p. 523), in a re-analysis, claims that "the requirement of special majorities or separate majorities in different legislative sessions or bicamerality is the key variable to explaining amendment rates." He continues by saying that "there is no evidence that a ratification requirement, whether involving states or a popular referendum, has any significant impact on amendment rates." In other words, Ferejohn suggests that special majorities in the legislature may be both necessary and sufficient to achieve a moderate amendment rate.

The empirical relationship between stringency and amendment rates found by Lutz and Ferejohn, however, is not robust. Perhaps more important, the number of constitutional changes is unfortunately an imperfect measure of constitutional stability. Not only do "document amendment counts" neglect other methods of change, but amendment counts assign equal importance to both major and minor amendments. For example, a change in rules governing alcohol consumption (as with the 18th and 21st amendments to the US constitution) has a trivial effect on a nation's fundamental political procedures and constraints, whereas a great expansion of suffrage, a change in governmental architecture (presidential or parliamentary system), new electoral system, or new policy constaints (bill of rights) may have very substantial effects on subsequent policy decisions. The latter suggests that the estimated relationships may understate the importance of amendment procedures insofar as those procedures may be more important for major than for minor reforms.

There are basically two requirements to consider, as noted above. Constitutional stability may be increased by increasing the degree of consensus required and by increasing the number of veto points in the amendment process. The data on amendment rates from Lutz (1994) can be combined with the institutional information of table 12.2 to create indexes of consensus and of the number of central government veto players or points of agreement required to secure a constitutional amendment. The number of governmental veto players is coded as 0 through 3, with a single point awarded for each center of institutional authority beyond parliament that must agree to a proposed amendment: bicameral, presidential, and federal. The number of veto points is the number of governmental veto players plus an additional point if an intervening election is required, and another if a referendum is normally used to ratify constitutional amendments. As noted above, several of these features also tend to implicitly increase the breadth of consensus as well, although less explicitly than the requirement of supermajority approval.

Table 12.3 summarizes the result of a series of estimates that regress the log of the Lutz amendment rates against institutional features of national amendment procedures. Relatively sparse models are necessitated by the small data set of OECD countries used here (19 countries). The results suggest that the number of veto players and veto points have systematic effects on the amendment rates of these OECD countries. Amendment rates fall as the number of veto players increases and with requirements for intervening elections and/or referenda. The requirement of supermajorities in the legislature and the age of the constitution have no systematic effect within the present sample. (The results are slightly weaker if New Zealand is dropped from the sample or coded as having supermajority and referenda requirements.) Overall the regression results are consistent with the existence of a significant cost effect on the demand for constitutional amendments. As the costs of passing an amendment increases, fewer amendments are adopted.

In contrast to Ferejohn's results, however, the salient factor seems to be multiple decisions with voter involvement rather than special majorities in the legislature. The lack of a discernible effect for supermajorities is a bit surprising, but this may reflect the kinds of

Table 12.3
Estimated amendment rates (in logs, LS)

	(1)	(2)	(3)	(4)	(5)
Constant	0.517	1.819	1.668	1.581	3.249
	(1.17)	(2.32)**	(3.07)**	(2.79)**	(2.35)**
Number of veto players	−0.789	−0.864			
	(2.17)**	(2.40)**			
Number of veto points			−1.045	−1.039	−0.911
			(3.82)**	(3.68)**	(3.14)**
Supermajority required		0.023		−0.564	−0.027
		(0.03)		(0.21)	(0.04)
Referenda threat		−1.537			
		(2.40)**			
Intervening election required		−1.278			
		(1.95)*			
Log of constitutional age					−0.486
					(1.37)
F-statistic	4.709**	3.44**	14.656**	6.940**	5.517**
R^2	0.217	0.496	0.462	0.464	0.524

Source: Data from Lutz (1994) and table 12.2.
Notes: New Zealand is coded as lacking referenda and supermajority requirements. Absolute value of *t*-statistics are in parentheses below coefficient estimates; * denotes significance at the 10% level and ** at the 5% level; $N = 19$.

amendments normally passed in these polities. In many cases the constitutional amendments more closely resemble ordinary public policies and legislative procedures than profound changes in the fundamental procedures and constraints of governance. As such, efforts to secure coalitions favoring a particular amendment will attempt to craft amendments that secure sufficient approval, much as the coalitions assembled (see chapter 5 in this volume) are formed with the rules for forming and dissolving governments in mind. For example, in Sweden there is no requirement of super majority for constitutional reform. Still most major constitutional reforms have been based on very broad support in the parliament. This support has been achieved by yielding a little to each interest in the parliament, with the result that the constitutional language is often lengthy (and quite often ambiguous).

The Demand and Supply of Constitutional Amendments in Norway

Just as the market demand for ordinary goods and services are affected by more than a product's cost, so are political demands for

Table 12.4
Formal amendments of articles in the Norwegian constitution, 1814 to 2001

	Number of changes 1814–1905	Number of changes 1905–2001
Section A (articles 1–2): Form of government and religion	2	2
Section B (articles 3–48): Executive power, the king and the royal family	13	36
Section C (articles 49–85): Rights of citizens and the legislative power	36	93
Section D (articles 86–91): Judicial power	1	8
Section E (articles 92–112): General provisions	4	16
Total number of changes to articles ($\sum = 211$)	**56**	**155**

Notes: Most of the articles on individual rights and freedoms are found in section E of the constitution. The table shows the number of articles that have been amended (some articles more than once). Thus, if two separate changes were made simultaneously to one article, both are counted as a single change. If the changes to two articles are related and were made simultaneously, the amendment is nevertheless counted as two changes. In practice, these kinds of complications are rare.

constitutional amendments. A variety of political and economic circumstances can clearly affect the overall pattern of demand for constitutional amendments.

Table 12.4 shows the number of constitutional changes to articles accepted for the Norwegian Constitution from 1814 until today. Amendment activity was significantly lower during the years 1814 to 1905 than in the twentieth century. The explanation certainly has something to do with the union with Sweden, which was dissolved in 1905. Constitutional conservatism was a deliberate strategy by the (Norwegian) parliamentary majority to restrict Swedish influence in general and the power of the Swedish kings in particular. Already in the early 1820s the Storting rejected a reform package from King Karl Johan to strengthen the executive branch of government. Conversely, major reform proposals from the Norwegian parliament often failed to attract the assent of the Swedish crown during this period.

The contents as well as the number of amendments are also of interest. The section of the constitution dealing with various aspects of the legislative branch accounts for a majority of the changes. Many of the articles concerning the electoral system are found here, and they have been altered in various ways quite frequently. The set of individual rights and freedoms in the constitution has been relatively stable and

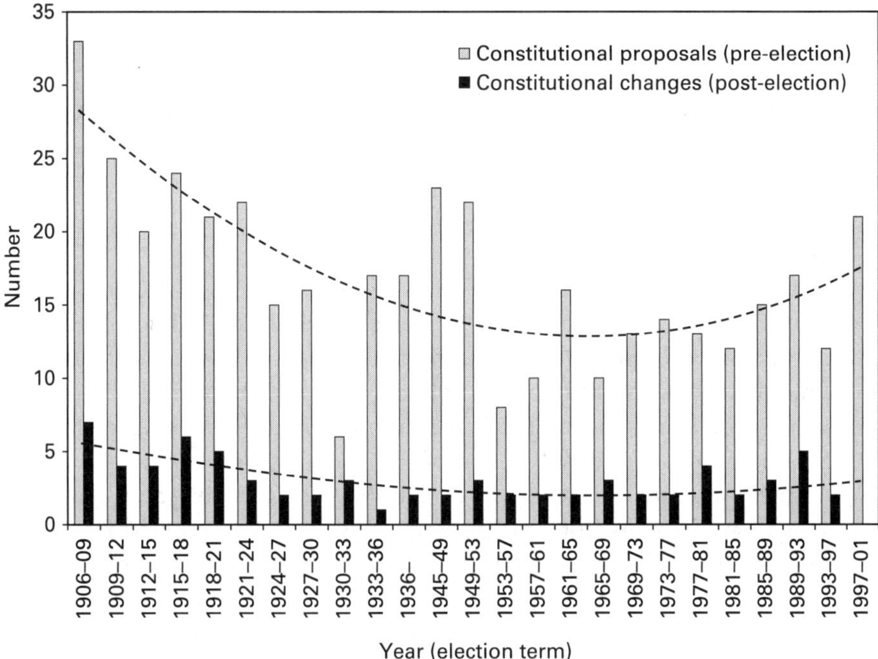

Figure 12.2
Proposals to amend the Norwegian constitution, and actual changes to the constitution, 1905 to 2001. Proposals are put forward before general elections (without a vote) and need a two-thirds majority in a vote after the election to be accepted (see article 112 of the constitution). The diagram is based on a total of 422 constitutional proposals and 73 constitutional amendments.

so far not been subject to any more fundamental upgrading or modernization.

A more complete picture of the demand and supply of constitutional reforms through time is found in figure 12.2, depicting the number of constitutional issues and the actual number of changes in each legislative period since 1905. Until 1936 the MPs were elected for three years only, making the yearly amendment rate much higher during the first decades of the century than later. There were no constitutional changes in the final legislative period recorded in the table (1997–2001), but this is in fact the only one without any revision of the constitutional text. The constitution has subsequently been revised several times.

The number of constitutional proposals is on average more than five times the actual number of changes. With time the number of proposals has diminished (in particular, the annual proposal rate), although the number of proposals in the 1997 to 2001 legislative period was the highest in nearly fifty years. This might indicate a new willingness to put constitutional questions on the legislative agenda. Nonetheless, almost all proposals for constitutional change are rejected with overwhelming majorities.

12.5 Conclusion

Unfortunately, the frequency of lawful constitutional changes cannot be understood by focusing on the number of veto players and degree of required consensus alone. The political demand for constitutional reform reflects economic, political, and cultural circumstances, as well as the magnitude of unresolved problems at any given point in time. External pressure for revision, constitutional traditions, and recent innovations in constitutional design, as well as the cost of formal amendments, will also affect the types of constitutional reforms proposed. It would be useful to have a more complete model of the demand for constitutional reform so that the effects of "demand" can be clearly separated from those of "supply."

Moreover measures of constitutional reforms can clearly be improved, insofar as formal constitutional documents do not include all of the core procedures and constraints of governance. That some core procedures and constraints are not fully specified by constitutional documents implies that significant reforms may be lawfully adopted through other means. Constitutions can be—and often are—changed without altering the text of constitutional documents. Election laws can often be reformed through ordinary legislation. The courts may reinterpret formal constitutional documents as well as "quasi-constitutional" legislation.

Moreover not all constitutional reforms have the same effect on a nation's fundamental procedures and constraints of governance. The constitutional reforms adopted in the first part of the twentieth century by many European parliaments included such radical changes as the adoption of universal male suffrage, women's suffrage, and proportional representation. The more recent constitutional histories of many countries include many dozens of reforms, but relatively few of these affect fundamental procedures or rights. Consequently the number of formal changes to constitutional documents is a far from perfect measure of constitutional stability.

Clearly, there is much more to be learned about the relationship between amendment rates and amendment procedures. We do not yet know exactly how to strike a good balance between flexibility and rigidity; a unique optimal solution may not exist at all. (The variation in amendment rates among successful OECD nations is clearly greater than that of per capita income.[10]) The new empirical analysis of constitutional stability remains very much a work in progress.

Nonetheless, the new empirical work clearly suggests that amendment procedures affect the stability of constitutional documents. Insofar as formal constitutional law and practice are similar in longstanding democratic states (an issue that we leave for further study), these results suggest that politics in both the large and small tends to be relatively more routinized, and consequently more predictable in polities with relatively demanding amendment procedures.

Appendix

Correlation matrix (Pearson's r): Variables measuring constitutional rigidity

	Constitutional rigidity (Rasch)	Super-majoritarianism (Rasch)	Index of difficulty (Lutz 1994)	Constitutional rigidity (Lijphart 1999)
Index of difficulty (Lutz 1994)	**0.380*** (0.099)	**−0.109** (0.649)		
Constitutional rigidity (Lijphart 1999)	**0.329** (0.157)	**0.407*** (0.075)	**0.480**** (0.032)	
Constitutional rigidity (Anckar and Karvonen 2002)	**0.489**** (0.029)	**0.716***** (0.000)	**−0.049** (0.838)	**0.496**** (0.026)

Notes: $N = 20$ (selected countries). *** $p < 0.01$ ** $p < 0.05$ * $p < 0.1$.
Index of difficulty (Lutz 1994): Additive index (continuous)
Constitutional rigidity (Rasch): See table 12.2. Four categories.
Supermajoritarianism (Rasch): See table 12.2. Dichotomy; qualified majority requirements (1) or not (0)
Constitutional rigidity (Lijphart): See table 12.1 in Lijphart (1999, p. 220).
Four categories: Supermajorities greater than two-thirds, two-thirds majorities or equivalent, between two-thirds and ordinary majorities, and ordinary majorities.
Constitutional rigidity (Anckar and Karvonen): Based on information from a forthcoming paper. Five categories: Ordinary majority, strengthened majority, weakened qualified majority, qualified majority, and strengthened qualified majority.

Notes

1. Denmark can serve as an example. The 1849 constitution was replaced by a new one in 1953. The fact that Denmark celebrated a 150-year constitutional anniversary in 1999 indicates that the change is evidently not considered to be fundamental. The most important part of the 1953 reform package was abolishment of the second chamber.

2. September 17, 1787, is the date at which the "present" US constitution was signed by members of the constitutional convention. It was formally ratified by the requisite nine states (article 7), often by narrow margins, in late 1788. The last of the original 13 states to ratify, Rhode Island, did not formally agree to the new constitution until 1790. The 1789 constitution replaced the Articles of Confederation negotiated in 1777 and ratified in 1781.

3. As mentioned above, only 4 percent of national governments today lack a constitution. Even dictatorships often adopt formal documents that characterize the formal procedures of governance. The traditional view is that rulers wielding absolute power cannot limit themselves by constitutional arrangements. Barros (2002) discusses the arguments against autocratic self-limitation and tries to specify conditions under which institutional constraints might be effectively introduced under an authoritarian regime. Congleton (2001) explores advantages that a dictatorship may realize by sharing power with a council or parliament.

4. See chapter 2 (on delegation and agency problems) of Kiewiet and McCubbins (1991) for an introduction to the principal–agent approach.

5. Indeed, the British constitution can be revised only in these ways insofar as its constitutional regime lacks formal methods of amendment. Ordinary legislation, judicial interpretation, and the evolution of binding intragovernmental norms are the normal method of British constitutional reform, and these methods are also widely used elsewhere.

6. New Zealand is an exception to this, because, the constitution is formally amended in the same way as ordinary legislation. Thus the Constitution Act 1986, as with other standard legislation, can be amended by a simple parliamentary majority. Only a subset of the Electoral Act 1993 requires a supramajority for amendments. The entrenching provision, however, is not itself entrenched and thus (in theory at least) can be amended or removed by a simple majority. Moreover, in practice, major changes of a constitutional nature are typically the subject of a binding referendum, but these have been few and far between.

7. This is the wording of article 112 of the Norwegian constitution: "If experience shows that any part of this Constitution of the Kingdom of Norway ought to be amended, the proposal to this effect shall be submitted to the first, second, or third Parliament [Storting] after a new General Election and be publicly announced in print. But it shall be left to the first, second, or third Parliament [Storting] after the following General Election to decide whether or not the proposed amendment shall be adopted. Such amendment must never, however, contradict the principles embodied in this Constitution, but solely relate to modifications of particular provisions which do not alter the spirit of the Constitution, and such amendment requires that two-thirds of the Parliament [Storting] agree thereto. An amendment to the Constitution adopted in the manner aforesaid shall be signed by the President and the Secretary of the Parliament [Storting] and shall be sent to the King for public announcement in print, as an applicable provision of the Constitution of the Kingdom of Norway." The article has been changed six times since 1814, but the stipulated amendment procedure is essentially unchanged.

8. Norway has a kind of bicameralism, but this fact has no relevance with regard to constitutional changes. After each election the Storting (parliament) divides itself into two sections: the Odelsting (the general chamber) and the Lagting (the permanent chamber). Politically there is no difference between the sections. Bills are first introduced to the Odelsting, and the Lagting has to agree for the bill to become law. (See article 76 of the constitution for details.) Financial matters (e.g., the state budget) are, just like constitutional amendments, handled by the Storting as a single chamber.

9. A recent trend in well-established democracies is increased instability at the polls (volatility). This makes it more difficult to amend those constitutions that require consent of the pre-election and postelection parliament. Thus an easily overlooked external factor may affect the difficulty of the amendment process significantly.

10. Average 30-year growth rates of real per capita GNP (1995 dollars) range from 1.1 percent a year (Switzerland) to 3.2 percent a year (Japan) within the sample of countries listed in table 12.2. Amendment rates are negatively correlated with growth rates within this sample but not at a statistically significant level. Particular features of constitutional amendment procedures are more strongly correlated with long-term growth. For example, federalism is negatively correlated with long-term growth rates within this sample.

References

Barros, R. 2002. *Constitutionalism and Dictatorship: Pinochet, the Junta, and the 1980 Constitution.* Cambridge: Cambridge University Press.

Busch, A. 2000. The Grundgesetz after 50 years: Analysing changes in the German constitution. *German Politics* 9: 41–60.

Brennan, G., and J. M. Buchanan. 1985. *The Reason of Rules. Constitutional Political Economy.* Cambridge: Cambridge University Press.

Congleton, R. D. 2001. On the durability of king and council: The continuum between dictatorship and democracy. *Constitutional Political Economy* 12: 193–215.

Congleton, R. D. 2003. *Improving Democracy through Constitutional Reform, Some Swedish Lessons.* Boston: Kluwer Academic Press.

Duchacek, I. D. 1973. *Power Maps: Comparative Politics of Constitutions.* Santa Barbara: ABC Clio.

Elster, J. 2000. *Ulysses Unbound: Studies in Rationality, Precommitment, and Constraints.* Cambridge: Cambridge University Press.

Ferejohn, J. 1997. The politics of imperfection: The amendment of constitutions. *Law and Social Inquiry* 22: 501–31.

Giovannoni, F. 2001. Amendment rules in constitutions. Paper presented at the European Public Choice Annual Meeting, Paris, April 18–21.

Hardin, R. 1989. Why a constitution? In B. Grofman and D. Wittman, eds., *The Federalist Papers and the New Institutionalism.* New York: Agathon Press.

Hylland, A. 1994. Konstitusjonell treghet. Bør noen saker være unndratt flertallets kontroll? In B. E. Rasch and K. Midgaard, eds., *Representativt demokrati. Spilleregler under debatt.* Oslo: Universitetsforlaget.

Kiewiet, D. R., and M. D. McCubbins. 1991. *The Logic of Delegation: Congressional Parties and the Appropriations Process.* Chicago: University of Chicago Press.

Lane, J.-E. 1996. *Constitutions and Political Theory.* Manchester: Manchester University Press.

Levinson, S., ed. 1995. *Responding to Imperfection: The Theory and Practice of Constitutional Amendment.* Princeton: Princeton University Press.

Lijphart, A. 1999. *Patterns of Democracy: Government Forms and Performance in Thirty-six Countries.* New Haven: Yale University Press.

Lutz, D. S. 1994. Toward a theory of constitutional amendment. *American Political Science Review* 88: 355–70.

Lutz, D. S. 1995. Toward a theory of constitutional amendment. In S. Levinson, ed., *Responding to Imperfection: The Theory and Practice of Constitutional Amendment.* Princeton: Princeton University Press.

Maarseveen, H. van, and G. van der Tang. 1978. *Written Constitutions: A Computerized Comparative Study.* Dobbes Ferry: Oceana Publications.

Maddex, R. L. 1996. *Constitutions of the World.* London: Routledge.

Mueller, D. C. 1999. On amending constitutions. *Constitutional Political Economy* 10: 385–96.

Murphy, W. 2000. Constitutional interpretation as constitutional creation. The 1999–2000 Harry Eckstein Lecture. Center for the Study of Democracy. University of California at Irvine. Available at: www.democ.uci.edu/papers/murphy.htm.

North, D. 1990. *Institutions, Institutional Change and Economic Performance.* Cambridge: Cambridge University Press.

Rasch, B. E. 1995. Parliamentary voting procedures. In H. Döring, ed., *Parliaments and Majority Rule in Western Europe.* Frankfurt/New York: Campus/St. Martin's Press.

Rasch, B. E. 2000. *Demokrati—Ideer og Organisering.* Bergen: Fagbokforlaget.

Salmon, P. 2001. Ordinary elections and constitutional arrangements. In R. Mudambi, P. Navarra, and G. Sobbrio, eds., *Rules and Reason: Constitutional Political Economy.* Cambridge: Cambridge University Press.

Smith, E. 1993. *Høyesterett og Folkestyret.* Oslo: Universitetsforlaget.

Taube, C. 2001. *Constitutionalism in Estonia, Latvia and Lithuania: A Study in Comparative Constitutional Law.* Uppsala: Iustus.

Tsebelis, G. 2002. *Veto Players: How Political Institutions Work.* Princeton: Princeton University Press.

Voigt, S. 1999. *Explaining Constitutional Change: A Positive Economics Approach.* Cheltenham: Edward Elgar.

13 Designing Constitutional Stability

Barry R. Weingast

13.1 Introduction

The failure of most constitutions (Weingast 2005b) forces us to confront the constitutional design question of what characteristics make a constitution more likely to survive? This question is especially interesting in the democratic context: Since most democratic constitutions have failed, what characteristics make them more likely to survive? Democracies typically fail in one of two ways: those in power fail to abide by the rules, such as ignoring an electoral defeat or abusing the rights of the opposition, and those out of power use force to take power (Przeworski 1991; Weingast 2005a). To survive, political officials must have incentives to honor the rules, including electoral defeats, and those out of power must have incentives to refrain from using force to take power. If either of these conditions fail, democracy is clearly unstable.

Stated in this way, the problem of constitutional stability becomes one of incentives. Those in power must have incentives to abide by the rules, and those out of power must have incentives to limit the contest for power to legitimate democratic means.

Drawing on the recent literature on self-enforcing democracy (Acemoglu and Robinson 2004; Fearon 2000; Przeworski 1991, 2005; Weingast 1997, 2004, 2005a) and self-enforcing constitutions (Gibbons and Rutten 1996; Hardin 1989; Milgrom, North, and Weingast 1990; Ordeshook and Svetsova 1997), I discuss two fundamental problems plaguing constitutional stability and two principles explaining how each problem might be resolved (Weingast 2005).

The first fundamental problem of constitutional stability concerns the *rationality of fear* model (de Figueiredo and Weingast 1997). When citizens feel threatened by changes in public policy, particularly when they believe their lives or livelihoods are at stake, they will take steps to defend themselves. The model holds that for with a given level of stakes, there exists a threshold probability. If the citizens believe that the probability of adverse policy changes is at or above the threshold, they will take actions to defend themselves against risk of loss. The rationality of fear defines one of the problems that all democratic constitutions must solve.

To survive, constitutions must short-circuit the rationality of fear mechanism. The first principle of self-enforcing constitutions reflects this insight. To see this, consider the observation of Przeworski (1991, ch. 2) that all successful constitutions lower the stakes of politics. This is because, as I will argue, constitutions that lower the stakes reduce the likelihood of triggering the rationality of fear mechanism: citizens are less likely to support extra-constitutional action to protect themselves when constitutions protect what they hold most dear.

The second fundamental problem of constitutional stability concerns the coordination problem underlying democracy, namely whether citizens have the ability to act in concert against political leaders who transgress constitutional rules (Weingast 1997, 2005a). The ability to coordinate provides a powerful deterrent to transgressions: citizens' withdrawal of political support following a constitutional violation provides a credible threat over those in power. In the presence of this threat, officials will adhere to the rules, since failing to do so risks being thrown out of office.

Concomitantly leaders are likely to transgress their citizens' rights when citizens lack the ability to coordinate. The absence of coordination implies that leaders can transgress the rights of some citizens while retaining sufficient support from others to remain in power.

This type of coordination problem is extremely difficult to solve for several reasons. First, large numbers of citizens are involved, and each must believe that the others will also react in concert (Chwe 2001). Second, there is no natural mechanism to help citizens coordinate. Because citizens' experience, interests, and values vary widely, they are unlikely to agree on how to coordinate: After all, how do they coordinate on the definition of what actions constitute a transgression? Finally, leaders can systematically defeat coordination through various divide and conquer strategies—maintaining a political support coalition sufficient to survive while transgressing the rights of others.

If coordination is difficult, what determines when citizens have this ability? The answer is in part that appropriately constructed constitutions create focal solutions to citizen coordination problems so that citizens can react in concert when the regime threatens a transgression (Hardin 1989; Ordeshook 1992; Weingast 1997, 2005a). First, constitutions specify "structure and process" (McNollgast 1989), including procedures for governmental decision making, various citizen rights, and a range of limits on governmental action. Second, when this structure and process protects what people feel most dear, it short-circuits the rationality of fear mechanism. Finally, successful constitutions create focal solutions to the problems of coordination against the government: by defining government structure and process and citizen rights, the constitution also defines what actions constitute transgressions so that citizens can coordinate against potential violations. For this to be self-enforcing, citizens must believe they are better off under the constitution and that unilateral defection ends the constitution, making them worse off.

The two principles of constitutional stability are logically dependent in the following sense. The first principle asserts that all successful constitutions must short-circuit the rationality of fear mechanism by limiting the stakes of power. They do so by imposing structure and process limiting governmental action. But all constitutions provide for structure and process, so what makes these provisions in some constitutions credible? The answer is given by the second principle: successful constitutions create focal solutions the citizen coordination problem. When citizens have the ability to react in concert to protect constitutional provisions—and when those provisions limit the stakes of power—constitutions are likely to survive.

In most countries the onset of constitutional democracy began with compromises called "pacts," agreements among contending—and often previously warring—elites that end hostilities.[1] For example, the various pacts ending the civil war in El Salvador in the late 1980s and early 1990s; in the United States, the constitution and the compromises of 1820, 1833, 1850, and 1877; and in Spain, the various pacts surrounding democratization in 1975 to 1978. As I show below, pacts are thus bargains critical for aligning the incentives of political elites.

In contrast to the literature on constitutional democracy, the approach here is more pessimistic. It suggests that stable constitutions cannot be designed at just any time or under any circumstances. Further in many cases it appears that powerful interests have to be protected even when the interests are morally questionable, such as those of southern slaveholders in the antebellum United States or drug lords in parts of modern Latin America. The reason is that, to succeed, a constitution must protect those with the power to disrupt democracy. Absent ridding the society of power interests, the theory of self-enforcing constitutions requires that these interests be protected.

I apply the stable constitution approach to two cases. The first involves constitutional democracy in the United States's first century, which fits the model of self-enforcing pacts. The United States's first constitution, the Articles of Confederation, was widely recognized as a failure: the national government under the Articles failed to provide basic national public goods, such as security and a common market. The constitution of 1787 resolved these problems by creating new structure and process that limited the national government. The horizontal separation of powers, federalism, delegation solely of enumerated powers, and the bill of rights all placed significant restrictions on the national government. Moreover the constitution qua pact satisfied the four conditions for a self-enforcing pact. I argue that, except for the issue of slavery, the constitution was self-enforcing.

The problems of slavery required additional institutions beyond the constitution to make the US constitution self-enforcing. Known as the "balance rule," the additional institution granted both sections a veto over national policy making through equal representation in the Senate (Weingast 1998). Nevertheless, periodic crises arose at moments when the country had been growing asymmetrically, allowing one section the potential to gain control over the national government. In each case, a crisis ensued, and in three of the four crises, a pact resolved it. I argue that these pacts, as with that creating the constitution, satisfied the four conditions noted by the theory for self-enforcing pacts.

The second application is to Spain. Spain had a tumultuous history for the first three quarters of the twentieth century. The 1930s witnessed a short-lived Second Republic that collapsed in civil war (1936–1939), leading to the stable, repressive dictatorship of General Francisco Franco. Following his death in 1975, a period of uncertainty and potential instability ensued, leading to stable constitutional democracy by the early 1980s.

The theory helps explain both the instability during the 1930s and the pacts that created constitutional democracy in the 1970s and early 1980s. Throughout this period Spain was deeply divided on a number of fundamental issues: monarchy versus republicanism, the degree of autonomy for the Basque region and Catalonia, the nature of the economic system (including whether Spanish society might be fundamentally redesigned according to a socialist program).

Three pacts following the death of Franco created a stable, self-enforcing constitution, each having the characteristics noted by the theory. These created a new focal set of attitudes of moderation, mutual accommodation, and compromise. Steering a middle course among the major issues, these pacts created self-enforcing constitutional democracy in Spain.

The chapter proceeds as follows. Section 13.2 develops a theory of democratic stability. Section 13.3 then applies the approach to the United States, while section 13.4 applies it to the Spanish case. My conclusions follow.

13.2 A Theory of Constitutional Stability

To understand the stability of democratic constitutions, I begin with *democratic consolidation*, the term political scientists use for stable democracy. According to Larry Diamond (1999, p. 66):

> For a democracy to be consolidated, elites, organizations, and the mass public must all believe that the political system they actually have in their country is worth obeying and defending.

Similarly Linz and Stepan (1996, p. 5) argue that consolidation occurs when democracy is the "only game in town"; and that citizens and politicians "become habituated to the fact that political conflict will be resolved according to the established norms and that violations of these norms are likely to be both ineffective and costly."

Reflecting these notions, I provide a twofold definition of democratic consolidation (Weingast 1997, 2005a): First, no significant group of citizens or parties out of power is willing to attempt to subvert power or secede. Second, those in power follow the constitutional rules (e.g., they obey election results and eschew transgressing the rights of their opponents).

Defined in this manner, consolidation requires that democracy is "self-enforcing": that is, it must be in the interest of all actors to adhere to the constitutional rules.[2] Incentives are central to both parts of the definition: First, actors out of power must have incentives to pursue their goals within the system. Second, political officials must have incentives to honor the rules, including election results. If either of these incentive conditions fail, democracy is not consolidated and is likely to fail.

The relevance of this approach is demonstrated by considering what I call the "Przeworski moment" after Adam Przeworski's famous book,

Democracy and the Market (Przeworski 1991, ch. 2). In the Przeworski moment, a party in power has just lost an election but retains power until the date of legal transition: Why would it ever give up power? Many democracies fail at such moments. Przeworski provides the answer in the abstract: it must be in the interests of those in power to give it up. To make use of this claim, we must derive conditions under which Przeworski's answer holds.

My approach begins with citizens, who are assumed to have preferences and values about their own fundamental rights and the appropriate limits on the state. These notions, in turn, define a transgression by the government—a violation of a fundamental right or limit on the state.

Yet rights and limits on the state are not self-actualizing. Because citizen's social and economic situations vary significantly, they are unlikely to agree about the form of rights or bounds on the state. Farmers disagree with merchants, landlords with tenants, workers with capitalists, and urbanites with those from the country. The manifold divisions in society imply that there is no natural consensus about the nature of the citizens' rights, the bounds on the state, and generally, the constitution.

Principles of Constitutional Stability

In what follows, I discuss two fundamental problems plaguing constitutional stability. Associated with each problem is a principle that explains how successful constitutions resolve the problem.

The first fundamental problem of constitutional stability concerns what de Figueiredo and I (1997) call the "rationality of fear." I have already mentioned that successful constitutions require that all actors must have an incentive to abide by the rules. One of the principal reasons people defect—or support defection, such as coup—is that they fear they are better off without the constitution.[3]

The rationality of fear model is based on the premise that when citizens or groups are threatened, they take steps to defend themselves. The rationality of fear has two important implications. First, suppose that citizens believe that a threat has a certain probability p of being realized. The model shows that given citizens preferences and the magnitude of the threat, there exists a critical probability threshold p^* such that if the probability of the threat is below this threshold, citizens will not act to protect themselves against the threat. If, however, the probability is at or above the threshold, they will act to defend themselves. Second, the model yields an important comparative statics result: *the larger the relative magnitude of the threat, the lower is the threshold probability triggering defensive action.* For very large threats—for example, those concerning people's lives and livelihoods—the probability triggering defensive reaction can be very low, such as one in ten.

The importance of the rationality of fear is that, for threats with very large consequences, citizens will support defensive action even when the act is not likely. The reason is that citizens are not social scientists—they are not trying to determine whether the threat is likely to be carried out; they are trying to maximize their expected value. For very large threats, even a small probability of an act yields large expected consequences. In the face of very large threats, citizens rationally act to defend themselves even when the probability is small.

The rationality of fear shows that constitutions are necessarily delicate: large stakes imply that citizens will react against democracy to even small threats. The rationality of fear has dozens of applications. For example, in Chile during the early 1970s, many on the political right felt their economic rights threatened by President Salvador Allende's government, leading them to support the military coup (Valenzuela 1978). Similarly, during the Second Republic in Spain (1931–1939), many agrarian landholders, leaders of the Church, and many industrialists felt threatened by the democratically elected regime, leading them to support General Francisco Franco in the civil war against the regime (Agüero 1995; Alexander 2002). In the early nineteenth century, large numbers of southerners in the United States felt their property in slaves threatened by the newly elected Republicans in 1860, leading to secession and Civil War (Weingast 1998). In each case a sufficiently large group of citizens felt threatened by a legitimately elected regime and supported extra constitutional action (e.g., civil war or coup) to defend themselves.

The second fundamental problem concerns the coordination problem underlying democratic stability (Weingast 1997, 2005a). When citizens are willing to act in concert in response to a governmental transgression, they deter leaders from doing so for fear of losing the support they need to remain in power. In contrast, when citizens fail to act in concert—notably, if they disagree about what constitutes a transgression—leaders can act in a way that retains the support of sufficient constituents while transgressing the rights of others. Indeed, as I argue elsewhere, the divide and conquer strategy is the most natural equilibrium for societies, and it characterizes most societies throughout history (Weingast 1997). In these societies the government respects the rights of some citizens—those whose support is necessary to remain in power—but not the rights of others. Only a small number of societies have been able to sustain democratic constitutions of universal rights.

The fundamental coordination problem of democracy is difficult to resolve because there is no natural focal solution on which citizens can coordinate. Citizen experiences differ so greatly that they disagree about the proper form of government, the rights of citizens, and what actions constitute a transgression. These differences are difficult to resolve because citizens have differing preferences over these issues, and no natural comprise exists.

The main point is that the natural situation for a society is the failure of coordination. And absent a coordination mechanism, citizens are unlikely to react in concert to governmental transgressions, allowing it to survive in power while transgressing the rights of some citizens. Democratic and constitutional stability therefore requires that a society resolve both of these problems. Resolving each involves the constitution, but in different ways.

The first principle of constitutional stability addresses the rationality of fear problem and follows an observation of Przeworksi (1991, ch. 2), namely that *all successful constitutions limit the stakes of politics.* When a constitution credibly limits the stakes of politics in ways valued by most citizens, political officials are far less likely to take actions that threaten citizens in ways that invoke the rationality of fear mechanism. Constitutions that limit the stakes of power imply that citizens are far less likely to resort to extra-constitutional means to defend themselves. Democracies that limit the stakes of political competition are therefore more likely to survive.

This principle also implies that the set of limits on government will differ across societies, at least to a degree. Because the pattern of assets, preferences, and values differ across societies, what citizens hold most dear will differ as well. This implies that what must be protected—limiting the stakes—differs across societies.

Limiting the stakes also implies that to be stable, constitutions must limit the power of majorities. This is a conclusion drawn by the founders and also emphasized in a wide range of public choice scholars (e.g., Buchanan and Tulloch 1962; Riker 1982). Unfettered majorities are more likely to threaten powerful minorities, raising the rationality of fear among these groups. When these minorities have the power to disrupt democracy, such threats mean democracy is likely to fail. Again, this implies that constitutions that impose limited government, protecting those with the power to disrupt the government, are more likely to succeed.

The second principle of constitutional stability, addressing the second problem, draws on an aspect of democratic consolidation identified by Diamond, Linz, and Stepan noted above, that is, the idea that sustaining democracy requires that citizens be willing to defend democracy against transgressions by political leaders. As noted above, leaders attempt to set aside the democratic rules in part based on the expectation that a sufficient portion of the population will support them. This condition holds for both leaders attempting coups and democratically elected leaders attempting to set aside constitutional rules.[4] Absent sufficient support, leaders are unlikely to survive in power.

This feature of majority rule in a consolidated democracy provides the incentives for the two parts of the definition. When citizens are willing to defend democracy, leaders cannot expect citizen support for extra-constitutional action; rather than risk failure, leaders are deterred from violating the rules by adverse citizen reaction.[5]

Thus the central question for democratic consolidation becomes What are the conditions under which citizens act in concert to defend the rules? As noted, citizen coordination is problematic because citizen disagree about the appropriate form of government, citizen rights, and hence about definitions of transgressions.

How Constitutions Implement These Principles to Create Credible Limits on the State

Here I explain how self-enforcing constitutions are achieved. My argument has two parts: Citizens must have a means of coordinating their reactions against governmental transgressions, and constitutions must lower the stakes of politics. When these two principles hold, they reduce the likelihood that the rationality of fear mechanism will be invoked.

Consider the first principle: appropriately designed constitutional institutions help lower the stakes of politics by creating self-enforcing limits on politics. But how do they do so?

First, constitutions place limits on government concerning structure and process (McNollgast 1989). Procedural limits specify how particular governmental activities take place. For example, legislation might require a majority in both chambers of a bicameral legislature and be signed by the president (or, if not signed by the president, then subject to a veto-override provision). A range of structural limits focuses on specific powers and prohibitions for the national government. The US constitution's federal structure denied the national government authority over a range of policies, such as religion, ad valorem taxation of property, and the form of economic property rights. These were powers reserved for the states, not the national government. Moreover the constitution limited the national government's authority by making it subject to a series of substantive limits, such as the commerce clause limiting national economic regulation to interstate issues, the contract clause preventing the government from abrogating private contracts, and the takings clause requiring that just compensation accompany public taking of private property. Constitutions that credibly guarantee private property rights limit the ability of governments to confiscate citizen wealth and thus reduce the likelihood of invoking the rationality of fear.

To bind those in power, structure and process are enforced through citizens' coordination. The critical ingredient in solving coordination problems is the creation of a focal point (Schelling 1960). Focal points help solve coordination problems by creating common expectations among citizens about what others will do in a given situation. In the face of multiple ways to coordinate, the existence of a focal point changes citizen incentives. Although many citizens may prefer to coordinate in different ways, the fact that they value coordination means that when others coordinate around a given focal point, they are better off doing so as well.

Constitutional focal points define the appropriate bounds on governments and rights of citizens. These in turn define transgressions so that citizens can react in concert to oppose them. As noted above, citizens are likely to disagree about what rights the constitution ought to include. The constitution must create a compromise among these different views. Constitutions that specify a set of rights become self-enforcing under one condition: these focal points not only create a compromise among these differing views about rights, but citizens must also believe themselves better off with these rights than without them. This condition provides citizens with the incentives to defend the rights: they understand that defending the rights of others is important to maintaining *their* rights. Thus the set of rights specified in the constitution cannot be arbitrary; that is, they cannot embody just any normative principle. Instead, the set of rights must be sufficiently valued by citizens so that they are willing to defend them.

So how are constitutional focal solutions created? The answer is that these cannot arise at just any time but must typically occur through *pacts*, agreements among opposing sides that modify or specify the rules of the political decision making (Higley and Gunther 1991; O'Donnell and Schmitter 1986).

I provide four conditions for self-enforcing pacts (Weingast 1997, 2005a, 2004). First, the pact must create (or be embedded in a context that has already created) structure and process—citizens rights and a set of rules governing public decision making—defining a series of limits on the state. Second, the parties agreeing to the pact must believe that they are better off under the pact than without it. If this condition fails for one of the parties, that party will be better off without the pact, so the pact will fail. In particular, the parties must believe that the structural and procedural limits on average lead the government to make them better off. Third, each party agrees to change its behavior in exchange for the others simultaneously doing so. Fourth, the parties to the pact must be willing to defend the pact against transgressions by political leaders. In particular, they must be willing to defend the parts of the pact benefiting themselves and also the parts benefiting others against transgressions by political leaders. This fourth condition occurs when each party anticipates that its rights will be defended by the others: that each party is better off under the agreement than not, and that if ever one party fails to protect the rights of others, the others will fail to come to its rescue. Put another way, the pact becomes self-enforcing when all parties are better off under the pact and when all realize that unilateral defection implies that the others will also defect, destroying the pact.

Pacts thus accomplish several goals at once. First, they are agreements to adhere to new structure and process, often including democracy. Second, they alter the parties incentives, again in part through structure and process. Third, they help solve the critical citizen coordination problem that plague nondemocratic states. By creating focal procedural and substantive limits, pacts help citizens act in concert to violations of the rules.

13.3 Self-enforcing and Self-destructing Democracy in the Antebellum United States

To modern Americans, democracy seems so stable that they rarely inquire into the sources of this stability. Yet consolidated constitutional democracy did not begin with the constitution in 1789. Indeed, constitutional democracy remained problematic for the America's first century. Crises with the potential disrupt the Union occurred in 1818 to 1819, 1833, 1846 to 1850, and 1876 to 1877. In each instance an important group of Americans was willing to disrupt the country if the crisis was not solved, demonstrating that America failed to satisfy the first part of the definition of democratic stability. Worse, in a fifth crisis, southerners did disrupt the constitutional in 1861 following the failure to resolve the crisis beginning in 1854, resulting in a devastating Civil War (1861–1865).

Applying the Theory

By the theory above, manifold political, economic, and social divisions characterized Americans in the first century. Perhaps the most important difference among Americans concerned slavery, which was concentrated in the south. On the eve of the Civil War, the outstanding value of slaves totaled on the order of the entire US GDP, a phenomenal figure generating the rationality of fear among southerners about national policies affecting slavery.[6]

The constitution of 1789 provided the basis for democratic stability by solving the problems of under the previous constitution, known as the Articles of Confederation, adopted during the American Revolution in 1781. I argue that except for the issue of slavery, the constitution of 1789 created self-enforcing constitutional democracy in the United States. I first apply the theory to show that the constitution conforms to the principles noted above. I then turn to the issue of slavery to show how additional institutions were necessary to solve the special problems created by this issue.

The constitution at once created a vastly new system of structure and process, and a series of focal solutions to the citizens' coordination problem. Consider the range of structure and process that helped to limit the stakes of politics:

• First, the founders explicitly designed the new separation of powers system to make legislation difficult. As Madison argued in the Federalist Papers, these institutions deliberately insulated national policy making from the whims of the majority. Multiple veto institutions were to pit ambition against ambition (Federalist 46).[7]

- Second, the vertical separation of powers—federalism—kept a wide range of powers at the state level. Many of the most divisive issues—such as slavery—remained under the purview of state authority. Similarly states retained authority over virtually all property rights, religious freedom, and all local economic and social regulation.
- Third, the national government was explicitly one of enumerated powers, with the residual (all those not explicitly delegated) retained by the states and private citizens.
- Fourth, the constitution contained a series of substantive restrictions on national power, such as the commerce clause and the contracts clause. The bill of rights added a wide range of additional substantive rights, including free speech, the right to bear arms, and the right to assemble. The bill of rights also restricted national policy making through the due process and takings clauses, the latter required that just compensation be paid whenever the government sought to take property for public use.
- Fifth, the constitution placed striking restrictions on the national government's ability to impose taxes. Americans concerns about the abuse of tax authority first arose in the struggles with Great Britain. These concerns were omnipresent under the Articles, and they were a major part of the ratification debate. The founders designed the constitution to restrict direct taxes to be in proportion to population. This restriction implied that the national government could not impose specific taxes on particular industries or regions.
- Sixth, the constitution created a rough parity between the sections, north and south, thereby creating another form of veto over national policy making.

This list demonstrates a wide range of structure and process imposed by the constitution to limit national policy making and hence to lower the stakes of the new national government.

Also per the theory, the constitution created a range of focal solutions to help citizens to coordinate against abuse of power by the national government. First, the separation of powers system, pitting ambition against ambition, was expected to create a set of alarms so that abuses by one branch would be widely signaled by the others. Second, the manifold ways in which the constitution placed limits on national power were designed to help citizens (and their representatives) to coordinate against abuses. The national government was of relatively small number of policies focusing on national public goods, such as defense, the common market, a stable currency, and the post office. Moreover the founders designed the restrictions on the national government in ways that would be easy for citizens to understand and coordinate against abuses. The restriction on direct taxes, the enumerated powers, and the takings clause all fit in this category. Similarly the strong system of federalism explicitly reserved a large number of issues for the states.

Madison explicitly noted in Federalist 46 the importance of coordination to prevent national government abuse of its authority:

> But ambitious encroachments of the federal government on the authority of the State governments would not excite the opposition of a single State, or a few States only. They would be signals of general alarm. Every government would espouse the common cause. A correspondence would be opened. Plans of resistance would be concerted. On spirit would animate and conduct the whole.

The states' ability to maintain their militias backed up this threat with force: it was expected that the state militias in the aggregate would be an order of magnitude larger than the national army.

Finally, the constitution, qua pact, satisfied the four conditions for a self-enforcing pact. First, as noted, it created a range of new structure and process. Second, by providing a range of public goods lacking under the Articles of Confederation, the constitution made nearly all Americans better off. Third, the movement out of the articles to the constitution was simultaneous. And last, any one group receiving their benefits of the Union required that they adhere to the agreement, lest the agreement fall apart. The threat of falling apart following the abuse of power provided a powerful restraint: since nearly all were better off under the constitution, abuse of power by some would cause the constitution to fail.

Slavery and the Problem of Maintaining Constitutional Stability

From the beginning of the Republic, southerners were concerned about the security of their slaves (Finkelman 1996; Rakove 1996). A necessary condition for their participation in the United States was that northerners agree to provide a credible commitment to protect rights in slaves. The constitution helped in several ways. The separation of powers divided the federal government among several branches, making legislation more difficult; the bill of rights placed a series of limits on the federal government; the "three-fifths" clause allowed southerners to count slaves as three-fifths of a person as part of the basis for the number of southerner members of the House of Representatives; federalism decentralized many critical issues dividing Americans, and thereby allowed southerners to provide the legal underpinnings of their "peculiar institutions."

At the same time northerners were quite nervous about southern dominance of the national government. Although most northerners were willing to help devise institutions to protect the south, they also wanted to prevent southerners from dominating the national government. This implied that any solution to the problem must be delicately balanced.

Although widely celebrated, the American constitution proved insufficient to protect slavery and hence to make early American democracy stable. An additional institution was necessary, called *sectional balance*. Sectional balance held that both sections, north and south, must have the same number of states, affording each a veto over national policy making through the US Senate (Weingast 1998). Americans recognized sectional balance from the beginning (e.g., in the projection of an equal number of new free and slave states in the territories in the 1780s). Balance was quickly achieved in 1796 and maintained for the next five decades.

Sectional balance provided a static security for southerners and their property in slaves. As long as the southerners held an equal number of slave states, they could veto legislation they found offensive. Similarly sectional balance provided protection for northerners against southern dominance. By granting northerners a veto, they could prevent southern attempts to grow too large.

Yet sectional balance was not dynamically stable. In a growing country, maintaining sectional balance required that the two sections grow in relatively equal proportions. Balanced growth proved difficult to engineer, setting the stage for the major controversies of the antebellum era. The reason is that in order to maintain this balance, the two sections had to grow in parallel. Yet a number of impediments made this difficult—the fact that their economies differed and hence responded to different forces, and because geography placed limits on the relative expansion of both sections.

Most of the era's major crises revolved around the status (free or slave) of the territories. Crises emerged over the territories in 1819, 1846, and 1854. In each case a significant group of Americans was willing to secede from the Union, as illustrated when the third of these crises led to secession and then Civil War in 1861. The American constitution was thus not consolidated or self-enforcing at these moments. In the first two crises, pacts in the form of the Compromise of 1820 and Compromise of 1850 resolved the problem. With several moments of disruptions, American constitutional democracy survived from 1787 until 1861. Unfortunately, Americans were unable to resolve the third crisis over the territories, leading to a disastrous Civil War.

13.4 Democratization in Spain, 1975 to 1982

Students of democracy have long held Spain as the paradigmatic case of a successful transition to constitutional democracy (O'Donnell and Schmitter 1986; Linz and Stepan 1996). Prior to the transition in the late 1970s, Spain had a turbulent history. Political instability characterized the early twentieth century. A short-lived Second Republic in the 1930s came to a violent end in the civil war of 1936 to 1939. This was followed by nearly four decades of peace born of a repressive authoritarian regime under General Francisco Franco.

Many of the issues that divided Spaniards in the civil war reemerged after Franco died in 1975. These included: Would the monarchy continue? What form would the institutions of public choice take? Would the capitalist system become sacrosanct or a battle ground? And would regionalists in the Basque country and Catalonia seek autonomy as a first step toward independence and hence threaten the integrity of Spain? New questions also arose: Would the left demand reprisals for repression, and would the right accept some form of amnesty for those persecuted under Franco?

Despite a history of violence over this wide range of fundamental controversies, Spaniards resolved their differences peacefully, with compromise and mutual accommodation. Central to the success of democratic consolidation in Spain was Aldofo Suárez, appointed by King Juan Carlos as president in July 1976 (Colomer 1995; Gunther 1992; Linz and Stepan 1996; Maravall 1978, 1982). A brilliant negotiator, Suárez initiated democratization in a series of steps. As I argue, these steps helped citizens solve their coordination problems through the creation of new rules, procedures, and the "invention" of new traditions (Perez-Diaz 1990).

Suárez proceeded through a series of pacts. He began by devising a pact with the Francoist elite, who sought to maintain as much of Franco's regime as possible. This pact used Francoist institutions to begin moderate reform, in part under the threat that failing to do so risked growing strikes, diminishing legitimacy, and possible political instability (Fishman 1990; Linz and Stepan 1996; Maravall 1978). This step represented a modest start toward representative government, providing for elections to create a new *Cortes* (parliament) and legalizing some political parties. Suárez's pact also created an electoral law, one biased toward the regime. Further, Suárez kept several issues off the table, including the monarchy and unity of the state.

In an important next step, Suárez sought to legalize the Communist party. He took this risk in part because failing to do so risked the legitimacy of his regime. His efforts at democratization would suffer if the Communist party, supported by a significant portion of the population, contested the regime's legitimacy.

This step also proceeded through a pact. In exchange for legalization, the Communists agreed to accept a series of rules and constraints, including abiding by the election results, accepting the monarchy (rather than insisting on a republican form of government), and to eschew demands of radical restructuring of society.

In a microcosm, this exchange represents the "invention of tradition" of inclusion and accommodation inherent in solutions to citizen coordination problems. This agreement had all four elements noted above in the theory of self-enforcing pacts: both sides agreed to abide by a series of structure and process, both sides gave up something to gain something of greater value, both sides agreed to change their behavior simultaneously, and both sides knew that their receiving benefits from the agreement required that they adhere to their part of the exchange.

The third step involved the pacts surrounding the new constitution in 1977 and 1978. Although more complex than the first two pacts, the agreements forming the new constitution reflected the same logic as the legalization of the Communist party. The constitutional pacts involved both Suárez and his centrist party, the parties on the left, and the most of the old Francoists on the right. A large exchange occurred in which the various parties gave ground on dimensions of lesser importance in order to gain on dimensions of greater importance (Colomer 1995, ch. 6; see also Gunther 1992; Linz and Stepan 1996; Maravall and Santamaria 1986).

A remarkable achievement, the new constitution resolved the conflicts that tore the society apart during the civil war. The right obtained the preservation of the monarchy, an electoral law biased in its favor, and the maintenance of the "integrity of Spain" (e.g., that the Basque regions and Catalonia would not receive significant special privileges and independence). The left obtained the right to participate, a political system (relatively) free of the military and church, and a set of political institutions that would allow a welfare state (if not a radical one). Although the regions seeking autonomy did not receive special privileges, a general decentralization was instituted that gave them much of what they wanted.

Nonetheless, these pacts did not consolidate Spanish democracy. The reason is that an important minority of the old-line Francoists, including a portion of the military, remained uncommitted to the regime. Because this group was potentially willing to disrupt constitutional democracy, Spain failed the first component of the definition of democratic consolidation. Indeed, in a dramatic moment, would-be coup leaders took over the *Cortes* at gunpoint on February 23, 1981. In part, their success depended on the acquiescence of King Juan Carlos, who had yet to prove himself as willing to risk his own future on democracy. Yet in a surprise move, the king stood up to the coup, forcing the military leaders to back down.

Observers agree that some time between the failure of the coup and the election of the socialists to power the following year, Spanish democracy became consolidated (Agüero 1995, ch. 7; Linz and Stepan 1996, p. 108). This argument shows how consolidation was constructed in Spain. The political and social divisions implied great difficulties in supporting a democratic constitution. Threats to both the right and left raised the rationality of fear. Yet these difficulties were solved as suggested by the theory. Suárez engineered three pacts that helped create the necessary solution to the citizen coordination problem, in turn creating incentives to sustain democracy. Per the theory these pacts had the four attributes noted by the theory for a self-enforcing pact. The new traditions of compromise and mutual accommodation underlay the new political institutions and the focal solution allowing citizens to coordinate so they could police the government. Most members of Spain saw themselves as better off under the new arrangements. A major motive was the possibility of joining the European Union, which held the promise of considerable economic benefits. To join the Union, however, required democratization.

After the 1981 coup attempt the right refrained from advocating violence as a means of controlling the government, and the left eschewed radical restructuring of the society, as they had threatened in the 1930s. Interestingly the king's role in the coup reveals an important element of randomness and fragility to a process that could have gone otherwise.

13.5 Conclusions

This chapter advanced an approach to the problem of self-enforcing democratic constitutions. To be stable, constitutions must be designed so that they provide political officials with the incentives to abide by the constitution's provisions. A particular constitutional provision, such as democratic elections, holds only if political officials abide by it. The literature on democracy and constitutions has accorded too little attention to the question of how constitutional provisions become self-enforcing.

Following the literature on democratic stability, the approach accords a critical role for pacts. Pacts are agreements among contending elites that help bring on democracy and other constitutional rules. Missing from the literature is an explanation of why some pacts work and others fail. This chapter argued that to succeed, pacts must be self-enforcing. The theory provides conditions under which pacts become self-enforcing, namely when all parties are better off under the pact and when all realize that unilateral defection implies that the others will also defect, destroying the pact.

More generally, the chapter advanced a theory of self-enforcing constitutions based on two fundamental problems of constitutional stability and two principles suggesting how these problems are resolves. First, the rationality of fear mechanism holds that when citizens feel what they hold most dear is being threatened by the government, they are willing to support extra-constitutional action. Appropriately constructed constitutions can short-circuit this mechanism by invoking structure and process to protect what people hold most dear. This structure and process lowers the stakes of politics. Lowering the stakes reduces the likelihood of the rationality of fear mechanism and therefore reduces the circumstances under which citizens support extra-constitutional action.

Second, constitutions must solve the citizen coordination problem so that citizens hold the ability to act in concert against potential constitutional violations. They do so by creating focal solutions that define transgressions.

The chapter applied this perspective to the evolution of democracy in the early United States. By the theory's first principle, the constitution provided a series of structural and procedural constraints on the national government, lowering the stakes of national politics. For example, the horizontal separation of powers divided power and made action based on narrow majorities less likely; the vertical separation of powers of federalism limited the national government's authority in a range of areas, reserving most policies for the states; the principle of sectional balance also provided each section, north and south, with a veto over national policy; and the constitution and the bill of rights defined a range of citizen rights that could be enforced against the national government. Moreover the shared experience of the founding era helped shape a strong consensus on a large number of issues. By the theory's second principle, this consensus combined with the constitution's structure and process to help to solve citizens' coordination problems. Along a wide range of dimensions, transgressions by the national government were well defined. Except for the issue of slavery, the constitution was self-enforcing as of the turn of the nineteenth century.

The issue of slavery plagued the nation for three generations, with a series of crises threatening the nation and the constitution. Hence the constitution was not fully self-enforcing during this period. The secession of the confederate states formally dissolved American democracy.

Yet American democracy reemerged after the Civil War, with the principal divisive issue of the era, slavery, decisively removed from national politics. The result was a final national pact in the compromise of 1877, ending Reconstruction, recreating American federalism, and allowing the creation of the Jim Crow south. The result was consolidated, self-enforcing democracy for white males.

This perspective may usefully be applied outside the American case. The chapter also applied the approach to the case of twentieth-century Spain. Although troubled by an unstable republic, a long dictatorship, Spaniards designed constitutional democracy following the death of Franco in 1975. They did so through a series of pacts creating structure and process limiting the government, but also creating new focal solutions to the citizen coordination problem.

Finally, the approach has a range of implications beyond those studied here. For example, it also applies to international agreements. In neither case—domestic or international—is there any external authority to enforce the constitution or agreement. This implies that in parallel with domestic constitutions, international agreements must also be self-enforcing to be stable. Similarly the approach has a range of implications for normative issues of constitutional and democratic theory. The principle that successful constitutions limit the stakes of power implies that constitutions are more likely to survive when they are designed to place limits the range of choices by majorities. To survive, a constitution must protect those with the power to disrupt it. In some cases this logic requires that interests inimical to freedom must be protected, such as southern slaveholders in the antebellum United States.

Notes

The author gratefully acknowledges Roger Congleton, Daniel Diermeier, Rui de Figueiredo, and Randall Holcolme for helpful conversations. This chapter is part of a larger project whose results are reported in Weingast (2005).

1. A large literature on pacts exists in political science. See, for example, Higley and Gunther (1991), Diamond (1999), and O'Donnell and Schmitter (1986).

2. To study the incentive problems surrounding consolidation, I draw on recent work on the conditions under which democracy is self-enforcing: Fearon (2000), Przeworski (1991, 2005), and Weingast (1997, 2000b).

3. BDM et al. (2003, 331–38 and 388–402) provides a specific model of this claim.

4. Many authors note that coups take place in democracies only when coup leaders expect considerable support. See, for example, Alexander (2002, ch. 1) and O'Donnell and Schmitter (1986).

5. As Diamond (1999, p. 70) suggests, "Only when [citizen] commitment to police the behavior of the state is powerfully credible ... does a ruling party, president, or sovereign, develop a self-interest in adhering to the rules of the game, which makes those constitutional rules self-enforcing."

6. The horror of slavery is that people were treated as property. Nonetheless, analyzing this system requires considering how southerners thought about this property.

7. Indeed, Wallis and Weingast (2005) show that these constraints were binding. For example, despite huge national demand for infrastructure development to promote economic growth, the national government failed to become the leader, lagging behind the states by an order of magnitude.

References

Acemoglu, D., and J. A. Robinson. 2005. *Economic Origins of Dictatorship and Democracy*. New York: Cambridge University Press.

Agüero, F. 1995. *Soldiers, Civilians, and Democracy: Post-Franco Spain in Comparative Perspective*. Baltimore: Johns Hopkins University Press.

Alexander, G. 2002. The sources of democratic consolidation. Unpublished MS. University of Virginia.

Bailyn, B. 1967. *The Ideological Origins of the American Revolution*. Cambridge: Belknap Press.

Bednar, J., W. Eskridge, and J. A. Ferejohn. 2001. A political theory of federalism. In J. Ferejohn, J. Rakove, and J. Riley, eds., *Constitutions and Constitutionalism*. New York: Cambridge University Press.

Bueno de Mesquita, B., A. Smith, R. M. Siverson, and J. D. Morrow. 2003. *The Logic of Political Survival.* Cambridge: MIT Press.

Carpenter, J. T. [1930] 1990. *The South as a Conscious Minority, 1789–1861*. Columbia: University of South Carolina Press.

Chwe, M. 2001. *Rational Ritual: Culture, Coordination, and Common Knowledge.* Princeton: Princeton University Press.

David, P. A., H. Gutman, R. Sutch, P. Temin, and G. Wright. 1976. *Reckoning with Slavery.* New York: Oxford University Press.

de Figueiredo, R., and B. R. Weingast. 1999. Rationality of fear: Political opportunism and ethnic conflict. In J. Snyder and B. Walter, eds., *Military Intervention in Civil Wars*. New York: Columbia University Press.

de Figueiredo, R., and B. R. Weingast. 2004. Self-enforcing federalism. *Journal of Law, Economics, and Organization* 21 (1): 103–35.

Diamond, L. 1999. *Developing Democracy: Toward Consolidation*. Baltimore: Johns Hopkins University Press.

Fearon, J. 2000. Why use elections to allocate power? Working Paper. Stanford University.

Finkelman, P. 1996. *Slavery and the Founders: Race and Liberty in the Age of Jefferson.* Armonk, NY: M.E. Sharpe.

Fogel, R., and S. Engerman. 1974a. *Time on the Cross*. Boston: Little Brown.

Fogel, R., and S. Engerman. 1974b. "Philanthropy at bargain prices: Notes on the economics of gradual emancipation. *Journal of Legal Studies* 3: 377–401.

Freehling, W. W. 1990. *The Road to Disunion, Vol I: Secessionists at Bay: 1776–1854*. New York: Oxford University Press.

Gibbons, R., and A. Rutten. 1996. Hierarchical dilemmas: Social contracts with self-interested rulers. Unpublished manuscript. Cornell University.

Gillette, W. 1979. *Retreat from Reconstruction, 1869–1879.* Baton Rouge: Louisiana State University Press.

Greene, J. P. 1986. *Peripheries and Center: Constitutional Development in the Extended Polities of the British Empire and the United States, 1607–1788.* New York: Norton.

Hardin, R. 1989. Why a constitution? In B. Grofman and D. Wittman, eds., *The Federalist Papers and the New Institutionalism*. New York: Agathon Press.

Higley, J., and R. Gunther. 1992. *Elites and Democratic Consolidation in Latin America and Southern Europe*. Cambridge: Cambridge University Press.

Holt, M. F. 1978. *The Political Crisis of the 1850s*. New York: Norton.

Holt, M. F. 2001. *The Whig Party*. New York: Oxford University Press.

Hoogenboom, A. 1988. *The Presidency of Rutherford B. Hayes*. Lawrence: University of Kansas Press.

Kaplanoff, M. D. 1991. Confederation: Movement for a stronger Union. In J. P. Greene and J. R. Pole, eds., *The Blackwell Encyclopedia of the American Revolution*. Cambridge, MA: Basil Blackwell.

Knupfer, P. B. 1991. *The Union as It Was*. Chapel Hill: University of North Carolina Press.

Linz, J. J., and A. Stepan. 1996. *Problems of Democratic Transition and Consolidation*. Baltimore: Johns Hopkins University Press.

May, R. E. 1973. *The Southern Dream of a Caribbean Empire, 1854–1861*. Athens: University of Georgia Press (new Afterward, 1989).

McNollgast, M. D. McCubbins, R. Noll, and B. R. Weingast. 1989. Structure and process, politics and policy: Administrative arrangements and the political control of agencies. *Virginia Law Review* 75 (March): 431–82.

McPherson, J. M. 1988. *Battle Cry of Freedom: The Civil War Era*. New York: Oxford University Press.

Middlekauff, R. 1982. *The Glorious Cause: The American Revolution, 1763–1789*. New York: Oxford University Press.

Morgan, E. S. 1977. *The Birth of the Republic: 1763–89*, rev. ed. Chicago: University of Chicago Press.

Milgrom, P., D. C. North, and B. R. Weingast. 1990. The role of institutions in the revival of trade: The medieval law merchant, private judges, and the champagne fairs. *Economics and Politics* 2 (March): 1–23.

O'Donnell, G., and P. C. Schmitter. 1986. *Transitions from Authoritarian Rule: Tentative Conclusion about Uncertain Democracies*. Baltimore: Johns Hopkins University Press.

Ordeshook, P. C. 1992. Constitutional stability. *Constitutional Political Economy* 3: 137.

Ordeshook, P. C., and O. Svetsova. 1997. Federalism and constitutional design. *Journal of Democracy* 8 (1): 27–42.

Peskin, A. 1973. Was there a Compromise of 1877? *Journal of American History* 60: 63–75.

Polakoff, K. Ian. 1973. *The Politics of Inertia: The Election of 1876 and the End of Reconstruction*. Baton Rouge: Louisiana State University Press.

Potter, D. M. 1976. *The Impending Crisis: 1848–1861*. Edited and completed by D. E. Fehrenbacher. New York: Harper and Row.

Przeworski, A. 1991. *Democracy and the Market*. New York: Cambridge University Press.

Przeworski, A. 2005. Self-enforcing democracy. In B. R. Weingast and D. Wittman, eds., *Handbook of Political Economy*. New York: Oxford University Press, forthcoming.

Rakove, J. N. 1996. *Original Meanings: Politics and Ideas in the Making of the Constitution*. New York: Knopf.

Rakove, J., A. Rutten, and B. R. Weingast. 2001. Ideas, interests, and credible commitments in the American Revolution. Working Paper. Hoover Institution.

Ransom, R. L. 1989. *Conflict and Compromise: The Political-Economy of Slavery, Emancipation and the American Civil War*. New York: Cambridge University Press.

Ransom, R., and R. Sutch. 1988. Capitalists without capital: The burden of slavery and the impact of emancipation. *Agricultural History* 62 (3): 133–60.

Reid, J. P. 1995. *Constitutional History of the American Revolution*, abr. ed. Madison: University of Wisconsin Press.

Riker, W. H. 1987. The lessons of 1787. *Public Choice* 55 (September): 5–34.

Robinson, D. 1971. *Slavery in the Structure of American Politics.* New York: Norton.

Schelling, T. 1960. *Strategy of Conflict.* New York: Oxford University Press.

Silbey, J. H. 1985. *The Partisan Imperative: The Dynamics of American Politics Before the Civil War.* New York: Oxford University Press.

Theriault, S., and B. R. Weingast. 2002. Agenda manipulation, strategic voting, and legislative details in the compromise of 1850. In D. Brady and M. D. McCubbins, *Party, Process, and Political Change in Congress.* Stanford: Stanford University Press.

Wallis, J. J., and B. R. Weingast. 2005. Equilibrium federal impotence: Why the states and not the American national government financed economic development in the antebellum era. Working Paper. Hoover Institution.

Weingast, B. R. 1997. The political foundations of democracy and the rule of law. *American Political Science Review* 91 (June): 245–63.

Weingast, B. R. 1998. Political stability and civil war: Institutions, commitment, and American democracy. In R. Bates, A. Greif, M. Levi, J.-L. Rosenthal, and B. R. Weingast, eds., *Analytic Narratives*. Princeton: Princeton University Press.

Weingast, B. R. 2004. Constructing self-enforcing democracy in Spain. In J. Oppenheimer and I. Morris, eds., *Politics from Anarchy to Democracy: Rational Choice in Political Science.* Stanford: Stanford University Press.

Weingast, B. R. 2005a. The self-enforcing constitution: With an application to uncertain democracy in America's first century. Working Paper. Hoover Institution.

Weingast, B. R. 2005b. Self-enforcing economic liberty. *Journal of Economic Perspectives*, forthcoming.

Wood, G. 1969. *The Creation of the American Republic, 1776–1787.* New York: Norton.

Wood, G. 1991. *Radicalism and the American Revolution*. New York: Vintage Books.

Woodward, C. V. 1951. *Reaction and Reunion.* New York: Oxford University Press.

Wright, G. 1978. *Political Economy of the Cotton South.* New York: Norton.

Wright, G. 2003. The role of nationhood in the economic development of the United States. In A. Teichova and H. Matis, eds., *Nation, State and the Economy in History*. Cambridge: Cambridge University Press.

Index